Selous & the Bulawayo Field Force

Selous & the Bulawayo Field Force
Tribal Conflict in East Africa 1895-1896

Sunshine and Storm in Rhodesia

Frederick Courteney Selous

The Matabele Rebellion, 1896

D. Tyrie Laing

LEONAUR

Selous & the Bulawayo Field Force
Tribal Conflict in East Africa 1895-1896
Sunshine and Storm in Rhodesia
by Frederick Courteney Selous
The Matabele Rebellion, 1896
by D. Tyrie Laing

FIRST EDITION

First published under the titles
Sunshine and Storm in Rhodesia
and
The Matabele Rebellion, 1896

Leonaur is an imprint
of Oakpast Ltd

Copyright in this form © 2014 Oakpast Ltd

ISBN: 978-1-78282-291-2 (hardcover)
ISBN: 978-1-78282-292-9 (softcover)

http://www.leonaur.com

Publisher's Notes
The views expressed in this book are not necessarily
those of the publisher.

Contents

Sunshine and Storm in Rhodesia   7
The Matabele Rebellion, 1896   249

Sunshine and Storm in Rhodesia

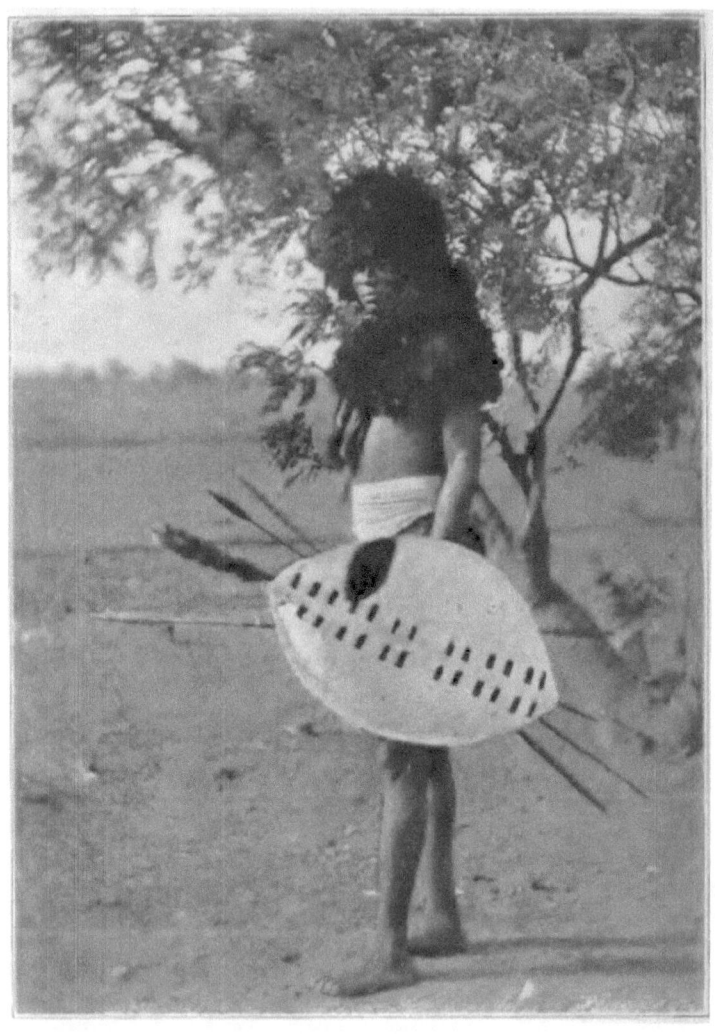

MAHOLI
An old servant of the author's who came in with his master and mistress from Essexvale, on the outbreak of the rebellion, and has been with them ever since.

Contents

Preface	13
I Return to Matabeleland	23
Our life at Essexvale	30
First Overt Act of Rebellion	39
Precautions Against Native Attack	45
Massacre of the Whites Near Edkins' Store	49
The Matabele Campaign of 1893	57
Effect of Removing the Police Force	63
Cattle Stolen by Matabele	70
Return to Essexvale	75
Skirmish With the Rebels	80
O'Connor's Wonderful Escape	86
Laager Formed at Bulawayo	95
Captain Grey's Timely Arrival at Tekwe Store	102
Mr. Dawson's Patrol	110
Escort a Convoy of Waggons to Bulawayo	116
Gilford's Fight in the Shiloh Hills	125
Despatch from Captain Laing	131

Matabele Advance on Bulawayo	138
Force Retire Without Fighting	146
I Rejoin My Troop at Dawe's Store	155
Proceed Towards Bulawayo	164
Matabele Impi Reported Near Tekwe River	172
Column Under Colonel Spreckley Sent to the South	181
A Scene of Desolation	189
A Large Impi Reported Camped on the Umguza	196
The Bulawayo Field Force Disbanded	204
A Few Thoughts and Opinions Upon Matters Rhodesian and South African	214
Appendices	228

To My Wife
Who During the Last Few Months
Has at Once Been
My Greatest Anxiety and My Greatest Comfort
I Dedicate This Book

Preface

It was during the early days of the recent insurrection that I first thought of utilising my spare time by writing some account of what was taking place around me, and these rough notes, written at odd moments during the campaign, I intended to have sent to the *Field* for publication in that journal, in the form of a series of articles dealing entirely with my own personal experiences. After the disbandment of the Bulawayo Field Force, however, and my own resignation as an officer in that corps, finding that I had leisure to do so, I determined to amplify these notes, and give some account of every skirmish which had taken place between the Colonists and the natives in Matabeleland up to the date of the disbandment of the above-mentioned Force.

To this I add a short account of my personal experiences in the country during the months immediately preceding the outbreak of the insurrection, and finding that I had then sufficient material to fill the covers of a small book, I abandoned my original idea of getting what I had written published in weekly numbers, and determined for the third time to launch a book—always about Africa—on the long-suffering British public.

What I have written as it were historically regarding the events which have lately taken place in Matabeleland may, I think, be received as a simple and unadorned statement of fact, for where I have had to go outside my own personal experiences, my information has always been obtained at first hand and checked by the corroborating accounts of others who were also eye-witnesses of the events described. As to any conclusions I may have arrived at from given facts, they may be right or they may be wrong, but at any rate I claim the right to express my opinions frankly and fearlessly as long as they are my honest convictions. It may be said that, as I am a friend of Mr. Cecil Rhodes and of Dr. Jameson, I ought not to have expressed the opinion that it was the removal of the police force from Matabeleland to the Transvaal which gave the natives their opportunity to revolt, since the expression of such an opinion may be held to reflect upon the administration of the Chartered Company.

My reply is, that I have written a history, which, to have any value, must be truthful, and that as Dr. Jameson cannot lay claim to infallibility, he was, like other mortals, liable to err. When he left Matabeleland he never dreamt that the removal of the police force would have any more effect upon the Matabele than the disbandment of the police in Mashunaland in 1891 had had upon the natives in that country. This opinion, moreover, must have been shared by the great majority of the inhabitants of Matabeleland, since no remonstrance was made by any public man at the time that the police left Bulawayo. We now know that the removal of the white police force was a mistake; but it is easy to criticise after the event, and as at the time the mistake was made no one in Rhodesia was wise or prescient enough to foresee the possible effect it might have on the natives of Matabeleland, it would be the height of meanness and injustice to hold Dr. Jameson morally responsible for the present insurrection.

Judging from the knowledge which we now possess of the secret history of the rebellion, it appears that the leaders of the movement must long ago have determined to revolt whenever a favourable opportunity occurred, and a rebellion would therefore in all probability have taken place sooner or later; so perhaps it is as well to have had it and got over it at the same time as the *rinderpest*. The latter plague will have far more lasting effects than the native rising; but when the railway from the south reaches Bulawayo, the country will once again be able to make a fair start, for with the greater knowledge now possessed by the authorities of the native character, the outcome of which will be a complete reorganisation of the native administration, no farther insurrection ought to be possible.

For the rest, it is very evident that the Matabele broke out in rebellion because they disliked their position as a conquered people, and imagined that they were strong enough to throw off the yoke of their conquerors. But I fail to see that the fact that they have rebelled is any more an indictment against the general principles of the government of the Chartered Company, than were the numerous rebellions which have taken place from time to time in the Cape Colony an indictment against the wisdom and justice of the Imperial Government.

Now that the rebellion has occurred, it will very possibly be said that it was brought about by systematic brutality to the natives on the part of the white men in the country. Such an allegation, however, cannot be supported by facts, for, as the records of the magistrates' court will prove, the present government has done all that any other civilised government could have done to protect the natives from ill-treatment at the hands of irresponsible individuals; and as a native commissioner thoroughly conversant with the Matabele language, and well in touch with the people, was stationed in each of the districts into which the country has been divided, it cannot be urged that the natives had no opportunity of making their grievances known.

Grievances of course they had, the chief of which, doubtless, was the loss of their independence as a nation, and the fact that they found themselves treated as a conquered people lately engaged in hostilities, who had only been permitted to return to the country from which they had been driven at the time of the first war under certain conditions, one of which was that the *indunas* should, through the medium of the native commissioners, supply miners and farmers with native labour—all the able-bodied young men in the country being required to work for a certain number of months per annum at a fixed rate of pay.

This rate of pay was fixed at 10*s*. a month with food; but as a matter of fact mining work was almost always paid much more highly, as much as 30*s*. a month with food being often given for unskilled labour, whilst the managers of mines made it their business to see that the boys in their Company's employ were well treated, and cruel treatment by individuals was, I do not hesitate to say, the exception to the rule. Owing to the excessive indolence of the people, however, there can be no doubt that the labour regulations were most irksome to them. The *indunas* grew more and more disinclined to exert their authority in the matter of inducing their people to work when applications were made to them, with the result that native policemen were sent to their kraals to insist on the labour regulations being carried out, and these policemen, I fear, sometimes exceeded their duties, and used their position to tyrannise over the people.

I remember well that when Umlugulu[1] visited me for the first time, after I had taken up my residence on Essexvale,[2] he complained bitterly of the high-handed manner in which the "*Ama Policey Minyama*," the "Black Police," behaved to him and his people. "I have no

---
1. One of the most influential men in Matabeleland in the time of Lo Bengula.
2. The name of my Company's estate on which I was living before the rebellion .

complaints to make," he said, "against the white policemen; but the black police, *wa duba, wa duba sebele*—they give me trouble; they really give me trouble." I myself complained to the acting administrator, Mr. Duncan, concerning the inconsiderate manner in which it appeared to me that the labour regulations were sometimes carried out, and I was led to believe that the whole question of native administration would shortly be gone into by the government, and all grievances remedied.

The cattle question I have dealt with in the course of my story. It was never sagaciously handled, and its mismanagement probably caused more discontent against the Chartered Company's rule amongst the pure-blooded Matabele, or Abenzantsi, than anything else, whilst the irritation excited by the regulation exacting a certain amount of paid labour yearly from every able-bodied man produced a feeling of bitterness and discontent throughout the other classes of the community, which made them ripe for rebellion when they were called to arms by the leaders of the insurrection. However, although no impartial critic can deny that the confiscation of so large a number of their cattle, and more especially the manner in which that confiscation was carried out, was impolitic if not ungenerous; whilst the manner in which the labour regulations were enforced was sometimes calculated to provoke serious discontent.

Yet neither of these causes, nor both combined, would, in my opinion, have been sufficient to induce the mass of the population to break out in rebellion had there not been amongst them many men who, having once belonged to the ruling class in the country, were so dissatisfied at their loss of position and power under the white man's rule, that they had determined to regain their independence as a nation, or to attempt to do so, on the first favourable opportunity which offered. The rebellion was not the spontaneous act of the mass of the people goaded to desperation by an insupportable tyranny. It was a drama into which they were surprised, and in many cases dragged against their better judgment, by a few leading spirits, who planned and carried out the first murders and utilised the *Makalaka Umlimo*,[3] as a prophet.

To show that neither the cattle nor the labour questions were the only causes of the rebellion, I may mention that on Mr. Arthur Rhodes' block of farms on the Impembisi River, extending to some 50,000 acres, there was a considerable native population which had been altogether exempted from the general labour regulations—al-

---

3. God. See Chapter 26.

though required to supply Mr. Arthur Rhodes himself with any labour necessary on the farm for agricultural purposes; whilst there had been distributed amongst them 1600 head of cattle, which they held, in addition to their own, on exactly the same terms on which they had been formerly accustomed to tend cattle for Lo Bengula. Now here was a population living, one would have thought, in a state of the most absolute contentment—for they were receiving the full benefit of the milk from a far larger number of cattle than they had ever had to look after in Lo Bengula's time; had been allowed to build their *kraals* wherever they thought fit, make use of whatever land they desired for cultivation, and in fact to lead their own life in their own way undisturbed by any one, for the number of boys who came voluntarily to ask for employment was far in excess of what was required for agricultural work on the estate.

And yet, when the rebellion broke out, these people to a man (always excepting Captain Fynn's Delagoa Bay boy) joined the insurgents, and not only burnt down Mr. Arthur Rhodes' homestead and swept off all his cattle, but murdered Mr. Edwards the surveyor, who happened to be working in the neighbourhood; against whom they could have had no personal animus, as he was a complete stranger to them. Then, again, if anyone had heard the natives living in the villages close round my homestead on Essexvale singing and dancing as they were wont to do on every moonlight night, he could not have maintained that they appeared to be weighed down by a sense of injustice and oppression, or, in fact, that they were anything but joyous and happy.

It is very difficult to understand the workings of a *kaffir's* mind, as anyone must admit who has lived long amongst natives, but the fact that the Matabele broke out into rebellion against the government of the Chartered Company, appears to me to be no proof of any special iniquity *per se* on the part of that government, since history has shown us, that wherever a savage race, entirely unaccustomed to order and restraint, has been conquered by a highly civilised people, who have forthwith essayed to govern that savage race as humanely as possible, but after all in their own interests rather than in the interests of the conquered people, a rebellion against the more intelligent ruling class has been the result; for the ways of the civilised man are not the ways of the savage, who, there can be no doubt, would rather put up with all the ills from which we consider we have freed him, than be subject to the restraints of a settled form of government. Practically, he says "hang your *Pax Britanica*"; give me the good old times of superstition and bloodshed; then, even if I did not know the day nor the hour when I might be "smelt out" as a witch, and forthwith knocked on the head, at any rate I could have basked in the sun until my time came; and then, too, when the "*impi*" went forth, what glorious times I had, and how I revelled in blood and loot!

As to any general charges of systematic injustice and cruelty towards the natives, which may and will now be made by the personal enemies of Mr. Rhodes, against the Chartered Company, with the object of providing a justification for the brutal murders of European women and children which have been committed during the present rebellion, I would point out that such charges come rather late in the day, for the natives of Matabeleland had lived for over two years in an apparently fairly contented condition under the government of the Company before the rebellion broke out, and during the whole of that time there were four missionaries belonging to the London Missionary Society, besides some people called "seventh-day Adventists"—whatever that may mean, for I have not the least idea myself—all of whom were working amongst, and avowedly for the benefit of, the natives.

Now, if systematic cruelty, injustice, and oppression of the Matabele by the government of the Chartered Company had been going on constantly for over two years, it must have been very well known to all these men, and it was their duty not only to have protested against such gross misgovernment to the Company's administrator in Bulawayo, but also to have reported such abuses to their directors in England. No such allegations, however, were ever made prior to the rebellion, and should any be now brought forward they ought to be received with the very gravest suspicion.

The fact, too, remains that although individual acts of brutality have occurred in Matabeleland—as they have done in every other country in the world—during the last two years, and although mistakes have been made, especially in dealing with the cattle and labour questions, yet, on the whole, the conditions under which the natives in that territory were living, were such that no one resident in the country, whether missionary or miner, imagined before the rebellion broke out that there could be any deep-seated discontent amongst them. That the government of the natives has been all that was desirable from their point of view I do not say, as it is my opinion that, when a black man's country has been conquered by Europeans, the laws by which that country will be subsequently governed will be made in the interests of the whites, and some of them will be very unpalatable to the conquered race, however just and equitable they may seem to their rulers.

We Europeans make the mistake of thinking that, when we free a tribe of savages from what we consider a most oppressive and tyrannical form of government, substituting in its place an orderly rule, under which every man's life and property is protected and witchdoctors are not recognised, we ought to earn their gratitude; but the fact is we invariably fail to do so, as the present insurrection, as well as all the many rebellions by the natives of the Cape Colony against the rule of the Imperial Government has shown. Yet, as in the Cape Colony, so also will it be in Matabeleland. The savages will discover the uselessness of rebelling against the white man, and as time goes on will become more reconciled to the ways of their conquerors; that is, if their grievances are inquired into and as far as possible remedied, as I have every hope and belief that they will be as soon as the present rebellion has come to an end; for not until mutual confidence has again been restored between the whites and the blacks can Rhodesia prosper.

From the black man's point of view the white man is probably not necessary as a factor in the prosperity of the country. He could get along very well without him. Unfortunately we cannot manage without the black man; he is absolutely necessary for the development of the country on the white man's lines. But a sulky, rebellious black man, only held in subjection by fear, is both a useless and dangerous personality, and, therefore, the dictates of policy will be at one with the promptings of humanity, in demanding that the natives of Matabeleland shall be governed both kindly and justly as well as firmly.

One word more. In the following pages I have given descriptions of many barbarous deeds which have lately been committed in Matabeleland. I have hidden nothing, but have told the naked truth, and related not only how white men, women, and children were lately murdered, und their senseless bodies afterwards cruelly mutilated by black men, but also how, subsequently, black men were shot down pitilessly by the whites, no mercy being shown or quarter given them by the outraged colonists. By those who seek it, matter will doubtless be found in some of my stories on which to found imputations against the colonists of Rhodesia, who will be held up to execration for the "slaughter" of "poor natives"; the insinuation being that the "poor natives" were ruthlessly killed, with little or no provocation, in order to gratify the lust for blood, which certain people in England appear to think takes possession of their countrymen whenever they set foot on African soil.

But by the great mass of the English-speaking race I feel sure that the conduct of their kith and kin in Matabeleland during the late rebellion will not be too harshly judged. It will be remembered that they were the avengers of the women and children of their own colour, who had but lately been so mercilessly slain, and that, fighting as they were against hordes of savages eager to spill the life-blood of every white man in Rhodesia, savages in whose vocabulary no such words as pity or mercy are to be found, nothing else could be expected than that in the hour of victory no quarter should be given to the murderous foe. It is as unfair as it is ridiculous to talk of the "slaughter" of natives who, having come with arms in their hands, not only to kill you, but your wife and child also, find they have reckoned without their host, and are themselves discomfited and shot down by their would-be victims.

Now, possibly, there might be found in England a philanthropist so meek and good that, were he suddenly confronted by a burglar who told him plainly that he meant to kill him and walk into his house, he would reply, although he carried a loaded revolver in his hand, "Kill me and walk on, for it would be against my creed and conscience to sully my hands with the slaughter of so fine a specimen of the human race as yourself." I do not say that so noble a character really exists within the four seas of Britain, but if he does, I suppose he ought to be looked for amongst the ranks of those who have been loudest in their condemnation of the British settlers in Rhodesia, and who thereby arrogate to themselves the possession of a nobility of nature to which ordinary mortals cannot hope to attain. For the sake of example, therefore, let us say that such a man does exist, and that he is none other than the editor of *Truth*, Mr. Henry Labouchere.

Well, granted then that Mr. Labouchere—the man whom, for the sake of example, I have endowed with such a noble nature—would be prompted to sacrifice his own life rather than sully his soul with the killing of a burglar, would he go yet farther and still spare the robber's life if he knew that, after he himself had been killed, his wife and child would also be put to death? I cannot believe that he would, but imagine rather that he would shoot as straight as possible to prevent such a catastrophe, and I for one would wish that in such a special case his practice might be better than his usual preaching.

Now the settlers in Rhodesia, on those occasions when they have been accused of slaughtering the natives, have only taken the same course as I think would have been adopted by the great-souled philanthropist, whom I hope I am not wronging by imagining that he would steel his heart to take the life of a burglar, if for no other reason than to save the lives of those dear to him; and therefore I would ask my readers not to judge too harshly of the deeds of the colonists which I have recounted in the following pages, but to remember, when judging of their actions, the terrible provocation which they had received. It may be that I have here and there shown a very strong racial feeling against the blackman; but it must be remembered that my story has been written in the midst of all the horrors of a native rebellion, that I have seen many gruesome sights, and have with my own hands collected together the broken skulls of murdered women and children—Dutch and English—in order to give them Christian burial.

Thus I have sometimes written under the influence of strong emotions, making too little allowance possibly for the black man smarting under what he perhaps had some reason to consider the arrogance and injustice of his white conquerors. However, my opinions after all are of little value, being those of a single individual; but I trust that whoever may take the trouble to read my narrative will accept my facts, and believe that the account I have written of events which have lately occurred in Matabeleland is a true and unvarnished one.

The Author

Bulawayo, 21st August 1896.

ADVENTURE WITH A LEOPARD.
"It was close to me before I could even swing my rifle over the horse's neck."

CHAPTER 1

I Return to Matabeleland

When, in the end of December 1893, immediately after the close of the first Matabele War, I rode away from Bulawayo and set out on my journey to England, I thought it more than probable that I should never again revisit the land over which Lo Bengula had so lately held sway. Destiny, however, willed it otherwise. Perhaps I found that the definition of "enough" as "a little more than you've got," when applied to income, was a true one; or perhaps I thought the ways of civilisation somewhat irksome, and at times pined for "a breath of the *veldt*" and one more look at the wild game in the wild country where I had already passed so many years of my life. At any rate, when I was asked by my old friend, Mr. Maurice Heany, to go out once more to Matabeleland to assist him in the management of a land and gold-mining company which he had recently floated, I gave the proposal my very serious consideration, and when I found that my wife was quite willing to face all the troubles and difficulties incidental to a life in a new country, I agreed to undertake the duties required of me for a period of two years.

We—my wife and I—left England for South Africa on 30th March 1895, but we did not reach Bulawayo until the end of the following August; as, after landing at Cape Town, we spent two months in the Cape Colony and the Orange Free State, and then taking ship round the coast to Beira, proceeded by river steamer to Fontesvilla, and thence by rail to Chimoio. Here my waggon was awaiting us, and in it we travelled slowly and comfortably for two months, keeping the main transport road—which I had myself laid out four years before—to Salisbury, but from there going across country to my old hunting camp on the Hanyani River; thence to Hartley Hills on the Umfuli, and from there along the old hunters' road to Bulawayo.

On this portion of our route I found game very plentiful, especially sable antelopes, large herds of which beautiful animals I saw almost daily. Near the River Sewhoi-whoi I was able to take my wife quite close up to the largest herd of these antelopes that I have ever seen. As they cantered past us within a hundred yards I counted them roughly and made their number between seventy-five and eighty. Having plenty of meat at the waggon I had no need to shoot; so we just sat on our horses and admired them, though there was one cow with a beautiful curved pair of horns that tempted me sorely. On several occasions we saw the fresh spoor of lions, but we never either got a sight of the animals themselves or even heard one roar. At the Sebakwe River I saw the tracks of a herd of elephants that had passed only a few days before; and on this same day I met with rather a curious experience, which, although I am not writing an article on shooting incidents, I will take the liberty to relate.

Early on the morning of the day in question I had left the waggon and ridden down to the river—the Sebakwe—intending to follow its course to the point at which the road crossed it. Having plenty of meat, I took no native attendants with me, and resolved not to shoot at anything but a small antelope, a wild pig, or some animal the greater part of which I could have carried behind my saddle. However, I saw no game at all, large or small, with the exception of one reed buck ram bounding through the long grass, and was approaching the ford across the river without having fired a shot, when I noticed what I took to be a jackal sitting on its haunches in the grass about a hundred and fifty yards to my right. The grass being rather long I could not make out very well what it was even from my horse's back, and when I had dismounted I could barely see that there was anything there at all. However, aiming rather low in the grass, I fired, and distinctly heard the bullet strike something with a loud thud.

Remounting my horse, and marking by a small bush the spot near which the now invisible animal had been before I fired, I rode leisurely up to see what I had shot. I was carrying my rifle across the saddle in front of me, without having reloaded it, and on nearing the bush I had marked pulled up my horse and was looking about for a jackal lying dead on the ground. However I could not see one, and was wondering how such a small animal could have moved away after being hit by an expanding bullet, when a loud grunting noise made me look up, and I saw a leopard rushing towards me through the grass. As it only charged from a distance of fifteen yards, it was close to me before I could even swing my rifle over the horse's neck, and I made sure that it would spring upon him and bite and claw him badly before I could load and shoot.

However, strange to say, it simply galloped past, almost, if not quite, brushing against my horse's fore-leg, and passing beneath my right stirrup. After going about thirty yards it stopped and sat down on its haunches. By this time I had another cartridge in my rifle; so I hastily dismounted and gave the leopard a shot behind the shoulder, killing it instantly. It proved to be a large female in good condition, with a beautifully-marked skin. The first bullet had struck it in the middle of the body, and going right through, had made a large hole on the further side, out of which a portion of the liver was protruding. This was of course sufficient to account for the animal's display of bad temper; but why it simply rushed past me without springing on to the horse, I don't quite know.

Had my horse turned, possibly it would have done so; but being an animal of a very imperturbable temper he never moved, and his immobility may have disconcerted the leopard, and caused it not to act quite up to its original intention. After disembowelling it, I lifted it on to my horse, and carried it behind the saddle to the ford across the Sebakwe, where I found my waggon outspanned. This very mild adventure is the only incident of interest which I have to record as having occurred on our journey to Bulawayo, which we finally reached on 20th August.

When just twenty months previously I had left Matabeleland, there was no other Bulawayo save a ruined *kraal*, but lately wrecked and destroyed by the order of the unhappy Lo Bengula, who in despair at the defeat of his bravest regiments, had blown up his European house, burnt his chief town to ashes, and abandoning the land won by his father's *assegais* to the victorious troopers of the Chartered Company, fled away to die heart-broken in the forests to the north. Just across the stream which runs below the *kraal* stood the camp of the white invaders, a rough, hardy lot of men, whom some have called heroes and others filibusters; a confusion of titles equally applicable, I fancy, to the followers of Drake or Clive or any other body of men who have helped to make the British Empire what it is. The site of the new township had indeed been marked out, but not a house of any kind stood upon it.

In the short interval, however, a European town had sprung up, containing many good, substantial buildings, whilst the bustle and movement in the dusty streets gave an air of life and vigour to the new Bulawayo, which is very commonly absent from the frontier towns of South Africa. In short, at this time—the autumn of 1895—everything was apparently *couleur de rose* in Matabeleland. Properties, whether farm lands, building sites in town, or mining claims, went up to very high values, whilst almost every one believed that within a year Bulawayo would contain a population of 5000 souls, and that the town itself would receive a plentiful supply of water from the reservoirs already in course of construction, and be lighted by the electric light. In fact, all was mirth and joy and hope in the future; for what was to hinder the ever-increasing prosperity of the country? Much good work had already been done on many of the reefs, and on the whole the promise was distinctly good. Then again, after a probation of eighteen months, the country had been pronounced favourably upon by Dutch and Colonial farmers, especially for cattle-ranching, whilst many predicted that much of the high *veldt* would carry sheep.

Apparently no difficulties with the natives were to be apprehended, and certainly were not foreseen, as no one could have recognised the identity in the quiet submissive native carrying nothing but a stick, to the arrogant savage of old times who was seldom seen without his shield and *assegais*, and who was usually insolent and brutal in his manner to the white man. No one dreamt that within a very few months the country would be well-nigh overwhelmed in calamity; that that terrible scourge the *rinderpest*, which has swept like a destroying angel from Masailand through Central and Eastern Africa, almost annihilating in its course all bovine animals as well as all the various and beautiful species of antelopes, was creeping ever nearer to the Zambesi River, and was destined ere long to cross that boundary, and travelling ever southwards destroy tens of thousands of cattle in Matabeleland, thereby paralysing its transport service, and rendering the cost of living almost prohibitive in a country separated by 600 miles of wilderness from the nearest railway station.

Still less, looking at the submissive behaviour of the natives, did anyone picture to himself in the furthest recesses of his mind, the vision of homesteads burned to ashes throughout Matabeleland, and around them the corpses of their owners, among them many women and tender children, all brutally murdered, lying unburied in their blood. Yet were these dire disasters, with partial drought and plague of locusts superadded, soon to crush all joy out of Matabeleland.

In spite of its air of prosperity and the light-heartedness of its inhabitants, Bulawayo with its constant dust-storms, scarcity of water, and general burnt-up appearance, had but few attractions either for my wife or myself, and we made our arrangements to get away to our Company's property of Essexvale as soon as possible. On this property a rough two-roomed house of poles, plastered with mud and thatched with grass, had been got ready for us temporarily, pending the arrival of a wire-wove bungalow that had been sent out from England in sections, and which was to be erected on a site chosen by myself.

On our way to Essexvale we spent a night with my old friends the missionaries at Hope Fountain, and I had a long talk over old times, and the present condition of the natives in Matabeleland. Mr. Helm told me that although doubtless the members of the royal family, and the men of position under the old regime, regretted the downfall of their king and the conquest of the country by the white man, yet the great mass of the people acknowledged that they were better off under the rule of the Chartered Company than they had been in Lo Bengula's time; for although individual white men were sometimes guilty of injustice and brutality towards individual natives, yet, speaking generally, the lives and property of the latter were now secure, and whatever they earned was their own, all of which blessings were unknown to them before the conquest of Matabeleland by the white man.

There was, however, one matter, Mr. Helm informed me, that was causing a great deal of discontent throughout the country. This was the periodical taking away of the cattle in small numbers by the Chartered Company, subsequent to the first confiscation immediately after the war. Probably if, after the subjugation of the country, the Chartered Company had at once taken all the cattle they ever intended to take, and given the natives the balance for their very own to do with as they liked, there never would have been any heartburning over the cattle question at all. However, after the first confiscation, all the remaining cattle in the country—about 90,000—were branded with the Company's brand and left with the natives to look after. They were told that the Company would take more from time to time as they required them, but at the same time they were given to understand that only cattle which had belonged to the king would be confiscated, and none belonging to private owners interfered with.

This promise was made under the belief that nearly all the cattle in Matabeleland had belonged to the king, and that the private owners had been but few in number. That this was a mistake I think there can be little doubt, as almost every man of any standing in Matabeleland had been a cattle-owner, some of the chief *indunas* possessing large herds of private cattle. But when a native commissioner received an order from the government to send to Bulawayo without delay a certain number of cattle from his district, he never could have done so had he listened to all the claims made to private ownership previous to the war, some of which were true, but others false; and he therefore had to use his own discretion in selecting the cattle necessary to make up the total required. In this way certain natives suffered wrong, more especially owners of perhaps only three or four cows, who in some cases lost their all, both in cattle and faith in the honesty and justice of the government of the Chartered Company, which they deemed had broken the promise given to them, as indeed was the case, though the mistake was made inadvertently and through not considering the investigation of the whole question of sufficient importance to take any great trouble about.

Mr. Helm said:

> If the Company would take, once for all, all the cattle they intend taking, and give the natives the remainder, it would restore their confidence, as they now believe that the cattle will be constantly taken away from them in small lots until there are none left to them. However, the Company can do what it likes with them, and treat them generously or otherwise as it pleases, for they acknowledge themselves to be a conquered people, and will submit to any terms imposed upon them.

This remark was made by a man who had lived in close intimacy with the natives of Matabeleland for twenty years, but as subsequent events show, it was far from the truth. Shortly after this conversation, the Government of the Chartered Company, acting on the advice I believe of the chief native commissioner, Mr. Herbert Taylor, decided to finally settle the cattle question. There were at this time about 70,000 head of cattle in the hands of the natives, and of this number the government determined to take two-fifths, leaving the remaining three fifths as the absolute property of the Matabele. A meeting was called at Bulawayo, at which all the chief *indunas* in the country were present, and when the proposition was laid before them, they expressed themselves as thoroughly satisfied, and assured Mr. Taylor that their people would also be satisfied; and from my own subsequent observation, I believe that this final distribution of the cattle caused a general feeling of relief throughout the country, and, in the district in which I was living at any rate, the people seemed well contented with this settlement of the question, which left them for the most part fairly well off.

CHAPTER 2

Our life at Essexvale

Of our life on Essexvale I have but little of interest to relate. In September and October the weather became intensely hot, but our well-thatched house we found to be much cooler than any building in Bulawayo, to which seat of light and learning we paid but occasional visits. Our wire-wove house did not arrive in Matabeleland until late in November, just as the rainy season was setting in, and it was not until towards the end of the year that it was put together and stood ready to receive us, on the site I had chosen for it. This was a very picturesque position on the top of a cliff about eighty feet above the Ingnaima River. Here we lived happily and contentedly for three months, and were apparently on the most friendly terms with all the natives living near us. Our Company bought about 1200 head of cattle, and these I distributed amongst the natives living on Essexvale—an estate of nearly 200,000 acres—to herd for us in lots of from ten to thirty in number, which they were very glad to do for the sake of the milk. To all the headmen living immediately round the homestead I gave a larger proportion of milk cows, on the condition that they brought me daily half the milk.

I was assisted in the management of the estate by a young German, Herr Blöcker, who had taken his diplomas in a German School of Forestry, as it was part of our Company's scheme to start a plantation of gum trees, the timber of which is valuable for mining purposes. We therefore cleared and ploughed up about forty acres of land, and planted out over 5000 trees raised from seed on a strip of eight acres near the house. The rest of the ploughed land we sowed with maize, reserving about an acre near the river for a vegetable garden. The ground round the house my wife laid out in flower-beds, and I had also beds prepared for the planting of orange and other fruit trees,

THE AUTHOR'S HOMESTEAD ON ESSEXVILLE, MATABELELAND
Destroyed by the natives in April 1896

which I had ordered from the Cape Colony; whilst several banana and *granadilla* plants, which had been given us by the Rev. Mr. Helm, were already growing well. Altogether, in spite of the most unseasonable drought which prevailed during January, February, and March, our homestead commenced to look quite pretty, and another year's work would have made a nice place of it; whilst the view from our front door up the river, with our cattle and horses grazing on the banks, and ducks and geese swimming in the pools or sunning themselves on the sand, was always singularly homelike.

As I have said above, up to the day of the native insurrection, which broke out towards the end of March, all the natives on Essexvale appeared to be on the most friendly terms with us, and were always most civil and polite to my wife, who had grown to like them very much. We had done them many good turns, and I believe they liked us as individuals. Umlugulu, a relation of Lo Bengula's, and one of the principal men in that king's time, as well as a high priest of the ceremonies at the annual religious dance of the Inxwala, was living about fifteen miles away, and often came to see us. He was a very gentle-mannered savage, and always most courteous and polite in his bearing, and by us he was always treated with the consideration due to one who had held a high position and been a man of importance in Lo Bengula's time.

It is now supposed, and I think with justice, that this man was one of the chief instigators of the rebellion; but if this is so, I have strong reasons for believing that he only finally made up his mind that the time had come for the attempt to be made to drive the white men out of the country when he learnt that the whole of the police force of Matabeleland, together with the artillery, munitions of war, etc., which had been taken down to the Transvaal by Dr. Jameson, had been captured by the Boers. My reason for thinking so is, that before he heard this news he asked mo several times to take some unbranded cattle from him, and have them herded amongst my own, or bought from him at my own price.

This request I could not grant, but advised him to go and tell Dr. Jameson the story he had told me, as to how these cattle came to be in his possession without the Company's brand on them. After he heard the news of Dr. Jameson's surrender, Umlugulu never said anything more about these cattle, but he often came to see me, and always questioned me very closely as to what had actually happened in the Transvaal. Although at that time I had no idea as to the lines on which I now think his mind was working, I gave him little or no information, the more so that I could see he was very anxious to get at the truth.

Towards the end of February, Mr. Jackson, the native commissioner in my district, who was living with a sub-inspector and a force of native police at a spot on one of the roads through Essexvale about twelve miles distant from our house, informed me that rumours of coming disaster to the white man, purporting to emanate from the "*Umlimo*" or god of the Makalakas, who dwells in a cave of the Matopo Hills, were being spread abroad amongst the people of Matabeleland. Shortly before this there had been a total eclipse of the moon. This the *Umlimo* told the natives meant that white man's blood was about to be spilt.

Further than this, they were informed that Lo Bengula was not dead, but was now on his way back to Matabeleland with a large army from the north, whilst two other armies were coming to help him against the white man from the west and east. "Watch the coming moon," said the *Umlimo*, "and be ready." He also claimed to have sent the *rinderpest*, which had just reached the cattle in the north of Matabeleland—though of what advantage that scourge was to the natives I don't quite see—and promised that he would soon afflict the white men themselves with some equally terrible disease.

Now, although these rumours of a native rising were current in Matabeleland some time before the insurrection actually broke out, and were reported to the then acting chief native commissioner, Mr. Thomas, and to the heads of the government, I do not think that they would have been warranted in taking any steps of a suppressive nature at this juncture; for there was absolutely nothing tangible to go upon, nor could any commission of inquiry have come to any other conclusion than that the natives had no intention of rebelling; for they were as quiet and submissive in their demeanour towards Europeans as they ever had been since the war, and there was absolutely no evidence of any secret arming amongst them. And the fact remains that, with one exception, all those Europeans in Matabeleland who had had a long experience of natives—that is, the native commissioners, missionaries, and a few old traders and hunters, amongst whom I must include myself—were unanimous in the opinion that no rebellion on the part of the Matabele was to be apprehended.

I say there was one exception, as I have been told that Mr. Usher, an old trader long resident in Matabeleland, and who since the first war has been living altogether amongst the natives, has always maintained that the Matabele would one day rise against the white man.

For myself, I had many conversations with Mr. Jackson on the subject, and we came to the conclusion, after talking with several intelligent natives regarding the rumours going about, that the Matabele were not likely to rebel until Lo Bengula appeared with his army. "However," said Mr. Jackson one evening, "it is very difficult to worm a secret out of a native, and if there should be an insurrection those are the devils we have to fear," pointing to his squad of native Matabele policemen, sitting about round their huts all armed with repeating Winchester rifles. At that time no one would have imagined that these native policemen—all fine, active-looking young fellows, and very smart at their drill—would have been likely to mutiny, since they were not only very well disciplined but most civil and obedient to their white officers; whilst, on the other hand, they were constantly at loggerheads with their compatriots, whom they had to bring to book for any transgression of the Chartered Company's laws, and more particularly for evasion of the regulations exacting a certain amount of labour annually at a fixed rate of pay from every able-bodied young man. However, as subsequent events have shown, Mr. Jackson was right in his prognostication, for when the rebellion did break out, about half the native police at once turned their rifles against their employers. The remainder were true to their salt, but had to be disarmed as a precautionary measure.

I will now before going further say a word concerning the "*Umlimo*" or god of the Makalakas, who has apparently played such an important part in the present rebellion, but who, I think, has in reality only been the instrument employed by the actual leaders of the insurrection to work upon the superstitions of the people, and mould them to their will. To the best of my belief, there exists amongst the Makalakas, as amongst all the tribes of allied race throughout South-Eastern Africa, an hereditary priesthood, confined to one family, though from time to time certain other young men are adopted by the high priest and initiated into the mysteries of his profession. These men in common with the actual sons of the high priest are known henceforth as children of the god.

The head of the family lives in the Matopo Hills, and is known as the *Umlimo*, but as far as one can understand from the rather conflicting statements made concerning him by the natives, he is not actually the *Umlimo*, but a being possessed of all the ordinary attributes of man,—in fact a human being, with a spiritual nature superadded which enables him to commune with the unseen Deity that pervades space, and communicate the wishes or commands of the invisible spirit to the people. The temple of the *Umlimo* is a cave in the Matopo Hills, whither the people repair to consult him; and I believe that the voice which is heard in answer to their questions from the depths of the cave is supposed to emanate not from the human *Umlimo* or priest, but to be the actual utterance of the invisible god.

The human *Umlimo* is kept wonderfully well posted up concerning everything that happens in Matabeleland, probably by the various members of his family, who live in different parts of the country, and who often visit him. He is thus often enabled to make very shrewd answers to the questions asked him, and to show himself conversant with matters which his interlocutors thought were known only to themselves; and in this way he has gained a great ascendency over the minds of the people.

If one asks who the *Umlimo* is, the answer is that he is a spirit or supernatural being of infinite wisdom, known to man only as a voice speaking from the depths of a cave. He is said to be able to speak all languages, as well as to be possessed of the faculty of roaring like a lion, crowing like a cock, barking like a dog, etc. On the other hand, the human *Umlimo* accepts or rather demands presents from those who visit his cave for the purpose of consulting the Deity, and possesses not only cattle, sheep, and goats, but also a large number of wives. The great mass of the Matabele people seem to me to have very vague ideas concerning the *Umlimo*; and sometimes I think that besides the priest in the Matopos through whom the voice of God is supposed to be heard, there are other priests,[1] or so-called *Umlimos*, in other parts of the country through whom they believe that the commands of the Almighty can be conveyed to them.

At any rate, both prior to and during the present rebellion, utterances purporting to emanate from the "*Umlimo*" have been implicitly believed in, and the commands attributed to him obeyed with a blind fanaticism, that one would not have looked for in a people who always seem to be extremely matter of fact and practical in everyday life. It may seem strange that this "*Umlimo*," or god of the despised Makalakas, should be accepted as an oracle by the Matabele, but I know that Lo Bengula professed a strong belief in his magical powers, and from

---

1. There can be no doubt as to this, as there is now an *Umlimo* or prophet with the insurgents in the north-east of Matabeleland, who has apparently no connection with the *Umlimo* in the Matopo Hills.

time to time consulted him. I believe, however, that the *Umlimo* was made use of for the purposes of the present rebellion by Umlugulu, and other members of the late king's family.

These men were naturally not content with their position under the white man's rule, and as ever since the war they had probably been rebels at heart, they only wanted an opportunity to call the people to arms. This opportunity they thought had come when they heard that the entire police force of Matabeleland, together with most of the big guns and munitions of war up till then stored in Bulawayo, had been captured by the Boers. For to them the police represented the fighting or military element amongst the white men, and they more or less despised all other classes, whom they usually saw going about altogether unarmed and defenceless. When the police were gone, therefore, they at once probably set about stirring up a rebellion, and got the *Umlimo* to play their game and work upon the superstitions of the people. This at any rate is my own opinion of the origin of the insurrection.

About the middle of March I was appointed cattle inspector for the district between the Umzingwani and Insiza Rivers, and had to do a lot of riding about in my endeavours to assist the government to arrest the spread of the *rinderpest*. However, one might as well have tried to stop a rising tide on the sea-shore, as prevent this dreadful disease from travelling steadily down the main roads, leaving nothing but rotting carcasses and ruined men behind it.

Therefore, while still strictly prohibiting all movement of cattle from infected districts to parts of the country yet free from the terrible scourge, the government declared the main roads open for traffic on Tuesday, 24th March, in order that as many wagon-loads of provisions as possible might be brought into Bulawayo, whilst any oxen were still left alive to pull them; for at this time the only calamities apprehended in Matabeleland were famine, and the complete dislocation of transport throughout the country owing to the terrible mortality amongst the cattle from *rinderpest*. These dangers indeed seemed so pressing that the government was called upon by a deputation from the Chamber of Commerce to at once purchase 2000 mules, to be used for the importation of food-stuffs into Bulawayo, and their distribution from that centre to the various mining districts.

On Sunday, 22nd March, I reached Bulawayo late in the evening, after a very long day's ride inspecting cattle, and I then heard rumours of a disturbance having taken place between some of Mr. Jackson's native police and the inhabitants of a Matabele *kraal* near the north-western boundary of our Company's property of Essexvale. On the following day I got a fresh horse and rode twenty-five miles down the Tuli road to Dawson's store on the Umzingwani River—the limit of my beat in this direction—issuing passes to all the waggons I met with to proceed on their way up or down the road on the following morning. Arrived at the store, I there met my friend Mr. Jackson, the native commissioner, and Mr. Cooke, and learned from them that a native policeman had been murdered by the Matabele on the previous Friday night, and that the murderers had fled into the Matopo Hills, taking all their women and children as well as their cattle with them. My friends were only waiting for a detachment of native police, under two white inspectors, to follow up the murderers and endeavour to bring them to justice.

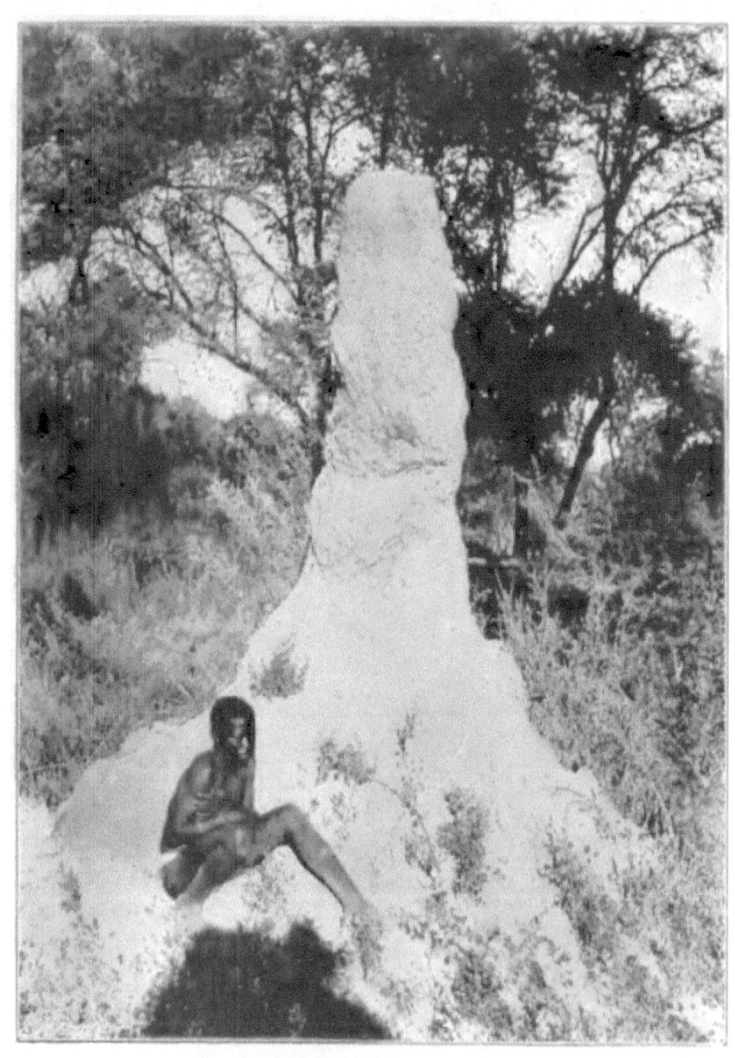

AN ANT-HEAP IN MATABELELAND.

Chapter 3

First Overt Act of Rebellion

Now this murder of a native policeman on the night of Friday, 20th March, was the first overt act of rebellion on the part of the Matabele against the Government of the British South Africa Company, and I will therefore relate exactly what occurred. On the evening of the aforementioned day, eight native policemen, acting on instructions of Mr. Jackson, arrived at the town of Umgorshlwini, situated in the hills near the Umzingwani River. Being accompanied by several boys carrying their blankets, etc., they formed quite a little party, and so camped outside the native town. They were sitting talking over their fires after the evening meal, when a number of Matabele came up, and ranging themselves in a line in front of them, commenced to dance. These men all carried *knobkerries*, and were led by a man named Umzobo,[1] who had held a post of importance at Bulawayo in Lo Bengula's time. The so-called dancing of all *kaffirs* of Zulu race is not dancing in the European sense, but consists for the most part in stamping on the ground, swaying the body and gesticulating with sticks. The stamping is usually accompanied by a chant, the words of which are often improvised for the occasion, and the effect of the whole dance is decidedly stimulating, as I have often watched a stolid, stupid-looking *kaffir* work himself up to a state of high excitability by this means.

On the present occasion Umzobo and his men very soon showed that they had come to dance before the representatives of the law with a purpose, that purpose being to pick a quarrel with them. They soon commenced to *"jia,"* or point with their sticks; then one of them ran out of the line, and coming close up to the police, stooped forward, and drawing his left hand rapidly backwards and forwards across his

---

1. His title was *"Umlisa go Bulawayo,"* or Lieutenant of Bulawayo.

throat, said: "You are killing us, you are killing us; why don't you cut our throats, and make an end of it?" Then another ran out, and repeating the formula, "you are killing us," pressed his finger on his temple, and said: "Why don't you shoot us? why don't you put the bullet in just here?" The expression, "you're killing us," so frequently used by Umzobo's men, meant "you're making life unpleasant to us by enforcing the Company's laws."

When these hostile demonstrations had gone on for some time, the sergeant in charge of the police told Umzobo that he had better take his men away, and tell them to go to sleep, as nobody wanted to fight with them; but his words were without effect, and the dancing was still going on, when one of the policemen saw a man creeping stealthily towards them round the back of the cattle *kraal*. At once suspecting mischief, he jumped up, and calling to his comrades "Look out, we're amongst enemies," rushed upon the crouching figure that at once stood up and revealed a *kaffir* armed with an *assegai*. Before he could make use of his weapon, however, the policeman caught him by the wrist, whilst another guardian of the law who had followed close behind seized his other arm.

They at once disarmed the man, and were putting the handcuffs on him, when a shot was fired out of the cattle *kraal*, aimed of course at the police, but so badly aimed that instead of hitting one of them, it struck their prisoner in the back, killing him almost instantly. Indeed, he fell dead with the handcuff on one wrist. Immediately the shot was fired some of the police rushed into the *kraal* and almost succeeded in capturing the man who had fired, so nearly in fact that he dropped his rifle in his hurry to escape.

Umzobo and his men had now disappeared, and the police having collected together, were standing in the light of their camp fires uncertain what to do, when a volley was fired amongst them from the bush outside the *kraal*. None of the police were hit, but one of their blanket-carriers was shot through the head and killed on the spot. Not knowing the number of their unseen enemies, the representatives of the law then thought it advisable to beat a retreat. They reached Mr. Jackson's camp at 1 a.m. on Saturday, handing him the captured rifle, and reporting the loss of two of their boys; for besides the one whom they knew to be dead, another small boy some ten or twelve years of age was missing. This boy Mr. Jackson found lying dead half under the *kraal* fence, when he visited Umgorshlwini with all the police he could muster on the morning after the disturbance. The town was then deserted, and Mr. Jackson thinks that this small boy must have been discovered trying to hide under the fence after the police had left. He had been murdered in a most brutal way, his skull having been smashed to atoms with *knobkerries*.

But the murder of these two police boys and the accidental killing of one of Umzobo's men was not the only deed of blood which occurred on this Friday night. Amongst Umzobo's men was one Ganyana. After the retreat of the police this man went alone to the *kraal* of a nephew of Lo Bengula—Umfondisi, the son of Lo Magazi—and waking him up, told him what had happened. According to the report of a stranger who was sleeping in Umfondisi's *kraal* that night, Ganyana was very much excited and called out, "Come, Umfondisi; why are you sleeping? don't you know we're fighting? we've killed some policemen, come; blood is running and men are lying dead; come with me and let us do some more killing." Umfondisi was nothing loath, and arming himself with an *assegai* went off with Ganyana to a neighbouring *kraal*, the headman of which they at once awakened in order to tell him the news. At this *kraal* there happened to be one of Mr. Jackson's native policemen. He was asleep in a hut when Ganyana and Umfondisi arrived, but the loud and excited conversation that was being carried on awoke him, and he got up and came out of the hut, asking as he did so what all the noise was about.

"Who are you? "said Ganyana.

"I am so and so, one of Mr. Jackson's policemen," was the answer.

"What!" responded Ganyana; "do you tell me that you are one of the witches who are always troubling us?" and running up to him he shot him, and as he fell down mortally wounded, Umfondisi, the king's nephew, plunged his *assegai* into him.

When on Monday evening, 23rd March, I heard from Mr. Jackson what had happened on the previous Friday night, I imagined that the disturbance was merely the outcome of local discontent, and little thought that this attack on native policemen was but the prelude to the most terrible massacre of Europeans that has ever yet taken place in a native rising in South Africa; and more than this, that even whilst I listened to the story, white men, women, and children lay freshly murdered not many miles away. On the following morning, Tuesday, 24th March, I rode through the hills to my own place, passing Umgorshlwini on the way. Riding round the *kraal* I found bloodstains where the three men had been killed, but the bodies had been taken away and buried by the order of Mr. Jackson. The *kraal* itself, together with many smaller ones in its vicinity, was absolutely deserted, and a splendid crop of corn left standing in the valley below.

Having been absent since the previous Sunday morning, I was still all unsuspicious of danger, but knowing now all that actually happened during that time within a short distance of my house, I shudder to think of what might have occurred there during my absence; for my wife had been quite alone in the house with two little native girls; Mr. Blöcker, my German assistant, and a young Scotchman, Mr. Notman, occupying huts some distance away.

I reached home about mid-day, and found everything going on as usual. My wife told me that during the morning several men—all of whom I knew well—had come over to see her from the chief village of the district—Intuntini—which had been a big military *kraal* before the war. These men were all true-blooded Matabele, and several of them were in charge of cattle belonging to my Company. They all wished to borrow axes from her, to be used for the purpose of strengthening their cattle *kraals*, they said, but I know now that they wanted them as weapons of offence, as many of the murders were committed with axes. As we were accustomed to assist the natives in any small matter of this kind, she let them have all the axes that could be spared, and allowed them to sharpen them on the grindstone.

About sundown some of these same men brought the usual evening's milk, and my wife and I chatted with them for some time. We spoke about the recent murders on the Umzingwani, and the conduct of Umzobo and Umfondisi, and my wife asked me to say that she thought they had acted very foolishly, as the white men would punish them. At this they laughed, and one of them said significantly, "How can the white men punish them? where are the white police? there are none left in the country."

Soon after these men had left us, George, a colonial *kaffir* in my employ, came and said he wished to speak to me, and on my going aside with him informed me that his wife—a Matabele woman—had just heard from another native woman that white men had been murdered on the previous day by the Matabele, on the further side of the Malungwani range, amongst them a native commissioner, who, it was said had had his throat cut by his own black police. On hearing this disagreeable news, which I did not doubt was substantially true, I began to think that we were going to have a native rising after all.

However, I did not consider that we were in any danger, except from natives coming from a distance, as I could not believe that any of the people living close round us would be keen to murder either my wife or myself or anyone living with us, as we had benefited them in many ways, and had certainly never given them any cause to dislike our presence amongst them. I, of course, said nothing to my wife as to what I had heard, but I told Mr. Blöcker and the young Scotchman to keep their rifles handy in case of accidents. I had, too, some very good watch-dogs that I knew would give me warning if any *kaffirs* came near the house, and I kept awake all night with my rifle and a belt full of cartridges alongside of me. But the night passed off quite quietly.

Why no attempt was made to murder us on that Tuesday night will always remain a mystery to me. I should like to think that because we had always treated them kindly and considerately, our immediate neighbours shrank from killing us; but after all that has happened I find it very difficult to believe this. They may have come with the intention of killing us on the Tuesday morning, but finding me absent, and Mr. Blöcker with a rifle in his hands—for when they arrived at the homestead he was just going off to shoot a cow whose hip had been dislocated in branding—may not have thought the opportunity a good one. My wife noticed that they seemed very excited, and they also seemed very anxious to know when I would return.

All things considered, I am afraid we owe them little, as if they did not attempt to murder us they at any rate gave us no warning, and went off on the Tuesday night with all the cattle I had entrusted to their care, and in all likelihood assisted in the murder of Messrs. Foster, Eagleson, and Anderson, all three of whom were carrying on mining work on Essexvale; Foster's camp being within four miles of my home.

The events of the last three months have taught me at least this, that it is impossible for a European to understand the workings of a native's mind; and, speaking personally, after having spent over twenty years of my life amongst the *kaffirs*, I now see that I know nothing about them, and recognise that I am quite incompetent to express an opinion 'as to the line of conduct they would be likely to adopt under any given circumstances.

On the following morning I got up early, and after seeing the *kaffirs* make a start on the work on which I was then engaged—which was the preparation of a piece of ground round the house for a plantation of fruit trees—I went up to George's hut and told him to try and get some farther particulars, through his wife, as to the murders said to have been committed on the previous Monday. Then I strolled back to the house and worked at one thing and another till breakfast time, and was just going indoors to sit down to that meal, when I saw George running down from his hut to our house, followed by a *kaffir* boy. As he came near he shouted out to the horse-herd who was standing by the stable, "Bring the horses, bring the horses; make haste!"

I knew then there was something wrong, and half thought that an attack was imminent, and having my wife's safety to provide for, was much relieved when George told me that no pressing danger threatened, but that armed *kaffirs* had driven off some of my Company's cattle. The boy who accompanied George belonged to a small *kraal*, to the members of which I had given some twenty or thirty head of cattle to look after for our Company, they getting full benefit of all the milk, a great boon to them, as they possessed no cattle of their own. He had been sent by the headman to inform me that just at daylight a number of Matabele from the *kraal* of Gwibu, a nephew of Lo Bengula, had opened the cattle *kraal* and driven off all the cattle, threatening the life of any one who interfered with them.

These men, he said, were all armed either with guns or shields and *assegais*, and wore white ox-tails round their left arms and necks. Whilst I was still speaking, another messenger arrived to tell me that all the Intuntini people had left in the night, taking all their cattle with them, the greater part of which belonged to my Company. I now knew that we were face to face with a native rising, but I thought—what was indeed the fact—that this rising had been fomented by members of the late king's family, and was confined so far to the Abenzantsi, or Matabele of pure Zulu descent, and I cherished the hope that if energetic measures were at once adopted by the government, the more numerous and useful section of the nation, of Makalaka and Mashuna descent, might be kept quiet and the rebellion speedily suppressed.

Chapter 4

Precautions Against Native Attack

The first thing to be done was to take my wife into Bulawayo, and then return at once with a body of armed men to Essexvale, in order to make a display of force which might deter those natives, who were still sitting quiet watching events, from joining the rebels; for I knew that the general idea was, that there being now no longer any police force in the country, the government was practically powerless to cope with an organised rebellion. I therefore had all our horses saddled up immediately to be ready for emergencies, and in order to guard against surprise placed George as a vidette on the top of a rise behind the house, from which a good view of the surrounding country was obtainable. Then, whilst we were having breakfast, I sent messengers to summon all the headmen of the *kraals* in the immediate vicinity of the homestead. These men, I may say, were all in possession of cattle belonging to my Company, and as none of them were pure-blooded Matabele, I imagined they would have no sympathy with the insurgents.

They all answered my summons, accompanied by many of their people, and before leaving I spoke to them, and did my best to impress upon them the folly of rebelling against the white man. They professed themselves in perfect accord with all I said; averred that they were quite content to live with me as their "*inkosi*," [1] and protested that they had nothing to hope for from the overthrow of the white man by the Matabele. In conclusion, I told them that I was going into Bulawayo to place my wife in a position of safety, but that I would return immediately with an armed force and endeavour to recover some of the cattle stolen by Gwibu and the rest of the Matabele. Mr.

---
1. Literally king; but the word is commonly used in addressing a European, as a complimentary title, conveying the idea of dependence on the part of the speaker.

Blöcker wished to remain at the homestead until my return, but this I would not allow, as I did not care to leave a white man all by himself; and besides I required him to help me in getting some men together. George—the colonial *kaffir*—however, stopped behind, as he considered himself quite safe with Umsetchi's people,—Umsetchi being the headman of several little *kraals* close to the house, with the inhabitants of which we had always been on the most friendly terms.

Our ride into Bulawayo was altogether uneventful, as our road lay almost entirely through uninhabited country, and did not cross the line that the rebel natives of the district would have been likely to take on their way to the fastnesses of the Malungwani Hills. As, however, it was a scorching hot day it was a very trying experience for my wife.

Just before reaching town we met Mr. Claude Grenfell, who, with Messrs. Norton and Edmonds, was on his way out to Essexvale with a cart and horses to bring in my wife, and from them we learned that the insurrection was becoming general all over the country, and that forces had already been raised and sent out to relieve miners and settlers in the outlying districts. The Hon. Maurice Gifford had left the previous day for the Insiza, whilst Messrs. Napier and Spreckley were just on the point of starting for other disturbed parts of the country.

After handing over my wife to the kind care of her good friend Mrs. Spreckley, I at once set to work to get together a mounted force with which to return immediately to Essexvale, and thanks to the energetic assistance of Mr. Blöcker and Mr. Norton I was able to leave Bulawayo again at eight o'clock the same evening with thirty-six mounted men. I had wished to raise a force of 100 men, but found it impossible to do so, nearly all the horses and rifles in the possession of the government having been given out to equip the forces already sent out before my arrival in town. There were men enough left, and good men too, ready to go with me anywhere, but the government could only supply six horses—and not good ones at that—and twenty rifles. However, I managed to raise thirty private horses, and some private rifles, and got away about two hours after sundown with a compact little force of thirty-six mounted men.

The moon was now getting near the full, and by its light we pushed on, and at 2 a.m. on Thursday, 26th March, were back at my homestead, which is just twenty-three miles distant from Bulawayo. Here I found everything as I had left it, George having installed himself with some of Umsetchi's men in the stable, which being built very solidly of stone, they might easily have held against any ordinary attack.

I had left Essexvale a few hours before, without any very bitter feeling against the *kaffirs*, for after all, looking at things from their point of view, if they thought they could succeed in shaking off the white man's rule, and retaking all the cattle that once were theirs or their king's, and all those brought into the country since the war as well, why shouldn't they try the chances of rebellion? I knew they would have to fight to accomplish their ends, and it was for them to consider whether the game was worth the candle or not. At that time, however, I was far from realising what had happened, and was inclined to judge the *kaffirs* very leniently. But my visit to Bulawayo had changed my sentiments entirely, and the accounts which I had there heard of the cruel and treacherous murders that had been perpetrated on defenceless women and children, besides at once destroying whatever sympathy I may have at first felt for the rebels, had not only filled me with indignation, but had excited a desire for vengeance, which could only be satisfied by a personal and active participation in the killing of the murderers.

I don't defend such feelings, nor deny that they are vile and brutal when viewed from a high moral standpoint; only I would say to the highly moral critic. Be charitable if you have not yourself lived through similar experiences; be not too harsh in your judgment of your fellow-man, for you probably know not your own nature, nor are you capable of analysing passions which can only be understood by those Europeans who have lived through a native rising, in which women and children of their race have been barbarously murdered by savages; by beings whom, in their hearts, they despise; as rightly or wrongly they consider that they belong to a lower type of the human family than themselves.

I offer no opinion upon this sentiment, but I say that it undoubtedly exists, and must always aggravate the savagery of a conflict between the two races; whilst the murder of white women and children, by natives, seems to the colonist not merely a crime, but a sacrilege, and calls forth all the latent ferocity of the more civilised race. For, kind and considerate though any European may be under ordinary circumstances to the savages amongst whom he happens to be living, yet deep down in his heart, whether he be a miner or a missionary, is the conviction that the black man belongs to a lower type of humanity than the white; and if this is a mistaken conviction, ask the negrophilist who professes to think so, whether he would give his daughter in marriage to a negro, and if not, why not?

At any rate the lovers and admirers of the Matabele would do well to caution their *protégés* not to commence another insurrection by the murder of white women and children, for should they do so, they will once more have cause to rue a war of retaliation, that will be waged with all the merciless ferocity which must inevitably follow upon such a course; as, although the murder of Europeans by savages may commend itself to certain armchair philosophers in England, who can see no good in a colonist, nor any harm in a savage, yet the colonists themselves cannot look upon such matters from the same point of view, and will take such steps to prevent the recurrence of any farther ebullitions of temper, as were taken by the United States troops after the massacres of Minnesota, or by the British troops at Secunderabad and other places in suppressing the Indian Mutiny.

Before resuming my personal narrative, I will give a short account of what had already taken place in the progress of the insurrection on Essexvale itself, and in those parts of the Insiza and Filibusi districts which border upon Essexvale.

There is reason to believe that the outbreak of the rebellion, commencing as it did with the murder of a native policeman on Friday, 20th March, was somewhat premature, and thus there was an interval of nearly three days between the date of this murder and the day when the first white men were killed by the natives. From the Umzingwani, the flame of rebellion spread through the Filibusi and Insiza districts, to the Tchangani and Inyati, and thence to the mining camps in the neighbourhood of the Gwelo and Ingwenia Rivers, and indeed throughout the country wherever white men, women, and children could be taken by surprise and murdered either singly or in small parties; and so quickly was this cruel work accomplished, that although it was only on 23rd March that the first Europeans were murdered, there is reason to believe that by the evening of the 30th not a white man was left alive in the outlying districts of Matabeleland. Between these two dates many people escaped or were brought in to Bulawayo by relief parties, but a large number were cruelly and treacherously murdered.

CHAPTER 5

Massacre of the Whites Near Edkins' Store

Not far from the once large military *kraal* of Gorshlwayo, near the southern border of Essexvale, was a trading station known as Edkins' store. In the neighbourhood were several mining camps and the residence of a native commissioner, and it is here probably that the first murders of Europeans were committed during the present native rising.

At any rate some time on Monday, 23rd March,[1] seven white men, two colonial boys and a *coolie* cook were murdered there. Among the murdered men was Mr. Bentley, the native commissioner, who was shot or stabbed from behind, whilst sitting in his hut writing—the date above the last words he ever wrote being 23rd March. Mr. Edkins and three other white men, together with their two colonial servants and the *coolie* cook, were killed in and round the store, whilst Messrs. Ivers and Ottens were killed, the former near the Celtic mining camp, and the latter about halfway between the camp and the store, from which it was distant about a mile and a half. The corpses of these poor fellows were found by Colonel Spreckley's relief party four days subsequent to the massacre.

A colonial native was also discovered still living, though terribly injured. He had evidently been left for dead by the Matabele, and besides the wounds which they had inflicted on him in order to kill him, they had slit his mouth open from ear to ear. It was not thought that

---

1 There is some doubt as to whether these murders were committed on the Monday or the Tuesday; Colonel Spreckley thinks on the Monday, whilst Mr. O'Connor says it was Tuesday. It is possible that the latter may have been a day wrong in his reckoning, whilst the entry in Mr. Bentley's books seems to favour the earlier date.

this man could possibly live, but his wounds were dressed, and food given him, and, wonderful to relate, he eventually made his way to Bulawayo, where, thanks to the skilful treatment and kind nursing he received in the hospital there, he in time recovered from his injuries.

He was able to give evidence concerning the murders, which he said were committed suddenly and without warning by native policemen, aided by natives from the surrounding *kraals* under two brothers of Lo Bengula, Maschlaschlin and Umfaizella, who, with Umlugulu, Gwibu, Umfondisi, and other members of the king's family, were the chief instigators of the rebellion; and this being so, no peace can be made that will satisfy the colonists until all the members of the late king's family, as well as every *induna* and every native policeman who it can be proved took part in the murders which marked the outbreak of the rebellion, have been either hanged or shot.

This may seem a big order to some people—who, however, do not probably contemplate residing on a lonely farm in Rhodesia—but it is necessary for the future safety of the country.

The bodies of Ottens and Bentley had been mutilated, and dry grass had been heaped up and burnt over the faces of all the dead, possibly with the idea of destroying their identity.

Almost simultaneously with the murders at Edkins' store, or at any rate on the same day, the massacre of the whites was commenced in the Insiza district, the first sufferers being probably the Cunningham family, who were living on a farm near the Insiza River. These poor people seem to have been attacked early in the afternoon, as when their homestead was visited on the following day by Messrs. Liebert and Fynn, the remains of the mid-day meal were still on the table, whilst old Mr. Cunningham seemed to have been murdered whilst reclining on a couch reading a newspaper. Here is the sworn deposition of Mr. Fynn, the assistant native commissioner for the Insiza district, as to the finding of the bodies.

Herbert Pomeroy Fynn's sworn statement:—

> I am an assistant native commissioner for the Insiza district. I accompanied last witness—Mr. Liebert—and Orpen to Cunningham's farm on Tuesday morning, 24th March. On arrival there I saw eight dead bodies lying on the ground about twenty yards from the homestead. We made a cursory examination and saw that the deceased persons had been murdered by means of *knobkerries* and battle-axes, or similar weapons. The ground was

covered with native footprints, and there were broken *knobkerries* lying about. I identified among the dead bodies those of Mr. Cunningham senior, Mrs. Cunningham, two Miss Cunninghams, Master Cunningham, and three children whom I identified as the grandchildren of Mr. Cunningham senior. The deceased persons appeared to have been killed inside the house and afterwards dragged out and thrown outside in the position in which we found them. From the fact that all the native *kraals* in the vicinity were quite deserted, I have absolutely no doubt that the persons who killed the deceased were Matabele natives. Young Cunningham, aged about fourteen years, was still alive when we arrived, but unconscious, and died immediately after our arrival.

Such is the bald account of the discovery of the battered and bloody remains of this unfortunate family, which, alas! was not the only one suddenly blotted out of existence, root and branch, during the first terrible days of the Matabele rebellion. The hideous barbarity of these murders, and the feeling of intense exasperation they would be likely to excite amongst the surviving settlers, seem to have been somewhat underrated in England; whilst for obvious reasons they have been carefully kept out of sight by those dishonest speakers who recently endeavoured to excite public opinion against the white population of Rhodesia. You can respect an honest enemy even if you can't like him; but when a fanatic endeavours to support either his or her theories by the suppression of truth, he or she becomes contemptible.

But we are thankful for the sympathy of that most determined enemy of everything Rhodesian—except the noble savages who therein dwell—Mr. Labouchere, who has professed himself "sorry for the women and children who have been killed." Sorry—only sorry! Wonderful indeed is the calm serenity of soul that enables that noble nature to view all mundane affairs from the same cold, passionless plane, whether it be the cruel murder of an English settler's wife and family in Rhodesia, or an accident to the wheel of a friend's bicycle in Hyde Park! But the men who have looked upon the corpses of the murdered ones, who have seen the shattered skulls of their countrywomen, the long grey locks of the aged and the sunny curls of the girls and little children all alike dabbled in their blood, are something more than sorry; indignation mingles with their sorrow, and they are determined to exact such punishment for the crimes committed, as shall preclude as far as possible their recurrence in the future.

At a distance of a few miles from the Cunninghams' farm was a mining property belonging to the Nellie Reef Development Company, where work was being carried on under the superintendence of Mr. Thomas Maddocks, the manager of the Nellie Reef Mine. At about a quarter to six on the evening of Monday, 23rd March, that is probably some four hours after the murder of the Cunningham family, Mr. Maddocks and two miners, Messrs. Hocking and Hosking, were sitting smoking outside their huts just before dinner, when some fifteen natives came up armed with *knobkerries* and battle-axes. The man who appeared to be their leader spoke to Mr. Maddocks and said that he and his companions had been sent by Mr. Fynn, the native commissioner, to work, and on being asked if he had a letter from that gentleman, called to some more natives who were standing not far off. What followed I will tell in the words of Mr. John Hosking, who, in his sworn statement regarding the death of Mr. Maddocks, deposes as follows:—

> The call was answered by a shout of '*Tchaia*,' 'strike.' A number of natives joined those who were with us, and the leader then struck deceased on the head with a *knobkerry*. I immediately retired into my hut for my revolver. When I came back three natives were hitting Hocking with *kerries* and axes. I fired a shot and dropped one man, and just as I had fired my second shot, I received a blow on the head causing the mark I now show. Hocking then managed to get into the hut, whereupon the natives cleared off; Hocking and I then went to Maddocks, but found him dead. We retired into an iron store, at which the natives fired a shot. The bullet passed inside through the iron, which caused us to retire again to the hut.

By this time it was growing dusk, so the two wounded miners, fearing that the natives would soon return and fire the hut, crept out, and getting into the long grass, made their escape to Cumming's store, three miles from Maddocks' camp, where about twenty men had already collected, many of whom, however, were unarmed. A *laager* was at once formed, and Mr. Cumming and another rode into Bulawayo for assistance. They first, however, warned several miners and farmers living in the neighbourhood, that the natives had risen, thus saving the lives of these people, as they all got safely to the *laager* and ultimately escaped to Bulawayo, whereas but for this timely warning they would most certainly have been murdered.

Mr. Cumming and his companion reached Bulawayo on Tuesday morning, and at once reported themselves to Mr. Duncan, the Administrator.

At this time no organised force existed in the country, with the exception of the few men of the Matabele Mounted Police under Captain Southey; and there were only some 370 rifles in the Government stores. However, no difficulty was experienced in getting men together who were ready to proceed at once to the relief of their countrymen and countrywomen; and, as I have already narrated, three small corps under experienced leaders were despatched to various outlying districts within a few hours of the time when the first alarm was given. The Hon. Maurice Gifford, as energetic as he is brave, got off that same evening with about forty men, including Captain Southey and twelve of his Mounted Police; his object being the relief of the men who had *laagered* up at Cumming's store.

The first sign of the rising seen by this party was near Woodford's store, about fourteen miles beyond Thaba Induna, or twenty-six from Bulawayo. Here an abandoned waggon was found standing in the road, the sixteen donkeys that had been harnessed to it lying all of a heap dead. They had for the most part been stabbed to death with *assegais*, but some had been shot. Nothing on the waggon had been touched, though it was loaded with flour, whisky, etc. No trace of those who had been in charge of the waggon could be discovered, but it has been subsequently ascertained that they were murdered in the bush some little distance away. They were colonial boys taking down a load of stores to the Insiza district.

Soon after this derelict waggon had been passed, three colonial boys were met making their way to Bulawayo, one armed with a rifle and another with a revolver. They reported to Mr. Gifford that the rising was general in the Insiza district, and said that a Dr. and Mrs. Langford had been killed on the previous day—Wednesday, 25th March—near Rixon's farm; but that Mr. Rixon, the Blicks, and others in the district had escaped to the *laager* at Cumming's store. They also told Mr. Gifford that they had seen several troops of cattle being driven by armed Matabele towards the Malungwani and Matopo Hills. On meeting Mr. Gifford these "boys" turned back and accompanied him to the Insiza, and did good service in the subsequent fight, in which one of them was wounded.

On Thursday night the relief party reached Cumming's store,

Hon. Maurice Gifford, C.M.G.

where they found about thirty men in *laager*. Of these, however, a large proportion were unarmed, so that Mr. Gifford had only about fifty rifles at his command altogether. The night passed off quietly, but at about 5 a.m., just before daylight on Friday morning, a most determined attack was made on the position by a large party of Matabele, who did not finally retreat until they had suffered heavy loss from the steady fire of the white men. The natives came on with the utmost fearlessness, as may be inferred from the fact that one was killed with his hands on the window-sill of the store, whilst six others lay dead close round; and it was afterwards ascertained that their total loss was twenty-five.

On the side of the whites, Sergt.-Major O'Leary of the Matabele Mounted Police was killed, as well as an educated American negro, a servant of Mr. Wrey's, whilst six white men were wounded. As soon as the attack had been completely beaten off, the waggons were inspanned, and the beleaguered white men broke up their *laager* and commenced their retreat to Bulawayo.

The first portion of the road to be travelled led amongst broken wooded hills, through which it was expected they would have to fight their way; but although the Matabele once gathered on the top of a neighbouring hill, and seemed about to attack, they did not do so, and thus allowed the whites to get out into the open country, where they were comparatively safe, without further molestation.

I think it will not be out of place to here reproduce, with the kind permission of Mr. Maurice Gifford, two letters written by him on the night after the fight, of which I happen to have copies, as they cannot fail, I think, to interest my readers.

14 miles from Lee s Store,
10. 5 p.m.

To A. H. F. Duncan, Esq.,
    Bulawayo.

Dear Sir—We have relieved Insiza, and brought away thirty-six men and one woman. At 5 a.m. this morning were attacked and enemy repulsed. Details of same will be given you by bearer. We have at present six wounded, and the woman with a child. One of the wounded is a serious case. Suggest the following for your consideration and for our assistance. Send out two large American spiders with mules to bring them in. Leave it to your judgment to say whether you consider escort necessary.

Suggest fifteen men. We can then bring in the remainder of the party. I am sending two men who have brought me dispatches this morning from Napier to advise him of the serious nature of this rising; but again leave it to your judgment whether you consider it advisable to send him advice from your end, taking into consideration the possibility of these two men not being able to reach him. If a doctor can come with the spiders, so much the better; also suggest making arrangements for beds for wounded. Advise me as to your knowledge of any possible attacks from natives en route from here to Bulawayo. Written by moonlight. We are all well and cheery, and hope to have a drink with you tomorrow night at 9 p.m.—Yours faithfully,

                      Maurice R. Gifford.

         Written at the Camp where Thackeray
               and friend left you,
                    10.30 p.m.

Dear Napier—Your dispatch duly received. Just a line from me to let you know that the *kaffirs* mean business this time. We were attacked this morning at one hour before sunrise by about three hundred natives, who came on in the most fanatical and plucky style—the old Zulu rush. Three natives were shot alongside the walls of our barricade. I mention this to you to put you on your guard, as you must have many new chums with you, and to advise great caution to prevent night surprises. We never thought an attack probable, but fortunately were well prepared. This, in my opinion, will prove a more Serious business than the old war, and I am sure that prompt action is necessary.—Yours,

                      M. R. Gifford.

CHAPTER 6

The Matabele Campaign of 1893

As will be seen from the last sentence of Mr. Gifford's letter to Colonel Napier, even at this early stage of the insurrection he predicted that it would prove a more serious business than the first war, and that this prediction has been fully justified will never I think be gainsaid by any man who has taken part in both campaigns. As, however, the difficulties experienced by the colonists in coping with the present rebellion have been very much underrated in certain quarters, and invidious comparisons instituted between Dr. Jameson's victorious march on Bulawayo in 1893 and the conduct of the present campaign, I will take the liberty of giving my own opinion on the subject; which is that the essential differences in the circumstances under which the two campaigns were conducted render it impossible to institute any comparison between them.

In 1893 Dr. Jameson marched from Mashunaland to Bulawayo with a compact force of 670 white men, 400 of whom were mounted, a small number of native allies, and a strong party of artillery consisting of 5 Maxim guns, 2 seven-pounders, 1 Gardner gun, and 1 Hotchkiss. Choosing its own line, and under the guidance of Nyenyezi—a Matabele of high position, whose whole family to the number of seventy had lately been put to death by the order of Lo Bengula, and who was himself a proscribed fugitive—this force kept in the open country as much as possible, but were obliged to pass through some broken wooded country in the neighbourhood of the Tchangani river. Here, at 4 a.m. on the morning of the 25th of October, it was attacked for the first time by the eastern division of the Matabele Army, computed at some 5000 strong, though it is improbable that all the regiments composing this division were actually engaged, as all the fighting seems to have been done by the Insukamini regiment, aided by small detachments of the Inhlati and Umquicho.

The attack failed, the Matabele being beaten off from the *laager* with heavy loss, whilst the column marched on towards Bulawayo, and was not again attacked until after the Impembisi had been crossed.

At a point a few miles beyond this river the *laager* was again attacked on 1st November, this time in perfectly open ground, and in the middle of the day. The attack was made by the Imbezu and Ingubu regiments, computed by Sir John Willoughby to number together about 1700 men; some 5000 more of other regiments who were hanging round never having come into action at all. In this engagement these two regiments suffered very heavily from the fire of the Maxim guns, although, as they have both reformed and taken a prominent part in the present rebellion, they were certainly not annihilated.

On hearing of the defeat of the Imbezu and Ingubu, one or other of which regiments he usually kept near him as a sort of bodyguard, Lo Bengula fled from Bulawayo, after first burning the *kraal* and blowing up his European house; but before doing so he recalled his son-in-law, Gambo, from the Mangwe Pass, thus leaving it open for the unopposed advance of the southern column under Colonel Gould Adams, who with the 400 men under his command was thus enabled to effect a junction with Dr. Jameson on 10th November. Gambo had been in command of all the regiments composing the Eegapa and the Umschlopay, the two largest military divisions of the four into which the country was divided, numbering together at least 8000 men. Excepting, however, a small detachment which attacked Colonel Gould Adams at the Singuesi River, none of the men composing this force took any part in the first Matabele war, although it numbered in its ranks some of the king's best regiments, such as the Inyama Nghlovu and M'schlaschlanglela.

Neither were the men under Sikombo, Umlugulu, and many other influential *indunas* living to the south-east of Bulawayo, ever engaged in the first war, as although they were all mustered and were close to Bulawayo at the time of the defeat of their compatriots at the Impembisi, they seem to have lost heart when they heard of the disastrous result of that fight, immediately followed as it was by the flight of their king, and so retired to the Matopo Hills, and subsequently surrendered without fighting.

The death of Lo Bengula probably closed the campaign, for but for this event his pursuit to the lower Tchangani, resulting as it did in the death of Major Wilson and all his brave companions, would scarcely have had any other effect than to show the Matabele that although white men were invincible when defending a *laager* with Maxim guns, they were by no means so when only armed with rifles, if they could be outnumbered and surrounded in difficult country.

But the death of their king left them like a swarm of bees bereft of their queen. Their councils were divided; their military arrogance crushed out of them by the heavy defeats their best regiments had sustained at the Tchangani, the Impembisi, and in a minor degree at the Singuesi. Short of food, and living like wild beasts in the rocks and forests, with all the bitter discomfort which such a life entails even on savages during the rainy season in a sub-tropical country, they saw their women and children sicken and die day by day, until their only hope of life seemed to lie in a speedy return to the high and healthy plateau from which they had fled. But there lay the *laagers* of the white men strongly defended with cannon and Maxim guns. From such positions they could not hope to drive them, nor without a leader or any cohesion between the numberless little parties into which they were divided did they dare to try conclusions with the mounted patrols which scoured the open country.

What wonder then that when liberal terms of peace were offered them, first one Induna with all his people, and then another and another, surrendered, until in a short time the whole nation had freely and frankly submitted itself to the white man's rule? Such is a brief account of the conquest of Matabeleland in 1893, which was practically settled by two battles, in which the Matabele attacked the white men in *laager* and were in each case driven off with heavy loss by the fire of the Maxim guns.

The brilliancy of the exploit, resulting as it did in the overthrow of one of the most cruel and barbarous despotisms that has ever existed even in barbarous Africa, and in the throwing open to European enterprise of a rich and fertile territory, blessed with a climate in which white men can live and thrive, will ever be remembered as one of the most brilliant episodes in the history of British colonisation in South Africa; and no one, in this country at any rate, would wish to detract one iota from the honour due to all those who took part in Dr. Jameson's historic march to Bulawayo in 1893. It was admirable both in the boldness of its conception and the steady and unflinching resolution with which it was carried out.

All I wish to point out is that in 1893 the fighting power and the military spirit of the Matabele nation was only scotched, not killed;

for more than half the regiments which had formed the king's army at the time of the war did not lose a single man during the hostilities, never having been engaged in any of the fights; whilst the only regiments which lost really heavily were the Insukamini, the Imbezu, and the Ingubu. It is difficult to state with any degree of exactitude the number of men lost by the Matabele in 1893, but personally I find it difficult to believe that their loss in men killed or who died from wounds can have exceeded 1000—that is, 200 at the Tchangani, 500 at the Impembisi, 100 at the Inguesi, and 200 killed during the fighting on the lower Tchangani. Be it remembered by those who consider this too low an estimate, that if more than 500 Matabele were killed at the Impembisi fight, it would mean over 30 *per cent* of the entire force engaged, as the strength of the Imbezu and Ingubu together did not exceed 1700, whilst the number of the survivors who have been and still are taking part in the present rebellion is by no means inconsiderable.

As regards the loss inflicted on the Matabele by Major Wilson and his brave companions during their last desperate stand on the lower Tchangani, we have nothing to go upon, except what natives who were there can tell us, and I think there is reason to believe that their loss there was not actually so heavy as at one time it was supposed to be, as they were always able to fire on the whites from behind the shelter of trees. Apart, however, from the direct loss sustained in the various fights, the Matabele must have suffered heavily from the ravages of sickness caused by exposure and want of food after the fighting had ceased. The greatest sufferers were naturally the women and children, the able-bodied men having been better able to withstand the unaccustomed hardships. Altogether, I think that if to the 1000, which is my estimate of those killed in battle, or who died from the effects of their wounds, another 1000 is added for the able-bodied men who died of sickness afterwards, the aggregate will be a very liberal allowance for the total losses sustained by the Matabele in fighting men during, and in consequence of, the war of 1893.

However, to avoid all cavilling let us add another 1000 to this number, making 3000 altogether. Subtract these 3000 from the entire fighting strength of the nation before the war, which has never been estimated at less than 20,000, and it leaves a residue of 17,000 able-bodied men. This total may be a thousand or two out one way or the other; but, whatever the fighting strength of the nation may be, every man composing it throughout the length and breadth of the land is now in arms against the white men, with the exception of some of Gambo's people and a few others, numbering in all under 1000 men, about whom I shall say a few words later on.

But, it has been said, however many Matabele may have rebelled against the government, they cannot be very dangerous foes, since the whole nation was disarmed after the first war. This is an error. After the war of 1893 a considerable number of guns were certainly given up, but that the total handed in and destroyed was but a small proportion of what they had possessed before the war no one who knew anything about the matter ever doubted. Besides muzzle-loading guns of every description, the Matabele were formerly in possession of at least 2000 breech-loading rifles, principally Martini-Henrys, a certain number of which were captured from them during the war or surrendered after hostilities were over. As no count seems ever to have been kept of the number of these rifles captured or handed in, no exact figure can be given. General report says 150 to 300, whilst the highest number I have ever heard ventured was "between 400 and 500."

Even taking the highest number to be correct, considering that a considerable number of Martini-Henry rifles have been illicitly sold to the Matabele during the last two years, that nearly 100 breech-loading rifles were taken over to the enemy by the rebel police, whilst many more were captured from murdered men during the first days of the rebellion, it cannot be denied that they have regained more than they lost, so that in the matter of breech-loading arms they entered upon the present insurrection with a larger supply than they possessed in 1893, whilst, as I have said before, however many muzzle-loading guns they may have surrendered, they kept back a great many which they are now using. As regards ammunition, I, for one, certainly thought when the present rebellion broke out that their supply would soon run short, but it has not yet done so, and, moreover, it seems to be fairly distributed through the whole nation, as every *impi* with which we have yet been engaged has shown itself to be well supplied, especially with Martini-Henry cartridges.

Thus we now see that after the first conquest of Matabeleland a very large proportion of the former military strength of the country was still available, and that although this large number of able-bodied savages were apparently without arms, their weapons were only hidden for the time being. Where the large supply of ammunition which they have proved themselves to be possessed of came from, I cannot say. Probably large quantities were buried with the rifles after the first war, and this store has been constantly added to by theft and illicit purchase ever since.

However, over two years of most submissive behaviour, unbroken by any attempt whatever to rebel against the authority of the Chartered Company, lulled every white man in the country into a feeling of security which events have not justified.

A native police force was raised, which was apparently working admirably up to the time of the rebellion; and even then, it is but fair to say, almost all the police who had been first enrolled, and who had done more than a year's service, held themselves aloof from the rebels, the great majority of defections occurring amongst those who had been but lately enrolled and amongst whom there was therefore little or no *esprit de corps*.

CHAPTER 7

Effect of Removing the Police Force

In spite of their submissive behaviour, it seems probable that all the members of the late king's family and many of the chief *indunas* were only biding their time, and waiting for an opportunity to try the chances of a rebellion against the white man.

This opportunity did not present itself as long as there was a strong police force in the country, but once that police force was removed, I think the malcontents began to act.

That the plague of locusts with which Matabeleland has been afflicted ever since 1890, the first year of the occupation of Mashunaland by Europeans; the partial drought of the last two years; and, finally, the outbreak of the *rinderpest*, would all be ascribed to the evil influence of the white man, and made use of by the witch-doctors to incite the mass of the people to join the insurgents, is doubtless true; but that the insurrection can be fairly ascribed to the bitterness caused by these visitations alone, I very much doubt, for it is remarkable that throughout the Umzingwani, Filibusi, and Insiza districts, where all the first murders of white men were committed, the rainfall had been plentiful, and the locusts had done but little damage, so that, as I can personally bear witness, the crops throughout these portions of the country were exceptionally good, whilst as the *rinderpest* had not yet approached this part of Matabeleland, the people living in these districts could have known little or nothing about it.

In its inception, the insurrection was, in my opinion, a rebellion against the white man's rule by the Matabele of Zulu origin alone, and I am convinced that, in the district where I was living at least, the other section of the tribe were at first not in the secret; however, the greater part of these soon joined, some unwillingly and under threats from their former masters, but most of them readily enough, believing, as they did, that with the assistance of the *Umlimo* they would be able to completely root out the white man, and revel once more in loot and wholesale murder. And a merry time they had of it, if it was but a short one, to be followed by a heavy retribution.

When the first news of the rising reached Bulawayo, Gambo was in the town on a visit to the chief native commissioner, by whom he was very wisely detained as a prisoner. Whether, if he had been at large, he would have joined the rebels or not, it is difficult to say. Since the war, he has lost control over the greater part of the people who formerly composed the Eegapa military division, and many of these have joined the ranks of the insurgents, but all Gambo's own people, under his head *induna*, Marzwe, have remained loyal to the government. Umjan, once the *induna* of the Imbezu regiment, and now quite an old man, has also refrained from taking part in the present hostilities, although he is one of the few whose cattle were shot by order of the government because they were infected with the *rinderpest*. He came in to Bulawayo soon after the outbreak of the rebellion with his wives and immediate attendants, and is now living quietly near the town. His sons, however, have joined the rebels, whilst the men whom he formerly commanded—the Imbezu—reformed themselves into a regiment, and have been fighting since the outbreak of the insurrection.

Besides Gambo's men, a few hundreds of Matabele Maholi (men of Makalaka and Mashuna descent) living on my Company's property of Essexvale, on Colonel Napier's land and round the Hope Fountain mission station, have thought it advisable to stand by the government, and have, therefore, come in to live near Bulawayo for protection. But putting aside these few hundreds of natives who have not joined in the rebellion, the fact remains that at least nine-tenths, I think I might safely say nineteen-twentieths, of the Matabele nation are now in arms against the whites.

And, now, let us see how the colonists were prepared to meet the onset of these hordes of savages. When the rising first broke out, with the exception of the native police, there was no organised force in Matabeleland worth speaking of; and as one-half of the native police at once went over to the enemy, and the remainder had to be disarmed, for fear lest they should follow suit, it may be said that there was no police force at all. Of the old Mounted Police there only remained forty-eight officers, non-commissioned officers, and men, in the whole of Matabeleland, under Inspector Southey. Of these, twenty-two were stationed in Bulawayo, and the rest distributed over the country at the police stations of Gwelo, Selukwe, Belingwe, Inyati, Mangwe, Tuli, Matopos, Umzingwani, and Iron Mine Hill. When the rebellion broke out only twelve of these men were available at Bulawayo for immediate service, and these, under Inspector Southey, accompanied Mr. Gifford to the Insiza.

The Rhodesia Horse, a volunteer force which had been raised and equipped the previous year, had also practically ceased to exist as an effective force fit for use at a moment's notice, for although there were some six hundred men in Matabeleland who had enrolled themselves as members of this corps, they were scattered all over the country at the outbreak of the rebellion. Some of these were murdered, whilst others had to take refuge in the laagers of Belingwe and Gwelo. However, about five hundred were soon mustered in Bulawayo, but the services of the majority could not be utilised except to defend the town, owing to the want of horses, since, so great had been the ravages of the fatal horse-sickness during the rainy season then just coming to an end, that when Colonel Napier, the senior officer of the Rhodesia Horse, called on the government for seventy horses for immediate use on 23rd March, he could only be supplied with sixty-two.

The actual number of horses in the possession of the government throughout Matabeleland on the day when the first tidings of the outbreak of the insurrection reached Bulawayo is as follows:—

Horses in Government stables	77
Horses in possession of members of the Rhodesia Horse Volunteers scattered over various parts of Matabeleland	117
In possession of cattle inspectors	28
Unfit for work	58

Of the 117 horses that had been issued to volunteers, a good many never returned to Bulawayo, as they either died of horse-sickness or were taken to Gwelo or Belingwe, so that in the first days of the rebellion the government could not command the services of more than 100 horses; but no expense was spared to procure more, and very soon all the private horses in Bulawayo were bought up, whilst others were sent up from the Transvaal, so that by the end of April there were nearly 450 horses in the government stables, the large majority of which were fit for active service.

The number of rifles belonging to the government throughout the country on 25th March was as follows:—

	Lee-Metford Rifles.	Lee-Metford Carbines.
At Gwanda	20	—
At Gwelo	40	—
With Colonel Napier's patrol	33	52
＂ ＂ Spreckley's patrol	36	2
To guard coaches	7	—
In stores	295	70
Permanent staff	25	—
Total	456	124

Making a total of 580 rifles all told.

Besides these, however, there were about eighty old Martini-Henry rifles in the Government stores, but these were nearly all unserviceable at the outbreak of the rebellion, though the armourer has since been able to get most of them into working order. Of ammunition there was a good supply, *viz.* 1,500,000 rounds.

In the way of artillery there was in Bulawayo when the insurrection broke out one 303 Maxim gun in good order, and a second so much out of repair as to be useless; two 2.5 screw guns in good order, but with only seventeen rounds of ammunition for the two; one Hotchkiss gun and limber, one Gatling, one Gardner, one Nordenfeldt—all in good order—and one seven-pounder, useless except at Bulawayo owing to carriage having been destroyed by white ants. In addition to this ordnance there arrived in Bulawayo from Macloutsie, on the very day on which Mr. Maddocks was murdered, two old Maxims and two seven-pounders. These, however, were unserviceable at the time, one of the seven-pounders being without a carriage and the two Maxims being also out of repair. The armourer here has now, however, I believe, put them all in working order.

Taking these figures as correct—and they are absolutely beyond question—it cannot, I think, be said that the colonists in Matabeleland were very well prepared to cope with a sudden and unexpected rising of at least 10,000 natives, about one-fifth of whom were armed with breech-loading rifles and well supplied with ammunition, whilst many more were in possession of muzzle-loading guns; and when it is remembered that at the time of the outbreak the food supply was very low in Bulawayo, owing to the ravages of the *rinderpest*, it must be acknowledged that the position was at one time a very serious one, which a little more intelligence on the part of the Matabele might have rendered absolutely disastrous.

But all through they have behaved in an incomprehensible manner, their leaders apparently never having arranged any settled plan of campaign, the consequence being that there has never been any understanding or community of action between the various hordes into which the nation is now divided. All through there appears to have been a general belief amongst them that they would receive supernatural aid from the "*Umlimo*," or god, but this belief must be getting a little thin now, and they would have done far better had they worked together under one intelligent general.

Why, when the rebellion first broke out, they never attempted to block the main road to Mangwe will ever remain a mystery. No one doubts that they might have done so, nor that, if they had placed a couple of thousand men in the Shashani Pass, we could not have raised a sufficient force on this side to dislodge them and open the road; for it must be remembered that as there were over six hundred women and children in Bulawayo a large force was always necessary to protect them. Possibly there is some truth in the report that the road to Mangwe has been purposely left open by command of the *Umlimo* in order to give the white men the opportunity of escaping from the country. That this was an error of judgment, if it is a fact, is very clear, as in the critical time but few men left the country, and such as did could be well spared, as they were of no use as defenders of the women and children, and were only consuming valuable food. On the other hand, owing to the road having been left open, stores of arms and food and horses were constantly being brought in.

It certainly seems very strange that no attempt has ever been made to stop waggons and coaches on this road, when it is remembered that at one time Government House—which is less than three miles from the centre of Bulawayo—was practically in the hands of the rebels, sometimes in the daytime and always at nights for a period of about ten days, their *impis* during that time lying in a semicircle to the west and north of the town, and being sometimes within two miles of it.

Yet although two Dutchmen, living in their waggon standing near the boundary of the town commonage, about four and a half miles along the road from Bulawayo, were murdered, no waggon or coach moving along the road was ever interfered with, nor was the Government House burnt, the reason for this being, it is said, because the

Umlimo told the people that when Bulawayo had been destroyed, and all the white men in the country killed, they would find Lo Bengula sitting there, ready to rule them once more; for, be it said, Government House has been built in the centre of the old *kraal* of Bulawayo, just where the king's house once stood.

For over a month, an *impi*, supposed to be at least a thousand strong, was camped just within the Matopo Hills, not ten miles from the nearest point on the road to Mangwe, and no one doubts that at any moment a portion of this *impi* might have moved over to the road by night, and, by shooting a mule or two, have had a coachload of white men at its mercy; and God help the unfortunate white man who has nothing else to trust to but the mercy of the Matabele!

Of course there were forts along the road, and patrols rode daily between the forts, but even so I maintain that much damage might have been done if the natives had determined at any moment to block the road. Now, however, that the *impi* of which I have been speaking has been driven from its position by the forces under Major-General Sir Frederick Carrington, it is not likely that the safety of the road will ever again be threatened.

And, now, let me hark back to the early days of the rebellion. I think I have shown by figures that on the outbreak of the insurrection the country was not over well supplied with either horses or arms, nor was there any superfluity of men, and the smallness of the number will, I think, astonish some critics of the present campaign in England. Turning to the *Matabele Times* of 6th April last, I find it stated under the heading "The Native Rising up to Date."

> A census was taken of all those who had been in the *laager* on Friday night as they made their exit on Saturday morning, or remained on the waggons. The count was carefully made, and showed that the refugees numbered 632 women and children, and 915 men, making a total of 1547.
> A general parade was held yesterday of the men now in town who have enrolled themselves in the Bulawayo Field Force. They fell in at ten o'clock, the scouts, under Captain Grey, in front making a splendid display of the class of men whom the hostile natives will not seek to tackle twice. The men on foot looked like business, and went through their movements with sufficient precision. The Africander Corps now consists of three companies, numbering 76, 64, and 73, with 6 on the staff. The total number on parade was over 500, of whom about 300 were

fully armed, and about 100 were engineers and artillerymen. To this number have to be added the 169 out under the Hon. M. Gifford and Captain Dawson, and the 100 men gone down to Gwanda under Captain Brand and Captain Van Niekerk. The total efficient force now available for the reconquest of Matabeleland may be put down at 700, nearer 800.

From these figures it will be seen that at the outbreak of the rebellion there were under 1000 men in Bulawayo, some 200 of whom were unfit for active service. The remainder of the male population of the country were shut up in the *laagers* at Gwelo, Belingwe, and Mangwe, and therefore unavailable for offensive operations against the Matabele; whilst of the 800 fighting men in Bulawayo, it was necessary to have at least 400 always in town to protect the women and children, and 130 were drafted off to man the forts on the Mangwe road, leaving less than 300 available for active operations against the enemy. This force was, however, augmented by about 150 Cape boys, chiefly Amaxosa *kaffirs* and Zulus. These boys were got together and formed into a regiment by Mr. Johan Colenbrander, and they have done most excellent service during the present campaign, being man for man both braver and better armed than the Matabele.

Thus, all things considered, I do not think the colonists have done so badly. With small patrols they first succeeded in bringing in many scattered whites from the outlying districts, and then after a series of engagements, always fought on ground of the enemy's own choosing, succeeded in driving them from the immediate neighbourhood of Bulawayo, and forcing them to take refuge in the forests and hills, from which they will be finally driven by the forces now in the country under the command of Major-General Sir Frederick Carrington.

It is worthy of remark that whilst in the first war the Matabele attacked strong positions defended by artillery and Maxim guns, thereby suffering very heavy loss themselves but killing very few white men, in the present war all the fighting has been amongst broken ground, and in country more or less covered with bush, and all the killing has been done with rifles; for in the first war the natives learnt the futility of attacking fortified positions, and now only fight in the bush in skirmishing order, giving but little opportunity for the effective use of machine guns; so that, although a good many rounds have been fired from Maxims at long ranges, only a very small amount of execution has been done by them.

CHAPTER 8

Cattle Stolen by Matabele

I will now again take up the thread of my own personal experiences. As will be remembered, I reached my homestead at 2 a.m. on Thursday, 26th March, and found everything as I had left it seventeen hours before. A mule cart carrying food supplies for my men was to have followed immediately behind us, but the men in charge lost the road, and the provisions did not turn up till late the next day.

On the following morning, just at daybreak, a native named Inshlupo, who had been in charge of a herd of over thirty head of cattle belonging to my Company, turned up and informed me that on the previous evening the headman of a small Matabele *kraal*, situated in the broken ground just below the Malungwani Hills, had paid him a visit, accompanied by several armed men, and taken off all the cattle.

On the receipt of this news I had the horses saddled up at once, as, it being still so early, I had little doubt that, if no time was lost, we should find the stolen cattle still in the *kraal* to which they had been taken the previous evening. Before moving, however, I said a few words to my men, telling them that my object in visiting Essexvale and other parts of the country with an armed force was twofold, namely, to endeavour by prompt action to strike terror into the hearts of some of the rebels before they had time to concentrate, and at the same time to reassure those who were content with the white man's rule, but who, in the absence of any display of power on the part of the government, might be led to believe that their only chance of safety from the vengeance of the Matabele lay in taking part with them in the rebellion.

In conclusion, I told them that any *kaffirs* we might find with arms in their hands, who had left their *kraals* and gone off into the hills with stolen cattle, ought to be shot without question and without mercy, as they were every one of them more or less responsible for the cruel murders of white men that had already been committed.

Under the guidance of Inshlupo we reached the neighbourhood of the *kraal* where I hoped to find my Company's cattle before the sun was an hour higher. Here I halted my men, and sent half of them round under the shelter of the bush to a certain point where they were to show themselves, that being the signal for a simultaneous advance as rapidly as possible on the *kraal* from both sides. However, although we found all the cattle still in the *kraal*, there were no men there, and in fact no one but a Matabele woman, the wife of the headman, and several children. The woman would offer no explanation of the undeniable fact that my Company's cattle were in her husband's *kraal*, and would give no information concerning his whereabouts, so, after driving out the stolen cattle, I had the whole place burnt, first allowing the woman to remove all her private effects. When this had been done, I sent the recaptured cattle back to the homestead, in charge of two of Inshlupo's boys, and then proceeded straight into the Malungwani Hills, in the hope of coming across some of the rebels who had gone off with the first lot of my Company's cattle that had been stolen on the previous Tuesday night.

As we proceeded, the hills became thickly wooded, and in the valleys between them we found the spoor of a good many cattle that had passed during the last two days, although we saw no fresh tracks.

About nine o'clock I gave the order to off-saddle in a little grassy hollow, after first placing sentries all round to guard against any sudden attack, for we were now, of course, in the enemy's country. After an hour's rest the horses were just being caught when one of the sentries reported that a herd of cattle was being driven up a valley at the foot of a high ridge to our left. I at once went up to have a look myself, but by this time the cattle were out of sight. However, I carefully examined the ground, and saw that by following another valley running parallel to the one in which the cattle had been seen, and then ascending the steep ridge at its head, we should in all probability drop right on to the rebels in charge of them.

And this is exactly what happened, as upon cresting the ridge we found that both *kaffirs* and cattle were immediately below us. Some of the former were driving the cattle, but most of them were in the bush ahead. We at once opened fire on them, which they made no attempt to return. Indeed, taken by surprise as they were, and having so much the worse of the position, and, moreover, not being in any force, they could scarcely be expected to do anything else but run for it. And run they did, throwing down almost everything they were carrying, and abandoning the cattle. I saw one man throw a gun away, probably fearing lest he should be caught with it in his possession, but most of them were, I think, only armed with *assegais*.

We chased them up and down several hills, and expended a lot of ammunition on them, but did them I am afraid very little damage, as the hills were all thickly wooded, and our horses were not able to climb up and down them any faster than the light-footed savages we were pursuing. In the second valley we found another herd of cattle, but could see no *kaffirs* near them, and I think they must have heard the firing, and run off before we came in sight. Altogether we captured over 150 head of cattle, every one of which had been taken from white men, a large number having Mr. Colenbrander's brand on them.

I have stated plainly that we fired on these *kaffirs* at sight, and that although they offered no resistance, but ran away as hard as they could, we chased them and kept on firing at them as long as we could see them, and this action may possibly be cited as an example of the brutality and inhumanity of the Englishmen in Rhodesia. The fact that the *kaffirs* whom we sought to destroy—with as little compunction as though they were a pack of wild dogs—were taking part in a rebellion which had just been inaugurated by a series of the foulest murders it is possible to conceive, and the ultimate object of which was evidently to stamp out the white man throughout the land, will, of course, be entirely lost sight of or quietly ignored.

In fact, I should not be at all surprised to see it stated that the rebellion was caused by the inhuman behaviour of the white men in Rhodesia, who, it will be said, were in the habit of shooting down the poor, meek, inoffensive Matabele.

The *kaffirs* upon whom we fired were, of course, caught red-handed, driving off a herd of cattle, every animal in which had been taken from a white man, and we afterwards learnt that they were the very men who had stopped Mr. Meikle's waggon two days before on the Insiza road (some eight or ten miles distant), murdered the colonial boys in charge of it, and *assegaied* the sixteen donkeys harnessed to it.

For breaking out into rebellion against the white man's rule, and for taking all the cattle in the country, I should have borne them no great animosity, especially as the great majority of these cattle had once belonged to their king or to them personally. Being a representative of the race that had conquered them, I should, of course, have lent the services of my rifle to help to quell the rebellion no matter what form it had taken; but had it not been accompanied by the cruel murders of white women and children, I should not have been animated by the same vengeful feelings as now possessed me, as well as every other white man in Matabeleland.

The kind-hearted, untraveled humanitarian may say:

> But, such incidents are the necessary accompaniments of a native rebellion against Europeans, and ought not therefore to excite any greater surprise or indignation in your colonist than they do in myself; and, moreover, given that you admit that, looking at things from their point of view, the Matabele were justified in rebelling against the white man's rule, go further and acknowledge that the white men were wrong in ever attempting the colonisation of any of the territories between the Limpopo and the Zambesi, since it was the occupation of Mashunaland in 1890 that led to the various disagreements between Lo Bengula and the Chartered Company which culminated in the invasion and conquest of Matabeleland in 1893.

To this proposition I would answer that the whole question of the colonisation by Europeans of countries previously inhabited by savage tribes must be looked upon from a broad point of view, and be judged by its final results as compared with the primitive conditions it has superseded. Two hundred years ago, the Eastern States of North America were inhabited by savage tribes who, by incessant internecine war and the practice of many abominable customs, constantly deluged the whole land with blood. Now the noble red man has disappeared from those territories—has been exterminated by the more intelligent white man—and in place of a cruel, hopeless savagery there has arisen a civilisation whose ideals are surely higher than those of the displaced barbarism.

In like manner, before Van Riebek landed at the Cape of Good Hope, the whole of South Africa was in the hands of savages, a people, be it noted, who were not living in Arcadian simplicity, a peaceful happy race amongst whom crime and misery were unknown quantities, but on the contrary, who were a prey to cruel superstitions, involving a constant sacrifice of innocent life, and who were, moreover, continually exposed to all the horrors of intertribal wars. Now an orderly civilisation has been established over a large area of this once completely savage country, and no one but an ignorant fanatic would, I think, assert that its present condition is not preferable from a humanitarian point of view to its former barbarism.

Well, the present state of Matabeleland is one of transition. Its past history—and this fact ought not to be ignored by the impartial critic of what is happening there today—has been one of ceaseless cruelty and bloodshed. But in time a civilisation will have been built up in that bloodstained land, as orderly and humane as that which has been established—in place of a parallel barbarism—in the older States of South Africa.

Yet, just as in the establishment of the white man's supremacy in the Cape Colony, the aboriginal black races have either been displaced or reduced to a state of submission to the white man's rule at the cost of much blood and injustice to the black man, so also will it be in Matabeleland, and so must it ever be in any country where the European comes into contact with native races, and where at the same time the climate is such that the more highly organised and intelligent race can live and thrive, as it can do in Matabeleland; whilst the presence of valuable minerals or anything else that excites the greed of the stronger race will naturally hasten the process.

Therefore Matabeleland is doomed by what seems a law of nature to be ruled by the white man, and the black man must go, or conform to the white man's laws, or die in resisting them. It seems a hard and cruel fate for the black man, but it is a destiny which the broadest philanthropy cannot avert, whilst the British colonist is but the irresponsible atom employed in carrying out a preordained law—the law which has ruled upon this planet ever since, in the far-off misty depths of time, organic life was first evolved upon the earth—the inexorable law which Darwin has aptly termed the "*Survival of the Fittest.*"

Now there may be those who maintain that the aboriginal savagery of the Red Indians in the Eastern States of North America, or of the *kaffirs* in the Cape Colony, was a preferable state of things to the imperfect civilisations which have superseded them. To such I have no reply. "*Chacun à son goût.*" Only I would ask them to endeavour to make themselves as well acquainted as possible with the subject under discussion, either by actual travel or by reading, and I would beg them not to accept too readily the assertions constantly made without any regard to truth or honesty by the newspaper opponents of British colonisation, which are broadly to the effect that no savagery exists in Africa except that practised on the blacks by Europeans.

CHAPTER 9

Return to Essexvale

When on the afternoon of Thursday, 26th March, we got back to my homestead with the recaptured cattle, both men and horses were tired out, as the heat had been intense, and the former had had no food since early dawn. However, the cart carrying provisions having arrived, the men were soon able to get a good meal, whilst the horses were turned into a twenty-five acre patch of maize, which, although it had been sadly destroyed as a crop by the locusts, still afforded an abundance of sweet succulent food for stock. In order to allow the horses time to recover from the effects of their hard day's work in the hills, I resolved to let them feed and rest until the cool of the afternoon of the following day, and then make a night march over to Mr. Jackson's police station at Makupikupeni, where I hoped to be able to get some news as to the whereabouts of Colonel Spreckley's patrol, with which I was anxious to effect a junction.

I should have sent the recaptured cattle at once in to Bulawayo, had it not been for the *rinderpest* scourge which would have rendered such a course worse than useless, since every one of them would have died within a week. The only other plan open to me was to commit them to the care of the natives living immediately round my homestead, who, at this time at any rate, did not seem at all inclined to take part in the rebellion.

As there were now at least 500 head of cattle collected together in a small area, I fully recognised the danger there would be lest so rich a bait should attract a Matabele raiding party as soon as it became known that there was no one left to defend them. However, no other course was open to me, so the cattle were left on the off chance that they would not fall into the hands of the rebels.

Some ten days later the not unexpected came to pass. Inxnozan, an old Matabele warrior, whom I knew well, and whose manly independent bearing I had always admired, descended upon my homestead with a following of some 300 men, burnt down my house and stables and all adjoining storehouses and huts, and either carried off or destroyed everything they contained. Then they collected all the cattle in the neighbourhood, all of which belonged to my Company by right of purchase or capture, and went off.

All the *kaffirs* who up to this time had been living quietly in their *kraals* looking after my cattle went away into the hills after Inxnozan's visit, and as they have never sent me any message, I do not know whether they have joined the rebels or have only taken refuge in the hills until the war is over. At any rate I shall do all I can to protect them, as they must have been placed in a very difficult position—fearing the enmity of the rebels on the one hand, if they refused to join them, and the vengeance of the white man on the other for suspected complicity in some of the outrages that had taken place in the district if they remained at their *kraals*.

On the Friday afternoon we made a start for Mr. Jackson's police station, passing the remains of the once large military *kraal* of Intuntini, and still the largest in the district. Such as it was, we set it alight, and as it was situated on the shoulder of a hill the burning huts must have been plainly visible to the people who had so lately deserted it, from almost any point in the Malungwani range, to which they had probably retired.

Shortly after midnight we reached the police station, which we found entirely deserted, though all the huts were still standing. A closer inspection showed that these huts had been very hastily evacuated by the native police to whom they had belonged, as they were still full of their personal effects, such as coats, hats, blankets, etc. In one of the huts we found a broken Winchester rifle, and in one of the coats a purse containing a few shillings in silver, about the last thing a *kaffir* would willingly leave behind him. We afterwards learned that Colonel Spreckley's patrol had reached the police station—which was situated on the main road to the Filibusi district from Bulawayo—late at night on the previous Wednesday. At this time there were seven native policemen with a sergeant in the huts.

These men, hearing the horsemen approaching, immediately fled, taking nothing with them but their arms and ammunition, and went over to the rebels. That they must have previously made up their minds to desert, is, I think, certain, otherwise there was no reason why they should have left the station of which they were in charge on the approach of the white men. In one of the huts we found several bags of maize, and so were able to give all our horses a good feed.

On the following morning I paid a visit to several *kraals* in the neighbourhood, the inhabitants of which were in charge of cattle belonging to my Company. These people I found in their villages. They were subsequently attacked by the rebels, who carried off a large proportion of the cattle in their charge. They however escaped with the remainder, which they brought in to Bulawayo, where they very soon all died of *rinderpest*. These *kaffirs* are amongst the few who out of the entire nation have stood by the government and rendered active assistance to the white men during the present crisis. They are Matabele Maholi of Makalaka descent, as I think are all the "friendlies," with the exception of a small leavening amongst them of "Abenzantsi" or Matabele of pure Zulu blood, and I think I am correct in stating that there is not a single Maholi of any other descent who is not in arms with the pure-blooded Matabele against the government.

The Makalaka proper, a numerous people living on the western border of Matabeleland, have—except possibly with some individual exceptions—held themselves resolutely aloof from any participation in the present rebellion, just as they took no part in the war of 1893. They are an industrious, peaceable people, and have found the rule of the Chartered Company if not perfect, at any rate a vast improvement on the oppressive tyranny under which they lived in the good old days of Lo Bengula.

At Makupikupeni we heard a rumour, which happily proved to be entirely false, though at the time it disturbed my peace of mind very much, to the effect that the ninety native police who had accompanied Mr. Jackson and his companions into the Matopo Hills, on the trail of Umzobo and Umfondisi, had mutinied and murdered their officers, Mr. Jackson having been bound to a tree, and then having had his throat cut. We also heard that Colonel Spreckley had buried the white men who were murdered at Edkins' store, and then crossed over to the Tuli road and returned to Bulawayo.

This being so, I determined to make for Spiro's store, situated just on the edge of the Matopo Hills on the main road from Bulawayo to the Transvaal, and about twelve miles distant from the Makupikupeni police station, as I was in hopes of there hearing something authentic concerning the fate of my friend Mr. Jackson and his companions. I knew the way across country to the store well enough myself, but had

I not done so, I had a good guide with me in the person of one Mazhlabanyan, a Matabele—not of Zulu blood, but of Makalaka descent—who had joined me that morning. This man had known me in former years when he was an elephant-hunter in the employ of the late Mr. Thomas, and on hearing that I was residing on Essexvale, had come with his wives and family to live near me, and I had given him a nice little herd of cattle—amongst them some good milk cows—to look after for our Company, for which he was very grateful. He fought in the war of 1893 against the whites and was with the Imbezu at the Battle of the Impembisi, on which occasion he was the recipient of a bullet through the shoulder.

During the present troubles, however, he has stood by the government, and joined the rest of the "friendlies." Shortly before sundown we reached Spiro's store, which we found had been deserted by its occupants not many hours prior to our arrival. The colonial boys in charge of the coach mules were still at their post, and reported everything quiet in the district as far as they knew, nor could they give any information concerning Mr. Jackson.

Since mid-day the weather, which had been intensely dry and hot for some time past, had changed suddenly, the sky became overcast and a light rain commenced to fall. Luckily, however, there proved to be sufficient accommodation in the out-buildings and beneath the broad verandah which surrounded the store for all my men, and we were thus spared the disagreeable necessity of sleeping out on the wet ground and beneath a rainy sky.

The next day—Sunday, 29th March—broke fine, but cool and cloudy, a very pleasant change after the excessive heat we had recently experienced. The question now arose as to whether any other course was open to me but to return at once to Bulawayo by the Tuli road. To my left lay the rugged mass of broken granite hills called the Matopos, within whose recesses it was believed by many people at Bulawayo that the Matabele had already massed in large numbers. Now I fully realised that had this been the case, it would have been madness to take so small a force as that at my disposal into so difficult a country. As, however, I had very good reasons for believing that as yet no large number of Matabele had assembled in this part of the country, I was anxious to make a reconnaissance through them in order to see what the difficulties of the country really were.

Before starting I paraded my men and told them what I wished to do, stating that in my opinion, although we should have some very rough country to get over, and should have to walk and lead our horses most of the way, we should not meet any large force of hostile *kaffirs*, or indeed be likely to fire a shot at all unless we met some of the revolted police who had murdered Jackson—for at this time I believed that he had really been murdered. However, I told them that I did not wish an one to go with me who did not care to do so, which was unnecessary, as no one was willing to be left behind.

CHAPTER 10

Skirmish With the Rebels

It was about seven o'clock when we entered the first gorge leading in amongst the foothills, which were here well wooded. Mr. Blöcker, who is an excellent walker and a very good shot, I told off to scout on foot a short distance ahead of us, whilst Messrs. Simms and Fletcher, two Cape Colonists and both steady, reliable men, scouted on the left and right flanks respectively.

After we had proceeded for about an hour through very broken and, for the most part, thickly wooded country, we emerged upon a huge bare granite rock. Here Mr. Simms rejoined us and reported that as he was scouting on the left flank, upon emerging from a patch of bush, he had come suddenly upon four *kaffirs*, one carrying a gun whilst the rest were armed with *assegais*. These men quickly moved out of sight, fearing to attack Simms lest there should prove to be more white men behind him, whilst he on his side did not care to fire on them, as he did not know how many more natives there might be close at hand.

Beyond us there now lay a large open grassy valley enclosed on every side by rocky granite hills. In its broadest part this valley was over a mile in width, but at its top end it gradually narrowed into a rocky gorge, which apparently led on to some higher ground beyond the farthest hills we could see. Much of the valley was under cultivation, and a splendid crop of corn was standing, still unreaped, in the fields. Mazhlabanyan told me that these cornfields belonged to Banyubi, a tribe allied to the Makalakas, and who are the aboriginal inhabitants of the district. After carefully looking over the country on ahead, I decided to keep straight up the valley, and make my way to the higher ground by the gorge I have spoken of.

When we were halfway through the open valley, *kaffirs* began to

VIEW IN THE MATOPO HILLS

shout to one another amongst the hills to our left, and presently we saw some, but they were a long way off and we could not make out whether they were armed or not. I now gave orders that any *kaffir* who approached us must be fired on if he was armed, but not unless.

We had just entered the neck of the gorge and were finding a good deal of difficulty in getting our horses through a stream that was too deep to ford and could only be crossed on flat slippery stones, when some shots were fired at us from a rocky *kopje* about 300 yards to our left rear. However, as the *kaffirs* who had fired were hidden behind rocks, we could see nothing of them, nor did we catch a glimpse of the enemy until we had all crossed the stream. We then saw a few natives amongst the wooded hills directly ahead of us, and at once commenced a skirmishing fight with them. They were in no great numbers, and they retired before us without firing many shots or giving us much of a chance at them.

In this way we had advanced slowly but steadily in extended order for about 300 yards through rocks and bush when we suddenly came upon a *kraal* filled with cattle, at the foot of a mass of bare castellated rocks. From these rocks we drove the enemy, without any loss on our side, though many of us were fired at at very close quarters, but, as has so often been remarked, *kaffirs* always make wretched shooting if at all hustled. Personally I had one little piece of luck. A *kaffir* had fired either at me or Mr. Blöcker —we were close together—from behind a buttress of rock, and as I knew that his rifle was therefore empty, and hoped he had been alone, I ran up the flat slope of rock on which I was standing, thinking to get a good shot at him round the corner of the rock.

When I got there, however, I did not see the man who had fired at me, but found another *kaffir* waiting for me with his rifle at his shoulder. He was on a lower level than the rock slab on which I was standing, and must have heard me approaching as he was evidently on the lookout for me to show myself. I was carrying my own rifle at the ready, but had to get it up to my shoulder before I could fire. There was no time to get a sight, so, looking at him, I raised my rifle as quickly as possible and fired, and at almost the same moment he fired at me. The result was mutually disappointing, as we both missed our mark. How I managed to make so bad a shot I don't know, as the *kaffir* was not more than fifteen yards from me. However, had I waited for the few seconds necessary to get the sight on him, he might very likely have shot me first, whilst my quick snap-shot very probably disconcerted him and made him miss. Immediately he had fired, he dodged behind a rock, and I did not get another chance at him.

We now took possession of the rocks above the cattle *kraal*, and got a few good shots at a lot of *kaffirs* running away amongst the trees to the left. Having placed several men as sentinels on the highest boulders, I went down to look at the cattle, considering it very bad luck having ever come across them, as I did not like to leave them and then continue my reconnaissance, nor did I think it would be possible to drive them out of the hills to the Tuli road without any *kaffirs* on foot to help. I first thought of shooting the lot, but as there were over a hundred, could not spare the ammunition that would have been required for the purpose. I therefore determined to try and drive them out of the hills and take them to Bulawayo.

With a great deal of trouble we got them down to the broken ground above the stream, but farther than this we could not drive them, as they scattered in all directions, but would not go down the rocks. Over and over again we rounded them up and tried to force them to go the way we wanted them to take, but without success, and I was once more thinking of shooting them all when some shots were fired at us from the broken ground to our left front. By a mistake the sentinels had left their posts on the top of the rocks and rejoined the rest of our party, and the *kaffirs*, now heavily reinforced, had got back to positions amongst the wooded cliffs above us without being observed.

I at once sent Mr. Blöcker and a few men who were good shots to take up a position beyond the stream, from which they could check the enemy's fire, whilst the rest of the men were crossing. I myself with Mr. Claude Grenfell and a few more men protected the rear. However, before we got down into the open ground, we had four horses killed and two men wounded, Mr. Stracey and Mr. Munzberg. How it was that more men were not hit, I don't know, as the bullets were pinging about pretty freely. Everyone, I think, although I spread the men out as much as possible, had some narrow shaves, and my sergeant-major got two bullets through his gaiter, and one through his trousers between his legs, yet he was not touched.

Not knowing how many *kaffirs* we had to deal with, nor whether some of them would not try to get round in front of us, I now sent Mr. Blöcker on with half the troop and the wounded men to take up a position on ahead, on our line of retreat; whilst Mr. Grenfell and I with the rest of the men remained behind to keep the *kaffirs* from coming out of the broken ground behind us. However, having lost a few of their number, they showed no disposition to leave the shelter of the rocks, so we retired slowly and off-saddled on an open spot just beyond the hills.

The *kaffirs* with whom we had been engaged had been for the most part, I think, members of the native police force, as I had seen several myself who were wearing the white knickerbocker trousers of the police uniform. They all, too, seemed to be young men, and were shooting with Winchester rifles; and did not shoot badly either—that is for natives. It was most fortunate that neither of the two men hit was mortally wounded, as if they had been we should have found it very difficult to carry them. Mr. Stracey was shot through the knee, though fortunately the bone was not much shattered, so he not only did not lose his leg, but will eventually, the doctor promises, have as good a limb as ever. Mr. Munzberg, a young German, was hit in the small of the back, and had a wonderful escape, as the bullet struck a kind of chain belt he was wearing round his waist. It went through this, but being much flattened out lost its velocity, and only inflicted a deep flesh wound.

In some ways the *kaffirs* may be said to have had the best of this encounter, as we left them in possession of the field. However, whilst we lost no men, we left a few of our opponents ready for burial, and our retreat, although it was a retreat, was of the slowest and most orderly character. Our horses were simply a nuisance to us amongst the granite boulders, and we could have done much better without them. Indeed, I saw enough this day to assure me that all subsequent fighting in the Matopos would have to be done on foot.

During the firing old Mazhlabanyan had behaved with great coolness. At first, when we were driving the *kaffirs* from the rocks above the cattle *kraal*, he had remained below holding my horse, but after recrossing the stream, I told him to go on with Mr. Blöcker. Finding that I did not immediately follow, the old fellow seems to have got very nervous about my safety, as after asking Mr. Blöcker a great many times where his master was, he came back to look. However, old Jack will be comfortably settled on my Company's land when these troublous times are over, and when the *rinderpest* has died out, and fresh cattle can be brought into the country, his fidelity will not be forgotten. After an hour's rest we again saddled up, and made straight across country to Dawson's store, at the Umzingwani ford on the Tuli road, twenty-five miles from Bulawayo. Here we were able to obtain a stretcher on which to carry Mr. Stracey, Mr. Munzberg still being able to ride.

As there could now be no doubt that there were hostile *kaffirs* at no great distance, I advised Mr. Boyce, who was in charge of the store, to lock up everything and accompany us to Bulawayo, which he did.

We started at sundown, all of us taking it in turns to carry our wounded comrade, and reached the post station, twelve miles from Bulawayo, soon after midnight. Here we passed a wretched night in the mule stable, as we were all wet through, a soaking rain having come on about an hour previously, which lasted for the rest of the night.

I sent two men on at once to Bulawayo, asking that a cart and a doctor might be sent out for the wounded men in the morning. The cart was sent, but no doctor could be spared. However, by mid-day we reached Bulawayo, and the wounded men were soon made comfortable in the hospital.

CHAPTER 11

O'Connor's Wonderful Escape

In the course of conversation, during our journey to Bulawayo, Mr. Boyce, the manager of Mr. Dawson's store on the Umzingwani, told me that, on the night before our arrival there, a miner named O'Connor had reached the store in a dreadful condition, having been terribly beaten about the head by *kaffirs*, from whose tender mercies he had escaped on 24th March. This poor fellow had been sent in to the hospital on the morning of the day on which we reached the store, and as his escape was a most remarkable one, I will tell it as I heard it from the man's own lips.

O'Connor, it appears, was engaged in mining work together with two other miners named Ivers and Ottens, on a reef called the Celtic, situated some mile and a half from Edkins' store.

On the morning of Tuesday, 24th March, after their early cup of coffee, the three miners were discussing matters in general, and more particularly the fact that during the last few days thirteen of their boys had run away for no apparent reason, unless it were that they had gone off to take part in a beer drink at the neighbouring *kraal* of Gorshlwayo. About seven o'clock they had an early breakfast, and shortly afterwards Ottens went off to see the Native Commissioner, Mr. Bentley, who was living at the police camp not far from Edkins' store. Then Ivers went away to see how the work was progressing at one of the shafts on the Celtic reef, leaving O'Connor alone. He, after kneading a loaf of bread and placing it in the sun to rise, went into his hut, and sitting down on his bed, threw his hat on a chair beside him, and lit his pipe.

He had been sitting smoking some few minutes, when he was suddenly startled by the loud and angry barking of Ottens' dogs, Captain and Snowball, just outside his hut. "The angry condition of the dogs was so unusual," said O'Connor, "that I give you my word I thought there was a lion in the camp." Jumping up, he ran to the door of the hut, only to find a *kaffir* standing just on one side of the entrance with a musket pointed towards him in his hands.

O'Connor said:

> For an instant I was paralysed, and retreated back into the hut, the door of which was immediately afterwards blocked by a crowd of *kaffirs* all armed with heavy *knobkerries*. Then, seeing that they had come to murder me, I became mad, and rushed in amongst them. I succeeded in wresting two *knobkerries* from them, and with these I fought desperately, always making my way towards the mouth of No. 1 shaft, which was something over 100 yards from my hut. I was repeatedly knocked down, and heavy blows were continually rained upon me, but, now on my knees, again on my feet, and sometimes rolling, I got to the mouth of the shaft with the remains of two broken sticks in my hands.

During this desperate struggle, O'Connor remembers hearing the *kaffirs*, who were attacking him with sticks, continually calling to the one with the gun, *u injani wena ai posa*—"why don't you shoot?"—and says that this man actually fired at him more than once, holding his gun at his hip, and always missing him. Just as he fell at the mouth of the shaft he was fired at for the last time. Then O'Connor rolled down the shaft "like a football," as he expressed it.

This was what is called an "incline shaft," going down for 136 feet at an angle of about 45 degrees. From the bottom of the incline shaft a tunnel had been driven into the reef 170 feet in length. Arrived at the bottom of the shaft, the hapless miner was at once attacked by his own boys—ten in number—who had been working in the tunnel. These devils fell upon him with hammers and drills, O'Connor defending himself as best he could with stones, and finally driving them all, as he thought, up the shaft.

After the terrible punishment he had received, which included thirteen scalp wounds—one of which had broken the outer table of the skull above the left temple—heavy blows with a hammer on each cheek-bone, and bruises and contusions all over the body, it may be wondered how O'Connor managed to retain his senses. But the fact remains that he did, and, thanks to a good old Irish head, still lives to tell the tale of the sufferings he endured, which, however, were not yet over by any means.

Believing that all his assailants had left the mine, he bethought him of a place of refuge, at a spot some halfway up the incline, where a vertical shaft had been cut into it. Here the shafts cut through some old workings, which formed a recess, into which O'Connor crept. Just as he was about to avail himself of this hiding-place, a *kaffir*, who, during the last fight, must have run back down the tunnel, rushed past him up the incline shaft. This man must have told the rest of the would-be murderers where the white man was hiding, and they did not leave him long in peace, for shortly afterwards several *kaffirs* came down the shaft, some with lighted candles, and four with guns. Two of these men carried muzzle-loaders, whilst the other two were armed with breech-loading rifles.

The latter O'Connor recognised by the light of the candles as "boys" who had been working for himself and his companions. Their names were "Candle," and "Makupeni," and they had been in the employ of the miners for nearly eighteen months, and as they were both good shots they had often been sent out with the only two rifles in camp to shoot game for the sake of the meat. Latterly, so implicit was the trust reposed in them by their masters that the rifles had been left entirely in their possession, but now they were among the first to volunteer their services to put an end to their employer in his sore extremity.

When O'Connor recognised his own trusted servants amongst his assailants he spoke to them, asking what harm he had done them, and why they wished to kill him, to which they answered, "We're going to kill you and all the white men in the country." However, although their would-be victim could see them, they could not see him, and seemed afraid to advance their heads into the recess where he lay—as they would have had to do in order to shoot him—for fear probably of being hit with a lump of quartz, which, even though it had been gold-bearing, might have made a nasty mark on their skulls.

During this time the *kaffirs* at the top of the shaft kept continually calling out to those below with the guns, "What are you doing; why don't you shoot the white man?" but still the cowardly murderers lacked the courage to creep into the recess and finish their victim. Suddenly there was a commotion at the top of the mine, and shouts of "*Amakiwa, Amakiwa*"—"white men, white men,"—and the four men with guns, together with those who were holding the candles, ran up the shaft, leaving the white man once more alone.

This cry of "white men" must have been a false alarm, as all the Europeans at the neighbouring police station and at Edkins' store were murdered without offering any resistance, having been taken completely by surprise. However, it gave O'Connor a few minutes' respite and enabled him to gain the shelter of another hiding-place where he thought he would be more secure from the guns of his enemies. This was a spot about halfway down the tunnel, where some loose ground had fallen in and rendered a certain amount of timbering necessary. Here, behind some boulders, O'Connor took refuge, but his enemies having recovered from their alarm and again come down the mine with candles, soon found out, probably by his tracks, where he had hidden.

And now the fruits of education were brought to the aid of native devilry to compass his destruction, for some of his own boys threw two charges of dynamite with short fuses into his hiding-place. Then the *kaffirs* all ran out of the mine, nor did they return, thinking probably that they had blown the white man to pieces. Having only seen the wonderful effects of dynamite when employed for blasting rocks and exploded at the bottom of a hole drilled deep into solid stone, they did not know that a loose charge exploded on the surface of the ground would have comparatively little effect. However O'Connor, except that he was nearly suffocated by the fumes of the dynamite, remained uninjured in the shelter of the boulder behind which he lay. Shortly after the explosions he thinks he must have become unconscious and remained so for many hours. When he came to himself, hearing no sound that betokened the proximity of his enemies, he crept from his hiding-place, and made his way to the mouth of the tunnel, and then ascended the incline shaft.

It was a bright moonlight night, and from the position of the moon he judged that it was about eight o'clock. A glance showed him that his camp had been destroyed and all the huts burnt down, but he could see no *kaffirs* about. He then made his way to an old mining camp about one and a half miles distant, called Nelson's Camp, from which he could look down on the police station, which he still hoped to find in the possession of white men. In the brilliant moonlight he saw the huts still standing; but there was no life or movement perceptible, and no lights or fires burning, and he therefore felt assured that the whites had either been murdered or left the camp. Then he went down to the stream which ran between the police camp and Edkins' store, and as he expressed it *"wallowed in it like a pig."*

After having quenched his thirst and washed the blood from his wounds he carefully approached Edkins' store, which he found had been burnt down, whilst the smell of murder was in the air, and the deathlike stillness was unbroken by even the bark of a dog. Then, indeed, the unfortunate man recognised to the full all the terrors of his dreadful position. All hope of succour from his immediate neighbours was gone; they had all been killed or forced to flee for their lives, whilst he stood alone amongst a nation of murderers. But his stout Irish heart never quailed, and weakened as he was by loss of blood he set out to the northwest, towards Bulawayo.

Leaving the Matabele *kraal* of Gorshlwayo as far as possible to his left, he at length reached the Insiza River some four miles from the camp he had left. By this time he was completely exhausted, and lay down in the reeds on the river's edge. Here he remained hidden all that night and the next day. On Wednesday night he again tried to get on towards Bulawayo, but by this time he was becoming more or less light headed, and unable to steer a good course, nor does he know exactly where he wandered. He lay hidden by day, and only moved at night, nor was it until Saturday night at about eleven o'clock, more than 110 hours after he had been attacked by the *kaffirs*, that he found his way to Mr. Dawson's store on the Umzingwani River.

All this time he had had no food. On approaching the store he found two men standing outside—Messrs. Schultz and Judge— whom he knew well, but who had looked upon him as dead. As he approached them in the moonlight, hatless, his face and head covered with wounds, he thinks they took him for an apparition come to call the white men to avenge his murder, for they fell back as if they had seen a ghost, and he said, "What, don't you know me—Joe O'Connor?" Then as they rushed up and seized him by the hands, he fell down senseless and they carried him to the store. Mr. Judge at once rode in to Bulawayo to try and get a doctor to come out and dress his wounds.

The following morning he was sent on by waggon from the Umzingwani store, and was met halfway by Mr. Lyons, the dispenser at the hospital, who, as no doctor could be spared, had volunteered to go to the wounded man's assistance. On Sunday afternoon he reached Bulawayo, where he lay a long time in hospital. All that medical skill and kindly nursing could do for him was done, and he eventually recovered from the dreadful injuries he had received; but the terrible experiences he has passed through have turned his hair partially grey,

O'Connor's arrival at the store.

As he approached them in the moonlight, hatless, his face and head covered with wounds, he thinks they took him for an apparition come to call the white men to avenge his murder.

he being a young man of only twenty-six years of age. He has, too, to mourn the loss of his brother and cousin, both of whom were murdered by the Matabele.

I was present in Colonel Napier's office, when a Zambesi boy, who had been working for them, gave evidence as to the manner in which they had been killed. He said, "I saw them killed with my eyes; they were killed by their own boys. O'Connor's brother was drawn up from the bottom of the shaft in which he was working by two men, who held the windlass still when his head came above the level of the ground, whilst others beat his brains out with *knobkerries*; the other man—O'Connor's cousin—was stabbed to death with *assegais*."

I have made many inquiries concerning O'Connor, and find that he bears the character of being a hard-working man, whilst he was known to the native commissioner of his district as one who always got on well with the natives.

From some remarks which he made, however, subsequent to the relation of his trying experiences, I judge that he has now abandoned any latent intention he may ever have had of becoming a member of the Aborigines Protection Society, nor do I think that the funds of that admirable institution are likely to be added to by any donation from Mr. O'Connor.

The worst feature in the foregoing history of the attempted murder of O'Connor and the actual murder and mutilation of his two companions, Messrs. Ivers and Ottens, is the participation in the crimes by two trusted servants who had been in the employ of the murdered men for so long a time as eighteen months, since the very fact that these boys had worked for so many months for the same white men shows conclusively that they must have been kindly treated by them, for no *kaffir* will remain long in the service of a master who ill-treats him.

Now I am not so unreasonable as to think that the natures of the Matabele natives ought to be judged of by the unamiable qualities shown by two individuals; indeed I know that as a set-off, even during the present rebellion, the lives of some few white men have been saved by the fidelity of natives in their employ. But unfortunately the evil deeds get more noised abroad, and they add to the bitterness of the exasperation felt by the whites against the blacks; for it seems inevitable that during an insurrection such as the present, the average nature of the native will be judged of by the average European on the spot, according to the worst atrocities that have been committed, and such an instance of treachery as I have related will harden the kindest heart and produce a feeling of distrust in the whole race that can never be eradicated from the mind. In many, too—and these by no means the most brutal or worst educated in the community—such acts, coupled with the indiscriminate murder of women and children, produce a conviction that beings who are capable of such deeds, who can lick your hand and fawn upon you for eighteen months and then one day turn and murder you, and afterwards perhaps mutilate your senseless corpse, are not men and brothers, but monsters in human shape, that ought to be shot down mercilessly like wild dogs or hyenas, until they are reduced to a state of abject submission to the white man's rule.

In time, however, let us hope that the cruel deeds of the last few months will be forgotten, and the fierce passions they have evoked on both sides gradually smoulder out and die from the lack of fresh fuel. Henceforth it will, I trust, be recognised by the authorities that the native question in Rhodesia is one of the very first importance, and that it is also one which demands the most careful handling in order to ensure the future peace and prosperity of the country. When this rebellion is quelled and the natives have once more submitted themselves to the white man's rule, they must know exactly the terms on which their submission has been accepted; and they must also understand precisely what will be required of them in the shape of hut-tax, labour, etc. Then if they are treated kindly and justly, as well as firmly, they ought not to have any valid reason for again rebelling against the government of their white conquerors; but lest they should ever be inclined to make such an attempt without any valid reason, they must now be so thoroughly and completely disarmed as to render any such action futile.

The Laager in the Market Square. Bulawayo. April 1896.

CHAPTER 12

Laager Formed at Bulawayo

On our return to Bulawayo, we found that a very strong *laager* had been formed in the large square round the Market Buildings. Within this *laager* the whole population of the town, with few exceptions, slept every night; the women and children within the buildings, whilst the men manned the waggons in readiness to resist any sudden attack.

The Bulawayo *laager* was probably the strongest ever constructed in South Africa, and the whole Matabele nation, I think, would never have taken it by assault. But if 2000 of them, or even a smaller number, had made a night attack upon the town before the *laager* had been formed, I think it more than probable that the entire white population would have been massacred. It appears that there was a terrible scare on the very night on which I had left the town for Essexvale, *viz*. Wednesday, 25th March. This scare was absolutely groundless and seems to have been caused by a drunken man galloping about calling out "The Matabele are here; the Matabele are here."

My wife was resting in Mrs. Spreckley's house at the time, being much fatigued by her long ride in the hot sun from Essexvale. However, she and her kind hostess, as well as all the other ladies living on the suburban stands, were hurried over to the new club-house, nearly a mile distant, in the centre of the town. Here the large number of women and children in Bulawayo, many of them hastily summoned from their beds, and most of them terribly frightened, passed a miserable night all huddled up together, but getting neither rest nor sleep, as they were constantly kept on the *qui vive* by fresh rumours, all equally groundless, as happily at this time there was no force of hostile natives within twenty miles of Bulawayo. On the following day the *laager* was formed, and by the time I got back to town Colonel Spreckley and

Mr. Scott (the town major) had, after an immense amount of hard work, got everything into good order.

These two gentlemen deserve the utmost credit not only for getting the *laager* into good order, but also for keeping it in that condition for the next two months. Major Scott was indefatigable in looking after the sanitary arrangements, whilst Colonel Spreckley, by his genial good nature, backed by great common sense and strength of character, kept all the various human elements shut up in that confined space not only in good order but in good humour. Nobody in Bulawayo, I think, could have performed the very difficult duties required from the chief officer in charge of the *laager* so ably as Colonel Spreckley during the first two months of the insurrection, and his conduct was all the more admirable because he was carrying out a very arduous and harassing duty against his inclination, or rather burning desire, to be out of town at the head of a patrol doing active work against the insurgents.

Soon after my arrival in town, I was delighted to meet the native commissioner of my district, Mr. Jackson, whom I had never thought to see again. He and his white companions had received warning of the rising from his sub-inspector, and were also cautioned lest there should be a plot on foot for their murder by the native police. At this time, however, the ninety men they had with them, each of whom was armed with a Winchester rifle and seventy rounds of ammunition, did not know that the rebellion had commenced, and they managed to bring them all in to Bulawayo without any trouble, where they were at once disarmed.

Now by this time it had become evident that the insurrection had become general throughout the length and breadth of Matabeleland, and I will give a brief account of what had happened so far as is known.

I have already related that Mr. Cumming and another man brought the first news of the murders of white men in the Insiza district to Bulawayo. On reaching Lee's store, twenty-four miles from the town, they found that their horses were completely knocked up, and they could thus only have proceeded on foot, had not Mr. Claude Grenfell just happened to be passing the store with a cart and horses on his way from Gwelo to Bulawayo.

On hearing the alarming news Mr. Grenfell took Mr. Cumming on with him at once to headquarters, his companion, Mr. Edmunds, giving up his seat to him, and walking. Before reaching Lee's store,

Colonel J. A. Spreckley.

Mr. Grenfell had met Mr. George Grey, travelling alone in a Cape cart with a coloured boy, on his way to inspect some of his mining properties near the Tchangani River, and when the news of the murders in the Insiza district became known, much anxiety was naturally felt concerning Mr. Grey's safety, as well as that of all other Europeans who were living at a distance from Bulawayo in mining camps or on lonely farms.

Early on Thursday morning, however, Mr. Grey returned to town, having escaped death by the merest chance, as he must only just have escaped falling into the hands of more than one party of murderers.

On reaching the Pongo store some twelve miles from the Tchangani River, Mr. Grey had found all the outhouses just burnt. The store itself seemed to have been looted, but was not at this time burnt down. No trace of the owners could be found, but the ground was thickly covered with the naked footprints of natives, and, more ominous still, a large pool of blood was seen in the road in front of the store. We now know that at this time the recently-murdered corpses of three white men were lying, two of them close to the store, and the third on the top of a rise a short distance away. I was present some six weeks later when the bodies were discovered and buried. The unfortunate men must have been suddenly attacked with *knobkerries* and axes, as their skulls had all been smashed in. In this instance the clothes were not removed from the bodies.

This was the first intimation that Mr. Grey got that mischief was brewing in the country. Soon after passing the Pongo store, he turned off the main road and went down to the Eagle mine some four miles distant. This he found had been only recently deserted by the Europeans employed there, and with his suspicions now fully aroused he returned at once to the main road, and made for the Tchangani store. On his way there he came across a white man on the roadside, who had escaped from a party of *kaffirs*, after receiving two severe battle-axe wounds, one of which had cut his face open from nose to ear, whilst the second had cut his arm to the bone and severed all the tendons of the wrist. This man had been working with two companions on a farm in the neighbourhood, when on the previous day—Tuesday, 24th March—they had been suddenly and without any warning attacked by a party of *kaffirs* armed with *knobkerries* and battle-axes. Although two of them were wounded, they managed to retreat to their hut, on which the natives, probably thinking that they had firearms there, retired.

These numbers refer to the four gentlemen with folded arms.

3   2   1   4

GREY'S SCOUTS.

1. Captain George Grey.   2. Lieutenant F. Crewe.   3. Lieutenant Jack Stuart.   4. Lieutenant Hodgson.

After sundown the three white men left their hut, intending to make for Stewart's store at the Tekwe. Unfortunately it was a bright moonlight night, and the *kaffirs* must have been watching them, as they immediately followed, and chased them into a maize field, through which they hunted them. During this pursuit the white men became separated. One of them reached Mr. Stewart's store in safety; the second, Mr. Scott by name, found his way to the road near the Pongo store and was picked up and taken to the Tchangani by Mr. Grey; but the third must have fallen into the hands of the *kaffirs*, and, of course, been murdered, as he has never again been heard of from that day to this. The man who made his way to the Tekwe had received a severe blow on the head with a *knobkerrie*.

Arrived at the Tchangani, Mr. Grey found seventeen Europeans in *laager* there, amongst them the men from the Eagle mine, who had been pursued on their way to the store. The natives, however, were afraid to come to close quarters with them as they were armed with rifles, and at this time the rebels in this district had not yet dug up the firearms which they had buried after the war of 1893, and were therefore only able to kill white men whom they could take by surprise with *knobkerries* and axes.

Now fully realising the very serious aspect of affairs, Mr. Grey, instead of remaining in the shelter of the *laager*, most pluckily determined to return to Bulawayo at once, making use of the post mules along the road, in order to warn all people with as little delay as possible that the *kaffirs* had risen.

A few hours after he had left the Tchangani, the garrison of the *laager* was augmented by the arrival of Messrs. Farquhar, Weston Jarvis, Currie, and Mr. Egerton (M.P. for Knutsford) and his son. These gentlemen had been on a hunting trip to the Sebakwe River, and were returning to Bulawayo only just in time, as had they remained out in the *veldt* any longer they would certainly have been murdered, for although they would doubtless have given a very good account of themselves, yet a few men cannot fight an army.

On the following day—Thursday, 26th March—two small patrols were organised and sent out from the Tchangani, one of which, consisting of Mr. Mowbray Farquhar and two companions, visited a mine where a white man was known to have been working a day or two previously, whilst the other, consisting of Mr. Robinson and two others, visited the Pongo store and the Eagle mine. A careful search was made by the latter all round the store, and the bodies of two out of the three men who had been murdered there two days previously were discovered and covered with blankets, which were still in their places when we buried the remains some six weeks later. The third corpse they did not find, as it was lying some distance from the store.

Mr. Farquhar and his two companions visited Comployer's camp, and found the unfortunate man lying murdered in front of the door of his hut. They tried to get on to Gracey's camp, but could not do so for fear of being surrounded and cut off by the *kaffirs*, who were all in their *kraals* watching them. It has since been ascertained that Gracey was murdered on the same day as Comployer.

On returning to the *laager*, they found that a mule-waggon had been sent from Gwelo, with orders from the officer commanding there that all Europeans should come in as quickly as possible to assist in the defence of the town against the *kaffirs*.

Leaving the Tchangani at 5 p.m. on Thursday evening, the whole party reached Gwelo in safety on Friday morning at half-past eight In the meantime Mr. Grey, travelling at express speed with relays of coach mules, reached Bulawayo early on Thursday morning. On passing the Tekwe store, he found assembled there Mr. Stewart, five other white men, and two women, who were endeavouring to fortify a hut. Promising them speedy relief, Mr. Grey hurried on to warn others of their danger, but beyond the Tekwe he found that the occupants of the roadside hotels and post stations had already taken the alarm and made their way to Bulawayo.

On Thursday, 26th March, Mr. Grey got together twenty-three good men, and started back for the Tekwe that same evening. These men formed the nucleus of a force which has done splendid service in the suppression of the present rebellion, under the name of Grey's Scouts. They were a picked body of men, and neither their name nor their brave deeds will ever be forgotten in Rhodesia, whilst I think we all regard Captain Grey as one of the finest specimens of an Englishman in the country—quiet, self-contained and unassuming, but at the same time, brave, capable, and energetic.

CHAPTER 13

Captain Grey's Timely Arrival at Tekwe Store

Captain Grey and his men reached Tekwe store about 2 p.m. on Friday, 27th March, and were only just in time to save the beleaguered whites there; for shortly before their arrival a party of *kaffirs* had driven off all Mr. Stewart's cattle, and killed a horse belonging to him. At the same time they had been kind enough to send him a message by the boy who had been looking after his cattle, to the effect that they meant to return and kill all the white people that night. However, they made no attack when they found that Mr. Stewart's small party had been reinforced by some twenty well-armed men.

On the following day Colonel Napier's column, which had left Bulawayo on the previous Tuesday, and had been patrolling the country in the direction of the Insiza River, came across country to the Tekwe store. Besides saving the lives of Mr. Stewart and his party, the presence of Colonel Napier and Captain Grey with the men under their command on the Salisbury road at this juncture was the means of saving the lives of nine other white men and two coloured boys, the latter being the drivers, whilst the former were the guard, sent down with the last mail coach from Gwelo.

This coach left Gwelo on Saturday, 28th March, arriving at the Tchangani early the following morning. Here they found the body of a white man, just murdered and stripped stark naked, lying in the middle of the road in front of the store. This was the body of a prospector named Wood in the employ of Willoughby's Consolidated Company, who had come across country from the Selukwe district. Unfortunately he arrived at the Tchangani store on the day after it had been evacuated by the white men who had been in *laager* there, and he probably found it in possession of the *kaffirs*, who of course murdered him.

On seeing this ghastly sign of the times, the men in charge of the coach determined to drive on at once without outspanning, and soon observed *kaffirs* running in the bush and keeping pace with the coach on both sides of the road. These natives, however, seemed to have no guns, and by continually firing at them the white men kept them from coming to close quarters. After a time the Pongo store was reached, but no halt was possible owing to the threatening attitude of the *kaffirs*. The mules were now almost done up, and could only get the coach along at a walk, but still the *kaffirs* hung on either flank, as thirsty for blood as a pack of wild dogs awaiting the moment to rush in upon a wounded buffalo.

Some three miles farther on the poor mules came to a standstill, and the white men were forced to leave the coach, and keep on on foot along the road, the *kaffirs* ever keeping pace with them in the bush on either side, and doubtless only waiting for the darkness of night to enable them to rush in and kill them with as little loss to themselves as possible. But just at dusk they reached Colonel Napier's column in a very exhausted condition.

Some six weeks later, when we found the bodies of the men who had been murdered at the Pongo store, we also found some three miles on this side of the store the coach which had been captured by the *kaffirs*. A linchpin had been removed, and one of the wheels taken off. The pole had also been sawn in two, and all the mail bags cut open, their contents being scattered all over the ground. The poor mules had all been stabbed to death with *assegais*, and lay in a heap together, still in their harness.

Altogether the combined patrols under Colonel Napier and Captain Grey collected and brought back with them to Bulawayo forty-three persons, including two women and a child, many, if not all of whom, had they not been thus timely rescued, would have fallen victims to the *kaffirs*. The names of the poor fellows murdered at the Pongo store are Frederick Hurlstone, J. Reddington, and H. Zeeburg. At midnight on the Saturday before my return to Bulawayo from the Matopo Hills, Captain Pittendrigh of the Africander Corps had left town with a small party only eleven strong, in order first of all to reinforce for the night a small party at Jenkins' store, and then push on some thirty miles farther, in order to relieve Mr. Graham, the native commissioner at Inyati, who with Sub-inspector Hanley and five other white men was believed to be in *laager* there. There were many volunteers for this expedition, but as the government was unable to furnish them with horses or rifles, only those could go who were in a position to equip themselves.

Jenkins' store was reached at half-past two on Sunday morning. Here ten men were found in *laager*, including a younger brother of Mr. Graham the native commissioner. He, with an assistant native commissioner, Mr. Carter, a cart and four mules and two spare horses, had been on his way to Inyati to bring his brother, who was suffering from an attack of fever, into Bulawayo. As an attack had been expected on the store that night, the thatch had been removed from the roof, and a rough fence put up round the building. However, no attack was made, and at 5 a.m. the whole party, now consisting of nineteen men, with the two spare horses and the cart and mules driven by two colonial boys, set out for the Bembisi,[1] twenty-three miles distant.

For the subsequent experiences of this small rescue party, I am indebted to the kindness of Mr. Moodie Thomson, the able editor of the *Matabele Times*, who accompanied Captain Pittendrigh and wrote an account of the expedition. This he has kindly placed at my disposal, and I will take up his narrative at the point when the start was made from Jenkins' store early on Sunday morning. It proceeds as follows:—

> We were now in a very different country from the open *veldt* of the earlier ride. *Kopjes* were close on either hand, the road was of the roughest, and progress with the mule cart consequently slow. The word was constantly given for a good look-out on either hand, but for over an hour not a man or a woman was seen, though tracks crossing the path were met with at frequent intervals. The *kopjes* in which we had expected to have trouble were passed, and the more open undulating ground at the Elibaini Hills reached. Progress was slow along this portion of the ascending road, and near the highest point skirting the base of the most prominent hill a strip of bush was entered. No sooner had we made our way into this cover than a shot was heard from the hill-slope.
>
> In a second it was seen to be occupied by half a dozen or so natives, who sent in another and another shot. It was impossible to make a sufficient reply from our position, and a dash was made

---

1. Correct name "Impembisi."

from the road through the strip of bush to the open slope of the hill. One or more of the natives was shot as they retreated over the crest, and a hot pursuit was made.

When those of our party who were foremost reached the top of the hill they found that affairs had assumed a different aspect from repulsing a handful of stray rebels. A glance was sufficient. The natives were there in a dense mass, throwing out skirmishers on either flank to surround us, one body proceeding rapidly around the lower slope to cut us off. Our advance men fell back, and the natives began to show themselves in the open. Firing became hot on both sides, but taking advantage of the strip of bush we were able at first to inflict considerable damage. The natives to the number of about three hundred were soon in the bush also, advancing in excellent open order and becoming formidable. Several rushed in to close quarters, and Captain Pittendrigh, who had dismounted, lost his horse.

Before he could get one of the spare horses, a native armed with an *assegai* grappled him, and a hand-to-hand struggle took place. The native, however, was thrown off and shot, and the captain escaped with some slits in his coat. At the same moment Thomas Haden, who had been fighting most determinedly in the front, received a shot on the upper part of his bandoleer, which exploded three of his cartridges, one bullet passing through his shoulder and with a ricochet entering his neck and passing through his cheek. Immediately after Mr. S. Carter received a bullet through his ankle. The natives began to approach closer in their attack despite our heavy fire, and as they were gradually surrounding us, it was found advisable, encumbered as we were with two wounded men, to retire to the road.

With a rush through without further casualty on our side, we regained the road and found that one of our boys at the mule waggon had vanished, and the other was getting away on one of the spare horses. The mules and cart had therefore to be abandoned, and at a good pace we cut across through the lower bush over rough ground, avoiding the curve round the hills, to where the road bent round on the open.

Here half-sections were again formed, the wounded in front, and a quick canter gave us a good start. Looking back, the natives could be seen in hot pursuit, and it was thought they might be able to reach one of the *kopjes* ahead whose base we must skirt. Suggestions as to taking up a position on a *kopje* were untenable on account of the wounded men, and there was nothing for it but to get over the seventeen miles to the Bembisi as rapidly as possible. Again and again the natives seemed to be closing up on us, and sundry indications were closely scrutinised as to the presence of hostile forces ahead. The ride was made heavier by two of the ponies becoming done up. It was an anxious time, as the road ran through the hollows, but the clearness of the day gave abundant scope for noting the absence of an enemy ahead and the black mass falling farther astern.

About eleven o'clock Campbell's store came in sight, and we crossed the Bembisi with gladdened spirits. These, however, were immediately damped. The news was awaiting us that the party at Inyati, eight miles farther on, which we had been sent to relieve, had been massacred. The intelligence was given by Patrick Madden, miner, who, and a native in his employ, were the sole survivors. This man told with most circumstantial and convincing detail how Native Commissioner Graham, Inspector Hanley, George Hurford, George Case, and S. H. Corke had fought against ever-increasing odds on the evening of the previous Friday—this was now Sunday—until they were killed. Madden, another miner named Tim Donovan, and a colonial native had made for the hills, and after two days' hiding Madden and the native had reached this store.

The narrative, it may be said, has been fully corroborated since from other sources, with the addition that Donovan was also pursued and killed. Further, there was the news that an *impi* of from 1200 to 1500 lay at Inyati. It was hard to decide to abandon the projected relief, but the facts were obvious that with an *impi* ahead, and with a body of 300 at least following us, and very shortly seen to be in the bush across the river, there was nothing for it but to take up the strongest position possible.

Across the river the natives could be seen in the bush, and were we even to venture with our wounded to go by the road, we were at their mercy. At the store we had found Mr. Campbell with a waggon and oxen, hourly expecting to be pounced upon, and it was resolved to set to work to fortify the store. The verandah thatch was cut away, passages were pierced so that there might be free communication through the large building, and loopholes were cut through the brick walls in every direction.

In addition, a case of dynamite was found in the store which was utilised to lay mines with ingeniously-contrived short fuse, and to make a score or so hand grenades with a radius of about fifteen yards that could be thrown at assailants. The large stock of meal in sacks was put into service to block windows, and then we were certain that, having about 2000 rounds of ammunition, we could hold out well against a night attack.

It was necessary, however, to send word to Bulawayo of our condition and the intelligence we had received, and to obtain reinforcements which we calculated could arrive in time to fall on the rear of the natives attacking us at daybreak. Messrs. Fincham and Mostert were mounted on the best horses as despatch-riders. A diversion was made by the whole party crossing the river as if returning by the road we had come, and as we saw the natives moving to meet us the despatch-riders went off at an angle by the Queen's Reef road, passing the Shiloh Hills. The rest of the day was spent in completing our fortifications. Strong guard was set at night, and we waited eagerly for the natives to come for the reception prepared for them. The wounded had been bandaged and made as comfortable as possible; the horses were stabled in the bar and store-room, and every man was at his post carefully looking out.

About four on Monday morning the silence was broken by the sound of firing, and speculation was rife as to its meaning. It came nearer and nearer, and it was soon decided that this was the reinforcing party fighting its way through the natives lying in wait for us. There was silence for a time, broken again by the cracking of shots, and with the dim dawn we could see a body of men emerging from the thick bush. As they came nearer it became plain that they were white men, and we left the store to send up a cheer to let them know we were still safe.

As day came more brightly, in they rode across the open *veldt*, and with answering cheers dashed up the river-bank to the store. They were thirty strong, fifteen from the Africander Corps under Commandant Van Rensburg and Captain Van Niekerk, and the remainder from various Rhodesia Horse Volunteers, troops or volunteers under Captain Macfarlane. They had ridden the whole night through, with only a brief halt at the Queen's Reef, and in our vicinity had been met in the black darkness of the bush with a volley fired not twenty yards off. They had replied, and a running fire had been kept up for about half an hour. No one in the party had been wounded, but two men in the advanced guard, Messrs. Celliers and Henderson, were missing. Several dead bodies of natives seen in the bush testified later to the effect of the replying fire.

About nine o'clock it was decided that the whole party should return by the Queen's Reef road and ride straight for Bulawayo. A start was made with strong flanking parties, Captain Pittendrigh's men being placed in the rear-guard after the waggon containing our two wounded. Cautious progress was made through the bush where the natives had been assembled and where spoor was thick, but without a sign of life visible. The Queen's Reef was reached about eleven o'clock, and at noon the column got again into dangerous bush.

Nothing occurred, however, until the Shiloh Hills were reached, when on the spur of a *kopje* and in the bush below natives were seen. They opened fire, but their aim was high. Those of them who were venturous enough to make the attack were summarily disposed of—nothing being more convincing of the perfection of the fire of our party than the manner in which seven, eight, or nine shots would simultaneously bowl over a native who exposed himself even for a moment. On our side a horse—one of Mr. Zeederberg's finest animals—was shot through the lower part of the stomach, and subsequently died from the effects of the wound. This was our only casualty, and on the other side there must have been a loss of a dozen men at least. The fire was fairly hot while it lasted, but a party of about fifty was too strong for the natives, even though they may have been several hundred. They had to depend upon their firing, as close quarters against such marksmen was almost an impossibility.

The Kotki River was reached after a heavy detour through the bush to avoid giving the natives around us too much opportunity at the *kopjes*, and a halt made for an hour. Just before reaching there a herd of native cattle had been met and seized, and heifer steaks cooked on ramrods proved refreshing after our twenty-mile ride at ox-waggon pace. Then on again, the remaining fifteen miles without further attack, until in the darkness a cheer from the pickets about ten o'clock announced that Bulawayo had been reached.

The wounded were conveyed to the hospital, and tired horses

and men had the satisfaction of seeking what comfort was available in a *laagered* town. The men in Captain Pittendrigh's party who had this experience of Matabele skirmishing, were, with one or two additional exceptions, members of the Africander Corps. It is useful to testify that their courage, their determination, their skill with the rifle, and their expert employment of every ruse in such fighting as we had at the Elibaini Hills, command the highest admiration. We were in a fairly tight place, as may be judged when hand-to-hand fighting was possible, and we were only nineteen against several hundreds; but the pluck and brilliant dash displayed, as well as the good comradeship throughout, are convincing that in a like or even a stiffer affray one could neither wish nor hope to have better men than these.

It remains to be said that the two missing men came in to Bulawayo on Wednesday morning. Celliers had had his horse shot under him and was himself badly wounded in the knee. With that consideration which is akin to heroism Henderson placed him on his horse, and walking beside him for three days they had hidden amongst the hills, making their way through most dangerous country. Henderson tended his wounded comrade in every way possible, and succeeded in keeping clear of natives, though at times they passed in unpleasantly close proximity. Such conduct is something more than typical of the men who are bent upon holding Matabeleland.

The devoted courage shown by Mr. Henderson in giving up his own horse to his wounded comrade and sticking to him for three days, during the whole of which time they were surrounded by the enemy, and in continual danger of being discovered, appears to me to be as brave a deed as has yet been chronicled in the annals of Rhodesia. I commend it to the notice of Mr. Labouchere, as I feel sure that it will be quite a revelation to him to learn that there exists amongst the "Buccaneers" [2] at least one man who has shown himself capable of a self-sacrificing and generous act. Yet all Mr. Henderson's gallantry could not save his comrade's life, as Mr. Celliers eventually died from the effects of the amputation of his leg, owing principally to the length of time which had elapsed between the time when he was wounded and the date when the operation was performed.

---

2. "Buccaneers" is the term of endearment commonly bestowed upon the Englishmen in Rhodesia by the editor of *Truth*.

CHAPTER 14

Mr. Dawson's Patrol

Besides the patrols of which I have already spoken that were sent out from Bulawayo during the first days of the insurrection, I must not forget that which was taken down to the Gwanda district by Mr. James Dawson. Mr. Dawson, who has lived amongst the natives of Matabeleland for many years, and both speaks their language and understands their character well, could not believe that a general rising throughout the country was possible, and even after hearing of the murders in the Insiza and Filibusi districts, and my own report as to what had taken place on Essexvale, imagined that the disturbance was only local. However, in order to assure himself of the true position of affairs, he got together some ten or twelve men, and leaving Bulawayo with them on Wednesday night, 25th March, proceeded down the Tuli road to his own store at "Amanzi minyama," situated in the Gwanda district, and distant about seventy-five miles from Bulawayo.

On his way there he found everything perfectly quiet along the road, all the wayside stores being still in the occupation of their owners, none of whom had heard anything about the native rising—a state of things which of course confirmed Mr. Dawson in his scepticism.

On the return journey, however, shortly before reaching Spiro's store, which is distant thirty-seven miles from Bulawayo, the fresh tracks of numbers of natives—men, women, and children—as well as of cattle, goats, and sheep, were noticed crossing the road. These were doubtless the trails made by the Matabele from the Filibusi district, who were making their way to the Matopo Hills, and at once aroused suspicion.

Spiro's store was reached on Sunday, a few hours after I had left it the same morning on my way into the hills. Here Mr. Dawson found no one, for after my departure the boys who had been looking after the coach mules became frightened and took them in to Bulawayo, leaving the cattle behind; and these were still in the *kraal*, with no one to tend them, when Mr. Dawson passed. Not quite liking the look of things, the patrol went on beyond the store, and slept some four miles away from it.

On the following morning early they reached the wayside hotel at the Umzingwani River, which we had left at sundown on the evening before. Here in one of the huts were found the bloodstained shirt of Mr. Munzberg, and also a sock soaked with blood that had been taken from Mr. Stracey. During Monday Mr. Dawson and his men remained at the Umzingwani, but sent messengers to Bulawayo to obtain news as to what was going on.

Late that evening an answer was received requesting him to come on to town at once, as the *kaffirs* were reported to be massing in the neighbourhood. Before this there had been several alarms, and it was believed that natives were on the watch round about the store. Thus when the start was made for Bulawayo, the lights were left burning, in order to make the *kaffirs* believe that some of the party were still in the house. Arrived at the river some 600 yards distant from the store, Mr. Dawson rode back alone to reconnoitre, but hearing natives talking, retired and rejoined his men.

Early on Tuesday morning Inspector Southey was met with a small force at the head of the pass leading down to the Umzingwani. He had been sent out to escort the coach to Bulawayo, which was now some time overdue from Tuli. However, as Mr. Dawson had heard nothing of this coach, it was thought that it must have turned back; so Inspector Southey, who had been ordered not to descend the pass, returned to town, where shortly after his arrival the coach turned up too without an escort.

This was the last coach that ran on the Tuli road, and it seems to have been missed by the natives by a miracle, as they had broken into the Umzingwani store and gone away again in the interval between the time of its arrival there and Mr. Dawson's departure.

This coach reached Bulawayo on the morning of Tuesday, 31st March, and on the same day—the day after my own return from the Matopos—I was asked to take a patrol of twenty five men down the Mangwe road, in order to ascertain if it was still clear, as a coach loaded with rifles and ammunition and ten waggon-loads of provisions were on their way up.

We left town about 2 p.m., each man carrying three days' rations with him, and reaching Mabukitwani, twenty miles distant from Bulawayo, the same night, arrived at "Fig Tree" by noon the following day, where we found a store and mule stable in charge of Mr. Elliott.

The people living in the neighbourhood are nearly all of Makalaka descent, and have taken no part in the present insurrection. At the time of my visit they were in a great state of alarm, and the greater part of them had left their villages and fled into the hills, fearing lest the white men should visit the sins of the insurgents upon them. I therefore sent one of Mr. Elliott's boys to call the principal *induna* to come and see me. With this man, an intelligent-looking Makalaka named Jackal, who bears a striking resemblance to the chief Khama, I had a long interview, and finally persuaded him to send messengers to the refugees ordering them to return to their *kraals*.

Jackal assured me that the first news of the rebellion was brought to him by the son of Umfaizella (the brother of Lo Bengula, who with Umlugulu and others is responsible for the murders at Edkins' store), who was sent by his father to incite some of the Makalaka to revolt. When he found that Jackal's people did not seem very anxious to assist the Matabele in their attempt to regain their independence, he said to him, "You say that your people don't want to fight; that they wish to sit still. Don't you know that the white men are killing all the black men they can catch? Don't you know that they have shot Gambo through the head, and thrown his body to the birds? Have you not heard that every *kaffir* boy who was working in Bulawayo has had his throat cut?"

"I did not believe him," said Jackal, "and soon afterwards one of my own men, who had been working in town, came home, and told me that the white men had killed no one in Bulawayo except a few Matabele spies. Then I knew that the son of Umfaizella had lied to me, but still the bad news frightened my people."

I may here state that Jackal expressed the opinion that if they were unable to kill all the white men, a large section of the Matabele would probably leave the country with as many cattle as they could get together, and seek a new home beyond the Zambesi. What amount of truth there may be in this view, and how far the original plan may have been modified owing to the destruction of all the cattle by the *rinderpest*, remains to be seen. At present, however, no section of the tribe seems actually to have made a move beyond the outskirts of Matabeleland proper.

In the afternoon we proceeded to the Shashani. Before reaching

"Fig Tree," the coach, loaded with ammunition, had passed us on its way to Bulawayo in charge of the escort that had accompanied it from Mangwe. As, according to the information I had received before leaving town, the convoy of waggons ought now to have been close at hand, and I did not wish to tire all my horses by taking them any farther than necessary down the road, I left Lieutenant Grenfell in charge of the patrol at the deserted shanty, which had done duty as an hotel, near to which we had off-saddled, and rode on alone.

Shortly before reaching the Shashani hotel we had met a light waggonette drawn by a team of horses on its way to Bulawayo. In it were two gentlemen, Captain Lumsden (late of the 4th Battalion Scottish Rifles) and Mr. Frost, on their way to Matabeleland on a shooting expedition. We halted and gave one another the news from up and down country respectively, and had a laugh and a joke about the kind of shooting one was likely to get in Matabeleland at the present time. When Captain Lumsden got out of the waggonette I saw what a fine specimen of a man he was—tall and broad-shouldered, with a pleasant face and keen blue eye—and I little thought that when next I met him, only a week later, it would be in the Bulawayo hospital, where, poor fellow, he lay with a leg shattered by a *kaffir's* bullet, on what soon proved to be his deathbed, for he died from the effects of the subsequent amputation of the limb.

After leaving my men I rode quietly on, but only met the waggons I was looking out for when close to Mangwe. Having many friends in the laager there, I determined to ride a little farther and pay them a visit. First, however, I exhorted the man in charge of the waggons to push on at once, as I was anxious to return to Bulawayo as soon as possible, in the hope of getting something more exciting to do there than escorting waggons.

When still some three miles from Mangwe I met a party of horsemen riding towards me along the road. They proved to be old friends who had come out to meet me, as they had heard by telegraph that I was coming their way. Amongst them was one of my oldest and most esteemed friends, Cornelius Van Rooyen, with whom in the good old days I had wandered and hunted for months together over the then unknown wilds of Mashunaland.

Arrived at the *laager*, I received a very warm welcome from both Dutch and English. Major Armstrong was in command, whom, though a very young man, I thought both shrewd and capable, and the excellent service he has done for the government during the present insurrection has, I think, been fully recognised.

Before leaving Bulawayo I had heard it said that in the Mangwe *laager* order and discipline were conspicuous by their absence; but this I did not find to be at all the case. On the contrary, it seemed to me that Major Armstrong and Commandant Van Rooyen, by the exercise of great tact, had between them got everything into excellent order; and this is no small praise, for it must be remembered that the occupants of the Mangwe *laager* belonged to two nationalities, Dutch and English, each of which has its own way of doing things, and the two can only be brought to work harmoniously together by the exercise of both forbearance and good sense on the part of the officer commanding the combined force.

All my Dutch friends at Mangwe had suffered terrible losses amongst their stock from the *rinderpest*; indeed, some who had been rich men a couple of months before, possessing several hundred head of stock, had now scarcely a beast left. All along the road, too, from Bulawayo to Mangwe the evidences of the ruthless severity of this plague were most lamentable. Hundreds of carcasses in every stage of putrefaction everywhere lined the track, whilst here and there were groups of empty waggons abandoned by their owners, who, having lost their means of livelihood through the death of their oxen, had left the rest of their property standing uncared for in the wilderness, and walked away ruined men.

At Wilson's farm, six miles from Bulawayo, where herds of infected cattle had been slaughtered in the hopeless endeavour to stamp out the disease, acres of carcasses were lying festering in the sun, and any one passing along the road did not require to look at them to know they were there. Strangely enough, in spite of the exceptional opportunities offering for free meals throughout Matabeleland at this time, not a vulture was to be seen. I have heard it said that too hearty an indulgence in *rinderpest* meat in the early days of the plague killed all the vultures, and whether this is so or not, certain it is that these useful birds are now as scarce as cows in Matabeleland.

HIS LAST OX

CHAPTER 15

Escort a Convoy of Waggons to Bulawayo

Leaving Mangwe on 2nd April, I rejoined my men on the following day, and we then escorted the convoy of waggons to Bulawayo, where we arrived early on the morning of Saturday, 4th April.

Before reaching Bulawayo, I had heard that a Greek trader had been murdered in the Bulilima district, near the Maitengwe river, and this news was confirmed by the Rev. Mr. Reed and Assistant Native Commissioner Gordon, both of whom had been stationed in the same district, and both of whom owe their escape to the fact that they received notice from friendly natives that their lives were in danger. Mr. Gordon was informed by his own native police that a Matabele *induna*, named Langabi, had given orders to his people to kill him, and they not only warned him of his danger, but escorted him by bypaths through the dangerous part of the country, and put him on to the main road to Bulawayo.

These police, thirty in number, have all remained loyal to the government. One of them was murdered by the rebels, but the remainder all reported themselves to the chief native commissioner, by whom they were disarmed, but they have since been employed on government service.

Mr. Reed was saved by the Makalaka amongst whom he was working. They informed him that the Greek trader living near him had been murdered, and told him plainly that he too would be killed unless he got away to a place of safety. At the same time a horse was sent to him by the Rev. Mr. Carnegie from Hope Fountain, together with a letter containing information concerning the generally disturbed state of the country. This decided him to leave his station for the time being and retire on Bulawayo, which place he reached safely the day before the return of my patrol from Mangwe.

During my absence two patrols, somewhat stronger than those first sent out, had been despatched to the Gwanda and Shiloh districts. The first, under Captains Brand and Van Niekerk, had left town on the previous Thursday, in order to relieve a party of prospectors and families said to be in *laager* in the Gwanda district. This patrol consisted of one hundred mounted men—fifty of C troop and fifty of the Africander Corps—and was accompanied by a mule waggon and a Maxim gun. The second patrol, numbering one hundred and sixty-nine men all told, and accompanied by a Maxim gun, was commanded by the Hon. Maurice Gifford, and had started on the Friday night to dislodge an *impi*, which it was reported had gathered in the hills near Shiloh. I will first give a short account of the proceedings of the Gwanda patrol, for the most interesting portion of which, namely the account of the return journey to Bulawayo, I am indebted to Lieutenant Webb of the Africander Corps, who has most kindly placed the graphic description which he has himself written of this fateful march at my disposal.

Leaving Bulawayo at six o'clock on Thursday evening, 2nd April, the first halt was made at Spargot's store, some six miles from town. Here the horses were off-saddled for an hour. During the halt one of the sentries found a wounded *kaffir* lying in the grass, who, on examination, proved to be the colonial boy "Jim," who had been so terribly knocked about by the Matabele at Edkins' store, that when discovered there it was not thought he could possibly survive many hours; and yet, thanks to the food that had been left with him, he had not only been able to keep body and soul together, but had recovered in the course of a few days sufficiently to enable him to make his way slowly and by easy stages, travelling always by night, to Bulawayo. Fortunately he was never short of food, as the rainy season being not yet over, the young maize cobs—green mealies—were standing ready for plucking in all the native fields.

After leaving Spargot's the next halting-place was Dawson's store at the Umzingwani River, which was reached late at night. The store it was found had been burnt and destroyed by the *kaffirs*, but the mule stables were still standing, and in them a plentiful supply of maize was obtained for the horses. The latter were all placed inside the stable fence, whilst the men lay down behind their saddles on the rising ground outside. The pickets were fired on during the night, but a few volleys from a portion of the Africander Corps drove the *kaffirs* off, though they were afterwards heard calling to one another in the hills near the river.

When day broke no natives were to be seen, and the horses were at once saddled up, and the march continued. Spiro's store, thirty-seven miles from Bulawayo, was found to have been totally destroyed by fire, but Grainger's hotel, twelve miles farther on, was still standing. The *kaffirs* had, however, apparently only just left it before the patrol arrived, as everything was in the utmost disorder, and water was discovered in a bucket which had evidently only just been brought up from the stream, as some of it had been spilt on the ground. A large supply of maize was again found in the mule stables, so the horses got another good feed.

In the evening the expedition moved on to Grainger's second store, which it was found had not been interfered with by the natives. Here Friday night was passed, the men again lying down behind their saddles. Early the following morning Dawson's store at "Amanzi minyama" was reached. It was found to have been very recently deserted by its European occupants, and since their departure had been partially looted by *kaffirs*. From here a move was made to Mr. Nicholson's camp, some four miles farther down the road, where it was thought that all the white men in the Gwanda district had probably collected. On arriving there a most excellent fort was discovered on the top of a *kopje* near the camp.

Whilst the fort was being strengthened, Mr. Zeederberg, the well-known post contractor, and three more men rode down the Tuli road to discover how far ahead the Gwanda people were. Mr. Zeederberg and one of these men rode through to Tuli, in order to despatch telegrams to Bulawayo; but the other two returned the following day, after having caught up the waggon with the people from Dawson's store, who were retiring on Tuli, and who reported that the Gwanda party was thirteen hours ahead of them, making for the same destination. On Sunday, 5th April, two more despatch-riders were sent to Tuli with farther messages for Bulawayo, asking that reinforcements and a Hotchkiss gun should be sent down to meet the patrol on its return, as, from information received from a native scout, it was believed that the *kaffirs* would attack them in force at some point along the road.

On Wednesday morning the despatch-riders returned, with a message informing Captain Brand that it was impossible to send the reinforcements asked for, and requesting him to return as soon as possible to Bulawayo. On Monday, the day after the despatch-riders had left,

Captain van Niekerk
who commanded the Africander Corps of the
Bulawayo Field Force in many
engagements during the last campaign.

an escort which had been sent in charge of a waggon to Dawson's store to bring in some supplies was fired on by the *kaffirs*. Captain Van Niekerk with some men of the Africander Corps, and some of C troop under Mr. Holland, immediately went off in pursuit, but beyond a few stragglers saw nothing of them. On the following day Captain Van Niekerk and Mr. Purssell went out with a force to patrol round the store and bring in all the remaining stores left. They found the country strewn for several miles with blankets, boots, etc., left by the *kaffirs* in their hasty flight on the preceding day, but again no resistance was met with.

From this point I will proceed with the narrative in Lieutenant Webb's own words, as follows:—

> We started early the next morning, 9th April, on our return journey. By lunch time we had marched fifteen miles, and reached Grainger's store No. 2. This place we found had been burnt to the ground by the Matabele during our stay at Gwanda, and judging by the spoor a large number of them had been at work. We decided to stay the rest of the day at this place, and were careful to take every necessary precaution in case of a night attack. Next morning we saddled up at daybreak, and covered twelve miles to Grainger's store No. 1, before halting. This store had in our absence shared the same fate as the other, and we recovered nothing from the ashes.
>
> As we were now entering a most dangerous section of the road, we were careful to use extra vigilance. At about ten o'clock we came up with some cattle at the foot of the range of hills on our left, but before capturing them, narrowly inspected the hills for natives, as we suspected a trap. Sure enough on a ridge about 1000 yards away we made out a body of men hiding under cover. We at once put the Maxim on them, and as they retreated in haste up the side of the hill, we found that several hundreds of them had been waiting in ambush. They only returned our fire with one or two shots. We were then going through thick bush, with hills a couple of hundred yards away towering on each side.
>
> Upon emerging from these, we came to the ruins of Spiro's store, and about a mile beyond we saw a column of smoke ascending, and rightly conjectured that this was the place where they meant to attack us. The situation was all in their favour. We

had to pass through a narrow neck amongst the hills in order to emerge into comparatively open country, though even this latter afforded them ample cover from our fire. The first evidence we had of the ambuscade was a steady and prolonged fire directed at the head of the column (composed of our corps) from the *kopjes* on the left flank. We at once returned the fire; but so well was the enemy concealed amongst the rocks, that I may tell you—though you will hardly credit my statement—that I scarcely saw one of them for half an hour. As the column was pressing on to get out of the dangerous position we were in, a few of Captain Brand's men fired just in front of the faces of the mules drawing the provision waggon. The mules swerved round suddenly, and broke the *disselboom*. Whilst the damage was being repaired, Mr. Jobson, who was in command of the Maxim, brought his gun into action with the greatest coolness and promptitude; but this unfortunate accident delayed us for half an hour, and was largely responsible for the wounds of many horses and men.

When we at last emerged from the pass, the disorganised appearance of the column showed the severity of the enemy's fire, and I firmly believe it was due to the fact that there were a number of old campaigners in the Africander Corps, which was commanded by our cool and experienced chief Captain Van Niekerk, that we escaped annihilation. When we had got the men into skirmishing order, we were better able to cope with the enemy; and when I tell you that the latter were over 1000 strong and followed us for over five miles at a distance of little more than 200 yards, you will be better able to judge of the task we had in hand. Our route lay over successive ranges of ridges and valleys, and afforded plenty of cover for the enemy, as the grass was about three feet high, and the country thickly studded with bush and trees. They formed a half-moon round us and skirmished excellently, taking advantage of every bit of cover.

They also fought with ferocious determination, and often showed pluck verging on lunacy. They were kept well in hand by their leaders, who constantly urged them to fire low. Our horses and men were now falling with deadly monotony, and we all saw the importance of getting into more open country. Our men were firing steadily and rapidly all this time, and the Maxim did good service; but being on the move and owing to the tactics of the enemy, did not do the execution we were accustomed to see in the first Matabele war.

At last, after about three hours' fighting, we saw about a mile ahead of us a round stone *kopje*, for which we made in order to take a short halt. The enemy at once saw through our movement, and a number of them endeavoured to defeat our object by out-flanking our advance. Our horsemen, however, were too sharp for them, and by hard riding reached the *kopje* first, and held them in check until the main body arrived. The *kopje* we thus reached was nothing but a huge flat rock, showing out about twelve or fifteen feet above the surrounding country. It was almost surrounded by broken rocks and trees, and under this cover—in some instances only some thirty to forty yards from where we were standing—the Matabele concealed themselves, and continued their fire upon us. This alone will give you some idea of their astounding audacity and bravery. We had to charge them four times to make them at last give in and retire. It was now about sundown (5.30 p.m.), and we had actually been about six hours fighting over five miles of country.

When at last we had time to look about us, we saw a scene that I for one shall never forget. The men still stood at their posts about the *kopje* keeping a good look-out. Across the plain through which we had come could be seen the carcasses of horses slain, and the bodies of men lying as they fell. On the *kopje* itself was the little ammunition waggonette, capable of holding two men comfortably, and now surrounded by the wounded and dying. We found that we had lost five men shot dead, and two more were dying, whilst over twenty others were wounded, and thirty-three horses had been killed. Of the enemy we estimated that we had killed and wounded between two and three hundred.

I do not think that any one of us had reckoned upon having such a tough job in getting through the pass, and even now our position was very grave. Prompt action was needed to get us out of our difficulty, and after consultation amongst the officers, we decided at once to move on, so as to give the Matabele no time for united action to surround us during the night. Our greatest difficulty was the conveyance of our wounded, and how any of the poor fellows survived that night will always remain a mystery. In the little waggonette we had to place eight, and on the Maxim gun-carriage we carried several more. The remainder were fortunately able to ride.

We left the *kopje* at dusk, and for the next sixteen miles had a most unpleasant section of the road to traverse, on any portion of which the Matabele had us at their mercy had they chosen to attack. Whether they had had enough fighting, or whether they did not suspect our departure, is not known, but we were all heartily glad to get through that section of the country unmolested. At half-past four on the morning of the 11th of April, we met the relief force sent to meet us, and two hours later we halted in front of the Government Offices in Bulawayo. That afternoon we buried one of my most intimate friends, poor Baker, who had been shot in the fight, and died on the homeward march.

From the foregoing narrative it is evident that this small patrol of 100 men narrowly escaped annihilation at the hands of the Matabele; and I should be doing an injustice if I did not state that, in the opinion of at any rate the majority of those who took part in the fight, they were only saved from destruction by the determined bravery combined with cool judgment—the result of long experience gained in many a previous fight with *kaffirs* in the Old Colony and the Transvaal—shown by Captain Van Niekerk, who took over the command during the action. Captain Brand, who was the senior officer, and who is as gallant a fellow as ever stepped, indeed brave to the point of foolhardiness, but who had had no previous experience of native warfare, showed both generosity of character and soundness of judgment in asking Van Niekerk to take over the command directly he saw that his men were in a tight place.

Van Niekerk himself speaks enthusiastically of the cool bravery shown throughout this trying time by all the men forming the patrol. They were all equally brave, he says. But amongst the Africanders there were many old *kaffir* fighters, such as old Mr. Steyn and Messrs. Loots and Ferreira, and these old campaigners were naturally more useful than inexperienced men. Lieutenants Webb and Holland, Purssell and Jobson—the latter in charge of the Maxim gun—did their duty throughout the engagement as coolly as if they were on parade. Five dead men had to be left on the field, *viz.* Messrs. Forbes, Pack, Greer, Hayland, and Green. Mr. Baker died on the Maxim carriage, and his body was laid on the roadside eight miles from Bulawayo.

On the following morning, Saturday, 11th April, a party was sent out to bring in the body, which they did, but they were fired on from a *kopje* near the road. No damage however was done, and poor Baker was buried the same afternoon.

About half-past eight on the previous evening, a messenger—Mr. White, attached to the Africander Corps—had reached town, with a despatch from Captain Brand, saying that he was in a tight place and feared that his ammunition might run short if the fight lasted much longer. Mr. White had left the patrol about four o'clock in the afternoon, and some two hours earlier had been struck on the head by a bullet, which luckily however only inflicted a scalp wound, stunning him for the moment.

On his arrival there was great excitement in Bulawayo, and a relief force was at once organised to go to Captain Brand's assistance. Being then in town, I and my men of course volunteered like every one else, and I well remember how bitterly disappointed we were that we could not go. As it happened, the relief force was not required to rescue the patrol, which had extricated itself from a very difficult position without assistance; but its appearance must have been most welcome to the jaded men, whose horses when they reached Bulawayo had been upwards of twenty-six hours under the saddle without food or rest. Thus ended one of the toughest fights of the present campaign, in which more than one-third of the men engaged were either killed or wounded, and more than one-third of the horses were likewise killed. Several men, whose wounds were slight, never reported themselves at all.

Brave Captain Van Niekerk was twice hit, one bullet cutting his bandoleer-strap and bruising his shoulder, and the second smashing the stock of his revolver and bruising his side. The *kaffirs*, although they probably lost heavily, had the satisfaction of getting possession of the dead bodies of five white men to mutilate, together with the saddles and other accoutrements of the horses killed; whilst, worst of all from our point of view, several Lee-Metford rifles and bandoleers full of cartridges fell into their hands.

CHAPTER 16

Gilford's Fight in the Shiloh Hills

For the following narrative of what is now known as Gifford's fight in the Shiloh Hills, I am indebted to an officer in Gifford's Horse, who has done very good service throughout the campaign, but who however has modestly asked me not to mention his name.

The patrol under Lieutenant Colonel Gifford—now commonly known as the Shiloh Patrol—consisted of Gifford's Horse, with thirty-one men of F troop under Captain Dawson, and eleven men of Grey's Scouts under Lieutenant F. Crewe—one hundred and eighteen Europeans in all, with one Maxim gun and forty-nine Colonial Boys under Captain Bisset. Captain J. W. Lumsden accompanied the patrol as chief of the Staff and second in command.

We left Bulawayo about one o'clock on Saturday morning, 4th April. It was bright moonlight, and we travelled on without any delay or anything exciting happening till the sun rose, when we outspanned at M'Kisa's *kraal*, about twelve miles from Bulawayo. I believe we had a sort of roving commission to go down to the Khami River, break up an *impi* or two there, then to go over to Inyati, do the same there, and finally to come out on the Salisbury road at the Bembisi.

At our first outspan however Colonel Gifford obtained information that there was an *impi* encamped down the Umguza, on Holm's farm, about fourteen miles to the north of us, and he determined to have a go at them. We therefore broke camp about two o'clock and trekked on through very bad country, heavy sand and thick bush.

We had just got into better and more open country when continuous firing was heard on our right, in which direction a few of our scouts were out, and shortly afterwards a party of two or three hundred Matabele were seen coming down from a ridge on our right, and the rear-guard—B troop, under Captain Fynn—were soon engaged with them. At this juncture Colonel Gifford sent back Captain Dawson's troop and the Colonial Boys to support Captain Fynn, and after about an hour's heavy firing the Matabele withdrew into the hills close by.

In the meantime, the rest of the column had drawn out into an open space and *laagered* up. The scouts turned up just before the Matabele attacked, having narrowly escaped being cut off. We passed a quiet night as the enemy made no move, though we could see them in the hills, and they fired occasional shots at the *laager* before it got dark.

Next morning we started again after breakfast, but had not gone more than a couple of miles, when the wily Matabele showed himself again, and in stronger force. Our advance guard, A troop, under Captain Meikle, were attacked, and at the same time a party of two or three hundred came down on our right and attacked the column. They did not come on very close—to do this they would have had to cross the Umguza River, and this they did not seem to care about doing, but kept on the other side of the river firing at the column and showing themselves in pretty strong force. Colonel Gifford then opened on them with the Maxim at about 600 yards, and this quite quenched their military ardour. It was funny to see the way in which they all immediately lay down in the grass and then spread out, and finally strutted off into the bush, bending down and hiding themselves as much as they could in the grass all the time.

During this time A troop had beaten off the attack on the advance, and Captain Bisset's boys who were on the left advance fell on the already defeated party and did some damage, killing twenty or thirty of them. As the enemy appeared to be all round us, we outspanned again, and, the men remaining at their posts, a biscuit each was served out all round, and the horses were allowed to graze. No further attack was made, and we trekked on again to Fonseca's farm without any further hindrance from our enemy, though we could see an *impi* on our right keeping along with us all the way, though at a safe distance.

We camped and *laagered* behind our saddles in an open glade. Behind us was a ridge of *kopjes*, on one of which was the homestead, on our left was thick bush, and on our right was a dry river-bed. Just beyond, and parallel to it, ran a stream in which were some deep pools of water. These riverbeds afterwards proved to be our salvation, or at any rate of great assistance in our defence.

We passed another quiet night, and next morning, Easter Monday, at daybreak, the men made the fires and were soon brewing their coffee, as it was bitterly cold. The usual patrol of five or six men was sent out to scout round, and the Colonial Boys were sent out to look for cattle, as we had so far only had "bully" to eat, and a change was desirable. They had not been out long when Lieutenant Rorke, who was in command of the morning patrol, came across the *impi* holding an *"indaba"* in a *kraal*. He and his patrol opened fire on them, to which they promptly replied by rushing our men. Lieutenant Rorke had a very narrow escape; his horse broke away from him, and he was compelled to retire as best he could on foot. The Colonial Boys, who were not far behind, and his own few men, however, checked the enemy, and saved his life.

This opened the ball; as soon as the firing was heard in camp, Colonel Gifford ordered Dawson's troop out in support, and B troop under Captain Fynn were ordered up into the *kopjes* where Fonseca's homestead stood. The battle soon became general, and there was heavy firing through the bush on our left, which was occupied by the Colonial Boys, Captains Dawson's and Fynn's troops. Colonel Gifford then gave the order for the men in *laager* to take cover in the bed of the stream to which I have already referred. The two small waggons, one of which carried ammunition, and the other our provisions, and on which the Maxim was standing on its tripod, were quickly drawn up alongside of the gully, and the men took up their positions and manned the banks of both streams, which formed a natural laager.

Colonel Gifford then sent out the gallopers to call the troops in to *laager*, not a minute too soon. Captain Fynn's troop, with whom was Captain Lumsden, were fairly rushed by the enemy, who poured a fire into them at close range. Here Trooper Kenneth M'Kenzie was shot through the head and dropped dead from his horse. Trooper Fielding was wounded in the leg, and his horse shot under him, and Captain Lumsden's horse also fell shot under him. Captain Fynn, however, brought his men into *laager* in good order, returning the enemy's fire. Captain Dawson and the Colonial Boys also retired in good order into *laager*.

The Matabele came on close behind, and our men were hardly in the *laager* when they rushed out into the open from the bush, with the evident intention of charging the *laager*. The steady fire from the men, however, soon checked them, and a few shots from the Maxim made them retire into the bush again. A few of their bravest, having taken cover behind some stumps and dead trees which were lying in the open, kept up a galling fire on the *laager*, but these were soon picked off by some of our good shots.

One man, however, came on in the open and appeared to bear a charmed life, as no bullets touched him; he had no gun or *assegai*, but came on alone down the valley towards us. He must have got to within about 150 yards of the *laager* when he fell shot in the leg. He rose again, and only then turned to fly, but the charm seemed to be broken, and he fell dead, shot through with several bullets.

In the afternoon, when we were able to go out to where he lay, we found he had in his hands a skin-bag full of fat, and some of the usual witchdoctor's throwing bones—no arms of any sort. Apparently he was a witchdoctor, or one of the priests of the much-talked-of '*Umlimo*,' who thought he'd do for the white man by means of his bones and incantations and that the white man's bullets were to turn to water before him as had been predicted. The Matabele lined the bush all down our front and took to the *kopjes*, from where, at about 600 yards, they kept up a continuous lire.

Colonel Gifford had all the time been standing on the waggon alongside of the Maxim directing the fire, and giving his orders to the men. The enemy on our front were not more than 200 yards away, and were making good shooting, aiming especially at the waggon and Maxim. Here poor Reynolds was mortally wounded, having been shot through the arm and lungs, and dying within a brief space. Soon afterwards Colonel Gifford was wounded in the shoulder. The men saw he had been hit;

but he called out, "It's all right, boys, don't mind me—give it to them—give it to them." He had soon, however, to be lifted down from the waggon and carried into the bed of the stream, at the same time calling on Captain Lumsden to take command. Troopers J. Walker (Gifford's Horse) and Eatwell (Dawson's) were wounded shortly afterwards.

The fire from the enemy slackened soon after this, but they kept up a desultory fire till about twelve o'clock, when they finally drew off and left us in peace, though we could see them every now and then in the bush.

Shortly after Colonel Gifford was wounded Captain Lumsden, after consulting the officers, sent in to Bulawayo a despatch by two of Captain Bisset's boys on horseback, reporting that Colonel Gifford was wounded, and asking for assistance, as both ammunition and food were running short.

As soon as the natives drew off the horses were let out to graze, and we spent the afternoon, as far as we could, strengthening our position. As the sun went down we could see smoke from what we judged to be the enemy's camp behind the *kopjes*, and on the top of one of these, against the sky, we saw what was evidently their sentry carefully watching us. We passed a quiet night, and next day had a repetition of our Monday's experience.

After an early breakfast of one biscuit per man all round, some of the Colonial Boys were sent up on to the *kopjes* to see where our enemy had got to. This was soon very evident, as the Matabele came up from beyond the *kopjes* and chased our boys down and back into camp. They came out into the open again exactly as on the previous day, but this time from the *kopje* side. The fire from our men soon checked them and drove them back into the bush, and they then spread right round us and opened fire from every side. Captain Lumsden was wounded in the leg while walking about the *laager*, giving orders and directing the Maxim, and immediately carried down into the *donga*, which was our place of safety. Captain Bisset then took command.

Lieutenant Hulbert was soon afterwards wounded in the leg by a Lee-Metford bullet. After keeping up a desultory fire till about mid-day, the enemy again retired, as we afterwards found out having had quite enough of the white men in the *dongas*. In the afternoon some of B troop and the Colonial Boys went out and recovered poor M'Kenzie's body, which was lying where he fell. Both he and Corporal Reynolds were buried by their comrades in the centre of our *laager*, between the two *dongas*.

At about two o'clock a despatch-rider arrived from Captain Macfarlane, who, with the relief column, was about five miles off.

Captain Macfarlane's column arrived soon afterwards, and we were very glad to see them, as provisions were running short. We had about a biscuit per man and seven tins of bully beef left, and not too much ammunition for another fight. Our troubles were then over, except for our poor wounded.

We broke *laager* next morning, and carried them off on the waggons as carefully as we could into town, arriving in Bulawayo that night (Wednesday), late. It was, however, a long weary journey for them, twenty-two miles over the stumps and stones of a South African road. Captain Lumsden died next day in hospital, to the universal regret of all who had met him and served under him. Our own brave colonel had to lose his arm, so our leaders suffered severely. Certainly they by their coolness and daring behaviour inspired confidence in their men, and helped to keep the fire steady. That the firing of our men was exceptionally steady there is no doubt.

After the first rush it was impossible for a Matabele to show himself without receiving three or four bullets most uncomfortably near him, if he did not receive his quietus. It was estimated that the patrol killed at lowest 200 of the enemy, and many more must have been wounded. The Maxim did not have much chance, as after the first rush the Matabele spread themselves out in the bush, and kept under very good cover, and it then became a matter of sharpshooting. On the Monday, and the last day's fight, the enemy must have been about 1500 strong. As we could see, they increased every day, and we afterwards heard from native reports that reinforcements were joining them all the time. We also heard that after the failure of the last attack the *impi* retired and sent round the country for still further reinforcements. When they arrived and the *impis* came back to the scene of their flight, they found the *dongas* empty—the white men had gone.

Chapter 17

Despatch from Captain Laing

On the day before the return of Brand's patrol, the first news was received from Belingwe that had reached Bulawayo since the outbreak of the insurrection. The despatch was from Captain Laing, who was in command there, and was to the effect that all the whites in the district were in *laager*, and that they felt confident of being able to resist any attack made upon them by the natives.

This news gave great relief to many people who had friends in the Belingwe district, for it was not known whether they had been able to collect together and form a *laager*, or whether they had been surprised and murdered before they were aware that anything was amiss; as indeed they would have been, in all probability, had not Mr. H. P. Fynn, the native commissioner in the Insiza district, sent a message to Captain Laing to warn him that a native rising seemed imminent immediately after he was informed of the murder of Mr. Maddocks. This message was faithfully carried by one of Mr. Fynn's native policemen, and Captain Laing, recognising the gravity of the situation, at once acted with the promptitude and decision which always distinguish him, and ordered all the whites in his district to immediately come in to laager at Belingwe.

They were only just in time, for the natives showed their teeth very soon afterwards, and although fearing to attack the *laager*, succeeded in driving off a considerable number of cattle. Captain Laing, accompanied by only nine men—all he was able to mount—then in his turn attacked the insurgents, and succeeded in recapturing some of the cattle, though these were of little value, as the *rinderpest* was amongst them. It is worthy of remark that the native policeman who took the message to Captain Laing, which probably saved many white men's lives in the Belingwe district, never returned to his duty, but as is now known, went over to the rebels with his rifle and bandoleer full of cartridges.

This fact, taken in conjunction with many other circumstances, goes to prove that the secret of the actual date of the outbreak of the insurrection was not known to the mass of the people, though probably, owing to the prophetic utterances ascribed to the *Umlimo*, which had been diligently circulated amongst them, they were in a state of expectancy; but this policeman, for instance, must have been thoroughly taken by surprise, and after the first murders remained loyal to the government until he was got at by some one capable of explaining to him the scope of the whole plot.

On 10th April, too, a further excitement was caused in Bulawayo by the arrest of three Matabele rebels. They were captured near Soluso's, some twenty miles west of Bulawayo, by Marzwe's Friendlies, and sent in to town by Josana, having been caught red-handed, looting and burning property belonging to white men. I was present when the evidence was taken, and it certainly seemed to me to be overwhelming, especially as one of them was known to Mr. Colenbrander, and they all three acknowledged themselves to be the subjects of a certain Induna named Maiyaisa, who with all his people has been amongst the rebels from the first outbreak of the insurrection. They were caught, too, with *assegais* in their hands, looting a white man's farm, so that it might very reasonably be asked "*que diable allaient-ils faire dans cette galère?*"

At any rate they were condemned to death, and hanged forthwith, all three on one tree on the outskirts of Bulawayo. Besides these three men who had been incontestably guilty of taking part in the rebellion, and who were hanged together, six others were hanged singly and at different times, all of whom, if they were tried in a somewhat rough-and-ready fashion, were undoubtedly spies and rebels.

These are the only Matabele who have been hanged during the present insurrection, and a letter therefore on the subject of hanging natives which appeared in the *Daily Graphic* of Saturday, 13th June, purporting to have been written by a young tradesman of Bulawayo, is a trifle incorrect, to say the least of it. A portion of the letter runs as follows:

> My stand has one big tree on it, and it is often used as a gallows. Yesterday there was a goodly crop of seven Matabele hanging there; today there are eight, the eighth being a nigger who was

heard boasting to a companion that he had helped to kill white men, and got back to town without being suspected.

This letter was reproduced by Mr. Labouchere in *Truth*, as well as another he got hold of at the same time, in which the writer expresses it as his opinion that "it is grand fun potting niggers off, and seeing them fall like nine-pins," while further on he speaks of it being "quite a nice sight" to see men shot as spies. I can quite believe that a man who can write in this strain would take pleasure in, or "would not object," as he puts it, to seeing *kaffirs* shot, but I doubt very much if such an one would ever risk his skin to enjoy "the grand fun" he speaks of.

It seems a pity that a writer who takes "*Truth*" as the motto of his paper, should seize upon every little scrap of published matter he can discover (apparently without inquiry as to its real value), and not only reproduce it as gospel in an ensuing number of his journal, but found a sermon upon it into the bargain on the iniquities of his fellow-countrymen in Rhodesia. However, we have the consolation of knowing that nothing has discredited the editor of *Truth* in the eyes of all fair-minded men so much as the hostile feeling he has ever shown against the British settlers in Rhodesia, whilst, happily for that colony, his rage is as impotent as that of "*a viper gnawing at an old file.*"

During the week in which the aforesaid *kaffirs* were hanged, some parties of Matabele approached the town very closely at nights, and on the night of 6th April one of them succeeded in capturing a herd of cattle within a mile and a half of the hospital, at the same time murdering some Zambesi *kaffirs* who were sleeping outside the cattle *kraal*. As at this time there was a herd of cattle which was penned every night in a *kraal* near Dr. Sauer's house, some two miles away on the other side of the town, I was asked to take some of my men and lie in wait for any Matabele who might attempt to capture them on the following night.

I went down and reconnoitred the position during the day, and after dark rode down with fifteen good men. We first off-saddled our horses, and tied them up within the paling round Dr. Sauer's house, and then took up our positions along two walls of the square stone cattle *kraal*. During the night, the weather, which had been fine and warm, suddenly changed; a cold wind sprang up, and masses of cloud spread over the sky from the south-east. It looked as if it was going to rain every minute, but luckily the wind kept it off. However, it was bitterly cold, and we were all of us very glad when day at last dawned and our weary vigil was over, for no *kaffirs* came near us; and when I examined the cattle I did not think it likely they would, as the *rinderpest* was rife amongst them, two lying dead in the *kraal*, whilst many others, the herd boy told us, lay rotting about the *veldt* all round.

About this time the authorities determined to carry out a scheme for keeping open communications with the south by means of forts which were to be built along the road between Bulawayo and Mangwe. As a commencement in this direction, Captain Molyneux left Bulawayo, on Saturday, 11th April, with sixty men to establish a fort at Fig Tree, distant thirty miles down the road, whilst at the same time Captain Luck was ordered up from Mangwe with fifty men to build a second fort some fifteen miles from that place, in the centre of the hilly country through which the coach road passes.

Two days later I was sent down the road to establish further forts between Fig Tree and Mangwe, and to take command of all garrisons on the road, the force with which I left town consisting of sixty men of H troop of the Bulawayo Field Force (my own), forty men of E troop under Captain Halsted, and twenty of the Africander Corps under Lieutenant Webb.

We left Bulawayo on the evening of Monday, 13th April, and slept that night at Wilson's farm, reaching Mabukitwani the following evening. From information I received there concerning the movements of the Matabele, I became convinced that the dangerous part of the road was that portion of it lying between Bulawayo and Fig Tree, and not the hill passes farther on, as the inhabitants of the latter are all Makalakas, the rebel Matabele who had been living amongst them having all come up nearer to Bulawayo, and joined their compatriots on the Khami river.

According to the plan which I had been asked to carry out, the thirty miles of road between Bulawayo and Fig Tree would have been left entirely undefended, which did not appear to me to be at all advisable in view of the fact that there was a large *impi* under the Induna Maiyaisa encamped on the Khami, only twelve miles below the ford on the main coach road. I therefore took it upon myself to send Lieutenant Webb with his twenty men back to the Khami river, to commence a fort there, at the same time despatching a messenger to Bulawayo requesting Colonel Napier to reinforce him with another twenty or thirty men. At the same time I gave it as my opinion that a fort ought also to be established at Mabukitwani.

On Wednesday afternoon we reached Fig Tree, where we found that Captain Molyneux had already nearly completed an almost impregnable fort, which had been built on a small isolated *kopje*, itself a natural stronghold, about 200 yards from the mule stables, hotel, and telegraph office at Fig Tree. The natural strength of this *kopje* had been most cunningly taken advantage of and increased by blasting a rock out here and there, and fortifying the weak places with sand-bags. Good water was obtainable in the bed of a stream at the very foot of the *kopje*, whilst a recess amongst the rocks near its base had been cleared in such a way as to form a stable within which some twenty horses could be completely sheltered from the bullets of any attacking force. Altogether, Fort Molyneux was a perfect little place of its kind, and did every credit to the very capable officer by whom it was built

On the following day we went on to Shashani neck, some five and a half miles beyond Fort Molyneux. Here the road descends for a distance of three miles into the Shashani valley, winding continually in and out amongst thickly-wooded granite hills. Had the *kaffirs*, at the commencement of the insurrection, put a force of 1000 men armed with rifles, backed by another 1000 with *assegais*, into this pass, it is my opinion that they would have completely cut off all communication between Bulawayo and the south until a body of troops at least 1000 strong had been sent up from Mafeking to open the road. However, luckily they missed this opportunity, as they have missed every other chance they have had of striking a really effective blow at the white men. In fact, they have shown a general want of intelligence that stamps them as an altogether inferior people, in brain capacity at least, to the European.

About one-third of the way down the pass Captain Halsted and I found a *kopje* close to water, which commanded the road, and at the same time could be rendered absolutely impregnable to such enemies as the Matabele with a comparatively small amount of labour. Here I left Captain Halsted with the men of E troop to build a fort, and on Friday morning, 17th April, went on with my own troop to the Matoli River where Captain Luck had already almost completed a strong fort of earthworks and palisades in the centre of a large open space amongst the hills, by none of which, however, was it commanded.

Here I met Major Armstrong from Mangwe, and as all I heard from him regarding the state of affairs in his district only confirmed me in the opinion that it would be a waste of time and men to build another fort between Matoli and Mangwe, as I had been instructed to do, whilst on the other hand I felt that it was of vital importance to establish forts without delay between Fig Tree and Bulawayo, I determined to return to town and lay my views before the administrator personally before proceeding farther southwards.

Major Armstrong having also official business to transact in Bulawayo, we arranged to ride in together forthwith. On passing Captain Halsted late in the afternoon we found that he had already made wonderful progress with the stronghold which is now known to fame as Fort Halsted. Just at dusk we reached Fort Molyneux, where we got an excellent dinner and were made comfortable for the night. Here I received a telegram from Colonel Napier, telling me that at the present moment he could not possibly spare any men from Bulawayo to reinforce Lieutenant Webb at the Khami River, as the *kaffirs* were massing round the town; and that as twenty men was too small a number to leave alone without reinforcements, he had ordered him to fall back on Fig Tree, or join Captain Halsted for the present.

At daylight Lieutenant Webb turned up, and as Captain Molyneux had over fifty men at Fig Tree, and Captain Halsted only forty, I sent him on to the latter. Major Armstrong and I then saddled up, and reached Bulawayo about two o'clock on Saturday, 18th April, having passed the down coach accompanied by a strong escort at the Khami River. The situation in Matabeleland was now a sufficiently curious one. In Bulawayo were some 1500 white men, women, and children, all of whom, although they were able to visit their houses in different parts of the town by day, had to seek safety within the *laager* at nights, and were not allowed to leave it before seven o'clock in the morning.

At this time the whole of Matabeleland, with the exception of Bulawayo, and the *laagers* of Gwelo and Belingwe, was absolutely in the hands of the *kaffirs*, although, apparently by the orders of the *Umlimo*, the main road to the south had not been closed. A large *impi* lay at Mr. Crewe's farm, Redbank, on the Khami River, about twelve miles to the west of the town, besides which some thousands of rebels, amongst whom it was said was Lo Bengula's eldest son, Inyamanda, were camped all along the Umguza, considerable numbers of them being actually within three miles of Bulawayo, whilst other two large *impis* had taken up their quarters amongst the Elibaini Hills, and in the neighbourhood of Intaba Induna, there being altogether not less than 10,000 hostile natives spread out in a semicircle from the west to the north-east of the town.

Had these different *impis* only combined and acted in concert under one leader they might have accomplished something; but each *impi* appears to have been acting independently of the others, and my own belief is that they kept hanging round the town without any general plan of action, in the expectation of some supernatural interference by the deity on their behalf. At least this is what we hear from themselves, and I think it is the truth. Besides the *impis* to the north and west, there were others encamped within the edge of the Matopo Hills. These latter, however, although they blocked the Tuli road and destroyed the mission station at Hope Fountain, which had been established for over twenty-five years, never approached Bulawayo.

CHAPTER 18

Matabele Advance on Bulawayo

It was, I think, on Thursday, 16th April, that it was first realised that the Matabele had really advanced to within a short distance of the town. On that day, information having been received that there was an *impi* on the Umguza just below Government House, a small force was got together to go out and ascertain the truth of the report. This force consisted of twenty-one Scouts under Captain Grey and twenty-two of the Africander Corps under Captain Van Niekerk, Captains Nicholson and Howard Brown accompanying them, so that there were only forty-five men and officers all told.

Leaving town before daylight on the Friday morning, this little force crossed the stream on this side of Government House just as the sun was rising. It then, after emerging on to the high ground, turned to the right towards the Umguza. Soon numbers of *kaffirs* were seen moving about in the bush on the farther side of the river, who, when they saw the white men advancing at once opened fire on them, at a distance at first of about 800 yards. This fire was not answered, but as soon as the Scouts and Africanders could be thrown out in skirmishing order, they were ordered to advance towards the river at a canter. On reaching it they at once crossed at two different places, the Africanders being on the right and Grey's Scouts on the left.

When the top of the farther bank was reached the white men found themselves within 150 yards of a number of Matabele advancing rapidly towards them in skirmishing order through the bush. These latter at once fired a volley, all their bullets going high, and then turned and ran as the horsemen came galloping towards them. As Grey's Scouts got amongst them it was seen that the line of skirmishers was supported by a large body of men some distance in their rear, from which two flanking parties had been thrown out on either side. Van Niekerk charged with his men right on to the head of the left-hand flanking party and drove it back, but Captain Grey with his Scouts, whilst driving in the skirmishers on the main body, passed the right-hand flanking party, which then attempted to cut off his retreat to the river.

At once recognising that the natives were in force, and that the number of men at his command was altogether too small to cope with them, he gave the word to retire, and then both the Scouts and Africanders got back across the river again as quickly as possible, closely followed by the *kaffirs*. On reaching a rise some few hundred yards on the near side of the river, the white men halted, and dismounting kept the *kaffirs* in check for a while, but it was soon seen that their numbers were such that they would have been completely surrounded, so, one man and three horses having already been wounded, it was deemed advisable to retire and leave the field for the time being in possession of the Matabele. The wounded man was Mr. Harker, who was shot through the leg, but eventually recovered without losing the limb. The three horses that were wounded all died subsequently.

Upon reaching Bulawayo I at once had interviews with Mr. Duncan and Colonel Napier, and convinced them both that it was more necessary to establish a fort on the road between Bulawayo and Fig Tree than to add one more to the two already existing between Fig Tree and Mangwe, and I then and there received instructions to bring my own troop back again from Matoli, in order to build a fort at Mabukitwani. I should have left the same evening, to rejoin my men and carry out these orders, but the question arose as to the best means of provisioning the garrisons of the various forts, amounting altogether to 180 men. It was most inadvisable that any more food-stuff should be sent out of Bulawayo at this juncture than was absolutely necessary, so as there were three government mule waggons at different forts along the road, I suggested that these should be sent down to Tati, where I understood that there was a good deal of food-stuff stored, to bring up full loads of the most necessary kinds of provisions, the balance of which, when the garrisons of the forts had been supplied with a month's rations, could be brought on to Bulawayo.

Colonel Napier at once telegraphed to Mr. Vigers, who was in charge at Tati, to ascertain what food supplies he had on hand, and requested me not to leave Bulawayo until an answer had been received. I therefore spent Saturday night in bed, instead of on horseback riding down the Mangwe road. About eight o'clock on the following morning, Sunday, 19th April, a horse came galloping into town riderless, and with its saddle and bridle covered with blood. This horse was soon identified as having belonged to one of three men of the Africander Corps, who had left Bulawayo on picket duty in the neighbourhood of Government House on the preceding evening. It was subsequently discovered that these poor fellows had been surprised and killed by the Matabele early in the morning, two of their horses being also killed or captured, whilst the third made good its escape and galloped back into Bulawayo with a bullet-wound through its neck. The names of the unfortunate men were Heinemann, Van Zyl, and Montgomerie.

The excitement caused by this incident had scarcely subsided when news was received that Colonel Napier's homestead at Maatjiumschlopay, only about three miles to the south of the town, was being attacked by a large force of Matabele. At this homestead there were a large number of friendly natives, mostly armed with *assegais*, and also sixteen white men who occupied a small fort which had been built on the top of a small *kopje* overlooking the farm.

The first news received was that the Matabele had carried off a lot of cattle, killed a large number of the friendlies, and were now besieging the white men in their fort. A small force of mounted men was therefore hastily got together and sent out to their assistance under Captain Macfarlane. This force consisted of a troop of the Africander Corps under Captain Pittendrigh, a few of Grey's Scouts, and some men of K troop under Captain Reid; about sixty troopers all told, with a Maxim gun in charge of Lieutenant Biscoe. It left town at about ten o'clock, taking the Tuli road.

At this time I had an appointment with Colonel Napier at his office, to get the answer expected to the telegram sent the day before to Mr. Vigers at Tati. However, on inquiry at the office, I found that Colonel Napier was out, and that no reply had yet been received from Tati. On asking where Colonel Napier was, I was told that he had accompanied Captain Macfarlane. Now I had been requested not to leave Bulawayo until Colonel Napier had communicated to me the contents of the telegraphic message he was expecting from Tati, and therefore, believing that he had gone out with Captain Macfarlane's patrol, and that I would not be able to make a start for Matoli until he returned, I thought that I might as well take a ride out and see what was going on too.

Major Armstrong very kindly lent me the pony which he had ridden from Mangwe, which I knew was a very steady animal, trained for shooting. It did not take me long to saddle up, and I was soon riding hard on the tracks of Captain Macfarlane's troopers. I came up with them on the racecourse, not far beyond the suburban stands, and learned from the officer in command that the attack on Maatji-umschlopay had been repulsed by the friendlies, with the assistance of the white men in garrison there. The Matabele had not been in any force, and had evidently intended to sweep off a herd of cattle which was kept on the farm, and which the sixteen white men were there to protect.

No doubt the rebels were ignorant of the presence of these latter, for they cleared off when they were fired upon, hotly pursued by the Friendlies, who overtook and killed six of their number with clubs and *assegais*.

As these marauders had had ample time to reach the thick bush bordering the Umguza, where they would have been able to scatter and hide, Captain Macfarlane determined to waste no time in pursuing them, but to make a reconnaissance down the Umguza towards Government House, in the hope of coming across a larger body of rebels who would be likely to make a stand.

We therefore crossed the Salisbury road and followed down the bank of a stream which runs into the Umguza some two and a half miles from Bulawayo, just beyond a deserted farmhouse belonging to Mr. Colenbrander. The farmhouse stands on a rising piece of ground, in the angle formed by the two streams, but is about 400 yards distant from the Umguza, though close to its tributary.

When we got near the farmhouse, being still on the near side of the stream we had been following, some Colonial Boys, who proved to be scouts sent out by Mr. Colenbrander, came up and informed Captain Macfarlane that there were a lot of Matabele along the river, and that a number of them had only just left the farmhouse opposite.

The right-hand flanking party, under Lieutenant Hook, had now crossed the stream, so I galloped after them to get a look round from the high ground. Standing near the house, we could see large numbers of *kaffirs* spread out in skirmishing order amongst the scrubby bush on the farther side of the Umguza. As soon as they saw us, they at once commenced their usual tactics, throwing out flanking parties on either side, no doubt with the idea of surrounding us, whilst at the same time skirmishers were sent forward from the centre, evidently to take up a position in the bed of the river.

At this moment a messenger arrived recalling Lieutenant Hook to the other side of the stream, and upon riding through with him Captain Macfarlane informed me that, having just heard that another *impi* was approaching from the direction of Government House, he intended to take up his position on a fairly open piece of ground, near the junction of the smaller stream with the Umguza, and let the *kaffirs* attack him there, his force being altogether too small to risk crossing to the other side.

As we advanced the *kaffirs* opened fire on us, and a skirmishing fight soon commenced. I was asked to take a few of the Africanders across the smaller stream, so as to keep the *kaffirs* from taking possession of it, which I at once proceeded to do, but as I thus became separated from the main body I can only give an account of our own little skirmish.

As we rode up the rising ground beyond the stream, some *kaffirs* sent a few bullets whizzing amongst us from the shelter of the river, and then as we still advanced they very foolishly abandoned a good position and ran up the farther bank, and then along the river in a line, and in such a manner that if the one aimed at was missed, the next was very likely to be hit. The men I had with me were all good shots, and I saw several natives drop to our fire before they got round a bend of the river. Keeping a sharp look-out on ahead, I noticed a lot more coming down from the scrubby bush beyond it and crossing to our side, and rightly divining that their object was to advance up the valley behind the next ridge and then close in on us, I called to the few men with me to gallop at once to the top of the rise to prevent being taken by surprise and fired on from above.

Just at this moment we were joined by Lieutenant Hook and a few more men, and spreading out in skirmishing order, we rode to the top of the rise. We were just in time to meet a number of *kaffirs*—I daresay fifty or sixty altogether—making for the same position from the opposite side. They were right in the open, the nearest being within 150 yards of us. Some were armed with guns and rifles, but many of them had nothing but *assegais* and shields.

As soon as we appeared on the rise in front of them they all stopped, and those with rifles fired on us, their bullets nearly all going high, but on two of their number falling they commenced to retreat towards a strip of thickish bush which ran from near the bank of the Umguza river right up behind Colenbrander's farmhouse. This bush was about 400 yards from the top of the ridge from which the men with me were firing, and from its shelter a number of *kaffirs* were answering us and covering the retreat of their men across the valley. However, as the horses were quickly taken behind the ridge, and the men showed as little of themselves as possible, their fire did us no harm. On the other hand, several of the *kaffirs* fell to our shots before they reached the cover of the bush. They made no attempt to run fast, but went off crouching down at a slow trot.

I myself was sitting down with my back against a stone, and shooting as carefully as possible, when a bullet struck a small stone close to my left foot and ricocheted with a loud buzzing noise close past poor Pat Whelan, a brave son of Erin, who had been with me on the first patrol to the Matopos, and who, having come out from Bulawayo on this day for the fun of the thing, thought it his duty to keep near me. "That was a fair buzzer," said Pat.

The *kaffirs* were now calling to one another, or someone was giving them orders in the bush, and we could see that they were all making up within its shelter towards the farmhouse. Thinking that their idea was to get behind it, and then fire on the position taken up by the Maxim, I gave the word to the men with me to mount and take possession of it first. This we promptly did, just getting there as the foremost of the enemy were about halfway between the bush and the house. They stopped and fired at us as before, and then retired to the bush again, from which they kept up a fusillade on the house, which, however, unless they had made a heavy rush, we could have held against them if necessary; but just then Lieutenant Moffat came up with a message from Captain Macfarlane, requesting me to retire on his position and endeavour to draw the *kaffirs* on to the Maxim.

As we withdrew from the house they at once came on out of the bush, and when we got down to the stream they were already firing at us from behind it, and, their advance not being opposed, some of them came right down into the bed of the stream.

At this time there was a really good chance for the Maxim to do some execution, for although the *kaffirs* were nowhere in masses, there was a straggling line of a couple of hundred of them right out in the open, and not more than 400 yards from the gun. But when the word was given to fire it most unfortunately jammed at the sixth shot, and the *kaffirs* had to be driven back by rifle fire. The cause of the mishap was that a cartridge-case had broken off at the rim in the barrel of the Maxim, rendering it for the time being useless. The natives now again commenced to try and get round us on both sides, and it being reported that the other *impi* was advancing from the direction of Government House, Captain Macfarlane gave the word to retire.

At this time I was with Captain Reid and the men of his troop, helping to keep the *kaffirs* from crossing the Umguza at a point where they were trying to do so a few hundred yards below us, and it was here that a man named Boyes, of the Africander Corps, was killed. He, with another man, seems to have gone down close to where the smaller stream joined the river, and was shot from the cover of the bank right through the chest, his horse being shot at the same time I think. He fell dead at once, and his companion galloped back to the main body.

Captain Macfarlane was already retiring, and the order had come to Captain Reid to do the same, acting as flanking party to the right of the main body. Unfortunately, the death of Boyes was not reported to the commanding officer until the patrol was halfway to Bulawayo, so that the poor fellow's corpse fell into the hands of the *kaffirs*. The only other casualty was one man badly wounded in the knee. Considering the number of bullets that pass pretty near to every one engaged in a small skirmish such as I have described, it is wonderful how few men get actually hit. The fact seems to be that in a running fight, when they are flurried and hustled, *kaffirs* cannot get the time they require to take good aim, and if you are near them they always shoot over you. The golden rule is to scatter out, each man firing independently in the Boer fashion.

But although *kaffirs* shoot very badly if hurried and kept moving, many of them are very fair shots if they can get all the time they require for aiming, as they can in hilly country, where they can take up positions behind rocks, from which they can fire at their enemy at their leisure and without exposing themselves.

On the day of which I have been speaking, some of them with whom my little advanced party was engaged were firing at us with some very peculiar bullets, which I think had probably been made by first putting a stone into the mould, and then pouring lead on to it, forming a very rough irregular projectile. At any rate you could hear these bullets coming on with a loud buzzing noise, which increased in intensity until they passed with a peculiar whizzing sound. The trouble was one did not know which way to dodge, for as you could hear them approaching but could not see them, it would have been as easy to dodge into one as out of its way.

As our small force retired the bush became more and more open, so the *kaffirs* made no attempt to follow us. I do not think that they realised that the Maxim was out of order, and if not they probably thought that the retreat was a ruse to draw them into more open ground. What their loses were it is difficult to say, but I think that the small advance party to which I had attached myself could not have killed less than twenty; indeed, I think I saw quite that number fall. My friend Pat Whelan had fired away almost all his cartridges, and on examining my belt I found that I had nineteen less than I came out with.

However, the *kaffirs* again retained their position, and it was evident that their numbers were so great—we having only engaged their advanced skirmishing line—that it would not be safe to cross the Umguza and attack them on their own ground without a considerable force, both of foot and horsemen; the latter to work in the more open ground, and the former to drive them out of patches of bush.

Before returning to Bulawayo, Captain Macfarlane took a sweep round across the open ground in the direction of Dr. Sauer's house, and we there came in sight of the *impi* which had been reported early in the day. The main body was standing in a dense black mass on the top of a ridge just below Government House, their skirmishing lines being thrown out on either side, and in advance of the centre. Now the fact that this *impi* had stood idly by, not exactly watching, but at any rate listening to the firing that had been going on during the skirmish between their compatriots and the white men, shows, I think, the extraordinary want of combination amongst them, of which I have before spoken, and which has been one of the features of this campaign.

CHAPTER 19

Force Retire Without Fighting

On the way back to Bulawayo we were met by Colonel Napier and Captain Nicholson, and it was arranged that as strong a force as could be spared from the town should be sent out again to the Umguza on the morrow, under the command of the former gentleman. Accordingly, at about eleven o'clock on Monday, 20th April, a force of two hundred and thirty white men and one hundred colonial natives, all told, left Bulawayo for the scene of the previous day's skirmish. With the force were a seven-pounder, a Hotchkiss, and a Maxim. Captain Macfarlane had command of the right flank, and Captain Van Niekerk of the left; whilst I was in charge of a detachment of men on foot, drawn from various corps, and a body of Colenbrander's natives were under the command of Captain Cardigan.

This was a most disappointing day for all those who wanted a little excitement, as the Matabele and the officers commanding our column were at cross purposes; the former wanting the white men to cross the river and fight them in the bush, and the latter being in favour of the *kaffirs* coming through to their side, and attacking a position defended with artillery. The result was that there was no fight.

The decision not to cross the Umguza may have been a wise one, but it was not popular with the men, who marched back to town in a very dejected frame of mind; so strong was the feeling, indeed, that it was decided to send out another patrol to the Umguza on the following Wednesday, and as I was anxious to see a good blow struck at them, I asked Mr. Duncan and Colonel Napier to give me another day's leave of absence from my work of superintending the building of forts and patrolling along the Mangwe road, in order that I might take part in the engagement. At the same time I sent a wire to Captain Molyneux at Fig Tree, requesting him to forward instructions to Lieutenant Grenfell at Matoli to march back with the men of my troop to Mabukitwani, where it had been decided that we were to build a fort, and where I undertook to meet him, unless anything unforeseen should happen, on Thursday evening.

Thus on Wednesday morning, 22nd April, for the fourth time a small force marched out of Bulawayo, in order to try and dislodge the *kaffirs* from their position on the Umguza, in the immediate vicinity of the town. This patrol was put under the command of Captain Bisset, a gentleman who had had some previous experience of native warfare in Basutoland and Zululand.

The patrol consisted of twenty Scouts under Captain Grey; forty men under Captain Van Niekerk; twenty under Captain Meikle, and twenty under Captain Brand, making, with some twenty others unattached, about one hundred and twenty mounted men, with a Hotchkiss and a Maxim under Lieutenant Walsh. Besides these mounted troops, there were a detachment of one hundred colonial *kaffirs* and Zulus recruited by Mr. Colenbrander, and some friendly Kaffirs who, however, were only armed with *assegais*, and who took no part in the fight. I was asked to take command of the Colonial Boys, which I could hardly do, as they had their own trusted officers with them, but I accompanied these gentlemen, and undertook to assist them in leading their men to the attack. Dr. Vigne went in charge of the ambulance waggon which accompanied the patrol.

After much valuable time had been lost in looking for the *impi* which was said to be behind the brickfields, but which as a matter of fact had never been there, we turned towards the Umguza, passing at the back of Government House. Here an accident occurred to the Hotchkiss limber carriage, which delayed us for more than an hour, and although the broken shaft was temporarily tied up with a chain, so that the gun could be drawn along, it was rendered useless for action until the damage done could be properly repaired.

On proceeding we changed our direction and made straight for the Umguza, and it was soon evident that the *kaffirs* intended to dispute our advance, as they commenced to fire on us from the low ridges covered with scrubby bush which here border the river on both sides. Captain Van Niekerk and his Africanders were soon hotly engaged on the left flank, and as the *kaffirs* were in possession of some ridges just in front of us as well, I was asked to advance with the Colonial Boys from the centre, and endeavour to chase them across the river. My instructions were to attack and, if possible, drive them before me, but to retire on the guns if I found them too strong.

The boys came on capitally, led by their officers, who were all mounted, and we soon drove all the Matabele in this part of the field through the Umguza, and following them up at once, pursued them for about a mile over some stony ridges covered with scrubby bush.

Up to this time I had not fired a shot, as I had been principally engaged in encouraging the Colonial Boys to come on quickly and give our enemies no breathing time. But by this time we had got right up amongst them, and I began to use my rifle.

A number of the Matabele had built little fortifications of loose stones near the bank of the river, from behind the shelter of which they fired on us; but the warlike Amakosa and Zulus charged them most gallantly, and engaging them hand to hand drove them out of their shelters into the river, and killed many of them in the water. Several of the Colonial Boys were here wounded with *assegais* and axes, but none were killed.

It was at this time that I saw John Grootboom, a Xosa *kaffir*—who has distinguished himself for bravery on many occasions both during the first war and the present campaign—galloping after a Matabele just in front of me, who was armed only with *assegais* and shield. As the horse came upon him he ducked down, and only just escaped a blow on the head from John's rifle, which was dealt with such vigour that the rider lost his balance and fell off, and his foot catching in the stirrup, he was dragged along the road for some yards. If the Matabele had but kept his presence of mind and been quick, he might have *assegaied* his antagonist easily, and possibly would have done so had not Captain Fynn and myself been close to him.

We had now got the Matabele fairly on the run in our part of the field, and the only ones who were still firing at us were a party who had taken shelter in a bend of the river under cover of the bank, some three hundred yards ahead of us. I was just going with some of the Colonial Boys to dislodge them, when I saw Grey's Scouts charging down on them from the other side of the river. Finding themselves attacked from this quarter, the Matabele left their cover and ran out into the open in large numbers, exposing themselves to a heavy fire which thinned their ranks every instant.

The position was now this.—The Matabele had been driven from the banks of the river, and two or three hundred of them, panic-stricken and demoralised, were running in a crowd across some undulating ground, but scantily covered with bush, and had only Captain

Meikle and Captain Brand been sent in support of the Colonial Boys and the Scouts, they might have galloped in amongst them, and could not have failed to kill a very large number of them. But no; although these officers and their men were chafing and cursing at their enforced inactivity, they were kept idly standing round the Maxim doing nothing, which was all the more inexcusable as Captain Van Niekerk with his forty Africanders had by this time silenced the enemy's fire on the left flank, and there was no farther apprehension of any heavy attack from that quarter. At any rate, one of the best chances of inflicting a heavy loss on the rebels which has occurred during the campaign was not taken advantage of.

At this time, that is just when Grey's Scouts were driving the Matabele out of the river, someone told me that an order had come recalling the Colonial Boys, so I galloped along the line of those that were farthest in advance, and told them that the order had been given to retire. Then I thought that before going back myself I would gallop forwards and try and get a shot or two at some of the Kaffirs armed with guns, who were retreating from the fire of Grey's Scouts.

In front of me lay a piece of perfectly open ground extending along the Umguza, some 200 yards broad, whilst from the edge of the open to the left the country was undulating and very scantily covered with low bush. The pony I was riding was the same that had been lent to me on the previous Sunday, and he had proved himself so absolutely steady, with rifles going off all round him, and bullets pinging and buzzing past him, that the last thing I thought of was that he might now play me false and run away. However this is what happened. I had dismounted and was sitting down to get a steady shot when someone said close behind me, "Look out, they're coming down on us from the left." I did not know that anyone was near me, but on getting up and looking round, saw one of the officers of the Colonial Boys—now Captain, then Lieutenant Windley—close behind me.

At the same time I saw Grey's Scouts retreating on the other side of the river, and recognised that Windley and I were a long way ahead of John Grootboom and five or six other Xosa *kaffirs*, who were the only members of the corps I could see, and who were also retiring; whilst I also saw that some of the Matabele we had been chasing had rallied, and seeing two white men alone, were coming down on us as hard as they could, with the evident intention of cutting off our retreat. However, they were still some 250 yards from us, and could I but have mounted my pony, we could have galloped away from them and rejoined the Colonial Boys easily enough.

A few bullets were again beginning to ping past us, so I did not want to lose any time, but before I could take my pony by the bridle he suddenly threw up his head, and spinning round trotted off, luckily running in the direction from which we had come. Being so very steady a pony, I imagine that a bullet must have grazed him and startled him into playing me this sorry trick at such a very inconvenient moment. "Come on as hard as you can, and I'll catch your horse and bring him back to you," said Windley, and started off after the faithless steed. But the brute would not allow himself to be caught, and when his pursuer approached him, broke from a trot into a gallop, and finally showed a clean pair of heels.

When my pony went off with Windley after him, leaving me, comparatively speaking, *planté là*, the *kaffirs* thought they had got me, and commenced to shout out encouragingly to one another and also to make a kind of hissing noise, like the word "*jee*" long drawn out. All this time I was running as hard as I could after Windley and my runaway horse. As I ran carrying my rifle at the trail, I felt in my bandoleer with my left hand to see how many cartridges were still at my disposal, and found that I had fired away all but two of the thirty I had come out with, one being left in the belt and the other in my rifle. Glancing round, I saw that the foremost *kaffirs* were gaining on me fast, though had this incident occurred in 1876 instead of 1896, with the start I had got I would have run away from any of them.

Windley, after galloping some distance, realised that it was useless wasting any more time trying to catch my horse, and like a good fellow came back to help me; and had he not done so, let me here say that the present history would never have been written, for nothing could possibly have saved me from being overtaken, surrounded, and killed. When Windley came up to me he said "Get up behind me; there's no time to lose," and pulled his foot out of the left stirrup for me to mount. Without any unnecessary loss of time, I caught hold of the pommel of the saddle, and got my foot into the iron, but it seemed to me that my weight might pull Windley and the saddle right round, so, as a glance over my shoulder showed me that the foremost *kaffirs* were now within 100 yards of us, I hastily pulled my foot out of the stirrup again, and shifting my rifle to my left hand caught hold of the thong round the horse's neck with my right, and told Windley to let him go.

He was a big strong animal, and as, by keeping my arm well bent, I held my body close up to him, he got me along at a good pace, and we began to gain on the *kaffirs*. They now commenced to shoot, but being more or less blown by hard running, they shot very badly, though they put the bullets all about us. Two struck just by my foot, and one knocked the heel of Windley's boot off. If they could only have hit the horse, they would have got both of us.

After having gained a little on our pursuers, Windley, thinking I must have been getting done up, asked me to try again to mount behind him: no very easy matter when you have a big horse to get on to and are holding a rifle in your right hand. However, with a desperate effort I got up behind him; but the horse, being unaccustomed to such a proceeding, immediately commenced to buck, and in spite of spurring would not go forwards, and the *kaffirs*, seeing our predicament, raised a yell and came on again with renewed ardour.

Seeing that if I stuck on the horse behind Windley we should both of us very soon lose our lives, I flung myself off in the middle of a buck, and landed right on the back of my neck and shoulders. Luckily I was not stunned or in any way hurt, and was on my legs and ready to run again with my hand on the thong round the horse's neck in a very creditably short space of time. My hat had fallen off, but I never left go of my rifle, and as I didn't think it quite the best time to be looking for a hat, I left it, all adorned with the colours of my troop as it was, to be picked up by the enemy, by whom it has no doubt been preserved as a souvenir of my presence amongst them.

And now another spurt brought us almost up to John Grootboom and the five or six Colonial Boys who were with him, and I called to John to halt the men and check the Matabele who were pursuing us, by firing a volley past us at them. This they did, and it at once had the desired effect, the *kaffirs* who were nearest to us hanging back and waiting for those behind to join them. In the meantime Windley and I joined John Grootboom's party, and old John at once gave me his horse, which, as I was very much exhausted and out of breath, I was very glad to get. Indeed I was so tired by the hardest run I had ever had since my old elephant-hunting days, that it was quite an effort to mount.

I was now safe, except that a few bullets were buzzing about, for soon after getting up to John Grootboom we joined the main body of the Colonial Boys, and then, keeping the Matabele at bay, retired slowly towards the position defended by the Maxim. Our enemies, who had been so narrowly baulked of their expected prey, followed us to the top of a rise, well within range of the gun, but disappeared immediately a few sighting shots were fired at them.

Thus ended a very disagreeable little experience, which but for the cool courage of Captain Windley would undoubtedly have ended fatally to myself. Like many brave men, Captain Windley is so modest that I should probably offend him were I to say very much about him; but at any rate I shall never forget the service he did me at the risk of his own life that day on the Umguza, whilst the personal gallantry he has always shown throughout the present campaign as a leader of our native allies has earned for him such respect and admiration that they have nicknamed him "*Inkunzi*," the Bull, the symbol of strength and courage. But Captain Windley was not the only man who performed a brave and self-denying deed on this somewhat eventful day, as I shall now proceed to relate.

When the Scouts were recalled, and commenced to retire from the Umguza, after having driven a body of natives from its shelter, as I have already related, they were suddenly fired on by a party of Matabele who had taken up a position amongst some bush to the left of their line of retreat. The foremost amongst the Scouts galloped past this ambush, but Captain Grey with a few of those in the rear halted and returned the enemy's fire. Trooper Wise was the first man hit, and seems to have received his wound from behind just as he was mounting his horse, as the bullet struck him high in the back, and travelling up the shoulder-blade, came out near the collar-bone. At this instant Wise's horse stumbled, and then, recovering himself, broke away from its rider, galloping straight back to town, and leaving the wounded man on the ground.

A brave fellow named Baxter at once dismounted and put Wise on his own horse, thus saving the latter's life, but, as it proved, thereby sacrificing his own. Captain Grey and Lieutenant Hook at once went to Baxter's assistance, and they got him along as fast as they could, but the *kaffirs* had now closed on them, and were firing out of the bush at very close quarters. Lieutenant Hook was shot from behind, the bullet entering the right buttock and coming out near the groin, but most luckily, though severing the sciatic nerve, just missing both the thigh-bone and the femoral artery. Nearly at the same time, too, a bullet just grazed Captain Grey's forehead, half-stunning him for an instant. "Texas" Long, a well-known member of the Scouts, then went to Baxter's assistance, and was helping him along, when a bullet struck the dismounted man in the side, and he at once let go of Long's stirrup leather and fell to the ground. No further assistance was then possible, and poor Baxter was killed by the *kaffirs* immediately afterwards.

Whilst these brave deeds were being performed, Lieutenant Fred Crewe, with some others of the Scouts, amongst whom I may mention Button and Radermayer, were keeping the *kaffirs* in check and covering the retreat of the wounded men. Just as Lieutenant Hook got near to Crewe, his horse was shot through the fetlock and buttock at the same time, and rolling over, threw Hook to the ground, causing him at the same time to drop his rifle. Hook got on his legs and was hobbling forwards when Crewe said to him, "Why don't you pick up your rifle?"

"I can't," was the answer; "I'm too badly wounded."

"Are you wounded, old chap?" said Crewe; "then take my horse, and I'll try and get out of it on foot."

Crewe then assisted Hook to mount his horse, and fought his way back on foot, only escaping with his life by a miracle, keeping several *kaffirs* who were very near him, but who had no guns, at bay with his revolver, whilst he retreated backwards. So near were these men to him, that one of them, as he turned, threw a heavy *knobkerrie* at him, which struck him a severe blow in the back. Nothing could have saved him had not the *kaffirs* been constantly kept in check by the steady fire of Radermayer, Button, Jack Stuart, and others of the Scouts, and also by a cross-fire from some of the Colonial Boys, directed by Captain Fynn and Lieutenant Mullins.

The splendid gallantry and devotion to one another shown by Captain Grey and his officers and men on this day will ever be remembered in Rhodesia as amongst the bravest of the brave deeds performed by the Colonists in the suppression of the present rebellion. Such acts, too, speak for themselves, and bear eloquent if silent testimony against the cruel and malicious calumnies on the character of the white settlers in Matabeleland which have so frequently disgraced the pages of a widely-read, if generally-despised, weekly journal.

As soon as Grey's Scouts and the Colonial Boys had reached the guns, these latter were limbered up and the whole patrol retired slowly on Bulawayo, the Matabele making no attempt to follow. Indeed their loss must have been severe, and had Grey's Scouts and the Colonial Boys only been supported instead of being recalled, the Matabele would never have rallied, but would have been kept on the run and killed in large numbers by the mounted men. At least this is my view, and it has been thoroughly borne out by the experience gained in subsequent fights during this campaign.

Our loss on this day was, Baxter killed and Wise and Hook wounded amongst Grey's Scouts, while five or six of the Colonial Boys were wounded, but none dangerously. Wise has long ago recovered from his wound, and Lieutenant Hook is on a fair way to do so. I have forgotten to mention that my horse must have been captured by the Matabele, as he did not return to Bulawayo, and has not since been heard of. The lucky savage into whose hands he fell became possessed at the same time of a very good saddle and bridle, and a brand new government coat.

CHAPTER 20

I Rejoin My Troop at Dawe's Store

On our arrival in town we heard that the wire was down or had been cut by the natives between Bulawayo and Fig Tree Fort. A patrol was therefore at once organised to proceed along the telegraph line, repair the break, and then go on to Fig Tree in order to act as an escort back to town for a coach now due containing a large and valuable consignment of rifles. This patrol was under the command of Captain Mainwaring, and consisted of thirty-five men of his own troop of the Bulawayo Police Force, and twenty-two men of the Matabele Mounted Police under Inspector Southey.

Being due at Mabukitwani on Thursday evening, I left town early on the morning of that day, and joining Captain Mainwaring travelled with him down the telegraph line. We found the wire broken about three and a half miles from Bulawayo. One of the poles had been chopped down evidently with small-bladed native axes, whilst the wire itself had been cut and the insulator broken.

After the wire had been repaired we continued our journey, and reached the Khami River at about 2 p.m., where we remained till about seven o'clock. Then, both horses and men being rested and refreshed, we saddled-up and rode on to Mr. Dawe's store, which is about half a mile from the old *kraal* of Mabukitwani. Here I heard that Lieutenant Grenfell had arrived with my troop from Matoli the same evening, and was encamped near the mule stable on the further side of the stream; so bidding goodbye to Captain Mainwaring, who decided to camp near the store, I at once rejoined my own men.

On the following morning Captain Mainwaring proceeded to Fig Tree, where he had not to wait long for the coach which he had come to meet, as he got back to my camp with it on Saturday evening. There were 123 rifles on board from which the locks and pins had been taken—each man of the escort carrying three of each—in order that, in the event of the coach being captured by an overwhelming force of Matabele, the rifles should be useless to them. However, both coach and escort reached Bulawayo safely, no rebels having been met with.

When about four miles from town they discovered the bodies of two white men lying on the roadside about 150 yards from their waggon. They had evidently been surprised by the rebels, and had made a bolt for life towards the road. The bodies had been terribly mutilated and hacked about, and seemed to have been lying where they were found for at least forty-eight hours. They were examined by Captain Mainwaring and Inspector Southey, as was also the waggon, but nothing was discovered by which to identify the murdered men except a branding iron. It was, however, subsequently ascertained that they were two Dutch transport riders named Potgieter and Fourie.

Strangely enough, these are the only white men who have been murdered on the main road from Bulawayo to Mafeking during the present insurrection, and it is noteworthy that they were not travelling along the road, but had been living for some time in their waggon some little distance away from it. I have no doubt that they were murdered by the party of rebels by whom the telegraph wire was cut on Wednesday, 22nd April. These men probably discovered their whereabouts the same evening, and were thus able to surprise and murder them during the night, or more probably at daylight on the following morning. The murderers were followers of Babian, one of the two envoys who visited England with Mr. E. A. Maund in 1899. The second envoy, Umsheti, is dead, or he, too, would be found in the ranks of the insurgents.

On Friday morning Lieutenant Grenfell and Mr. Norton rode into Bulawayo on business, and on the following day the former gentleman took part in the memorable fight with the Matabele on the Umguza, when for the first time the rebels were driven from their position in the immediate vicinity of the town, near Government House, which they have never since reoccupied.

During Mr. Grenfell's absence, Messrs. Blöcker, Marquand, and myself chose a site for a fort on a *kopje* near the site of the old *kraal* of Mabukitwani, from the top of which a magnificent view of the surrounding country was obtainable, whilst with a certain amount of work the *kopje* itself could be turned into an impregnable fortress. Now that work has been accomplished, and Fort Marquand will long remain as a memento of the present struggle in Matabeleland. I chris-

FORT MARQUAND, ON THE ROAD BETWEEN BULAWAYO AND MANGWE; WITH A PORTION OF H TROOP OF THE BULAWAYO FIELD FORCE IN THE FOREGROUND.

1. The Author (commanding H Troop).
2. Lieutenant Claud Grenfell.
3. Lieutenant Marquand (who superintended the building of the Fort).
4. Lieutenant H. H. Brücker.
5. Sergeant-Major Robertson, standing behind Author.
6. Sergeant Gates, standing behind Lieut. C. Grenfell.
7. Sergeant Norton, standing behind Lieut. Marquand

tened it Fort Marquand, after my lieutenant of that name, whom, he being an architect by profession, I put in charge of the working parties, so that the fort was built entirely under his direction and superintendence, and whosoever may care to examine it will see for himself that it is a very good fort, built with great care and sagacity.

On Monday evening Lieutenant Grenfell and Mr. Norton returned to Mabukitwani, in company with a detachment of the Africander Corps which had been sent down under Commandant Barnard to meet Earl Grey, who was expected by the next coach. From Lieutenant Grenfell and Commandant Barnard and his men I heard all about the fight on the previous day at the Umguza, as they had all taken part in it. All agreed that the *kaffirs* had suffered very heavy loss, and been most signally discomfited, and Lieutenant Grenfell was kind enough to write for me the following account of the engagement:—

> On Friday, 24th of April, it was not difficult to discern that a determined move against the *kaffirs* on the Umguza was in contemplation. The situation was getting unbearable, the town being surrounded by the Matabele, and the operations against them with a view to clearing the country round Bulawayo not having hitherto been at all successful. In fact, an uncomfortable feeling was prevalent that we were in process of being closed in upon every side.
>
> It was therefore with great satisfaction that we learnt this Friday night that Captain Macfarlane was to be given as many men as could be spared, two guns, and a free hand, and go out in the morning. Great was the scrimmaging for horses among the unattached, unexpectedly sudden the popularity of the remount officer. There is a good deal to be said in favour of fighting when the state of affairs is such that you can go out after morning coffee to a certain find, with every chance of a gallop and a kill, and return to a late breakfast at say 2 p.m. There were rumours, too, that this time we really meant business, and that the natives would be encouraged to surround us on all sides, in order to give every opportunity to the machine guns and rifle fire.
>
> Such were the directions actually given by Captain Macfarlane to his officers, when on the march, and the tactics proved to be sound enough. The patrol consisted of 35 Grey's Scouts under Captain Grey; 25 B troop under Captain Fynn; 15 of

Captain R. Macfarlane.

Captain Dawson's troop; 35 of the Africander Corps under Commandant Van Rensburg; 100 Colenbrander's Cape Boys under Captain Cardigan, and 60 to 70 Friendlies under Chief Native Commissioner Taylor; 1 Hotchkiss and 1 Maxim under Captain Rixon, and an ambulance with stretchers under Dr. Vigne; making in all some 120 whites and about 170 Colonial Boys and Friendlies all told, all under the command of Captain Macfarlane. Mr. Duncan, Colonel Spreckley, Captain Nicholson, Town Major Scott, Captain Wrey, and several other unattached officers and scouts, also accompanied the force. It is worth mentioning that Messrs. F. G. Hammond, Stewart, Anderson, Farquhar jr., and two or three more, shouldered their rifles and marched out on foot, in order to participate in the day's work.

The patrol left Bulawayo at 7.30 in the morning of the 25th of April, and proceeded in a north-easterly direction, taking the road to the right of the scene of the recent engagements on the Umguza River. The Scouts went on ahead as usual, the Africanders opening out on the left, and Captain Dawson taking command of the right flanking party, the guns bringing up the rear with an ambulance waggon and the Friendlies. This order was kept until a small bare eminence was reached on which stood four old walls, the wreck of a small farmhouse some three miles out of Bulawayo. There was a circuit of bush in front of this position, then the Umguza river, and beyond that rocky ground with thick bush rising from the river, the lines of the native "*scherms*" showing up black on the heights in the distance.

Up to now nothing had been seen of the enemy, only some smoke from their fires. The Scouts rode down to the river with orders to draw the enemy on, while the rest of the men took up their places round the two guns. The position was very suitable for both the Maxim and the Hotchkiss; but afforded absolutely no cover for the men. The rebels, several hundred in number, no sooner saw the Scouts than they streamed down to the river, shouting out a loud challenge to come on, which was answered by our side. The Scouts drew back slowly, bringing the *kaffirs* well on, but were finally driven in on our position with a rush, and the *kaffirs* pulled up about 200 yards off in the bush, firing very rapidly. Bullets of all sorts came whistling along, from elephant-guns, Martinis, Winchesters, and Lee-Metfords, and for about an hour things were decidedly unpleasant, though up to this time we had only one man killed and one wounded.

Our firing was incessant, and the shooting, though mostly at long range, very steady, and as effective probably as our exposed position and the cover afforded our assailants by the bush would allow. After the rebels had made two determined efforts to approach the Maxim, in both of which they were foiled, their fire slackened, and they apparently sent their best marksmen to the front to see what they could do.

At this juncture, however, Captain Macfarlane ordered the Africanders to charge those on our left, and the brilliant manner in which this was carried out will not soon be forgotten by those who witnessed it. The enemy had cover here behind some rocky ridges, but the Africanders rode them out of this ground in the cheeriest way possible—they use rather more "noise" fighting than the Britishers do—and sent them flying over the river, killing no fewer than seventy-four at the crossing, and completely breaking up that wing of the enemy's line. The Hotchkiss planted several shells very well among the flying natives; whilst on our side only one horse was lost in the charge.

About this time the Scouts were ordered to drive off the rebels to our front, and in this they succeeded admirably, but owing to the bad ground they had three men wounded. Lovett was shot here, and subsequently died from the effects of his wound, whilst John Grootboom, a very plucky colonial native, well known in Rhodesia, was also hit in two places while trying to drive some natives out of a *donga*.

Meanwhile Captain Dawson with his men on the right had been holding his own under a galling fire in open ground, unable to have a good shot at the enemy who were in the bush. They were having a very warm time of it, and had lost two men killed and one wounded, when Burnham was ordered to clear the bush with 100 of the Taylor's Friendlies, wearing red capes and carrying *assegais*. The charge was successful, and, backed up by Captain Taylor and Colenbrander's Cape Boys armed with rifles, the Friendlies cleared the bush and relieved Dawson from the hidden enemy.

About this time a message arrived from Captain Colenbrander that a fresh *impi* from the west meant to attack us, and sure enough they turned up very soon after, but seeing how the others had fared they kept fully half a mile off, sending a number of shots after the Africanders, whom they tried to cut off. The Maxim and Hotchkiss, however, kept them from coming nearer. The main body of the enemy having now partially reformed, the Africanders went to assist the Scouts, and the enemy were driven off fully two miles, one of our men and one horse being wounded in the sortie.

Captain Macfarlane thought it was now time to get home, as the wounded would take some time to see to, and there was a chance of his having to fight his way back to town; so orders were given for the ambulance to prepare to return to Bulawayo, and the whole column marched back in good order, having had by far the most successful day since the commencement of the rebellion. Our loss was four white men killed and four wounded, two Cape Boys and one Friendly wounded, one horse and one mule killed. It is very difficult to estimate the number of natives engaged, but there were probably at least as many as 2000 in all opposed to us.

How many were killed it is difficult to say, but from the bodies which were counted, and from the reports of the wounded brought in by Captain Colenbrander and his boys, who were over the ground in the afternoon, the enemy's loss must have been considerable. A vidette party of four mounted men, who were sent out to Government House in the morning, allowed themselves to be surprised and surrounded by the rebels, and one, unfortunately, got killed, namely Trooper B. Parsons of D troop, the other three just escaping with their lives.

After the return of the column in the afternoon from the Umguza, a small patrol under Lieutenant Boggie, consisting of thirty dismounted men of C troop, fifty of Colenbrander's Cape Boys, and ten of Grey's Scouts mounted, with one Maxim gun, went out in the direction of Sauer's house, and turning to the left, past Government House and Gifford's house, picked up Trooper Parsons' body, and returned to town *via* the Brickfields, not having seen any of the enemy. A seven-pounder was placed in position on the rise at the back of Williams' buildings, trained ready on to the ridge at the left of Government House, in order to shell the position if necessary.

After the return of the patrol the Observatory reported the

appearance of a large body of the rebels, who came over the ridge to the east of Government House down as far as the *spruit*. Trooper Edward Appleyard, seriously wounded on the Umguza in the morning, died on Saturday night, and at 11.30 on Sunday morning his body, together with those of Troopers Whitehouse, Gordon, and Parsons, was accorded a military funeral.

CHAPTER 21

Proceed Towards Bulawayo

Lieutenant Grenfell having brought me a despatch on Monday evening, acquainting me that my presence was again required in Bulawayo, I handed over the command of Fort Marquand to him on the following morning, and rode in to town alone, meeting Lieutenant Parkin and a second escort which had been sent down to meet Earl Grey at the Khami River.

On arriving at Matabele, Wilson's farm, six miles from Bulawayo, I found Captain Dawson with his troop and a lot of the "Friendlies" busily engaged in building a fort on a commanding position some four hundred yards away from the homestead and mule stables. With Captain Dawson, too, were my old friends, the well-known American Scouts Burnham and Ingram, and that very plucky English Scout Mr. Swinburne.

Although this detachment had only arrived here on the previous day, very considerable progress had already been made with the fort, which I was very pleased to find was being built at this place, as I had long advocated it, as also that another should be established at the Khami River, about halfway between Wilson's farm and Fort Marquand.

This last link in the chain of forts between Bulawayo and Mangwe did not come into existence until some few days later, and only then could it be said that it was possible to have the road properly patrolled. Whilst resting my horse for half an hour at Dawson's Fort I heard more details from him and the Scouts concerning the fight on the Umguza on the previous Saturday, which they considered to be the greatest reverse which the Matabele had yet suffered; or perhaps it would be fairer to say the only reverse, since, although, in every encounter their losses must have been very heavy compared with those of the whites, yet this was the first time that they had deemed it expedient to retreat from their position after the fight was over.

On reaching Bulawayo, however, I found that, although the *impis* which for the last ten days had been encamped along the Umguza in the immediate neighbourhood of the town had now moved some miles farther down the river, yet parties of them were still hanging about ready to murder any defenceless persons that they might be able to surprise, even on the very outskirts of the town, as was sufficiently proved by the fact that on the very morning of my arrival, that is on Tuesday, 28th April, several *coolies* had been murdered in their vegetable gardens just beyond the native location.

The following account of this affair I have taken over from the *Matabele Times* of 2nd May, by kind permission of the editor:

> On their arrival in camp on Tuesday morning after night duty in the *laager*, the Mounted Police found a number of terrified *coolies* awaiting them, who informed them that they had been attacked by a large body of Matabele at their vegetable gardens, situated about two miles beyond, the Matabele Mounted Police camp, and that eight of their number had been murdered. Some twelve or fifteen of the police promptly seized their rifles and bandoleers, and proceeded—on their own accord—in skirmishing order to the scene of the massacre, which they reached after a sharp twenty minutes' walk. The enemy had disappeared from sight, but the tale of those *coolies* who had been fortunate enough to escape proved only too true. No less than eight *coolies*, including one young woman, were found lying foully murdered in different parts of the gardens, and every one, though pierced through over and over again with *assegai* stabs, was still warm. This proves that the enemy must have rushed down on the unprotected *coolies* in broad daylight.
>
> Shortly after the return of the police to camp, a couple of unarmed mounted men rode down to the gardens. They had not been there five minutes when they were fired upon from the adjacent *kopjes*, and they had to retire precipitately. This goes to prove that the enemy do not intend to give up their present position unless they are driven from it, and the sooner that is effected the better.
>
> The following information was also given to the public committee. Sedan deposed:

I slept at my garden near the Butts last night with an American negro called Smith. Smith this morning before sunrise started to go to his own garden. I heard shots fired just after he left me. His Zambesi boy ran over and told me Smith had been killed. I saw about forty or fifty *kaffirs*. I saw one man with a gun, whilst the rest had *assegais* and sticks. I hid myself in a ditch, and saw the *kaffirs* in the gardens. I saw them kill Indians with the gun and the *assegais*. About half an hour later I saw a picket of four white men come to the gardens. I ran to the picket and came in to town. I was too frightened to say anything.

Ahchelrising deposed:

I slept in my garden and heard a shout from a lot of Indians early this morning that the Matabele were on to us. I ran away, and saw my brother Isree shot in front of me. I came to town and reported in the *laager*, and then went back to my garden. I saw the bodies of Goolab, Yitian, Venctayelee and his wife, Ramsamee and Chinantoniem. Smith's Zambesi boy was also killed.

On Tuesday night, 28th April, Earl Grey, accompanied by his secretary Mr. Benson, and General Digby Willoughby—who had been down to Mafeking in order to hurry forward the food supplies and relief forces—arrived in Bulawayo. The coach which brought the administrator and his party was escorted into town by Lieutenant Parkin and his men, whom I had met on their way down to meet it. They seem to have narrowly missed, or been missed by, a portion of Babian's *impi*, which was reported on Wednesday morning to have crossed the road near the Khami River early on Tuesday night just after the coach had passed.

On the following morning, Wednesday, 29th April, an *impi* of several hundred *kaffirs*, in all likelihood a portion of Babian's force, suddenly appeared on the rising ground about 1000 yards away from Dawson's Fort. They were probably on their way to Wilson's homestead with the intention of destroying and burning it down, but on seeing the fort manned by a number of white men, were evidently a bit taken aback, as they halted and held a council of war. They then spread out in skirmishing order, and getting down amongst the thorn trees in the river-bed below the house, advanced towards the fort as if about to attack it. However, after approaching to within 800 yards they thought better of it and withdrew, probably imagining that the place was defended with Maxim guns.

After retiring from the neighbourhood of the fort, they went down to Captain Molyneux's farm, some two miles distant, and destroyed and burnt everything they could, even *assegaiing* the pigs, the carcasses of which animals they left untouched, as the Matabele of Zulu descent do not eat the flesh of the domestic pig, although they are very partial to that of both species of the wild swine found in Southern Africa, *viz.* the Wart Hog and the Bush Pig.

During my visit to Bulawayo it was at last decided to build a fort at the Khami river, and I was asked to take the work in hand forthwith. As only thirty men could be spared from Bulawayo, it was arranged that twenty more should be withdrawn from Fort Halsted, five miles beyond Fig Tree, and I requested that Lieutenant Howard, an old member of the Bechuanaland Border Police, who was at present with Captain Molyneux at Fig Tree, and who had done very good service in the first war during Major Forbes' memorable retreat along the Tchangani River, should be placed in command of the two troops combined.

On Friday, 1st May, I left Bulawayo with Lieutenant Parkin and thirty men, accompanied by a mule waggon carrying kit, tools for fort-building, and provisions. We had first to take the waggon to Fort Marquand, there off-load it, and then send it on to Fort Halsted to bring back the twenty men from that place, who on their arrival at Mabukitwani could be at once despatched, together with the thirty under Lieutenant Parkin, to the Khami River, to commence building the fort there. This was all arranged by the Sunday evening, and everything got ready to proceed to the Khami River early the following morning. That evening, my old friend Cornelius Van Rooyen, commandant of the forces at Mangwe, accompanied by three of his men, arrived at my fort on his way to see Earl Grey, by whom he had been called to Bulawayo. He was, of course, an honoured guest with us, and we did all we could to make him and his men comfortable.

At this time, Marzwe, Gambo's head *induna*, was camped with many of his people round the base of the hill on which my fort stood. As he had often expressed a fear lest the remainder of his people, who were living at their *kraals* some eight miles to the west, should be attacked some fine morning by Maiyaisa's *impi*, I had repeatedly told him to bring all his women and children to the immediate vicinity of the fort, since, as I had only ten serviceable horses at my disposal, it was out of the question to attempt any attack on a large *impi* in a thickly-wooded country, although I should be able to protect any of his tribe who were willing to take quarters round the walls of my fort.

On my last return from Bulawayo, I found that Marzwe had taken my advice, and had sent messengers on the Saturday morning to call all his people in to the fort. These men ought to have returned with the women and children on the following day, but owing to their dilatory ways, and their unfailing habit of *"never doing today what can be put off till tomo*rrow," they did not do so.

On the following morning, Monday, 4th May, Lieutenants Parkin and Webb started off early for the Khami River, taking the mule waggon with them, Lieutenant Howard and myself intending to follow them up and choose a site for the fort immediately after breakfast. Just before discussing this meal, Marzwe came out and reported to me that one of his men had heard shots fired in the direction of his *kraal*. None of my sentries or horse-guards having heard these shots, I half thought there was no truth in the report. However, I sent Mr. Simms and two other good men to scout round the back of some *kopjes*, about two miles to the west of our position, beyond which the shots were said to have been fired.

Shortly after the scouts had left, two of the men sent on the previous Saturday to bring in the women and children turned up, saying that Marzwe's town had been attacked at daylight by a portion of Maiyaisa's *impi*, and some of his people killed. A little later a young girl arrived at the fort with an *assegai*-wound in her right side just above the hip-bone. The wound was not a dangerous one, and after it had been washed and dressed, the child was able to tell her story, which was to the effect that Marzwe's *kraal* had been surrounded in the night, and every man, woman, and child in it murdered just at dawn.

Although, with the few mounted men at my disposal, I knew it would be madness to engage any large number of Matabele, unless I could get them in perfectly open country where there was no chance of being surrounded, I was not inclined to let this affair pass without endeavouring to ascertain exactly what had happened. Van Rooyen at once agreed to put off his visit to Bulawayo and accompany me with his three troopers to the scene of the reported massacre, and I sent a messenger to tell Lieutenant Parkin to return immediately to Mabukitwani with ten good men mounted on his best horses. When he arrived, my three scouts had also returned, having seen nothing, and I found myself in command of about twenty-five mounted men; some of the horses, however, were in wretched condition, and altogether unfit for hard work.

When the report of the massacre of his whole family, as well as a large number of his people, was brought to Marzwe, he received it with the utmost stoicism, only saying, "They wanted me; they were looking for me; they wanted my skin." Whether he believed it or not I cannot say, but he never betrayed the slightest sign of emotion.

It was already past mid-day when I was at last able to get away with my little force, travelling across country under the guidance of an elderly savage armed with a shield, and two long-bladed insinuating-looking *assegais*, and at the same time adorned with a chimney-pot hat, of all things in the world, thus combining in his own person the attributes of primitive savagery and the most advanced civilisation of Western Europe.

Before we were a couple of miles from camp we met a lot of women and children making for the fort, who said that they had fled from some of Marzwe's outlying villages early that morning as they had heard firing going on in the direction of the chief's *kraal*. Soon after passing these people we got into country where a small force such as mine might have been very easily surrounded and cut up by a hostile *impi*, as the ground was very broken and on every side of us were small hills and rocky ridges, the whole being covered with dense, scrubby bush, in many parts of which a *kaffir* would have been invisible at a distance of thirty yards.

Had this sort of country continued for any great distance, I would not have risked taking my men on indefinitely over ground so very favourable to any force of hostile Matabele which might chance to be there. However, after a time we emerged into country of a more open character, where the bush was much less dense, and where one was not constantly shut in amongst *kopjes* and scrub-covered ridges.

Just here one of my flanking parties came on a woman carrying a large bundle of blankets and other household goods on her head. On being questioned, she told us that at daylight that morning Marzwe's *kraal* had been attacked and three of his men killed, as well as one girl who had endeavoured to escape with the rest of the men. The girl referred to proved afterwards to be the damsel who had been wounded in the side by an *assegai*, but who had managed to evade her enemies and make her way to our fort at Mabukitwani. All the rest of the women and children, together with the cattle, sheep, and goats, the woman said, had been captured by Maiyaisa's people, who, however, she thought were in no great force, being only a small raiding party detached from the main body at the Khami River.

But now comes the sequel, about which the wounded girl had known nothing. Amongst Marzwe's men who had escaped from the first onslaught on the *kraal* was one Obas.[1] This man had recognised that the attacking force was not a large one, and he at once went round to all the outlying villages and collected a very considerable number of his chief's retainers, and taking command of them, followed up the raiders, and not only rescued all the women and children who had been taken captive but also killed eleven of the enemy, and retook all the cattle, sheep, and goats they were driving off. This good news was soon confirmed by Obas himself, whom we met coming on with all the recaptured women and children and cattle. He was a well-built, active-looking *kaffir* of middle height, light in colour, and with good features, altogether a good specimen of the best type of Matabele. He was armed with a Martini-Henry rifle, as were some few of his followers, whilst all carried *assegais*. He told us much the same story as we had heard from the woman who had just passed, except that he informed us that the number of Marzwe's men who had been killed was four, instead of three.

There was now no necessity to proceed any further, so we turned back to the fort, where all Marzwe's people arrived safely the same evening.

Early the following morning I rode over to the Khami with Lieutenant Howard, and after selecting a site for the fort which was to be built there, and leaving Lieutenant Howard in charge, returned to Mabukitwani. Here I found a telegram from Colonel Napier, which had been sent on to me by Captain Molyneux from Fig Tree. It was to the effect that I was to at once collect a force of forty mounted and eighty dismounted men from all the forts along the road, including Mangwe, and march them in to Bulawayo by Friday evening, as they were required to form part of a column which was to leave for the Tchangani on the following day, Saturday, 9th May.

As the time was so short, I rode the same evening (Tuesday) to Fig Tree in order to despatch a telegram as soon as possible to Major Armstrong, asking him to send me up twenty mounted men from the garrisons of Matoli and Mangwe, and on Wednesday I made all arrangements at the other forts. As Colonel Napier particularly wished Captain Molyneux and Lieutenant Howard to accompany the col-

---

1. "*Oude Baas*" or "Old Master," so named after Mr. Hartley, the veteran elephant-hunter, who must have been in the country when he was born (1864 to 1870).

umn, I put Lieutenant Stewart in command at Fig Tree, whilst Lieutenant Parkin took charge of the fort at the Khami River, Lieutenant Grenfell taking over the command of my own fort.

On Thursday evening I had all the men from the lower forts mustered at Mabukitwani, and after a cold rainy night we marched to Bulawayo, picking up the other detachments on our way, and reaching town before sundown on Friday evening, 8th May.

CHAPTER 22

Matabele Impi Reported Near Tekwe River

Owing to various circumstances, it was found impossible to get the column off for the Tchangani on the following morning, and the start was not actually made until Monday, 11th May. This column, the largest yet sent out from Bulawayo, was despatched with the object of opening the road to the Tchangani River, where it was hoped that the relief force from Salisbury under Colonel Beal, with which was Mr. Cecil Rhodes, would be met, when the future movements of the combined columns would be determined according to circumstances.

The composition of the force was as follows: Artillery, four officers and thirty-four men under Captain Biscoe; Grey's Scouts, four officers and forty men under Captain Grey; Africander Corps, three officers and fifty-nine men under Commandant Van Rensberg and Captain Van Niekerk; A troop (Gifford's Horse) two officers and nineteen men; B troop (Gifford's Horse) two officers and twenty men—the combined troops under Captain Fynn; F troop, one officer and twenty men under Lieutenant H. Lamb; four officers and 100 dismounted men under Captain Selous, consisting of detachments from H, C, D, K, and L troops, under Captains Mainwaring and Reid, and Lieutenants Holland and Hyden; also four engineers; making altogether 312 Europeans, supported by 150 of Colenbrander's Colonial Boys under Captain Windley, and 100 Friendly Matabele under Chief Native Commissioner Taylor. Also one seven-pounder, one 2.5 gun, one Hotchkiss, one Nordenfeldt, one Maxim; fourteen mule waggons carrying provisions, kit, and ammunition, and one ambulance waggon.

Of this force Colonel Napier was in command; Colonel Spreckley, second in command; Captain Llewellyn, staff orderly officer; Captain Howard Brown, staff officer; Captain Bradley, remount officer; Captain Molyneux, adjutant; Captain Wrey, heliograph officer; Captain Purssell, quartermaster; Dr. Levy, medical officer, with Lieutenants Little, Dollar, and Burnham as gallopers; whilst Captain the Honourable C. J. White and Mr. A. Rhodes also accompanied the expedition unattached, making I believe a total force of forty-two officers and 613 men.

With the column was one of two colonial natives who had been despatched on horseback a few days previously to try and carry a message through to Gwelo. They saw no signs of the enemy until after they had passed Mr. Stewart's farm, but near the Tekwe River they rode into the middle of a Matabele *impi*, in the middle of the night, which was watching the road and had no fires burning. They were immediately attacked, and the boy who got back to Bulawayo had his horse killed under him almost immediately, and received an *assegai* wound in the arm. However, in the darkness he managed to elude his enemies, and made his way back to town. His companion neither reached Gwelo nor ever returned to Bulawayo, but he apparently galloped through his assailants at the Tekwe, only to be again waylaid, and this time killed, at the Tchangani, where his corpse was discovered a few days later lying in the road by Colonel Beal's column.

To quote the words of the correspondent with the column representing the *Bulawayo Chronicle*:

> To the martial strains of the town band, on Monday, 11th May, the column under Colonel Napier left the citadel, and boldly started forth into the country lately taken from us by the Matabele. Within two hours our men had crossed from British territory into the Matabele country—to wit, the Umguza brooklet.

Arrived at the Umguza, it was found that we could not proceed until certain stores, which had been left behind in Bulawayo, reached us; and as these did not come to hand until the following morning, we did not again make a move until shortly before noon on Tuesday. For some miles our route lay through perfectly open country, but on getting abreast of Thaba Induna we came to a strip of thorn bush through which the road passes. Here a halt was made, whilst Colonel Spreckley went forward with Grey's Scouts to see if the bush was clear of *kaffirs*. He soon sent a messenger back reporting that the enemy were just in front of him, so Colonel Napier asked me to go on and obtain further particulars before he advanced with the whole column.

I found Colonel Spreckley about 600 yards in advance, the bush between where he had halted his men and the main body being much less dense than I had imagined, whilst in front of him the country was very open indeed. However, the grass was three or four feet high, and as some *kaffirs* had been seen on the rise only a few hundred yards ahead, it was impossible to tell how many of them there might be there. Colonel Spreckley therefore wanted some men on foot to be sent forward to assist the Scouts in driving the *kaffirs* out of the long grass.

I at once galloped back to the column, and was ordered to go forward again with two of the three troops of infantry under my command, Colonel Napier bringing on the remainder of the force behind us. As soon as my footmen reached the advance guard, we all spread out in skirmishing order and went forwards as rapidly as possible. The *kaffirs*, however, who had been seen in the long grass could only have been a few scouts, who, on seeing the mounted men, had retired on the main body, for until we came within a mile of the little pyramidal hill which stands by itself about a mile to the south of the low flat-topped hill known as Thaba Induna, we never saw a sign of the enemy.

Then, however, standing as we were on the crest of a rise, from which the ground sloped off into a broad valley which lay between us and the aforesaid hill, we suddenly came in sight of a considerable number of the rebels. A detachment of them was on the hill itself, whilst considerable numbers were scattered over the open ground below it. Altogether some hundreds of them must have been in sight. Between the single hill and the wooded slopes of Thaba Induna itself there is a space of perfectly open ground over a mile in breadth, and it certainly looked to the eye of an old hunter, accustomed in the pursuit of game to measure distances and take in at a glance the details of the ground before him, that, had the whole of the mounted men with the column at this juncture galloped as hard as they could go to the point of Thaba Induna, and then swept round at the back of the single hill, a large number of the rebels would have been cut off from the bush and killed in the open ground.

These tactics, however, were not adopted, and the natives got off scot free, for although a few shots were fired at them with a Maxim and seven-pounder at an unknown range, none were hit, and they all

Colonel William Napier who commanded the Bulawayo Field Force during the late rebellion.

retreated into the thick bush to the north of Thaba Induna. Our column then advanced for another couple of miles, and *laagered* up near Graham's store on the Kotki River.

On the following day the column remained in laager, and Colonel Napier took out a patrol, consisting of some 150 mounted men of Grey's Scouts, Gifford's Horse, and the Africander Corps, to ascertain if any of the rebels were still in our vicinity, and Captain Wrey accompanied the patrol in order to send some heliographic messages to Bulawayo.

Leaving the *laager* about 8 a.m., this force first returned about three miles along the road to Bulawayo, and when abreast of the single hill I have spoken of as having been occupied by the rebels on the previous day, turned to the right, and spreading out in skirmishing order advanced towards the hill, which was reached without a *kaffir* having been seen. Here Captain Wrey was left with his heliograph party, and a further advance was made towards the bush on the north-east corner of Thaba Induna, where were found the "*scherms*," or military camps of the Matabele who had been seen on the previous day. These encampments appeared to have been evacuated early that morning, their occupants having probably moved off to join the *impis* which had retired from the vicinity of Bulawayo a short time before and taken up their quarters on the lower Umguza.

After these *scherms* had been burnt, a portion of the patrol was detached to the right, consisting of Grey's Scouts, a section of the Africander Corps, and a small party of Gifford's Horse, in all about eighty men. This detachment, after having advanced for a couple of miles through undulating country more or less covered with thorn bush, which in some places was fairly thick, came suddenly upon a small *impi* of 200 or 300 *kaffirs*, which I believe was a section of the Ingubu regiment.

These men had taken up a position along the crest of a rough stony ridge covered with bush, and when the approaching horsemen were still some four hundred yards distant they opened fire on them. Captain Grey immediately ordered his men to charge, which they did in extended order.

The sight of the long line of cavalry thundering down upon them seems to have turned the hearts of the savages to water, as their saying is, for after having fired a few more shots, they turned and ran, trusting to evade their enemies in the bush. A considerable number of them no doubt succeeded in doing so, but the chase was continued for a mile and a half, and when it was at last abandoned a long line of corpses marked the track where the whirlwind of the white man's vengeance had swept along. *Vae victis!*—"woe to the conquered!"—woe indeed; for amongst the men who took part in the pursuit of the *kaffirs*, on this, to them, most fatal day, were many who, maddened by the loss of old chums foully slain in cold blood by the natives, were determined to use their opportunity to the utmost to inflict a heavy punishment for the crimes committed, while all were bent on exacting vengeance for the murders of the European women and children who had been hurried out of existence during the first days of the rebellion.

Once broken, the *kaffirs* never made any attempt to rally, but ran as hard as they could, accepting death when overtaken without offering the slightest resistance; some indeed, when too tired to run any farther, walked doggedly forward with arms in their hands which they never attempted to use, and did not even turn their heads to look at the white men who were about to shoot them down. No quarter was either given or asked for, nor was any more mercy shown than had been lately granted by the *kaffirs* to the white women and children who had fallen into their power. This realistic picture may seem very horrible to all those who believe themselves to be superior beings to the cruel colonists of Rhodesia, but let them not forget the terrible provocation. I cannot dispute the horror of the picture; but I must confess that had I been with Captain Grey that day, I should have done my utmost to kill as many *kaffirs* as possible, and yet I think I can claim to be as humane a man as any of my critics who may feel inclined to consider such deeds cowardly and brutal and altogether unworthy of a civilised being.

This claim to humanity, coupled with the defence of savage deeds, may seem paradoxical, but the fact is, as I have said before, that in the smooth and easy course of ordinary civilised existence it is possible for a man to live a long life without ever becoming aware that somewhere deep down below the polished surface of conventionality there exists in him an ineradicable leaven of innate ferocity, which, although it may never show itself except under the most exceptional circumstances, must and ever will be there—the cruel instinct which, given sufficient provocation, prompts the meekest nature to kill his enemy—the instinct which forms the connecting link between the nature of man and that of the beast.

The horrors of a native insurrection—the murders and mutilations of white men, women, and children by savages—are perhaps better calculated than anything else to awake this slumbering fiend—the indestructible and imperishable inheritance which, through countless generations, has been handed down to the most highly civilised races of the present day from the savage animals or beings from whom or which modern science teaches us that they have been evolved. I have been told that Mr. Labouchere often jokingly says that we are all monkeys with our tails rubbed off, but with natures still very much akin to those of our simian relatives; and however that may be, we are certainly the descendants of the fierce and savage races by whom Northern and Central Europe was peopled in prehistoric times; and I am afraid that the saying of Napoleon, that "*if you scratch a Russian you will find a Tartar*," may be extended to embrace the modern Briton or any other civilised people of Western Europe, none of whom it will be found necessary to scratch very deeply in order to discover the savage ancestors from whom they are descended.

On Wednesday afternoon subsequent to the dispersal of the natives, several *kraals* were burnt and a good deal of corn taken, which proved most valuable, being urgently required to keep the horses and mules in condition. About eighty head of cattle and some sheep and goats were also captured by Captain Fynn and Lieutenant Moffat. As during the time when the *kaffirs* were being chased by Grey's Scouts and the Africanders, Captain Wrey had received a heliographic message from Earl Grey, requesting Colonel Napier not to proceed any farther until some waggons loaded with provisions for the Salisbury column, which had already left Bulawayo, had reached him, we spent another day in *laager*.

The weather had now turned very cold, and on the Wednesday night heavy storms of rain had fallen all round us, though we had escaped with only a few drops; but on the following night, or rather very early on Friday morning, a soaking shower passed over us, and as we were lying out in the open, our blankets got wet through, rendering a very early start impossible; although, the convoy having reached us on Thursday night, the order had been given to have everything packed up ready to move by daylight.

However we got off by eight o'clock, and reached Lee's store, distant twenty-four miles from Bulawayo, before mid-day. This store and hotel, noted as being the most comfortable on the whole road between the capital of Matabeleland and Salisbury, had, like every other building erected by a white man in this part of the country, been burnt down and as far as possible destroyed. After our horses and transport animals had had a couple of hours' feeding, we proceeded on our way, and *laagered* up for the night on the site of the camp where Dr. Jameson was attacked on 1st November 1893 by the Imbezu and Ingubu regiments, during his memorable march from Mashunaland to Bulawayo.

On every side of this camp but that facing towards the west, the country consisted of open rolling downs, entirely devoid of bush for miles and miles. On the western face there was a space of open ground bounded at a distance of 500 or 600 yards by a strip of open thorn bush, and it was through this thorn bush that the Matabele warriors made their advance. Naturally, as they had to face the fire of several Maxims and other pieces of ordnance, they never got beyond the edge of the bush. It seems a marvel that they should have been foolish enough to advance as they did, but it was doubtless their ignorance of the impossibility of taking a *laager* by assault in the face even of a heavy rifle fire, let alone Maxim guns and other destructive toys of a similar character, which led them to expose themselves so vainly. But they learnt a lesson that day which has never been forgotten in Matabeleland, as the present campaign has shown.

The three following days were entirely without incident, as we never saw a sign of a *kaffir*, though every wayside hotel and store had been burnt to the ground. On Monday evening we *laagered* up at a spot a few miles short of the Pongo store, where it was known that some white men had been murdered. Mr. Burnham, the American scout, who had ridden on ahead in the afternoon, returned to the column at dusk from the store, with the news that a scouting party from the Salisbury contingent had been there also the same day, but had returned towards the Tchangani just before his own arrival.

On the following morning, Tuesday, 19th May, we reached the Pongo store early, having passed the coach which had been captured by the *kaffirs* some three miles on this side of it. As I have already stated, one wheel had been removed from the coach, and the pole had been sawn in two, whilst the contents of the mail-bags had been torn up and strewn over the ground in every direction. The sun-dried carcasses of the mules still lay all of a heap in their harness, just as they had fallen when they were *assegaied* some six weeks previously.

On reaching the store we found and buried the bodies of the two poor fellows (Hurlstone and Reddington) who had been murdered there just seven weeks previously, on Tuesday, 24th March. Both their skulls had been battered and chipped by heavy blows struck with *knobkerries* and axes. The bodies had not been touched by any animal or *kaffir* since the day when the murders were committed, as their clothes and boots had not been removed, and the blankets thrown over them by the patrol party sent out from the Tchangani, two days after they were killed, were still covering them. The poor battered remains of what had so lately been two fine young Englishmen were reverently placed by their countrymen in a hastily-dug grave, and a prayer said over them by the good Catholic priest Father Barthélemy. The remains of the third white man murdered here were found at some little distance from the store.

CHAPTER 23

Column Under Colonel Spreckley Sent to the South

On resuming our journey, we had not proceeded a couple of miles, when on cresting a rise we came in sight of the Salisbury relief force coming out of the bush ahead of us and just entering the valley which lay between us. The two columns were soon laagered up in the open ground some 500 yards apart on either side of a small stream. With the Salisbury contingent were Mr. Cecil Rhodes, Sir Charles Metcalfe, and several gentlemen who, having left Bulawayo on a shooting trip some two months previously, had been obliged on the outbreak of the rebellion to take refuge in the Gwelo *laager*, where they had been cooped up ever since.

Mr. Rhodes, I thought, looked remarkably well, and yet the fast grizzling hair and a certain look in the strong face told the tale of the excessive mental strain undergone during the last few months. Amongst those who had joined the Salisbury column at Gwelo were Mr. Weston Jarvis, Mr. Farquhar, the Hon. Tatton Egerton (M.P. for Knutsford) and his son. That evening Mr. Rhodes and Colonel Napier dined with our mess, and in course of conversation after dinner it was decided that, instead of returning at once with the combined columns along the main road to Bulawayo, a flying column should be sent under Colonel Spreckley through the country to the south of the hills bordering the Insiza River, whilst Colonel Napier should travel down the valley of that river itself with the main body; the two columns to meet in the neighbourhood of the ford across the Insiza, on the road from Bulawayo to Belingwe.

Early on the morning of Thursday, 21st May, Colonel Spreckley's column of about four hundred men left us and bore away to the south; the main body to which my own troop was attached making a move very shortly afterwards. We first kept the road as far as the valley beyond the Pongo store, but there turned off to the south, outspanning at about eleven o'clock amongst a lot of *kraals*, all of which had evidently been hastily vacated on our approach, as they were all full of grain, and pots were found cooking on fires that had only lately been lighted. The corn-bins in these villages were one and all quite full of maize, *kaffir* corn, and ground-nuts, showing not only that the harvest in this part of Matabeleland had been a very plentiful one, but also that the people thought they had got rid of the white men for good and all and had no reason to fear their return.

After all the grain had been removed that we could carry, the *kraals* were burnt and the remainder of the corn destroyed, in order that it might not again fall into the hands of the rebels, for a good food-supply constitutes "the sinews of war" to a savage people, who are not likely to come to terms as long as such supplies hold out.

In the afternoon we moved on a few miles farther, destroying several more *kraals*. The huts in some of these had been newly built and plastered, and we found that ground had been freshly hoed up to lie fallow until the sowing-time came. In every village were found goods of some kind or another which had belonged to the many white people murdered in this district, and the articles of women's clothing, and especially a hat that was recognised as having belonged to a young girl of the name of Agnes Kirk, made the troopers simply mad to exact vengeance on the murderers.

About two miles distant from the spot where we *laagered* up for the night, the huts of some white prospectors were found, but no trace of their former owners. These huts had been made use of by the *kaffirs* as store-rooms, and were found to be full of every conceivable description of merchandise, taken from neighbouring farmhouses and the hotels and stores along the road. The goods were all carefully packed up, and included bags of sugar, flour, and Boer meal, as well as boxes of soap and candles, tinned provisions, blankets, and many other articles. Outside the huts stood a waggon and a coach, the latter of which was known to have been brought from the Tekwe store, some five miles distant.

As it was evident that we were now in the midst of a native population, who were not only responsible for the murders of the white men in the district, the destruction of their homes, and the looting of their property, but who also seemed so infatuated by their success that they appeared to think that the compatriots of the murdered people "would never come back no more," it was determined to make an effort to prove to them in a practical manner that there is some truth in the French proverb which says that *"tout vient à qui sait attendre."*

Therefore at 4 a.m. on the following morning, the 22nd May, Grey's Scouts and a portion of the Africander Corps under Captain Van Niekerk, in all about one hundred men, were sent out down the valley of the Insiza in order to try and discover the whereabouts of the main body of the rebels in this part of the country. The members of the patrol at first proceeded on foot, leading their horses until day broke, when the order was given to mount. Shortly afterwards smoke was seen rising from a valley amongst the hills to the left, and the horses' heads were at once turned in that direction, and presently, after the first range of hills which bounds the Insiza valley had been passed, a herd of cattle was seen amongst the broken country on ahead. These cattle were found to be in charge of a small force of *kaffirs*, who abandoned them to the white men without making much resistance.

It was the firing which took place during this skirmish which was heard in camp soon after sunrise, and which caused Colonel Napier to send Commandant Van Rensberg and myself with a small party to ascertain what was going on. Just after these cattle had been captured, Mr. Little and some of Gifford's Horse under Captain Fynn, forming the right-hand flanking party to Colonel Spreckley's column, which was then moving forwards some four miles to the south, rode up, having been attracted by the firing.

After a few minutes' conversation, no more *kaffirs* being anywhere in sight, Colonel Spreckley's men went on their way, whilst the Scouts and Africanders started on their return with the captured cattle towards the *laager*. A little farther on a halt was made, and some of the men produced some provisions from their wallets and were proceeding to discuss the same, when *kaffirs* were suddenly seen on the crest of a rise in front.

At this moment Captain Grey was missing, but he turned up immediately afterwards with seven of the Scouts, who had been foraging with him, each man having a dead sheep tied behind his saddle. These, however, had to be immediately cut loose and abandoned, as large numbers of *kaffirs* were now seen both in front and to the right, where they had previously been hidden in a deep river-bed.

A running fight was now commenced, which was kept up for some four miles before the *kaffirs* were shaken off. When it was first seen that the Matabele were in force, and meant to try and cut off their enemy's retreat, Captain Grey sent the American Scout Burnham, together with a compatriot named Blick, to the top of a hill on ahead, to try and ascertain the numbers and disposition of the rebels; but Burnham and his companion were cut off from the main body, and had to gallop for their lives, and had they not both been very well mounted, they would probably not have got away, as the *kaffirs* nearly surrounded them in a very rocky bit of ground. The cattle which had been captured had to be abandoned by the men who were driving them, and very hurriedly too, as a party of the rebels made a determined attempt to cut them off from the main body.

Early in the fight Trooper Rothman of the Africanders was shot through the stomach, and, as a comrade named Parker belonging to the same corps was assisting the wounded man to mount his horse, he was himself shot through the upper part of the body, from side to side, and died almost immediately. Poor Parker had to be left where he fell, as there was no means of carrying him.

Just as the white men were descending the last hill-slope into the level valley of the Insiza River, a young Dutchman named Frikky Greeff, the son of an old elephant-hunter long resident in Matabeleland, had his horse shot through both forelegs just above the fetlocks. On being struck the poor animal fell heavily, pinning its rider to the ground. He, however, soon extricated himself, and one of the Scouts, Trooper Button, who was riding a strong, quiet horse, took him up behind him. Up to this time poor Rothman had been able to retain his seat on his horse, but being greatly weakened by loss of blood, and in fact in a dying condition, he now fell off. Lieutenant Sinclair of the Africander Corps, on seeing this, dismounted, and with the assistance of others placed Rothman across his saddle, and, mounting behind him, carried him in this way for over three miles. By this time it was apparent to all that the man was dead, so, as the *kaffirs* had now given up the pursuit, the body was placed on the ground in a shady place, there to remain until it could be recovered and brought in to camp.

After getting out into the open country the horses were off-saddled for an hour on the banks of a stream which runs into the Insiza, and the patrol then returned to *laager*. Besides the two men who were killed, two more were wounded, though not seriously, Trooper Niemand being shot through the fleshy part of the arm, and Trooper Geldenhuis getting something more than a graze just above his ankle. Singularly enough, as all the men were mixed up together, all the casualties occurred to members of the Africander Corps.

Just at sunrise the same morning Colonel Napier asked me to take a few mounted men of the Salisbury column and proceed, together with a small detachment of the Africander Corps under Commandant Van Rensberg, to a ridge of hills on our left rear, in order to burn some *kraals* which could be seen with the glasses in that direction.

We were just getting ready to start, when shots were heard straight ahead of us down the Insiza valley; and as the firing, though never very heavy, was kept up until our horses were all saddled up, Van Rensberg and myself asked permission to take our men in the direction of the firing, as we knew that it meant that Captains Grey and Van Niekerk were engaged with a party of Matabele, and we thought that we might be able to render them some assistance.

Colonel Napier at once granted us permission to do as we wished; so we lost no time in making a move, and before we had ridden much more than a mile heard two shots at no great distance on our left front. We immediately turned in that direction, and after having crossed a small stream, again heard two more shots which sounded quite close, in fact, only just beyond a ridge of low stony hills on our left. On hearing these shots we rode to the crest of the ridge as quickly as possible, and then saw a broad open valley beyond us, in the centre of which stood a good-sized native *kraal*. We however could see nothing, either of our friends or our enemies, nor did we hear any further shots.

We therefore crossed the ridge, and a deep river-bed beyond it, and rode towards the *kraal*, with the intention of burning it. Before reaching it, however, we caught sight of a few natives running through some corn stubble, and galloping after them found them to be a young woman and three little girls. These were taken prisoners and sent back to camp, as it was thought that Colonel Napier might be able to obtain some information from them regarding the whereabouts of any *impis* that might be about.

Just then a man carrying a shield and *assegais* was seen running to our right. He was soon caught and shot by some of the Africanders, just as he threw himself under a bush, where he then lay on his face, dead. "Pull him out that I may look on the murderer's face," I said in Dutch to the men, which they did, revealing the features of a middle-aged evil-looking *kaffir*, whom, however, I did not remember to have ever seen before.

After killing this man we rode back towards the *kraal*, but before reaching it, made out a number of Matabele standing on the slope of a hill overlooking a deep river-bed, about a mile distant. On looking at these natives through the glasses, I could see that they were all men, many carrying shields, and as there were too many of them to make it possible to suppose that they all belonged to the *kraal* near which we were standing, I surmised that they probably belonged to the *impi* with which Captains Grey and Van Niekerk had been engaged.

Not knowing their numbers, and recognising the impossibility of getting at them in the hills with mounted men, Van Rensberg and myself judged it advisable to send back to the *laager* for a reinforcement of men on foot. A man was therefore at once despatched with a verbal message to Colonel Napier, and whilst waiting for his return we took up our position on the crest of the rise we had previously crossed, in order both to guard against a surprise and keep a watch on the enemy. These latter gradually retired round the shoulder of the hill and disappeared from view.

From where we had taken up our position we could see the *laager*, which was little more than a mile distant, and the reinforcement of footmen we had asked for had already left it, when a heavy fusillade broke out which sounded amongst the hills to our left front. Immediately after this heavy firing commenced, large numbers of Matabele, who up to that moment had been hidden in the river-bed below the hill on which we had seen the others standing, suddenly showed themselves, and streamed out across a cornfield with the evident intention of taking part in the fight which it seemed was going on between the Scouts and Africanders under Captains Grey and Van Niekerk and another body of Matabele.

Our party consisted of only twenty-two men all told, and it was rather difficult to know what was the best course for us to pursue; but we had just decided to go on and try and reach our friends without waiting for the reinforcements, when the heavy firing ceased, being succeeded by scattered shots, which showed that the fight was moving more and more to the right. The Matabele whom we had seen leaving the shelter of the river-bed must also have recognised this fact, as they soon returned, marching in lines across the cornfield where we had first seen them, and again taking up their old position.

Shortly after this Captain Windley and Lieutenant Frost came up with thirty Colonial Boys, and Captain Taylor and Lieutenant Jackson also brought a contingent of Friendly Matabele; but as but few of these latter were armed with rifles, they could not be expected to be very useful in attacking a position, though no doubt they would have done excellent service in following up a defeated foe. Mr. Cecil Rhodes, Sir Charles Metcalfe, Mr. Weston Jarvis, and Lieutenant Howard also came up with the Colonial Boys.

On their arrival we at once proceeded as quickly as possible towards the point in the hills from which the heavy firing had seemed to come, and after having advanced for about a mile and a half through thick thorn bush we found ourselves in a valley bounded on one side by the main range of hills, and on the other by a single hill very thickly wooded at the crest. At this point several natives were seen on the hills above us to the left, and a few shots were fired at them, which they returned, whilst at the same time some shots were also fired at us from the crest of the rise to our right.

I therefore ordered the Colonial Boys to charge up the hill and take it, which they at once did, led by their officers and Lieutenant Howard; the few natives who had been firing from the summit at once giving up their position, and running down into the thick bush on the farther side, several of them leaving blankets and other goods behind them, whilst in one case a handkerchief had been abandoned, which was found to contain about twenty Martini-Henry cartridges. After we had taken possession of the hill, a few odd Matabele fired a shot or two at us from the valley below and from the hills above, but their fire was soon silenced by the heavy fusillade kept up by the Colonial Boys.

From the position we had taken we commanded a good view over the country to our front and right front, but we could see nothing of the mounted men under Captains Grey and Van Niekerk, and therefore judged that they had found it necessary to retreat from the Matabele by a circuitous route to the *laager*; and we soon saw that it would be expedient for us to do the same, as we could see a large number of rebels on a hill about 1000 yards to our right, amongst them being a man on horseback, and knew that besides those actually in sight there were many others in the riverbed under the hill, as well as the *impi* which had been engaged with the Scouts and Africanders, which we afterwards discovered was lying in a deep river-bed hidden from view only a short distance ahead of the hill on which we were standing.

In the valley beyond this river-bed were two small herds of cattle in a cornfield, but this seemed such a very obvious bait to entice us onwards that Van Rensberg and myself at once saw the advisability of getting back to the more open country beyond the thick thorn bush through which we had come as quickly as possible, in order not to allow ourselves to be outflanked by the *impi* to our right, which had now disappeared in the bush behind the hill on which we had seen it.

Had we crossed the river-bed in front of us and endeavoured to capture the cattle, we should have been completely cut off from the *laager* by two separate *impis*, which our small force would have been altogether inadequate to cope with. By keeping well to the right, however, on our return to the open country we avoided coming in contact with the enemy in the bush, and saw nothing more of them.

Chapter 24

A Scene of Desolation

On reaching the *laager*, Van Rensberg and myself, backed by Mr. Cecil Rhodes, were very anxious to have the base camp moved at once to the *kraal* near to which we had captured the woman in the early morning, and then at once attack the *impis* we had seen that same afternoon with as large a force as could be spared from the *laager*. However, as Captains Grey and Van Niekerk had then not yet returned, Colonel Napier thought it would be better to move the *laager* round the hills to the vicinity of the Insiza River and attack the rebels from that side on the following day.

This plan was at once acted upon, and the Scouts and Africanders turning up just as we had inspanned, we moved round the broken country in which the Matabele had taken up their positions, and camped in open ground beyond it, on a small stream running into the Insiza River.

Early the following morning we moved to the bank of the river itself, just opposite the spot where a Dutchman named Fourie had been building a house for a Mr. Ross, whose temporary residence whilst the house was being built could be seen still standing on a rise some mile and a half farther down the river.

At the latter end of March Mr. Fourie had been living here with his wife and six children, whilst Mr. and Mrs. Ross with an adopted daughter named Agnes Kirk were occupying temporary dwellings some little distance away from them. These eleven people—two men and nine women and children—were all murdered on the outbreak of the rebellion, Miss Johanna Ross being the only survivor of her family, and owing her escape to the fact that at the time the murders were committed she was on a visit to friends living near the main road, who, having received warning of the rising, took her with them to Mr. Stewart's store at the Tekwe River, where they were relieved by Captain Grey and his men on Thursday, 26th March.

With others I went down to the scene of the massacre of the Fourie family early in the morning and found the remains of four people—a woman and three children, the body of Mr. Fourie and those of three of the children being missing. The murders had evidently been committed with *knobkerries* and axes, as the skulls of all these poor people had been very much shattered. The remains had been much pulled about by dogs or jackals, but the long fair hair of the young Dutch girls was still intact, and it is needless to say that these bloodstained tresses awoke the most bitter wrath in the hearts of all who looked upon them, Englishmen and Dutchmen alike vowing a pitiless vengeance against the whole Matabele race.

At about ten o'clock a force of about 300 men under Captain Grey was despatched to the scene of yesterday's fighting, Colonel Napier and staff taking up a position with a seven-pounder gun on the top of a hill which commanded the valley in which we had seen the two small herds of cattle on the preceding day. I was placed in charge of the infantry division, which, spread out in skirmishing order, formed the centre of the line of attack.

After what had been seen that morning of the ghastly remains of the Fourie family, everyone was most eager to come to close quarters with the *kaffirs*, but we were not able to do so, as, although we found the *scherms* where they had slept, with the fires still burning in them, the *impis* had left apparently at daylight in the morning, and it was impossible to tell in which direction they had gone, as their camp was surrounded by rough stony hills, on which their footsteps had left no trace.

As the number of their *scherms* showed that the rebels must have been at least a thousand strong, I don't quite know why they did not wait for us and have another day's fighting, the more especially as they had been successful in repulsing about one hundred mounted men of the Scouts and Africanders on the previous day. I am half inclined to think that several rocket signals sent up from our *laager* during the early part of the preceding night, to notify our whereabouts to Colonel Spreckley, may have had something to do with their unexpected retreat, or possibly a peep at our *laager* at daylight may have given them an exaggerated idea of our numbers. At any rate they were gone, and the blow which might have been struck at them on the afternoon of the day before was now not struck at all.

On the site of the engagement of the previous morning between Grey's Scouts and the Africanders and the one section of the Matabele, we found the body of Parker, absolutely stripped of clothing, even to the socks, and riddled with *assegai* stabs inflicted after death. The corpse was carried back to camp, together with that of Rothman, which latter, as it had been carried to some distance from the scene of the fight, had not been found and mutilated by the *kaffirs*. The Matabele must have removed their dead, as none were lying on the hill-side below Parker's corpse, where many had been seen to fall. However, in a small *kraal* situated just under the hills and within a mile of the scene of the fight, we found a *kaffir* lying stretched out on his back close to the door of a hut, who could not long have been dead, as his body was still warm, and his limbs quite limp.

He had evidently been wounded during the fight, the bullet having passed through both thighs, and broken the right femur. Then I suppose he had been carried or had crawled to the village where we found him lying, and a cord tightly twisted round his neck showed that he had been strangled shortly before our arrival on the scene. Whether he had thus compassed his own death on hearing or being informed of our approach, or whether he had been strangled by a friend to prevent his falling into the hands of the white men, I cannot say, but as, besides having been strangled, he had a fresh *assegai*-wound in the right side, I fancy that he had been killed by his friends, who had fled at our approach and were unable to carry the wounded man with them.

Besides this man, another was found in a dying condition—a young fellow of two or three and twenty who must have been some one of importance, as his friends had made a stretcher of oxhide lashed to poles, on which to carry him. They seem to have been surprised in the act of carrying him away, as the stretcher was first found, and then the wounded man was seen crawling away at a little distance, but he was nearly spent, having been shot right through the chest, and died soon afterwards. His shield and *assegais*, and many little personal belongings, were found tied on to the stretcher.

After having burnt a few *kraals* and picked up a flock of sheep and goats and a stray cow or two, we returned to *laager* very much disappointed that we had had a ten-mile walk for nothing, so far as meeting with the rebels was concerned. The Hon. Tatton Egerton (M.P. for Knutsford) accompanied us on this outing, walking and shouldering a rifle with the rest of us, and unless I am very much mistaken no one was more eager to let off his piece at a *kaffir* than was he. In the afternoon a military funeral was accorded to the bodies of Parker and Rothman, and also to the poor scattered remains of the Fourie family, which having been carefully collected were all buried in one grave dug close alongside that in which the two dead troopers had been placed. The funeral service was read by the Rev. Douglas Pelly, who was attached to the Salisbury contingent.

After the service was over I took a few men of the Africander Corps, and some friendly Matabele with a stretcher, and went off to collect the remains of the Ross family. These we found had been scattered and dragged about in every direction by dogs or wild animals. We could find no trace of Mr. Ross, and it is quite possible that he had been murdered at some distance from his homestead. The broken skull of a young woman which we found close to the door of one of the huts must have been that of Miss Agnes Kirk, but of old Mrs. Ross all we found by which to identify her was a mass of long grey hair, the skull having disappeared. Besides these sad relics we also found the remains of three children, the one a boy by his clothes, and the other two, little girls, their fair hair being still plaited into several short plaits in the Boer style. These three poor children must have been members of the Fourie family who had probably been visiting the Rosses on the day when the murders were committed.

Thus, of the eleven people murdered here some remains of all were found, except of Mr. Fourie and Mr. Ross, and these being the only men were very likely led away on some pretext, such as looking at cattle, and murdered at a distance from their dwellings where there was no chance of their getting hold of rifles or revolvers. Then, the men being disposed of, the noble savages came down fearlessly to the homesteads and smashed in the heads of the women and children comfortably and at their leisure.

On Sunday, 24th May—the Queen's Birthday—we continued our march down the Insiza valley, burning a large number of *kraals* as we advanced. All these *kraals* had only just been deserted by their owners, and they were all full of grain, while, in addition, in every one were found articles of some kind or another which had been taken from the homesteads of white men. All the grain that could not be carried with us was destroyed as far as possible. In many of the *kraals* were found large accumulations of dried meat, and many dried skins of bullocks, cows and calves, proving that the *rinderpest* had been brought into this district by the natives since the outbreak of the rebellion, and had been playing havoc amongst their cattle.

As we advanced, burning *kraal* after *kraal*, on the northern slope of the range which runs to the south of and parallel to the course of the Insiza River, column after column of smoke continually ascending into the clear sky from the southern side of the hills let us know that Colonel Spreckley's column was devastating the murderers' country on his line of march as effectually as we were doing on ours.

On the following day we still pursued our way unopposed down the Insiza valley, burning *kraal* after *kraal*, but never seeing a sign of the native inhabitants, who had evidently received timely notice of our approach and fled into the hills. On the morning of Wednesday, 27th May, we reached the Belingwe road at about nine o'clock, and were soon joined by Colonel Spreckley's column which had been waiting for us a little farther down the road. Colonel Spreckley's force had had no general engagement with the enemy, but his scouts had captured about seven hundred head of cattle and twenty-three donkeys. They had also found the remains of several murdered Europeans, amongst whom the bodies of a miner named Gracey and those of Dr. and Mrs. Langford and a Mr. Lemon were recognised. Mr. Gracey's body lay just outside his hut, but he had evidently been killed when lying on his bed inside, as a blanket still lying there was soaked through and through with blood.

The case of Dr. and Mrs. Langford is one of the saddest of the many sad episodes of the late native insurrection in Matabeleland. They had been married but a short time, and had only left the old country three months before the rebellion broke out. Unfortunately fate ordained that they should reach Bulawayo, and leave it in order to take up their residence in the Insiza district, just before the outbreak. Thus they were suddenly surprised by a party of murderous savages when travelling in their waggon. Mr. Lemon was with them, and his body was found lying close to that of Dr. Langford; but poor Mrs. Langford's corpse was discovered some two miles away under the bank of a stream flowing a few hundred yards below Mr. Rixon's farmstead.

It looked as if when first attacked the two men had held the murderers at bay, and given Mrs. Langford time to run on to Mr. Rixon's house in the hope of obtaining assistance. But when she reached the homestead she found it unoccupied, Mr. Rixon having left the day before. The poor woman then probably waited at the house for the husband and friend that never came, and then knowing that they must have been killed took refuge under the bank of the river which ran below the house. Here she seems to have lain hidden for some days at least, as she had made a sort of bed of dry grass to lie on under the bank, and as a pie-dish was found beside her body, she probably visited the house at nights to get food of some sort. The agony of mind this poor young woman must have suffered, one shudders to think of. But at last the *kaffirs* found her, and then, poor soul, her troubles were nearly at an end, for they lost no time in killing her. They appear to have stoned her to death, as her skull was terribly shattered and some large round stones taken from the river-bed were lying beside her corpse. None of her clothes had been removed, and two rings were still on her finger, on the inner side of one of which were engraved the words "Sunny Curls, *Mizpah*."

On the afternoon of the day on which the columns rejoined, the Insiza River was recrossed by the ford on the main road leading from Belingwe to Bulawayo, and on the following day, 27th May, the Salisbury contingent, reinforced by sixty men of Gifford's Horse, left the Bulawayo column, and went off southwards with the intention of visiting the Filibusi district, where it was thought that an *impi* might be met with, and thence making their way to Bulawayo by the road which passes Edkins' store, where it may be remembered a number of white men were murdered at the first outbreak of the insurrection. As soon as the flying column under Colonel Beal had left us, Colonel Napier gave the word to inspan, and an hour later the remainder of the troops under his command were on their way back to the capital of Matabeleland, which was finally reached after an uneventful journey on Sunday, 31st May.

As on the road home the column passed near the northern boundary of my Company's property of Essexvale, I asked and obtained leave from Colonel Napier to pay a visit in company with Mr. Blöcker to the homestead where I had been living in the midst of an apparently happy and contented native population at the outbreak of the insurrection. Leaving the camp at daylight, just as the mules were being inspanned for the morning's trek, we reached the scene of our agricultural labours after a two hours' ride, only to find that the house was absolutely gone, literally burnt to ashes, there being nothing left to mark the spot on which our pretty cottage had once stood but the stone pillars and solid iron shoes on which it had rested. The roof of the stable had been burnt too, as well as all the outhouses, and a waggon, under which last wood must have been piled in order to set it alight. The only building which had not been destroyed was the kitchen, which, having been built very solidly of stone with an iron roof, was practically fireproof.

The mowing machine and rake had not been touched, nor had the ploughs been interfered with. In the vegetable garden we found any amount of cabbages, cauliflowers, onions, carrots, parsnips, beetroot, tomatoes, etc., which had ripened since the natives had left, and we loaded up our horses with as much as they could carry. The potatoes had all been dug up by some animals, probably porcupines. We visited some of the native villages close round the homestead, but found them entirely empty, having been probably deserted since the time when the Matabele burnt my house down. After having off-saddled our horses for a short time, we rode back with our load of vegetables to the column, which we found *laagered* up some six miles farther along the road than where we had left it in the morning.

CHAPTER 25

A Large Impi Reported Camped on the Umguza

Shortly after the return of Colonel Napier's column from the Insiza district, Major-General Sir Frederick Carrington reached Bulawayo with his very able and carefully-chosen staff, and at once took over the command of all the forces in Matabeleland. And here I ought perhaps to close my narrative, which I only intend to be a history of the efforts made by the colonists themselves to suppress the native insurrection, before the arrival in Matabeleland of the relief forces sent up to their assistance. However, at the risk of wearying my readers, I will ask them to have patience yet a little longer until I bring my story up to the date of the disbandment of the Bulawayo Field Force.

Some time before the return of Colonel Napier's column, the force raised by Colonel Plumer (of the York and Lancaster Regiment) for the relief of the colonists in Matabeleland had reached Bulawayo, and had already had a successful engagement with the rebels, whom he had dislodged from the positions they had taken up on the Umguza, some twelve miles from Bulawayo, to which they had retired after having been driven from the immediate vicinity of the town by the sortie under Captain Macfarlane on 25th April.

As a detachment of the Bulawayo Field Force and some of Colenbrander's colonial natives took part in this expedition, I will, before proceeding further, give a short account of what took place. Acting under instructions from headquarters, Captain Knapp of the Bulawayo Field Force left Bulawayo at 10 p.m. on the night of 24th May in command of a detachment of forty men of Gifford's Horse, with orders to report himself to Major Watts at Government House. On his arrival there the latter officer was found to be in readiness to move with the men under his command, and at about 11.30 p.m. the whole force marched in a north-westerly direction, holding a course across country between the Umguza and Khami Rivers, whilst at the same time Colonel Plumer moved out of Bulawayo with another column, taking a line parallel to the course followed by Major Watts. During this night march Captain Knapp was in command of the advance, himself leading the one detachment of Gifford's Horse on the right front of the column, whilst Lieutenant Warwick led the other half on the left. Colenbrander's boys under Lieutenant Mullins were placed in the centre of the advanced line.

At about 2.30 a.m. Captain Knapp came suddenly in contact with the enemy's outposts, who immediately opened fire on his party in the darkness. Captain Knapp at once dismounted his men and kept the rebels from charging by pouring volleys into the thickets where they were concealed. He was soon joined by Lieutenant Warwick and the Colonial Boys under Lieutenant Mullins, but it was not until Major Watts had come up with the main body and the Maxim had been brought into action that the enemy's fire was completely silenced.

When the firing commenced, Colonel Plumer and his men were not very far off on the left flank, and their course was at once directed towards the spot where the engagement appeared to be proceeding. Thus the two columns joined forces soon after the enemy had retired, when a square was formed, and a good watch kept during the remaining hours of darkness. However, no further attack was made.

During the first attack, Mr. Hamilton, who was acting as galloper to Captain Knapp, was shot through both legs, whilst one of the Colonial Boys was badly wounded and several horses killed.

At daylight the following morning Captain Knapp and Captain Coope were sent out to look for the enemy, and the latter officer coming across a small party of them, he at once attacked with the force under his command, consisting of twenty white men and some of Radikladi's Bamangwato natives, and drove the rebels back on their main body, which was found to be in a strong position amongst some thickly-wooded ridges about two miles to the west of Colonel Plumer's camp.

At about half-past seven or eight o'clock the whole column was moved forwards to attack them, Captain Coope's Scouts being in advance on the right, whilst Captain Knapp with the troopers of Gilford's Horse occupied a similar position on the left. These two officers, after galloping to the foot of the first ridge occupied by the rebels, there dismounted their men, and then in the face of a heavy fire, led them on foot most gallantly against the hidden enemy, whom they succeeded in driving from their most advanced position.

In this attack two of Captain Knapp's men were severely wounded, Sergeant Peacock being shot in the stomach, whilst Trooper Slowey had his right leg so badly shattered that amputation of the limb was found necessary.

The enemy's first line of defence having been taken in this brilliant manner by the advance guard, the whole column under Colonel Plumer then came into action, and the rebels were driven from three densely-wooded ridges successively into the open valley of the Umguza, and were then pursued for a distance of three miles. When the pursuit was over, the horses were off-saddled on the bank of the Umguza and allowed to rest until 2 p.m., at which hour a start was made for Mr. Crewe's farm of Redbank on the Khami River, some sixteen miles from Bulawayo, where it was believed that a large *impi* was camped in a very strong position. Captain Knapp now took charge of the right-hand section of the advance guard, and Captain Coope with his Scouts was placed on the left.

After having proceeded for about two hours, the latter officer sent a messenger to Captain Knapp to inform him that the enemy were in force on his left. They then joined forces and attacked the *kaffirs*, who were in a strong position on a wooded hill, to reach which two deep gullies had to be crossed under a very heavy fire. Here one of Coope's Scouts was shot dead (Trooper Hays), whilst Mr. Gordon Forbes, who had accompanied the expedition as a volunteer, had a very narrow escape. He had crossed a dry gully with four of Captain Coope's Scouts, when *kaffirs* showed themselves on either side at a distance of only thirty yards and fired on the white men.

Mr. Gordon Forbes' horse was shot in two places, and, falling with him, pinned him to the ground, the men who were with him retreating under the heavy fire, and had not some more of Coope's Scouts come up and pulled him out he would undoubtedly have been killed. At this time, too, one of Radikladi's boys was wounded in the face and another horse killed. The main column then coming up, the enemy were driven from their position and pursued through the bush till dusk, Colonel Plumer taking up his quarters for the night in the camp on the top of the hill from which the rebels had been driven.

On the following day scouts were sent out to endeavour to discover the position of the enemy, but no trace of them could be found, so, as the horses were very much knocked up, a return to Bulawayo was decided upon. During these skirmishes Captain Knapp lost five horses, in addition to the two men of his troop who were badly wounded, whilst Captain Coope also had several horses killed. These two officers and their men, being always in advance of the main column, naturally got the lion's share of the fighting. They were both thanked for the gallant way in which they had led their men by their commanding officer, Colonel Plumer, who also complimented Mr. Maurice Gifford on the excellent service rendered by the troop of horse which bore his name.

During the first week in June, General Carrington determined to send out three patrols simultaneously with the object of thoroughly clearing the country of rebels to the west, north, and north-east of Bulawayo, before making an attack with the combined forces on the *impis* of Babian, Umlugulu, and Sikombo, who, it was known, had taken up strong positions in the Matopo Hills, from which they could only be driven with great difficulty and at the expense of a heavy loss of life on the side of the attacking party. Thus, towards the end of the week Colonel Plumer proceeded with a force of some 600 men to the Khami River, the course of which stream it was his intention to follow to its junction with the Gwai, whilst on Friday, 5th June, Captain Macfarlane got off with 300 mounted white men and 100 Colonial Boys for the Umguza, which he was determined to thoroughly clear of rebels along its whole course. Mr. Cecil Rhodes, Sir Charles Metcalfe, and Mr. Weston Jarvis accompanied the latter force.

Both these patrols were unsuccessful in coming up with any large body of the rebels, who dispersed and fled as the white men advanced. Thus, although some *kraals* were burnt and a good deal of grain taken and destroyed, no decisive engagement took place, and no heavy blow could be dealt at the ever-vanishing foe. Colonel Plumer's column got back to their quarters on the Khami River on Wednesday, 24th June, whilst Captain Macfarlane's men did not return to Bulawayo until Friday, 3rd July.

Before these patrols left, Colonel Beal, who it may be remembered had parted company with Colonel Napier at the Insiza River, reached Bulawayo and formed a *laager* about two miles out of town to the right of the main road to Salisbury. It had been arranged that on the morning after Captain Macfarlane got away with his men to the lower Umguza, another patrol was to leave town under the command of Colonel Spreckley for the purpose of establishing forts at Shiloh and

Inyati, and to this patrol I had been attached with a few of my men, the majority of my troop being stationed at Fort Marquand.

Every preparation had been made for an early start on the Saturday morning, when late on Friday evening a report came in that there was a large *impi* camped on the Umguza, at the ford on the main road to Salisbury. It appeared that Sir Charles Metcalfe and the American Scout Burnham, who had been riding out to Colonel Beal's camp, having missed their way in the dark, had ridden down the main road to the Umguza, and had there seen a line of camp-fires, extending over half a mile of ground, along the wooded ridge beyond the river, which could betoken nothing else but that a Matabele *impi* had taken up its position there.

This news that a large *impi* was within six miles of the town having been confirmed by scouts sent out later on during the Friday night, Colonel Spreckley received orders to make an attack upon it on the following morning with all the mounted men he could muster in town, supplemented by the contingent under Colonel Beal. By nine o'clock a force of some 200 mounted men with three guns was ready, and forthwith set out for the Umguza. This force was composed of the Scouts under Captain Grey, a large contingent of Africanders under Captain Van Niekerk, thirty men under Captain Brand, and fifteen of my own troop which was all for which horses could be found.

On reaching the rising ground about a mile on this side of the Umguza, we found the Salisbury men drawn up all ready waiting for us, and they informed us that they had been watching the Matabele for some time past, and had seen them leave the camps in which they had slept in a very leisurely way and take up their positions in the open bush behind, where they were waiting for us.

They had not to wait long. The Africanders under Captain Van Niekerk were ordered to cross the river about half a mile below the ford, which they did at the same time that the remainder of Colonel Spreckley's force and the mounted men of the Salisbury contingent crossed by the main road, the latter then deploying to the left.

At this time we were hidden from the *kaffirs* by the slope of rising ground behind which they had retreated, but when this was crested they were seen in the bush little more than a hundred yards in front of the foremost horsemen. The order was at once given to charge, on which a whirlwind of horsemen bore down on them, Grey's Scouts and Brand's men being in the centre, the Africanders on the left, and the Salisbury men on the right.

On this occasion the *kaffirs* must have been quite 1000 strong, spread out in skirmishing order through the open bush in face of the long line of advancing horsemen, yet they never stood for a moment, but were seized with a panic just as the smaller number of their compatriots had been when charged at Thaba Induna, as I have already related. In the same way as these latter, they fired a hurried ill-aimed volley and then turned and ran. In the chase which followed, a large number of them were shot down, and the pursuit was only abandoned when the fleetest-footed amongst them had gained the shelter of the belt of thick bush which runs down from the western side of Thaba Induna towards the Umguza.

I am of opinion myself that the Matabele lost more heavily on this occasion than at any other fight during the campaign, for the very reason that it was not a fight but only a pursuit in which the natives were killed as fast as they were overtaken. Just as on the day at Thaba Induna, so on this occasion the panic-stricken savages accepted death when the horsemen came up with them without making any attempt at resistance, except in a few instances. One man turned on Trooper Davey of Grey's Scouts and shot him through the thigh with an old musket at close quarters, the large bullet smashing the thigh-bone and necessitating the amputation of the limb; whilst another, leaping out of a bush, rushed on to Trooper Hamilton of the Salisbury contingent and stabbed him in the right side, the *assegai* entering his liver.

Hamilton wrenched the *assegai* out of his assailant's hand and then shot him. My old friend, Mr. F. C. Farley of Grey's Scouts and a well-known figure in the Bulawayo of today, as he was also in the native *kraal* of Lo Bengula many years ago, had too a very narrow escape. He had dismounted to shoot a *kaffir* running a short distance in front of him, when the latter turned and rushed at him shaking his shield in front of him. Farley luckily carried a double-barrelled rifle, for he missed the *kaffir* with the first shot, and only brought him down with the second barrel when his assailant was so near him that his *assegai* struck the ground close to his feet. Two other men were slightly wounded, but these were the only casualties on our side, whilst the loss sustained by the Matabele was very heavy, not only in number, but in the rank of the men who were killed, for it was naturally the young and nimble who were able to make good their escape, whilst the greater part of the older men were overtaken and slain. Some of the latter, however, outlived this fatal day by hiding themselves in the midst of thick bushes.

That this *impi* should have dared to come close up to Bulawayo and take up its quarters at a point on the Umguza where the bush was not nearly so thick as it is farther down the river, at the point where several large *impis* had already tried conclusions and failed to hold their own against the white men, certainly took everyone by surprise; but since then several hundred men of this *impi* have surrendered to Mr. W. Fynn, and we now know that when they approached Bulawayo they did so under the superstitious belief that their enemies would be delivered into their hands by the *Umlimo*, and that they would be able to kill them all without any loss to themselves,

The story is as follows: Since the outbreak of the rebellion there has appeared amongst that section of the insurgents to which the defeated *impi* belonged a man who professes himself to be the prophet and mouthpiece of the "*Umlimo*" or invisible spirit. This man, it is said, possesses the power of throwing himself into an ecstatic condition, under the influence of which he swallows stones, rolls on the ground, dances on hot ashes, puts burning coals into his mouth, and goes through many other strange performances. He is known to the Matabele by the name of "*Si ginya amachi*," "He who swallows stones," and his utterances have come to be implicitly believed in, insomuch that when he called for an *impi* to go and destroy all the white men in Bulawayo, he had no difficulty in getting a number of picked men from seven different regiments to obey his behests.

His orders were that the men composing this *impi* should take up their quarters where we found them on the Salisbury road, and there wait for the white men to attack them. They were on no account to endeavour to prevent their enemies from crossing the Umguza, but were to offer them every encouragement to do so, "for," said the stone-swallower, "once they have crossed to the east of the river the *Umlimo* will strike them all blind, and you will then be able to kill them without trouble, and then go on and murder all the women and children in Bulawayo."

As the white men were not struck blind, whilst on the other hand a large number of the prophet's dupes lost their lives through their superstitious belief in his supernatural gifts, it would be interesting to know how "*Si ginya amachi*" has accounted to the survivors for his most dismal failure; for the fact that he has not yet" been put to death seems to show that he has been able to offer some excuse which has saved his life up to the present time.

It is this episode of the killing of a large number of Matabele at the

Umguza by the colonists *whom they had come to kill,* of which Mr. Labouchere has made so much capital lately, and which has enabled him to indulge in so many sneers against the white settlers in Rhodesia; his stock phrase being "that the natives are being shot down like game at a *battue,* with apparently as little danger to the shooters as to those killing hares and rabbits."

Now no one knows better than Mr. Labouchere himself the utter recklessness of such a statement if applied to the whole campaign, since it is evident that he is ever on the watch for every scrap of news emanating from Rhodesia, in the charitable hope of picking up something discreditable to the settlers or to the government of the Chartered Company, and he must therefore be well aware that the number of white men who have been killed and wounded in the various engagements and skirmishes that have lately taken place in Matabeleland is very considerable.

But should anyone who does me the honour to read my story be either a constant or a fitful reader of the pages of *Truth,* and be inclined to believe that the editor of that journal is correct in his oft-repeated assertion that the white men in Matabeleland have suffered an insignificant loss in their encounters with the natives during the present rebellion, I would ask such an one to turn to the Appendix at the end of this book, and look over the lists which I have there given both of the settlers who were murdered on the first outbreak of the rebellion, and also of those who have since been killed and wounded in battle. These lists, if compared with Mr. Labouchere's statements, will, I think, prove to the most prejudiced that Truth—the everlasting Truth which we are told is great and will prevail—is one thing, whilst Mr. Labouchere's *Truth,* sold at all the bookstalls at 6d. a copy, is quite another.

Chapter 26

The Bulawayo Field Force Disbanded

Owing to the delay caused by the attack on and pursuit of the *impi* from the Umguza, as I have just narrated, Colonel Spreckley's patrol did not leave Bulawayo for Shiloh until the afternoon of the following day, Sunday, 7th June. This patrol comprised about 330 white men, about half of whom were mounted, 100 Colonial Boys, and 100 Friendly Matabele—over 500 men altogether.

As we did not proceed along the main road, but first took a branch track to the old Imbezu *kraal*, and then followed the course of the Kotki River until we struck the main road, we did not reach the site of the old police camp near Shiloh mission station until Thursday, 11th June. Up to this time we had not seen a single native, whilst all the *kraals* we passed had been long deserted and all stores of grain removed, so that our horses and mules, having to depend entirely on the dry scanty grass for their sustenance, lost condition rapidly.

One day we outspanned close to a miner's camp, which was situated on a rise above the Kotki River, and as I was field officer for the day and had to post the videttes, I placed two of them on the site of the mining camp. Here we found the dead bodies of three natives, who proved to be Zambesi boys who had been working at the mine at the time when the rebellion broke out. On inquiry I found that this camp had belonged to an American miner named Jack Stuart—a lieutenant in Grey's Scouts—from whom I learned, that on hearing rumours towards the end of March that a native rising was imminent, he and his partner had gone in to Bulawayo to ascertain if there was any truth in the report. Six Zambesi boys were left working in the shaft, which had been sunk on a reef just alongside of the camp, and two days later one of these boys came to town and reported that on the previous evening a party of Matabele had visited the mine, and forthwith proceeded to murder all the Zambesi boys they found there. He himself, he said, had managed to escape by running, but he thought that all his companions had been killed. A few days later, however, another of these boys turned up who had been very badly wounded and left for dead by the Matabele.

It appears that, on seeing two of his friends attacked, this boy had made a bolt for it, but was overtaken and knocked down by a heavy blow on the back of the head from a *knobkerrie*. He fell on his face stunned, and was then stabbed in the back with an *assegai*, the weapon being driven clean through him, and then twice nearly but not quite withdrawn from the wound, and again driven through him, so that, although there was only one wound on his back, there were three in front, where the point of the *assegai* had come through, just below his breast-bone, and his right lung must have been punctured in three different places. This boy would seem to have lain a day and a night, insensible, where he fell, but on regaining consciousness had found strength enough to walk to Bulawayo, some twenty miles distant from the mining camp where he had been knocked down, *assegaied*, and left for dead.

On his arrival in town he was at once taken to the hospital, and, owing to the kind nursing and skilful treatment which he received there, he in a few weeks' time completely recovered, and although he still bears the scars of the wounds which he received, his general health appears to be as good as ever it was.

On Friday, 12th June, the day after our arrival on the site of the old police camp, a fort was built, and here Native Commissioner Lanning was left in charge with a garrison of about seventy white men and twenty Friendly Matabele and a stock of provisions sufficient to last for two months.

On the following morning we struck across country towards the Queen's Mine, a property belonging to Willoughby's Consolidated Company. That night we slept on the way there, and the fresh tracks of *kaffirs* and cattle having been seen late in the afternoon, a patrol was sent after them very early the next morning, the column shortly afterwards getting under weigh and arriving at the mining camp at about eight o'clock.

Here it was found that although a good deal of property had been destroyed by the *kaffirs*, but little damage had been done to the machinery and pumping gear, the savages probably not having recognised its value nor been sufficiently energetic to give themselves the trouble of smashing it up. Another short trek in the afternoon brought us to the ford of the Impembisi River, on the main road between Bulawayo and the mission station of Inyati. Here the patrol which had left us in the early morning under Captain Gradwell rejoined us just at dusk, having been unsuccessful in coming up with any *kaffirs* or cattle, all of whom seemed to have gone down the Impembisi river.

As the mules and horses were now getting into very low condition, it was determined not to take the whole column on to Inyati, but only to send on the contingent who were to remain in garrison there under the command of Lieutenant Banks-Wright, together with another 100 men who were to return to the main column as soon as the fort was in a fair way towards completion. This force was accompanied by four waggons carrying provisions and other necessaries for the garrison of the fort, and the Rev. Mr. Rees also went with it, in order to bury the remains of the six white men who had been murdered near the police camp of Inyati on 27th March.

Five of these bodies were found lying on the roadside near together, about a mile on this side of the police camp, while the sixth was discovered near the camp itself. The corpses had been partially mummified by the dryness of the atmosphere, and were all quite recognisable. Mr. Graham, the native commissioner, and his four companions had evidently been attacked by a large force of *kaffirs* soon after they had left the police station, and were killed whilst defending the waggon on which they were travelling to Bulawayo. In addition to their bodies the remains of two Colonial Boys were also found who had been murdered at the same time as their white masters.

That Mr. Graham and his companions had made a good fight of it, and sold their lives dearly, was evident from the number of empty cartridge-cases which were found on the ground round their dead bodies, Lieutenant Howard having picked up and counted eighty-five. As, however, the Matabele had removed their dead, it is quite impossible to say what loss they had suffered. The murdered men were all buried with military honours in the cemetery near the old mission station by Mr. Rees.

This gentleman himself, with his wife and family, must have had a very narrow escape, as they only left the mission station on the 26th March, the day before Mr. Graham and his companions were attacked and killed; and they must too have only just passed through the Elibaini Hills on their way to Bulawayo before the rebels collected there. Both mission houses at Inyati were found to have been burnt down and destroyed, as well as the church, in which it was evident that large quantities of wood had been piled up in order to set light to the heavy beams supporting the roof. The natives had also taken the trouble to chop down fruit trees and ornamental shrubs growing round the mission houses, and had evidently done their best, not only to rid themselves of the presence of all white men in the country, but also to destroy as far as possible all traces of their ever having been there.

On Wednesday morning the men who had been sent to assist in building the fort at Inyati returned to the Impembisi, and in the afternoon the whole column moved some four miles up the river to Mr. Fynn's farm. On the morning of the same day Lieutenant Mullins— Mr. Colenbrander's brother-in-law—had been sent on to this point with some fifty Colonial Boys to look for grain, and had come across a considerable number of armed *kaffirs* in a very broken, densely-wooded piece of country, just to the east of the Impembisi River. As it was impossible for Lieutenant Mullins to tell the numbers of the rebels in the broken country, he retired with his Colonial Boys to the top of a single hill to the west of the river, and sent back to camp for reinforcements. Captain Grey was at once sent on with his Scouts, and the whole column followed more leisurely, arriving at Fynn's farm just before sundown.

Captain Grey had seen a considerable number of natives, evidently watching his men from the tops of different *kopjes*, but as the country they were in was altogether impracticable for horses, he was unable to attack them, and they on their side showed no disposition to come out of the hills. At a council of war that evening it was determined to endeavour to clear the hills in the morning with as large a force of footmen as could be spared from the *laager*; Grey's Scouts at the same time being sent round at the back of the hills in order to cut off any *kaffirs* who might be driven out of them into the level country beyond. The general impression in camp was that the *kaffirs* were in force, and that we should have all our work cut out to drive them out of their positions. And so we should have had, if they had only remained to dispute our advance.

However, leaving the *laager* on the following morning just as day was breaking, we entered the hills at sunrise, and went right through them without seeing a sign of the rebels, who we found had decamped during the night and fled to what they considered a more secure stronghold—to wit, the "*Intabas a Mambo*," a sort of miniature Matopos some twenty miles farther eastward.

To this fastness it was not possible for Colonel Spreckley to follow them, so, as we met no other natives during our farther progress up the river to Mr. Arthur Rhodes' homestead, nor on our return journey from there to Bulawayo, we had absolutely no fighting during the whole trip.

Curiously enough, the temporary huts in which Mr. Fynn had been living before the outbreak of the insurrection had not been burnt, and on going up to a *kraal* some few miles higher up the river, where had dwelt a native to whom he had entrusted some Merino sheep, pigs, and a number of very handsome black Spanish fowls, Mr. Fynn found the fowls and pigs still there and in very good condition, and on making a closer examination observed fresh *kaffir* footprints, and therefore came to the conclusion that the man he had left in charge of his live stock was still looking after it, retiring into the hills by day and feeding his master's pigs and fowls by night. Mr. Fynn therefore asked Colonel Spreckley to allow him to take two friends that evening, and return to the *kraal* in the hope of being able to intercept his servant, and bring him down to the camp.

The plan succeeded perfectly, for just after dusk the man came along the footpath leading from the river to the *kraal*, and was suddenly confronted by Mr. Fynn, who had been waiting for him concealed behind a bush. The *kaffir* was at first very much taken aback, but when he recognised his master, he burst out laughing and said: "Why, is it you, Willy? you've caught me now." This man was a native of Delagoa Bay, and being lame had been able to escape being forced into taking part in the rebellion, and ever since the outbreak had been able to surreptitiously look after a portion of his master's property, for though the Merino sheep had been driven off to the "*Intabas a Mambo*," the pigs and fowls had been left, and these the faithful servant had fed and watered regularly every night.

He was able to give us a great deal of useful information, and told us that the men who had been seen the day before amongst the hills on the other side of the Impembisi River were a portion of the *impi* which had suffered so heavily at the Umguza, on Saturday, 6th June. He informed us that they were thoroughly disheartened, and wished to surrender, but were afraid to do so, knowing that they had made the white men very angry by murdering their women and children. He gave the names of thirteen headmen of *kraals* who had been killed on that fatal day, all of whom had been personally known to Mr. Fynn, as they had been one and all living on Mr. Arthur Rhodes' block of farms before the rebellion broke out.

The next three days were spent in collecting grain, an immense amount being found stored in all the *kraals* on Mr. Arthur Rhodes' farms. In almost every *kraal* was found something or other which had been taken from his homestead, which had evidently been completely looted before it was burnt down. Several hundred head of cattle were also recovered which had been stolen from Mr. Rhodes, but the *rinderpest* was amongst them and they died by the score every day. As it was very important to get as much corn as possible to Bulawayo for the use of the horses and mules stabled there, and it could not be all carried in at once on the waggons at Colonel Spreckley's disposal, a large amount was stored in a *kraal* near Mr. Fynn's dwelling-house, and Captain Robinson with fifty men and some Friendly Matabele left in charge of it until it could be sent for.

When this matter had been arranged, the column moved up to Mr. Arthur Rhodes' desolated homestead, which was reached at mid-day on Sunday, 21st June, and leaving again the same evening arrived in Bulawayo two days later after an absence of seventeen days.

On our arrival in town we heard for the first time of the insurrection which had broken out in Mashunaland, and learned the sad news that many settlers had been murdered in the outlying districts of the country. Colonel Beal was at this time already on his way back to Salisbury with the entire force under his command, and two days after our return to Bulawayo sixty more mounted men of Grey's Scouts and Gifford's Horse, under the command of Captain the Hon. C. White, were despatched to the assistance of their fellow-colonists in Eastern Rhodesia.

When the secret history of the rebellion in Mashunaland comes to be known, I fancy it will be found that it was brought about by the leaders of the Matabele insurrection through the instrumentality of the *Umlimos* or prophets, who exist amongst all the tribes in Mashunaland, where they are known as "*Mondoros*," *i.e.* "Lions." In the district to the north-west of Salisbury there lives a prophetess known as "*Salugazana*," whose magical powers were apparently believed in by Lo Bengula, as he was in the habit of sending messengers to consult with her.

Now, we know that messages have been sent to this wise woman either by the leaders of the Matabele or the agents of one of the *Um-*

limos or priests during the present rebellion, and I think that she was in all probability informed that the white men had all been killed in Matabeleland, including the column under Colonel Beal, and asked to disseminate this news amongst all the members of the priestly families throughout the country, bidding them at the same time to call upon the people to destroy the few surviving white men still left alive in the eastern province of Rhodesia.

As for the rising in Mashunaland proving that the natives of that country have been very cruelly treated by the whites, as Mr. Labouchere has asserted, it really demonstrates nothing of the kind; it only shows that the Mashunas imagined that they would be able to possess themselves of a vast amount of valuable loot with little danger to themselves, and no fear of punishment. The kindness or otherwise of the government of the whites would not be likely to weigh with them one way or the other, given the belief in their own power to kill the whites and take possession of their property without fear of retribution.

That is the crux of the whole question; for no one who has lived long amongst the various peoples generically known as Mashunas, whose principal characteristics are avarice, cowardice, and a complete callousness to the sufferings of others, will be inclined to doubt that were they governed by an angel from heaven, they would infallibly kill that angel, if his wing feathers were of any value to them, provided that they believed at the same time that the crime might be committed with impunity.

Towards the end of June Captain Laing arrived in Bulawayo in command of the relief forces which had been sent to him from Tuli and Victoria, Lieutenant Stoddart being left in command of the *laager* at Belingwe. On his way to Bulawayo, Captain Laing had had several successful engagements with the tribes in rebellion living between Belingwe and Filibusi, who are all Mashunas, with a small number of Matabele living amongst them; these latter having been the ringleaders of the rebellion in this part of the country. Captain Laing received very valuable assistance from Matibi, a Mashuna chief living near the Bubyi River, who sent several hundred of his men to accompany him on his march to Bulawayo. These men did good service and fought well when supported by white men. They accompanied the column as far as the Umzingwani River, twenty-five miles from Bulawayo, returning home from this point loaded up with loot of all kinds which they had taken from their rebel countrymen.

Captain Tyrie Laing who was in command at Belingwe on the outbreak of the native insurrection.

Besides Matibi, it is worthy of remark that Chibi and Chilimanzi, the two most important chiefs in the district between Belingwe and Victoria, have both not only held aloof from the present rebellion, but have given active assistance to the whites since the outbreak of hostilities, whilst Gutu's people—the Zinjanja—have also remained loyal to the government.

I have now, I think, given a fairly comprehensive history of the late insurrection in Matabeleland up to the time when, relief forces having arrived in the country, it was deemed expedient to disband the volunteer troops which had been originally raised to suppress the rebellion, and I will therefore leave to abler and more accustomed pens than mine the task of describing all the subsequent incidents of a campaign which we will hope is now fast drawing to an end. I will only say that no one appreciates more than myself the excessive difficulties that have been encountered in dislodging the rebels from such fastnesses as the Intabas a Mambo and the Matopo Hills, or recognises more fully the brave work which has been done under the guidance of Major-General Sir Frederick Carrington, by Colonel Plumer, Major Baden Powell, and all the officers and men under their command.

The Bulawayo Field Force was not actually disbanded until Saturday, 4th July, upon which occasion the assembled troops were addressed by Lord Grey after they had been first inspected by Major-General Sir Frederick Carrington. The administrator concluded his address to the members of the force in the following words:—

> All of you have acquitted yourselves as brave men, and I would particularly commend the conduct of Colonel Napier, who throughout the campaign has performed his very arduous duties so satisfactorily. But mingled with our enjoyment there must be some pain in looking back upon many of the episodes of this rebellion. The Company has done its best to look after your comfort, but you have undergone notwithstanding some severe hardships, which, however, you have borne like men; and the only complaint I have heard is that you were not always able to go out against the enemy, but had to perform as well the hard and monotonous work of *laager* and fort duty. Many of you have a Matabele memento in the shape of a wound, the mark of which you will carry to your graves. Many too have lost friends; and possibly none of us realise the loss of life which has taken place both before and during hostilities; for

our losses have been heavy, and form a large percentage of the total number of people who were engaged in the exploitation of the country. I cannot refer to individual cases of bravery where all have done so well, but I would again especially mention Colonel Napier's services to the country. He has exhibited remarkable tact and judgment, and has freely given great assistance to the government.

I regret that he is today retiring from the service, but I hope that he will continue to give us the benefit of his experience. I do not like to mention any particular troop, as each has acted so creditably, but I would note the excellent services rendered by the Africander Corps in this war, as showing the whole world the complete brotherhood which exists between the two races of Dutchmen and Britons in Rhodesia. I trust that an Africander troop will again form part of the new force which is now being raised by the government. Information reached this country by last mail that Her Majesty has been pleased to allow a medal to be worn for the last Matabele war, and I shall represent strongly to Her Majesty that the same honour ought to be conferred on the members of the Bulawayo Field Force. You have as much right and title to the distinction as those who fought in the first war, and I hope there will be a sufficient number struck for both those who fought in the first war and those who have fought during the present rebellion. I thank you for your assistance in the past, and I hope you will remain in the country to witness the prosperity which is certain to come.

And now, Lord Grey's speech to the members of the Bulawayo Field Force having formed the closing scene in the history of the corps, whose deeds in the cause of civilisation, and for the preservation of British supremacy in Rhodesia, it has been my endeavour to describe in the foregoing pages, it only remains for me to bid *adieu* to my readers, and to hope that the intrinsic interest of the scenes I have attempted to describe in very plain and homely fashion may be sufficient to atone for the deficiencies which will doubtless be only too apparent in my literary style.

SUPPLEMENTARY CHAPTER

A Few Thoughts and Opinions Upon Matters Rhodesian and South African

No one, I think, who has carefully read the little history which I have just brought to a close, can fail to have been struck by the conspicuous part which has been played by the Dutch settlers in Matabeleland in the recent struggle for supremacy between the white invaders of that country and the native black races; and it will probably come as a surprise to many to find that the Boer element is so strong as it is in Rhodesia, for that country has always been considered more exclusively British as regards its white population than any other State in South Africa, not except Natal and the Eastern Province of the Cape Colony, both of which territories, though almost purely British in the large towns, yet possess a large Boer population in the farming districts, whose ancestors were living on the land before the arrival of the British colonists.

But, in the opening up and colonisation of Rhodesia by means of the pioneer expedition of the British South Africa Company, which took possession of Eastern Mashunaland in 1890, a new departure was made in South African history, for the British became the pioneers instead of the Dutch, and a British colony was established in the far interior of the country many hundred miles to the north of the most northerly Dutch state; and it is the fact that the occupation of Mashunaland in 1890 and the invasion and conquest of Matabeleland in 1893 were purely British enterprises, which has, I think, created the belief generally held in England that Rhodesia at the present day is a purely British colony.

Yet this is not the case, for within the British state there are two Boer colonies, the one of which has been established subsequent to the Matabele war in the country to the south of Fort Charter, whilst the other has occupied the hills and valleys of Gazaland since the latter part of 1891. Besides these agricultural colonies, where a number of contiguous farms are occupied by Boers who have settled on the land with their wives and families, there are many other Boer farmers scattered throughout Rhodesia, whilst up to the time when the *rinderpest* destroyed all their cattle, a large number of Dutchmen were constantly present in the country, earning their living with their waggons and oxen as carriers from one district to another.

When the rebellion broke out, Commandant Van Rensberg at once formed an Africander Corps, the great majority of whose members were Boers, although it numbered in its ranks a certain proportion of colonists of British blood, and it is a matter of history that these Dutchmen under Commandant Van Rensberg and Captains Van Niekerk and Pittendrigh have done splendid service during the recent insurrection in Matabeleland, and have fought side by side with Grey's Scouts and Gifford's Horse, and all the other troops of the Bulawayo Field Force, in a way which has won for them the admiration and respect of their brothers in arms and fellow-colonists of British blood; and that the mutual esteem and good fellowship engendered between the two races during the recent time of common peril may be fostered and maintained in the coming years ought not only to be the earnest desire of all thinking men, but should be also one of the main objects constantly kept in view by the English administrator of these territories.

Many years ago, at a time when the scheme for the colonisation of the high and healthy plateaus lying between the Limpopo and the Zambesi had not yet assumed definite shape in the fertile brain of Mr. Cecil Rhodes, I remember writing in the course of an article, published, I think, in the *Fortnightly Review*, that those territories were in my opinion the natural heritage of the British and Dutch colonists in the older states of South Africa. My forecast was true enough, for although in its first inception the colonisation of Rhodesia was a purely British enterprise, yet today, (at time of first publication), in less than six years from the date when the Union Jack was hoisted at Fort Salisbury and the country proclaimed to be a province of Britain, it already numbers amongst its inhabitants a very considerable number of Dutch Boers, who form an element of the population, which in

COMMANDANT VAN RENSBERG WHO RAISED THE
AFRICANDER CORPS OF THE BULAWAYO FIELD FORCE.

all South African history has been found indispensable for the gradual conversion of vast uncultured wastes into civilised states.

Now I might, I think, have gone further, and said that the whole of temperate South Africa (in which must be included the high plateaus lying between the Limpopo and the Zambesi) was the joint possession of the British and Dutch races; for in all the states of that country, the old and the new alike, we find the two races living side by side, whilst, curiously enough, in the British province of the Cape Colony the Dutch outnumber the British, and in the Boer State of the Transvaal the British outnumber the Dutch.

Throughout South Africa the Dutch live away from the towns on their farms, and, speaking generally, form the agricultural and pastoral population of the country. They are naturally a kindly, hospitable race; but as the inevitable result of their surroundings and the circumstances in which they have lived for generations, they are for the most part very poorly educated, and therefore ignorant, unprogressive and bigoted; whilst among the descendants of the "*voortrekkers*," who some forty years ago abandoned their farms in the Cape Colony and fled, with their wives and their children, their flocks and their herds, into the unknown interior beyond the great Orange River, in order to escape from what they considered the injustice of British rule, there exists an ingrained hatred and distrust, not of the individual Englishman, but of the government of the country under whose flag they believe their fathers suffered wrong, and it is this sentiment which at the present moment, unfortunately, is being used as a political lever, which threatens nothing but disaster to the whole of South Africa, by the anti-British, but non-Boer adventurers, who are fighting for their own hands in Pretoria.

The recent deplorable invasion of Transvaal territory by a British force in defiance of all international law, to accomplish I still fail to understand what, has naturally exasperated the Dutch of the Transvaal, and caused them to look upon everything British with more distrust and suspicion than ever; but the history of that disastrous expedition, evoking as it did the most intense national sentiment, not only amongst the Boers of the Transvaal, but also in a somewhat milder degree perhaps, though still in a most pronounced manner, amongst their compatriots in the Orange Free State, coupled with the very notorious fact that in the exclusively Dutch districts both of the Cape Colony and Natal a very strong anti-British feeling was excited, must have convinced even the most infatuated that a conflict between

Dutchmen and Englishmen, in whatever portion of South Africa it may arise, will be but the prelude to a war between the two races throughout every province from Cape Agulhas to the Zambesi—a war which would retard the general progress of the country for a generation, which would be infinitely disastrous to both races engaged in the struggle, and yet could be beneficial to neither, no matter which proved victorious.

In future let us hope that neither young military aspirants to fame, who, being ignorant of everything concerning South Africa, would yet climb their way to glory over the dead bodies of British and Dutch South Africans with the most light-hearted carelessness, just in the way of their professional business, nor cold-hearted self-seeking foreign politicians, who would use the ignorance and prejudice of the Boer to assist them in gratifying their jealous hatred of England, will be allowed to sway the councils of the statesmen, British or Boer, on whose decree the fate of South Africa really depends.

Not being a politician nor anything else but a wandering Englishman with a taste for natural history and sport, it may be held most presumptuous on my part to have written as I have done; but yet I have the most profound conviction that a war between the Boers and British in South Africa can only be a calamity of incalculable dimensions to both races; whilst the name of that statesman, whether Boer or Briton, who should without just cause on the one hand "cry havoc and let loose the dogs of war," or on the other compel the slipping of such dogs by fatuous obstinacy, and a cynical disregard for all the principles of enlightened government, will be assuredly held in execration by unborn generations of Boers and Britons alike. Neither race can get away from or do away with the other, and therefore both must try and rub off their mutual prejudices, and live harmoniously together.

This is not difficult in a new country like Rhodesia, where the representatives of the two peoples are in the nature of things thrown much together, and where there has always been a good understanding between them, which has of late been very much strengthened by the mutual assistance given by each to the other during the recent troublous times; and the fact that in these territories a very good understanding prevails between the Dutch and British gives one reason to hope that in time a similar state of things may be attained in the Transvaal, although unfortunately in that State there are several factors which militate against such a result being speedily arrived at.

In the first place, the great mass of the European population in the Transvaal, the greater part of which is British, resides in one great city, where it leads its own life, and does not come in contact with the Dutch farming population, of which it knows neither the language nor the history, and with whose modes of thought and manner of life it is altogether out of sympathy; whilst, on the other hand, the rough Boer, in too many cases, despises the ultra-civilised, sharp-witted, faultlessly-dressed European, and does not recognise that many amongst them are fine fellows and good sportsmen, and are capable of throwing off their coats and doing a day's work, hunting or fighting, with the roughest Boer amongst them, should occasion serve.

And yet these mutual prejudices and misunderstandings between the two peoples might easily be rubbed away if it were not for the presence of an anti-British clique of Hollanders and Germans in Pretoria, whose object it is to widen the breach between the Boers and the British; and as many of these men occupy official positions in the government of the country, and are therefore more in touch with the Boer legislators than the citizens of Johannesburg can hope to be, they have opportunities which they do not fail to use of increasing the distrust and suspicion already existing between the two races who alone have got to work out the destiny of South Africa between them, and amongst whom they are only meddlesome self-seeking interlopers.

All the various States of South Africa will no doubt be united sooner or later under one flag, but I am beginning to have my doubts as to what flag that will be. It is true that at the present time there exists in South Africa a very large British population of highly intelligent and energetic men, who have been attracted to that country by the diamond and gold fields. That population is constantly increasing, but it is not one which settles on the land. It is rather a population which has come to the country on a visit, in the endeavour to make a fortune with which to retire to the old country, and as the recent census taken in Johannesburg has shown, it is for the most part composed of young men, the greater number of whom are unmarried.

Now I suppose it is conceivable that a day may come, say in fifty, eighty or a hundred years time, when all the treasures have been dug up out of the South African earth; and should such a day arrive, is it not also conceivable that the great mining populations which have built the cities of Kimberley and Johannesburg in what a few years ago was a sparsely-inhabited wilderness, may dwindle down to comparatively small proportions, leaving the Boer population, which during all that time will have been increasing at a very rapid rate, once more numerically very much in excess of the British?

It does not appear to me very probable that during the present generation at least the Boers, either of the Transvaal or the Orange Free State, are likely (except under compulsion, which presupposes a deplorable war) to enter any confederacy of South African States, on any terms whatever, under the British flag; and therefore should the large British mining population now existent in the country gradually vanish, and the Boer population at the same time very much increase, the eventful confederation may take place under some other flag than the Union Jack. After all, as the Boers hold as large a stake in land, if not in wealth, as the British in South Africa, and as they were the first comers, and can lay claim to having killed off as many natives, and generally prepared as much country for occupation by white men, as the British, I think they are entitled to some consideration in the matter of the flag which is eventually to fly over the confederated States of South Africa; and for my part I would rather see a confederation take place under a compound flag, composed of equal parts of the Union Jack and Dutch ensign, with a bit of a French flag let in, to represent the Huguenots who, on their first arrival in South Africa, formed one-sixth of the entire white population of the country, and to whom the South African Boers of today owe many of their most estimable qualities, than have the country plunged into war in order to enforce its acceptance of the Union Jack.

However, this flag question is a problem of the future, and in the meantime it is the duty of all South Africans who have the welfare of the country as a whole at heart to do all they can to obliterate the remembrance of events galling to the national pride either of Dutchmen or Englishmen, and to endeavour to bring about once more a feeling of mutual trust and confidence between the two races. The Dutch must forget Slagter's Nek and Boomplaats, and the English must learn to think no more of avenging the defeats of Laing's Nek and Majuba Hill than they do of avenging the battles lost by the British troops in America which culminated in the surrender of Cornwallis and the declaration of American independence.

Now there has been for some years past an association in South Africa called the African Bond, which in some quarters at least must be considered anti-British, since another association called the Loyal Colonists' League has been inaugurated to counteract its effects. This latter society, judging by some speeches which have lately been made by some of its members, is frankly anti-Dutch. Now, would it not be better, if, in place of the latter society, whose object seems to be to widen and accentuate the breach which, in the Transvaal at least, is existent between the two races, an association should be formed, which all clergymen of all denominations, including ministers of the Dutch Reformed Church, should be invited to join, whose object should be the gradual obliteration of race-hatred and race-jealousy between the Dutch and British throughout South Africa, by the promotion of knowledge amongst the ignorant and prejudiced of both peoples?— for that, after all, is what is most required in order to bring about mutual respect and mutual forbearance, and enable every member of every State in South Africa to work under equal laws for the general prosperity of the whole country, a prosperity which can never attain to full fruition until the Dutch and British have attained to a political unity throughout South Africa as complete as it is today in the Cape Colony.

And now, after this long digression upon matters South African, and the expression of many opinions which, should they be read at all, will possibly only excite ridicule, coupled with a rebuke upon my presumption in wandering from the fields of sport and natural history, where I may be at home, into the arena of politics, where, it will be said, I certainly am not, let me say a few words about the present position and future prospects of Rhodesia.

Should the lists I have given at the end of my book be glanced through, it will be seen that the number of the settlers who were murdered in Matabeleland alone at the outbreak of the native insurrection, added to those who have since been killed and wounded in the subsequent fighting, amounts to over 300, or more than ten *per cent* of the entire white population of the country at the time of the outbreak of the rebellion, a proportion, I think, which ought to be entirely gratifying to even the most determined enemies of colonial expansion in Africa, whilst it gives the lie direct to the statement which has so frequently been made, that the settlers in Matabeleland have run no greater risks in fighting with the Matabele in order to put down the rebellion than would be incurred by a sportsman engaged in shooting hares and rabbits at home.

I do not expect that the publication of these lists will call the blush of shame to the cheeks of those who have been so eager to vilify their countrymen in Rhodesia, but I do hope that it will arouse a feeling of indignation in the minds of many who have hitherto been more or less led astray by these dishonest, spiteful, and unpatriotic mentors, and at any rate they must be sad reading to all but the most prejudiced. However, the rebellion can now, I think, be considered as almost at an end. The *kaffirs* have entirely failed in their attempt to kill all the white men in Matabeleland, and to re-establish themselves as an independent nation. To the west, northwest, north, north-east, and east, the *impis* which four months ago had formed a cordon round all those faces of Bulawayo have one and all been driven from their positions, and have now broken up into hundreds of little bands, living in the forests with their wives and children.

From all the information one can gather, the vast majority of these people are already suffering from want of food, as their cattle are all or nearly all dead from *rinderpest*, and a large proportion of their year's supply of grain has been taken possession of or destroyed by the white men. Under these conditions they cannot hold out much longer, and they would probably have already come in to surrender were it not that on the one hand, knowing the exasperation caused amongst the whites by the crimes they have committed, they are afraid to throw themselves on their mercy, and on the other they are kept from doing so by their chiefs, who having been the ringleaders of the rebellion, and fearing that in case of surrender their own lives at least would be forfeited, are still doing all they can to prevent their people from submitting.

In the Matopos, Mr. Cecil Rhodes and Mr. Johan Colenbrander are at the present moment carrying on negotiations with the insurgent chiefs, which may or may not end in peace. Should no satisfactory arrangement be arrived at, and the war be continued, the natives will be driven to desperation, and it will not only require a much larger force than there is at present in the country, but the expenditure of a vast amount of money, and the loss of many valuable lives, before they can be absolutely all killed or hunted out of the almost impregnable fastnesses and hills honeycombed with caverns which exist all over the large area of country known as the Matopos.

Now I think that, in view of the enormous cost and great loss of life that would be entailed by the decision to make no terms with the natives, it would be better to accept their submission on lines consistent with the future safety of the country. The chiefs must stand their trial, but the lives of all those who have had no part in the murder of white men, women, and children, could be guaranteed. The whole nation must of course be disarmed as completely as possible, and the actual murderers of white people during the first days of the rebellion must be shot or hanged. But should these conditions be complied with, whilst at the same time a large police force is maintained in the country, and the native administration carried on in such a way that, although the natives are treated with firmness, their grievances will always be heard, and as far as possible remedied, I do not think we need fear another rebellion.

Of course there are those who say that it is a great mistake to hold any parley with them at all. Go on killing them, they say, until the remnant crawl in on their hands and knees and beg for mercy. Well, that end could only be attained, as I have already said, at a cost of much money and many lives; so I think that there are many here, who, some for the sake of expediency and others for the sake of humanity, would now wish to see this rebellion ended as soon as possible, if it can be done in such a way as to ensure the future safety of the settlers in the country. As soon as the chiefs submit and their people are again located on the lands from which they have been driven, I think there can be no doubt that the country will, for the time being, be perfectly safe for white men; for history has shown us that when a *kaffir* tribe submits it does so absolutely for the time being, and no murders of isolated individuals are committed until the chiefs are ready for another insurrection.

It may of course be said that the Matabele have not yet been thoroughly beaten, and that, having gained a good deal of experience during the last five months, their idea in submitting is to get in their next year's crops and then begin again, on the principle of *"reculer pour mieux sauter."* But is this at all probable? After the first war they were more or less surprised into submission to the white men, the greater part of them never having fought for their country at all. Then they found that the shoe of the white man's rule began to pinch, but they wore it for two years, and did not attempt to throw it off until the country appeared to them to have been left in an absolutely defenceless condition by their conquerors.

They have now had their rebellion, and it has absolutely failed, and they have lost at least twice as many men in the recent fighting as they did in the first war. Nor is there any longer a cattle question to excite their resentment, for the cattle are all, or almost all, dead from the *rinderpest*. Therefore it appears to me, that if they are disarmed as far as is possible, and if a strong police force is maintained in the country for the next few years, their submission can be safely accepted, and the mass of the people be allowed to go unpunished; but justice and common sense both demand that all who are proved to have been implicated, either directly or indirectly, in any of the murders which marked the outbreak of the rebellion, shall be most summarily dealt with. They will be gradually discovered, and some, it may be, may not be brought to justice for years to come, but no mercy must be shown them whenever or wherever they may be found.

In less than two years' time the railway now being pushed on through the Bechuanaland Protectorate will have reached Bulawayo; and if the natives can be kept quiet by a firm and just rule until the advent of the iron horse in Matabeleland, there is little fear of their ever again rising in rebellion against the white man.

In the meantime the development of the country must remain at a standstill, and the country retained as a British possession, by an occupation which will be almost purely military, as not only has the cost of living been rendered almost prohibitive through the destruction of all the cattle in Matabeleland and Bechuanaland by the *rinderpest*, and the consequent substitution of mules and donkeys in the place of oxen for draught purposes, but farming also has been rendered very difficult, as, putting aside stock and dairy farming, no ploughing can be done without oxen, nor can agricultural produce be carried to market without the assistance of those useful animals, for salted and acclimatised horses and mules are too scarce and expensive to be reckoned on for farm work. The *rinderpest*, therefore, has for the present put an end to all European enterprise in the way of mining and farming in Matabeleland.

People in England can only realise the disastrous effect which this dread disease has had on the prosperity of the country by endeavouring to picture to themselves what the consequences would have been had a disease suddenly made its appearance in Great Britain in the early part of the present century, before the introduction of railways, which destroyed ninety-nine *per cent* of all the horses in the British Isles; yet even that would scarcely represent the extent of the calamity from the effects of which we are now suffering, when it is considered what an immense tract of barren wilderness yet lies between Matabeleland and the nearest railway station.

In the early part of this year there were over 100,000 head of cattle, all sleek and in excellent condition, in Matabeleland, but when it closes, I think it very doubtful if 500 will be still left alive in the whole country. Even this loss is small as compared with that sustained by Khama and his people, who were the largest cattle-holders in South

Africa, and whose loss it has been computed, from reliable data, exceeds 800,000 head of horned cattle.

However, the *rinderpest* is a calamity which is not likely to occur again, but which, when it does occur, sweeps everything before it both in Europe and Africa. That Matabeleland as a whole is a country second to none in South Africa for cattle-breeding is the opinion of everyone who has lived there for any length of time and had the opportunity of studying the matter. When, therefore, the *rinderpest* has died out, and the railway has reached Bulawayo, the country will be gradually restocked; and then, too, mining machinery will be imported, and our mines will at last be worked with a result which will give the final death-blow to all those who have for the last six years been engaged in disseminating falsehoods concerning Rhodesia.

From the statistics supplied to me by the Compensation Board, which I have given in the form of an appendix, it will be seen that a good deal of farming work had already been done at the time of the outbreak of the rebellion, and that the population of Matabeleland were not all "gin-sellers" or "men who had gone out to Matabeleland in order to swindle the British public, by inducing them to subscribe for shares in worthless companies, whose so-called gold claims contained no gold." The fact, too, that farmers and prospectors were living all over the country in perfect health rather explodes the theory of a noxious vapour rising to some four feet from the ground which is so deadly to Europeans that all colonisation of the country is impossible; but this, if I remember aright, was the theory propounded by one of Mr. Labouchere's "reliable" correspondents—a fit contributor, forsooth, to the pages of *Truth*.

It is now known throughout South Africa that Matabeleland and Mashunaland are white men's countries, where Europeans can live and thrive and rear strong healthy children; that they are magnificent countries for stockbreeding, and that many portions of them will prove suitable for Merino sheep and Angora goats; whilst agriculture and fruit-growing can be carried on successfully almost everywhere in a small way, and in certain districts, especially in Mashunaland and Manica where there is a greater abundance of water, on a fairly extensive scale.

As for the gold, there is every reason to believe that out of the enormous number of reefs which are considered by their owners to be payable properties some small proportion at least will turn up trumps, and, should this proportion only amount to two *per cent*, that will be quite sufficient to ensure a big output of gold in the near future, which will in its turn ensure the prosperity of the whole country.

Once let the railway reach Bulawayo, and given intelligent legislation in the best interests of the settlers and miners in the country, Rhodesia will soon prove its value to the most sceptical; but the prosperity which I predict will, I am afraid, be very much retarded, if not completely destroyed, by the revocation at the present moment of the Charter which was granted to the British South Africa Company in 1889, and the substitution of Imperial rule for the present form of government. For this reason:—Under the present regime the Company's administrator is always accessible to the people living in the country, and whatever local reforms may be deemed necessary by the latter are always capable of discussion, and can be acceded to by him on the spot, without despatches having first of all to be forwarded to the High Commissioner at the Cape, by whom they would be sent on to the Colonial Office, with the result that a local reform, urgently required, might be delayed for months or never granted at all.

Under the Company's Government, too, the administrator himself would always be a man acquainted with the history of the territories he was governing, and would be probably one who not only had the prosperity of the country he was governing deeply at heart, but who also would have a very good idea as to how that prosperity was likely to be attained. During the next few years, too, which will be a very critical period in the history of Rhodesia, such an administrator would always have the benefit of the advice of the man through whose energy and genius the territories forming that state have been secured for the British Empire.

But should this territory be converted into a Crown colony and governed from Downing Street on hard-and-fast lines, some of them not at all applicable to local requirements, with an administrator very likely ignorant of his local surroundings, and possibly out of sympathy with the settlers—Dutch and British—who have made the country their home, nothing but disaster is to be expected.

Surely the people who have stuck to Rhodesia through good and evil times, and who, under the auspices of the Chartered Company, have added a vast territory to the British Empire and laid the foundations of what will soon be a prosperous colony, which, given an intelligent and adaptable form of government, will be able to pay its way, ought to have some say in this matter, and not be transferred unwillingly to a rule which they know would be ill suited to local requirements, and under which local enterprises would surely languish for want of the fostering care which only a local administrator can provide.

The white population of Rhodesia have had many a growl at the government of the Chartered Company, but in most cases they have got what they growled for—to wit, the extension of the railways, both from the Cape Colony and the East Coast; the reduction of the Company's percentage of interest in the mines; and full and most generous compensation, where the claims were just, for cattle destroyed in the endeavour to stay the progress of the *rinderpest*, and for all losses sustained owing to the late native insurrection. Under Imperial rule they know that no compensation has ever been granted for losses sustained through a native rebellion, and they also know that little or no assistance could be hoped for in the construction of railways or other public works.

Recognising all these things, having as an object-lesson just before their eyes the wretchedly slow progress made in Bechuanaland under the Imperial administration, and knowing, moreover, that the Transvaal war of 1880-81, if not the loss of the Transvaal itself as a British possession, was brought about solely by a government from Downing Street, through an administrator entirely ignorant of local requirements and absolutely out of sympathy with the people he was chosen to govern, can it be wondered tit that at a recent meeting of the Chamber of Commerce in this town, the people of Bulawayo expressed confidence in the government of the Chartered Company and in Mr. Cecil Rhodes, representing as they do a corporation of capitalists who hold the largest financial stake in the country, and whose aims and objects are identical with those of the people living in the country, whilst they resented the idea of being handed over to Imperial rule without having their wishes in the matter consulted, in order to please the Little Englander party at home?

One of the most noteworthy features at the meeting to which I have referred was the remarkable unanimity shown by the British and Dutch on this subject, for the Dutch up here believe in Mr. Rhodes, and have the most absolute confidence in his ability to insure the prosperity of the country. The natives, too, as has just been shown, look upon him as their father; and I believe that through his influence and the strength of his personality, a peace will soon be arranged with them, which would have been impossible at the present time but for his presence in the country.

Bulawayo, 26th August 1896.

Appendices

APPENDIX A

HEADQUARTERS, INTELLIGENCE DEPARTMENT,
BULAWAYO, *August* 1896.

Amended List of Persons murdered in Matabeleland during the recent native insurrection.

Names.	District.	Date (1896).	Details.
Anderson, Joscelyn Hepburn	Sebakwe	End March	On way to Mafungabusi; engineer.
Anderson, Alex.	Boola Boola	25th ,,	Reported killed by F. Evans, his mate, who escaped.
Bertlesen Family (6) (father, mother, and 4 sons)	Shangani River	End ,,	Farming 12 miles north of Hartley Hills Road.
Baragwanath, John Albert	Filibusi	24th May	Brother in the B.F.F.
Bentley, Arthur.	,,	,, ,,	A N.-C. from Queenstown district.
Barr, W. A.	Shangani	End March	Family, contractors at Bristol.
Barnard, Harry Edgar	Umvungu	25th ,,	Partner of West Brothers, Umvungu Store; late with Parker Wood, Johannesburg.
Bolton	Inyati	End March	Killed with Cyril West (Williams' Ex. Coy.)
Bowen, Jimmy	Mavene	30th ,,	Hammond's Mines; killed with S. Van Blerk.
Borgen or Vorgen	Shangani	...	Prospector.
Bowker, Trooper	Lower Gwelo	30th ,,	M.M.P. sent to warn people, Lower Gwelo.
Colas, Dionysius	Inyati	End ,,	A Greek trader.
Cunningham, James Samuel	Filibusi	24th ,,	One of Cunningham family, away carting wood.
Clark, W. E.	Mavene	End ,,	Body found—Gwelo patrol.
Carpenter, John Loran	Filibusi	24th ,,	Body found near Filibusi Store.

Names.	District.	Date (1896).	Details.
Cunningham Family (8) (father, mother, and 6 children)	Filibusi	24th March	Farmers near Store (brother, F. H. Cunningham, Dundee, Natal).
Classen, Henry	Makukapene	26th ,,	Body seen.
Case, George	Inyati	,, ,,	M.M.P., killed with Graham, Handley, Hurford, and Corke.
Corke, Leighton Huntley	,,	,, ,,	Ex. M.M.P., do.
Comploier, P.	Gwelo	,, ,,	Prospector; body buried by Napier's Gwelo patrol.
Cumming, Percy H.	Filibusi	25th ,,	Son of Mr. and Mrs. Cumming, Bulawayo; body seen near Filabusi Store.
Crawley, Alaine M.	,,	,, ,,	Working with J. Schultz.
Cato, Colin	,,	,, ,,	Body seen at edge of shaft.
Donovan, Timothy (? S. A.)	Inyati	,, ,,	Killed with Seward near Ancients Reef; working for Mallert.
Durden, Charles	Ingwena	,, ,,	Killed with Surveyor Fitzpatrick.
Dufra	Lower Gwelo	30th ,,	Killed at Shangani.
Daly, John (? James)	Filibusi	25th ,,	Left for Gambo's kraal.
Davies, Harold John	Bembisi	2nd April	Killed near Thaba N'Couga.
Danby, Lewis	Bulawayo	...	Prospector.
Daly, James M.	Bubi	25th March	Managing Glen's farms; sick at time of death.
Edwards, Norman	Inyati	,, ,,	Surveyor (of Fletcher and Espiro).
Edkins, E. C.	Filibusi	24th ,,	Storekeeper (brother in Johannesburg); body seen in store.
Eaglestone, Charles Percy	Makukapene	End March	Partner of Joseph Clinton.
Ehlert, Ferdinand (known as "Bill")	Filibusi	,, ,,	Working with J. Jeffries. Family in Kimberley.
Earst, Ayerst Alfred	,,	,, ,,	Working with J. Jeffries.
Edgell, E. R.	On way from Gwelo to Hartley Hills	,, ,,	Murdered by natives, as reported by Adjutant Taylor, Gwelo.
Fitzpatrick	Lower Gwelo	25th ,,	Surveyor; body seen.
Farquharson, James John Edward	Bulawayo	...	Storekeeper.
Forster, Wilson	Makukapene	,, ,,	Prospector; body seen.
Fourie Family (8) (Stephanus, wife, and 6 children)	Tekwe River	2nd April	Farming; bodies buried by Napier's Gwelo patrol.

Names.	District.	Date (1896).	Details.
Fourie, Caspar Hendrick	Near Bulawayo	20th April	Transport rider, killed with Potgieter.
Farrar	Lower Gwelo	End March	Prospector, with companion (name unknown).
Foxkerk, Stanley	Shangani	25th ,,	Prospector
Grenfell, Pascoe St. L.	Inyati	End ,,	Left Inyati for Bubi; Manager Company.
Gordon, John	Gwelo	,, ,,	Miner.
Graham, A. M.	Inyati	26th ,,	A N.-C. Family in Glasgow.
Grant, John M'Innes	Filibusi	25th ,,	Mining with Robert Sharpe.
Grant, Jock M'Leod	,,	,, ,,	Killed with Jock Nimmo at Godlway's kraal; body buried by Salisbury column.
Greenhaugh, John	Hotel, Filibusi	,, ,,	Working with Whawill and Roddan.
Gracey, Robert	Shangani	End ,,	Body buried by Napier's Gwelo patrol.
Hunter, H. E.	Bembisi	,, ,,	Body seen.
Handley, Mark	Inyati	,, ,,	Sub-Inspector M.M.P., son of Henry Handley, Natal.
Hurford, George	,,	,, ,,	Late M.M.P., killed with Graham, Handley, Case, and Corke.
Hurlstone, Frederick	Pongo River Hotel	,, ,,	Partner of H. P. Selmes. Family in Coventry.
Harbord, H. M.	Mavene	,, ,,	Store on Hartley Hill Road (brother, A. G. Harbord, Longton, near Nottingham).
Hammond, And. Robt.	Shangani	,, ,,	Killed with Palmer and Johnson, engineers.
Hartley, Joseph	Ingwena Store	,, ,,	Body found at Harbord's Store; age about forty-five, height 5 ft. 8 in.
Holstein	Shangani	...	Prospector.
Ivers, Colin Campbell	Filibusi	24th ,,	Body found Celtic Reef.
Johnson, W. H.	Shangani	30th ,,	Killed with Hammond and Palmer.
Jensen, Charles	,,	,, ,,	A Swede.
Johnston	Filibusi	25th ,,	
Jeffries, J.	,,	,, ,,	Working with Ehlert and Earst.
Kirk, Agnes	Tekwe River	2nd April	J. Ross's stepdaughter; body buried by Napier's patrol.
Keefe, Charles	Shangani	2nd March	Working with Webster.
Keefe, Christopher	,,	,, ,,	,, ,,
Koch	Filibusi	25th ,,	Killed with Jeffries, Ehlert, and Earst.

Names.	District.	Date (1896).	Details.
Livesay, E. R. Eustace	Filibusi	End March	Late Lieutenant 3rd Dragoon Guards.
Luckcass, Herbert	,,	25th ,,	Killed at O'Maker's waggon; others escaped.
Lennock, George	Gwelo	End ,,	Body found Mavene; almost unrecognisable.
Langford (2), Dr. and Mrs.	Insiza	,, ,,	Bodies found on Rixon's farm and buried by Napier's Gwelo patrol.
Lemon, C. J.	,,	,, ,,	Father G. D. Lemon, Raleigh, Bedeford, North Devon; money at Standard Bank; buried by Napier's Gwelo patrol.
Lewis, Arthur B.	Filibusi	25th ,,	
Lund, Severin H. C.	Gwaai River	End ,,	A Dane.
M'Heugh, Harry	Bembisi	,, ,,	
Maddocks, Thomas	Filibusi	23rd ,,	
Melford, William B.	Gwelo	End ,,	
Matthews	Shangani	,, ,,	With Van der Doorten; a Jew from Melbourne.
Mathey, Ernest	Filibusi	25th ,,	Body recognised near Store.
Marcussen, Andreas E.	Hartley Hills	...	Prospector.
Morrison, James E.	Queen's Reef	29th ,,	Refused to leave.
M'Cormack	Ingwena Store	End ,,	Working with H. B. Taylor; body not seen.
Macdonald, Colin	Filibusi	25th ,,	Killed with Classen.
Nimmo, Walter (known as Jock or Watty)	,,	,, ,,	Murdered with John M'Leod Grant.
Palmer, H. M.	Shangani	30th ,,	Killed with Hammond and Johnson.
Potgieter, Derk Rainer	Bulawayo Road	20th April	Transport rider.
Ottens, Wilhelm O.	Filibusi	24th March	Family lives near Assen, Holland.
O'Reilly, T.	Gwelo	End ,,	Murdered on Leechdale Co.'s property.
O'Connor, ("Jack") John	Filibusi	25th ,,	Brother saved; in Bulawayo.
Reddington, Reginald	Pongo River	End ,,	Clerk to Hurlstone.
Reddan, Valentine	Filibusi	25th ,,	Murdered with Greenhaugh and Whawill.
Rowe, F. R.	Shangani	30th ,,	Miner of St. Austell.
Richards, John Edward	Bulawayo	...	Prospector.
Ross (2), Joseph and wife	Tekwe River	2nd April	
Rowlands, John James	Bembisi	...	Miner of King William's Town.
Radford, A.	Shangani	End March	Partner of Leech.

Names.	Districts.	Date (1896).	Details.
Raw	Lower Gwelo	...	Prospector.
Sharpe, Robert . .	Filibusi	25th March	Killed with Grant.
Stanley, Frank Harrison	Sebakwe	End ,,	Brother, late Lieut. Royal Irish Rifles, c/o Armstrong Bros., bankers, 93 Bishopgate St., London.
Stobie, James . .	Mavene	25th ,,	Murdered with Joseph Hartley, both working for G. R. Ainnocks.
Smith . . .	Lower Gwelo	...	Miner.
Seward, George E.	Filibusi	25th ,,	Killed with Cato, near Ancients Reef; working for Mallett.
Talman, Frank . .	Gwelo	End ,,	Near Pongo Store; body recognised by Robinson. Age 24; 5 ft. 5 in.; light.
Taylor, George . .	Shangani	,, ,,	
Thomas, Jock . .	,,	,, ,,	
Tyass, George (of Natal)	Bembisi	,, ,,	Sent with medicine to J. H. Daly.
Van Blerk, Sid. .	Mavene	30th ,,	Hammond's Mines; age 30; killed with Jimmy Bowen.
Vaughan, Thomas	Pongo River	25th ,,	
Van Gorckim, Martinus Gerhardus	Bulawayo	...	Bricklayer.
Vavaseur, Robert .	Stoneybrook Thabas M. Simbi	June	Reported murdered to Charter.
Van der Doorten .	Shangani	30th March	From Rotterdam.
White, Robert . .	Inyati	End ,,	Left Inyati for Bubi.
West, Cyril (Willoughbys)	Inyati	End ,,	Killed with Bolton.
West Bros. (2) . .	Shangani	,, ,,	
Wren . . .	,,	25th ,,	Cattle-inspector in district.
Wyllie, David . .	Gwelo	End ,,	Working for Warwick Colliers.
Wright, James . .	Bembisi	...	Storeman (of Johannesburg).
Woods, Arthur W. P.	Filibusi	25th ,,	Working and killed with E. Mathey.
White, Charles . .	Shangani	,, ,,	
White, Edward . .	Filibusi	,, ,,	Killed with Jack O'Connor.
Walsh, William . .	Mavene	End ,,	Body found Gwelo patrol; aged 40; buried Mavene patrol.
Whawill, John . .	Filibusi	25th ,,	Killed with Reddan and Greenhaugh.
Webster, R. . .	Shangani	End ,,	Killed with Keefes, a partner of Peacock's.
Weinand . . .	,,	,, ,,	Cattle-inspector.
Zeeburg, H. . .	Pongo River	26th ,,	Trader.

List of Persons supposed to have been in Matabeleland at the time of the outbreak of the insurrection, of whom nothing has since been heard, and the greater part, if not all, of whom must therefore be numbered amongst those murdered by the natives.

Names.	Details and Address.	Last heard of.
Ansterhauzen	Thabas Mamba	Trading at Thabas Mamba.
Bird, Robert George	...	Left Cape Town 13th April.
Band	...	Late of Johannesburg Police.
Burch, Dr.	...	Reported to be in Matabeleland.
Bridge, Walter.		
Batchelor, Franc D.	...	Reported to have been on some mining property near Bulawayo.
Bruce, Stewart	...	A Trooper in Dr. Jameson's force.
Bent.		
Bowen, O.		
Beaton, James	Johannesburg	Left Scotland in 1880 East for London, afterwards in Kimberley and Johannesburg, and left latter place probably for Bulawayo. Height 5 ft. 10 in.; black curly hair; well built; 42 years of age.
Cook, James P.	Bulawayo	Photographer's assistant, Bulawayo.
Cook, Thomas.		
Cook, Robert	...	Late of M.M.P.
Carstens, John E. A.	Bulawayo	Formerly in Captain Selous' Troop.
Carter, James	,,	Civil engineer in Bulawayo.
Dickson or Dixon	Gwelo	Gwelo district.
Douvre	,,	,,
Dixon, R.	...	Formerly in army.
Doveton, W. T.	Inyati	Seen in Bulawayo between 1-13 April, and not heard of since.
Evers, Harold Cecil	Bulawayo	Bulawayo district.
Greyling (5), John, wife, and 3 children	,,	On road to Bulawayo.
Grant, Jimmy	,,	Bulawayo.
Hill, John Shutter.		
Jacobs, Charlie	...	Gwelo camp, 2nd June.
Jones, William Stevens	Bulawayo	Bulawayo at time Matabele War.
Kerr	Gwelo	Shangani district.
Kroger, Frans J.	Chemist	Delagoa Bay.
Lee, Thomas	Gwelo	Gwelo district.
Mackenzie, Thomas	Bulawayo	Bulawayo.
Morrison, Wm. Hutchinson	...	Late of B.B.P.

Names.	Details and Address.	Last heard of.
Matthews, Stuart	Bulawayo	Late of Dunraven mines.
Honey, Clifford Francis	...	Formerly of B.B.P.
Mitchell, Basil.		
Magee, Joseph.		
Nieuwenhaus	...	Bulawayo road.
Oosthuizen	Gwelo	Shangani district.
Orton, Henry Sambourne	...	Sebakwe drift.
Palmer, William R.	Johannesburg	Bulawayo, end February.
Reet, P.	Transport rider	Pietersburg.
Rothman, John	Bulawayo	Bulawayo.
Reynard, J. J.	...	Believed to be in Colonel Plumer's force.
Reed, William James	late Johannesburg	Bulawayo.
Richardson, Arthur	...	A prospector.
Stalmp, Frank J.	London	Bulawayo.
Spalteholz, Kurt	Dresden, Germany	Left Johannesburg for Bulawayo, December 1895.
Spalteholz, Kurt	Amsterdam	Last heard of, Pietersburg, 2nd Jan. 1896, when on road Bulawayo with party by ox waggon. Height 6 ft.; age 24; smooth face; light brown hair; sharp features. Papers of his have been found on Rixon's farm, and bag (possibly belonging to him) at Thabas Mamba.
Smith, Sidney Z.	Mafeking	Reported to have left Mafeking with M.R.F.
Tilbury, George	...	Mafeking, 24th April.
Taylor, Alfred West	...	Possibly passing under his stepfather's name of Bent.
Wright, James	Bulawayo	Bulawayo.
Wilson, Edward E.	...	Bulawayo, June 1895.
Walsh, Frederick Byron.		
Webster, R.		
Walsh, I.	Bulawayo	Came in from Golingena at beginning of rebellion.

APPENDIX B

HEADQUARTERS, INTELLIGENCE DEPARTMENT,
BULAWAYO, *August* 1896.

List of Officers, Non-Commissioned Officers, and Men killed in action during the Matabele rebellion.

No.	Rank.	Name.	Where killed.	Date (1896).
1	Sergeant	O'Leary, T., M.M.P.	Cumming's Store	27th March
2	Corporal	Reynolds, Ernest E., R.H.V.	Gifford's patrol	6th April
3	Trooper	Mackenzie, S. Kenneth, R.H.V.	,, ,,	,,
4	,,	Baker, Richard Arthur, R.H.V.	Gwanda patrol	10th April
5	,,	Hayland, Edward, R.H.V.	,, ,,	,,
6	,,	Packe, Christopher J., R.H.V.	,, ,,	,,
7	Corporal	Greer, Stewart George, R.H.V.	,, ,,	,,
8	Trooper	Forbes, J. M'Ainsch, R.H.V.	,, ,,	,,
9	,,	Boyes, George Walter, B.F.F., Afcr. Corps	Macfarlane's patrol	19th April
10	,,	Heinemann, J. J., B.F.F.	Vedette duty	,,
11	,,	Van Zyl, W., B.F.F.	,, ,,	,,
12	,,	Montgomerie, Henry, B.F.F.	,, ,,	,,
13	,,	Baxter, Frank Wm., B.F.F.	Grey's Scouts, Bisset's patrol	22nd April
14	,,	Whitehouse, Henry George, B.F.F.	Ambulance, Macfarlane's patrol	25th April
15	,,	Gordon, Charles, B.F.F.	Dawson's Scouts, Macfarlane's patrol	,,
16	,,	Parsons, Benj, B.F.F.	D Troop, vedette duty	,,
17	,,	Hay, Carrick, B.F.F.	Coope's Scouts, Plumer's patrol	25th May

No.	Rank.	Name.	Where killed.	Date (1896).
18	Trooper	Parker, Arthur, B.F.F.	L Troop, Napier's Gwelo patrol	22nd May
19	,,	Rothman, George, B.F.F.	L Troop, Napier's Gwelo patrol	,,
20	,,	Langton, Courtney, E Squad, M.R.F.	Thabas Mamba	6th July
21	,,	O'Reilly, John, Brand's Troop, B.F.F.	,, ,,	,,
22	Corporal	Pringle, James F., A Squad, M.R.F.	,, ,,	,,
23	Sergeant	Warringham, Fred. Chas., A Troop, M.M.P.	Matopos, Babian's impi	20th July
24	Corporal	Hall, John, Belingwe F.F.	Inugu engagement, Matopos	,,
25	Trooper	Bennett, Peter, E. Troop, M.M.P.	Inugu engagement, Matopos	,,
26	,,	Bush, William Henry, E. Troop, M.M.P.	Inugu engagement, Matopos	,,
27	,,	Matheson, R. B., Major Hurrell's Troop	Bezury Hills engagement	21st July
28	Corporal	Hayes, Dan., Major Hurrell's Troop	Sinango kopje engagement	7th July
29	Major	Kershaw, C Squad, M.R.F.	Sikombo engagement	5th August
30	Sergeant	M'Closkie, Oswald, C Squad, M.R.F.	,, ,,	,,
31	,,	Gibb, William, D Squad, M.R.F.	,, ,,	,,
32	,,	Innes, Kerr, Maxim gun, M.R.F.	,, ,,	,,
33	Battery Sergt.-Maj.	Ainslie, Alexander, M.M.P.	,, ,,	,,
34	Lieut., Dismnt. Troop.	Hervey, Herbert John Anthony, died from wounds, late Paymaster-General	,, ,,	,,

APPENDIX C

HEADQUARTERS, INTELLIGENCE DEPARTMENT,
BULAWAYO, *August* 1896.

List of Officers, Non-Commissioned Officers, and Men wounded; or died in hospital from wounds received in action during the Matabele rebellion.

No.	Rank.	Name.	Details.	Date (1896).
1	Trooper	Hill, Eustace	Gifford's patrol, Insiza	27th March
2	,,	Hocking, John	,,	,,
3	,,	Luis, Wilton	,,	,,
4	Corporal	Strutt, M.M.P.	,,	,,
5	Trooper	Saunders, Charles	,,	,,
6		O'Connor, Joseph	Prospector, escaped from Filibusi	,,
7	Trooper	Stracey, A. H.	Selous' patrol	28th March
8	,,	Munzberg, Berthold	,,	,,
9	A.N.C.	Carter, Samuel	Shiloh patrol	29th March
10	Serg.-Maj.	Haden, Thomas	,, (Afric. Corps)	,,
11	Trooper	Celliers, John	Shiloh patrol (died in hospital, 16th May 1896)	,,
12	,,	Anderson, August	Shiloh patrol	,,
13	Lieut.-Col.	Gifford, Hon. M. R.	Fonseca's Farm	6th April
14	Captain	Lumsden, J. W.	Fonseca's Farm (died in hospital, 10th April 1896)	,,
15	Lieutenant	Hulbert	Fonseca's Farm	,,
16	Trooper	Eatwell	,,	,,
17	,,	Fielding	,,	,,
18	,,	Walker	,,	,,
19	M.O.	Levy, Dr. J.	Gwanda patrol	10th April
20	Trooper	Harvey, F. J.	,,	,,
21	,,	Whitlow, Chas. Ern.	,,	,,
22	,,	Stowell, W.	,,	,,
23	,,	Ormsby, O.	,,	,,

No.	Rank.	Name.	Details.	Date (1896)
24	Trooper	Ferreira, J.	Gwanda patrol	10th April
25	,,	De Villiers, Isaac James	,,	,,
26	,,	Wilson, J.	,,	,,
27	,,	Collins, C.	,,	,,
28	,,	Ashley, W.	,,	,,
29	,,	Kramer, S.	,,	,,
30	,,	Blackwell, J.	,,	,,
31	,,	Wallace, E. C.	,,	,,
32	,,	Farrell, E.	,,	,,
33	,,	Swift, Henry	Gwanda patrol (died in hospital, 14th April 1896)	,,
34	,,	Harker, George, B.F.F.	Local patrol	17th April
35	,,	Ter. Blanche Esiah Michael, Afric. Corps	Macfarlane's patrol	19th ,,
36	Captain	Grey, George	Bisset's patrol	22nd April
37	Lieutenant	Hook, Godfrey Blair	,,	,,
38	,,	Crewe, F. H.	Bisset's patrol (Grey's Scouts)	,,
39	Corporal	Wise, George	Bisset's patrol (Grey's Scouts)	,,
40	Lieutenant	Lyons, M. H., Hosp. Corps	Macfarlane's patrol	25th April
41	T.S.M.	Botha, Joh. Christian	Macfarlane's patrol (Afric. Corps)	,,
42	Trooper	Howell, Thos. Easton	Macfarlane's patrol (Grey's Scouts)	,,
43	,,	Price, F. H. Talbot	Macfarlane's patrol (Maxim detachment)	,,
44	,,	Appleyard, Edward	Macfarlane's patrol (Dawson's Scouts). Died in hospital same evening	,,
45	,,	Lovatt, Ronald Venables	Macfarlane's patrol (Grey's Scouts). Died in hospital, 29th April 1896	,,
46	,,	Beatty-Pownall, W. C.	Laing's Camp, Belingwe	2nd May
47	,,	Hamilton, H. Rice	Unattached, Plumer's patrol	25th May
48	Sergeant	Peacock, Arthur W.	Plumer's patrol (B Troop)	,,
49	Trooper	Slowey, W. John	Plumer's patrol (A Troop)	,,
50	,,	Beinedell, Pieter	Napier's Gwelo patrol (L Troop)	22nd May
51	,,	Niemand, Jac. P. Joh.	Napier's Gwelo patrol (Mangwe detachment)	,,

No.	Rank.	Name.	Details.	Date (1896).
52	Trooper	Geldenhuis, Elias Jac.	Napier's Gwelo patrol (Mangwe detachment)	22nd May
53	Corporal	Combrink, Jacobus, Afric. Corps	Spreckley's patrol	6th June
54	Trooper	Davey, Cecil, A Troop, B.F.F.	Spreckley's patrol. Serious gun-shot, right hip since amputated	,,
55	Sergeant	Hamilton, Geo. Michael, R.V.H.	Spreckley's patrol. Assegai wound	,,
56	T.S.M.	Morrison, S., 8 Troop, M.R.F.	Macfarlane's Gwaai patrol. Bullet wound on head	8th June
57	Trooper	Clark, A Troop, Gifford's Horse	Macfarlane's Gwaai patrol. Slight wound	,,
58	T.S.M.	Blatherwick, S. M., M.R.F.	Macfarlane's Gwaai patrol	,,
59	Trooper	Hill, John H., A Squad, M.R.F.	Thabas M'amba. Dangerously wounded; died same day	6th July
60	,,	Meyer, George, A Squad, M.R.F.	Thabas M'amba	,,
61	,,	Cooper, David E., A Squad, M.R.F.	,,	,,
62	,,	Dupreez, Arthur, M.R.F	,,	,,
63	,,	Dunn, George, ,,	,,	,,
64	,,	Potgieter, L., Belingwe F.F.	Belingwe patrol	26th June
65	Lieutenant	Taylor, Scouts, M.R.F.	Matopos, Babian's impi	20th July
66	Sergeant	Halkett, C. H., Belingwe F.F.	Matopos, Inugu engagement	,,
67	,,	Eadio, Malcolm, A Troop, M.M.P.	Matopos, Inugu engagement	,,
68	Trooper	Dick, Duncan, Belingwe F.F.	Matopos, Inugu engagement	,,
69	,,	Judge, T., Belingwe F.F.	Matopos, Inugu engagement	,,
70	,,	Toulson, John George	Matopos, Inugu engagement	,,
71	,,	Parker Parker, F.F.	Severe bullet wound, thigh	,,
72	,,	Morgan, Charles Oglethorpe A., M.M.P.	Matopos, Inugu engagement (died 23rd July, buried at Usher's Farm)	,,
73	,,	Stewart, A. M., Belingwe F.F.	Matopos, Inugu fight	,,
74	,,	Sell, Charles A. T., M.M.P.	,,	,,
75	,,	Millar, Fredk., M.M.P.	,,	,,

No.	Rank.	Name.	Details.	Date (1896)
76	Trooper	Roger, Scott, Belingwe F.F.	Matopos Inugu fight	20th July
77	,,	Wilson, Campbell, A Squad, M.R.F.	Hope Fountain	12th ,,
78	,,	Cheres, Laurence, M.M.P.	Nicholson's patrol, Inugu gorge (died and buried at Usher's Camp, 27th July)	25th July
79	,,	Bern, William, M.M.P.		
80	Trooper	Heathfield, Richard, Jr., M.M.P.	Nicholson's patrol, Inugu gorge	,,
81	,,	Bell, James, M.M.P.	Nicholson's patrol, Inugu gorge	,,
82	Corporal	Porter, Joseph Kirk, M.M.P.	Nicholson's patrol, Inugu gorge (died in Bulawayo hospital, 3rd August)	,,
83	Lieutenant	Norton, Frederick Cunningham, M.M.P.	Taylor's patrol, Sobisi	27th July
84	Captain	Lloyd, Chas. P., Engineer Train	Inyandi engagement	3rd Aug.
85	Trooper	Little, Edward Runnell, M.R.F.	Gun accident, Spargo's (died 3rd August)	,,
86	,,	Champion, William Lewis, M.R.F.	Gun accident, Spargo	,,
87	,,	Silberhazen, George, M.R.F.	,,	,,
88	,,	Macdougall, Lorne Somerlea	Fort-Spargo	5th Aug.
89	Lieutenant	M'Culloch, Robert H., Royal Art.	Sikombo engagement	,,
90	,,	Frazer, Norman Warden, West Riding Regt.	,,	,,
91	Captain	Fowler, Charles H., M.R.F.	,,	,,
92	Staff-Sergt.-Major.	Josephs, William, M.R.F.	,,	,,
93	Sergt.-Maj.	Dumeresq, Rawlings, M.R.F.	,,	,,
94	Sergeant	Brabant, Arthur E., M.R.F.	,,	,,
95	Corporal	Turnbull, Richard, M.R.F.	,,	,,
96	Trooper	Currie, William, M.R.F.	,,	,,
97	,,	Holmes, Evelyn, M.R.F.	,, (Died 9th August)	,,
98	,,	Gordon, Thomas, M.M.P.	Sikombo engagement	,,
99	Lieutenant	Howard, Hon. H.	,, (Robertson's Cape Boys)	,,
100	Captain	Windley	Robertson's Cape Boys	,,

APPENDIX D

**HEADQUARTERS, INTELLIGENCE DEPARTMENT,
SALISBURY,** *August* **1896.**

List of persons murdered in Mashunaland during the recent native insurrection.

Names.	District.	Date (1896).	Details.
Birkett, W.	Salisbury	...	Body supposed to be his recovered on 5th August.
Kentenge, Frank	,,	18th June	Killed at the Gwibi River.
Wills, M.M.P.	,,	,,	,, ,,
Loeford, S.	,,	15th June	Killed at Beatrice Mine.
Tait, James	,,	,,	,, ,,
Van Rooyen	,,	16th June	Killed at Hartley Road.
Fourie, Benj. John	,,	,,	,, ,,
Norton Family (3), Joseph, Mrs., and infant	,,	17th June	Killed at Norton's Farm, on the Hungani River.
Fairweather, Miss	,,	,,	Killed at Norton's Farm, on the Hungani River.
Alexander, H.	,,	,,	Killed at Norton's Farm, on the Hungani River.
Grahener, H.	,,	,,	Killed at Norton's Farm, on the Hungani River.
Harvey, J. L.	,,		No particulars of murders; but six or seven weeks having elapsed without any news of these persons, and who were known to have been surrounded by rebels at the time of the rising, it is beyond all doubt that they are dead.
Dixon, James	,,		
Briscoe	,,		
Hite, W. D.	,,		
Dowenbrock, R.	,,		
Basson, Nicholas	,,		
Joubert, J.	,,		
Gray, Harry	,,		
Curtis, J. H. (surveyor)	,,		
Saunders	,,		
Calcott	,,		
Cass, J.	Mazoe	18th June	Killed near Salvation Army Camp.

Names.	District.	Date (1896).	Details.
Faull, W.	Manzoe	18th June	Killed near Salvation Army Camp.
Dickenson, J., Mining Commissioner	,,	,,	Killed near Salvation Army Camp.
Routledge, J. J.	,,	,,	Killed near Telegraph Station (telegraphist).
Blakiston, J. J.	,,	,,	Killed near Telegraph Station (telegraphist).
Pollard, H. H.	,,	...	Killed near Mount Hampden.
Nunesty, C.	,,	...	Missing.
Fletcher, John	,,	...	,,
Salthouse	,,	...	,,
Smith	,,	...	,,
Short, Henry	Charter	...	Killed.
Bester, Mrs.	,,	...	,,
Smith	,,	...	,,
Moore, John	,,	...	Dunstan estate; killed Umtala Road; body recovered 3rd August.
Milton (transport rider)	,,	...	Killed at Homestead Store; body found on 3rd August.
Graham, Harry	,,	...	Killed at Homestead Store; body found on 3rd August.
Weyers Family (4), Jan, wife, and 2 children	,,	...	Bodies recovered.
Bekers, C. D.	,,	...	Killed at Campbell's Store.
Campbell, J. D.	,,	...	,, ,,
Phillips	,,	...	Killed at Graham's Store.
Law, Horace, M.M.P.	,,	20th June	Killed near Campbell's Store.
Tucker, M.M.P.	,,	,,	,, ,,
Dickenson, A. J.	,,	...	Killed near Law's Store.
White, James (Willoughby's consolidated)	,,	7th July	Killed at Marandellas Mission Store.
Bremner, Lieut.	,,	...	Killed near Marandellas.
Eyre, Herbert H., M.M.P.	Lo Magondi	21st June	Killed at Umvokwe Mountains.
Young, Arthur Liston, M.M.P.	,,	,,	Killed at Umvokwe Mountains.
Gambier, J. C.	,,	22nd June	Killed at Menin River.
Boijes, W. H.	,,	,,	,, ,,
Drysdale	,,	,,	,, ,,
Mynhardt (native commissioner)	,,	21st June	Killed at Mynhardt's Camp.
Shooter, F.	,,	,,	,, ,,
Dougherty, J.	,,	31st May	
Watkins, Charles H.	,,	...	Medical officer; killed at Hinnan's Store.

Names.	District.	Date (1896).	Details.
Jameson, Arthur John	Lo Magondi	...	Mining Commissioner.
M'Gowan, J. } Hodgson, A. }	,,	...	{ Were at Jameson's Camp and have not been heard of.
Bent, F. L.	,,	...	Missing.
Box, James	,,	...	,,
Box, Duncan	,,	...	,,
Kerr, Carr, or Care	,,	...	,, United States man.
Ireland	,,	...	,,
Hermann, Louis	Abercorn	21st June	Killed at Macombis.
Tupnell, W.	,,	,, ,,	,, ,,
Steel, J.	,,	,, ,,	,, ,,
Austin, F.	,,	,, ,,	,, ,,
Smith, Newman H.	,,	...	Missing.
Horn, J.	,,	...	,,
Jansen	,,	...	,,
Steele, W.	,,	...	,,
Cronchly, J.	,,	...	,,
North, A.	,,	...	,,
Hawkins	,,	...	,,
Hornby	,,	...	,,
Gibson, J. G.	,,	...	,,
Sagus	,,	...	,,
Newman	,,	...	,,
Hermann, Harry	,,	...	,,
Ruping (native commissioner)	,,	28th June	Killed by his native police at Tahoskos.
Rhapiro, Renten	,,	21st ,,	Shot at Abercorn Store.
Fletcher	,,	,, ,,	,, ,,
Eaton, J.	,,	19th ,,	Killed at Chipadgus.
Thurgood, A.	Hartley Hill	15th ,,	
Hepworth, J. C.	,,	17th ,,	Killed at Wallace's farm.
Wallace, "Friday"	,,	,, ,,	,, ,,
Moonie, D. E. (native commissioner)	,,	15th ,,	Killed at Mashingontis.
Hunt, A. J.	,,	,, ,,	,, ,,
Skell	,,	,, ,,	,, ,,
Purser, A. L.	,,	19th ,,	Killed near Hunyani River.
Carrick Edward (mining commissioner)	,,	,, ,,	,, ,,
Wickslorn, A.	...	...	Killed while prospecting near Hartley.
Nelson	...	...	Killed while prospecting near Hartley.

The following were killed in action :—

Names.	District.	Date (1896).	Details.
M'Geer, C. M.	...	20th June	Mazoe patrol.
Van Staden, H. J.	...	,, ,,	,,
Jacobs	...	,, ,,	,,
Dillon	...	,, ,,	,,
Mitchell, J. Bentley	...	...	Wounded first Hartley patrol ; died 27th June.
Stevens, Charles Trelawney	...	25th ,,	Killed Cheshwasha patrol.
Gwilkin, W. H.	...	20th July	Killed second Hartley patrol.

The following were wounded in action :—

Grey, Dr.	...	...	First Hartley patrol.
Bottemley, Trumpeter (Natal Contingent)	...	...	,, ,,
Finucase, E.	Salisbury	...	,, ,,
Burton, Arthur	,,	...	Mazoe patrol at Jwito River.
Hendrikz, C.	,,	...	,, ,,
Neibuhr	,,	...	,, ,,
Ogilvie	,,	...	,, ,,
Berry	,,	...	,, ,,
Judson, Captain	,,	...	,, ,,
Cartwright, Trumpeter, M.M.P.	Charter	...	
Van de Merwe	...	...	At Hunyani.
Fitzpatrick	...	...	Beal's column on second Hartley patrol.
Arnott	Salisbury	...	
Kerr	,,	...	
Lee	...	...	White's column in foraging patrol.
Fraser	...	...	Beal's column.
Brown	...	...	,,
Millar	...	...	,,

APPENDIX E

For the following statistics I am indebted to the courtesy of Colonel Heyman, the President of the Compensation Board, which up to 15th August 1896 had paid claims for the following items :—

Growing Crops Destroyed

Mealies	896	acres
Kafir corn	270	,,
Oats	70½	,,
Barley	17	,,
Potatoes	67	,,
Wheat	7	,,
Various	151½	,,
Total	1479	acres

Trees Destroyed

Fruit trees	1,092
Gum trees	290
Various trees	19,957
Total	21,339

Domestic Animals Carried Off or Killed

Imported bulls	59
Kafir bulls	58
Oxen	4,440
Cows and heifers	9,592
Mixed cattle	7,394
Sheep and goats	5,114
Pigs	842
Horses	33
Mules	6
Donkeys	548
Imported fowls	4,348
Matabele	7,133
Ducks and geese	514
Turkeys	58
Total	40,139

No. of homesteads destroyed	150

FARMING AND AGRICULTURAL IMPLEMENTS STOLEN OR DESTROYED

Ploughs	112
Harrows	30
Carts, various	15
Waggons	85
Scotch carts	52
Picks and shovels	2349
Cream separators	5
Churns	19
Sundries	5121 including mining implements
Total	7788

Note.

Up to 15th August 371 claims had been adjudicated upon.

The full amount claimed in settlement of these claims amounted to £166,829 : 19 : 9.

The amount awarded in settlement of the same being £111,439 : 10 : 11.

The total number of claims filed amounted on 15th August to 637, the total amount of compensation claimed for which amounted to £266,237 : 19 : 4.

Since 15th August other claims have been filed bringing the total number up to about 800 for losses sustained in Matabeleland alone.

The total amount of compensation which will be paid by the Chartered Company in settlement of these claims will, it is thought, reach the sum of £230,000.

APPENDIX F

SCHEDULE showing the number of Native Policemen in the employ of the Government throughout Matabeleland, at the time of the outbreak of the rebellion, and the proportion of the same which remained loyal in the different districts.

Station.					Loyal.	Rebels.	Doubtful.
Headquarters	.	.	.	60	45	...	15
Bulawayo	district	.	.	30	15	15	...
Bulilima	,,	.	.	30	28	2	...
Umzingwani	,,	.	.	30	11	19	...
Mangwe	,,	.	.	30	6	24	...
Usiza	,,	.	.	30	2	28	...
Gwanda	,,	.	.	30	18	...	12
Belingwe	,,	.	.	30	Nil.	25	5
Gwelo	,,	.	.	30	Nil.	30	...
Bubi	,,	.	.	30	1	29	...
	Total	.	.	330	126	172	32

These figures must be taken as only approximate, as it is known that three or four of the police were killed by the rebels, and it is doubtful whether others did not meet the same fate. It will not be known exactly what number of the police were murdered by the rebels until the war is over.

For these statistics I am indebted to Mr. H. Morrison Jackson, the native commissioner, who was living on my company's property of Essexvale.

F. C. SELOUS.

APPENDIX G

Gold Output

Reef.	District.	Tons crushed.	Approx. output in ounces.
Alice	...	2	7
Auriga	...	41	49
African	...	150	97
Birthday	...	100	104
Beatrice	...	100	563
Bonanza	...	201	80
Cotapaxi	...	4857	2328
Congress on Hill	...	20	$15\frac{1}{2}$
Concession	...	4	$7\frac{1}{2}$
Dickens	...	1090	1084
Golden Quarry	...	23	96
Golden Horse Shoe	...	100	71
Glendarra	...	3	$7\frac{1}{4}$
Hidden Secret and Rob Roy	...	120	60
Heathfield	...	2	$20\frac{1}{2}$
Inez	...	40	97
Just in Time	...	$\frac{3}{4}$	27
Lion	...	2	$5\frac{1}{2}$
Matchless East	...	20	12
Matchless West	...	12	20
Natal	...	6	7
Old Chum	...	20	49
Nil Desperandum	...	2	$2\frac{1}{2}$
Panhalanga	...	50	50
Pioneer	...	18	$10\frac{3}{4}$
Standard No. 2	...	278	222
Shepherds	...	6	$10\frac{1}{2}$
Salamander	...	799	$439\frac{1}{2}$
Shankaru	...	25	75
Vesuvius	...	40	90
		$8131\frac{3}{4}$	$5707\frac{1}{2}$
Ancient Ruins	...	...	357
Alluvial	Manica	...	$84\frac{1}{2}$

For these statistics I am indebted to the courtesy of Mr. Arnold, Secretary of the Chamber of Mines.   F. C. Selous.

The Matabele Rebellion, 1896

Major D. Tyrie Laing

Contents

Introduction	253
Apprisal of Rebellion	257
Treachery and Desertion of Native Police	263
Capture of a Native Spy	271
Attack by Matabele	281
Strong Patrol Goes Out	288
Arrival of Captain Hopper's Relief Party from Victoria	294
A Prisoner is Captured	301
Arrival at Dooboolelo's Kraal	307
A Slight Brush with the Enemy	309
Captain Brabant Arrives with Despatches from Earl Grey	317
M'Tipi's Men Score a Victory	325
Relief of Belingwe Garrison	333
A Council of War	341
Description of the Engagement	345
The Rebels Send Peace Offerings	350
March to Buluwayo	357
A Brush with the Enemy	364
Attack on Matopos Postponed	369

The Battle of Inugu   376
Return of Column to Belingwe   385
Arrival of Column at Buluwayo   392

Introduction

My purpose in writing this book is to discharge a duty I owe to the officers, non-commissioned officers, and men of the Belingwe Field Force, lately under my command, by placing on record their share in the quelling of the Matabeleland rebellion of 1896.

Firstly, to the men of Belingwe, who gallantly stuck together, held their position, and the district in practical subjection, until Mr. Rhodes was enabled to send a force to the relief of the beleaguered garrison and who afterwards marched out, aided to subjugate the rebels, and restore order. Nothing could be more striking and pleasing a feature to me than the behaviour of the enrolled volunteers, and that of many men of different nationalities, amongst whom I have much pleasure in mentioning Lieutenant Malcolm McCallum and Sergeant Douglas, Americans of the very best stamp; Descalzie, an Italian, and several others, who might have lain under our protection, but preferred to share the duties of their comrades in misfortune. They voluntarily and cheerfully joined in the hardships, which they so nobly helped to lighten. I thank them now for all the assistance they rendered so willingly, and shall ever remember with pride that such good fellows placed themselves under my command.

The behaviour of the volunteers, under all circumstances, was worthy of every praise. Their work was hard and trying, rendered all the more difficult by their having to sleep in the new earthworks in a tropical country. Most of them suffered from fever in consequence. Still they did their duty without a grumble, and never once questioned the authority of their officers. I appreciated their valuable assistance, and shall ever remember them with gratitude and pleasure. Their loyalty made everything so much easier and saved the lives of every one in the Belingwe garrison. Where all did so well, it would indeed be invidious to mention names, but I cannot pass without mentioning

Mr. A. J. Wilson, the late quartermaster of the Belingwe garrison, as all the fever-stricken men will remember. Before we had a doctor, Mr. Wilson's presence was seldom absent from the hospital, and to him all of us are indebted for many kindnesses. For the others, I can only say I was proud to be one of them.

Our Cape boy servants, too, behaved splendidly, and as they had all been in the service of white men for years, were a most valuable addition to the garrison. Being, as a rule, good shots, they were armed, and did their duty in turn with the white men, whom they emulated, and assisted in the very best manner. To show that they were to be trusted, I may mention that two of them rode through with despatches from Belingwe to Gwelo, which enabled Mr. Rhodes to send us the much-needed reinforcements.

Secondly, to Captain Harman Hopper and the twenty brave fellows who volunteered to follow him from Victoria to march to our assistance, strengthening us by their numbers, as well as bringing with them a much-wanted supply of ammunition and a Maxim gun. Little has been said or heard of Captain Hopper up to the present, but I feel certain that of those who are indebted to him and his companions, the men of Belingwe will always be glad to recall his name and those of the men who followed him. I am also sure that none of the garrison will ever forget the pang of pleasure and relief that shot through their breasts when Hopper's advance-guard appeared on the crown of the ridge, about a mile east of the Belingwe fort.

Lastly, I must pay a tribute to the men who, under orders of Mr. Rhodes, marched from Tuli, under the command of Lieutenant Yonge, for the relief of Belingwe. Of this party I desire to make particular mention for the following reasons—namely, that, with the exception of about thirty of them, who belonged to Rhodesia, the remainder had come from all parts of South Africa, with the simple, and. I may say, heroic intention of assisting their distressed fellow-countrymen in Rhodesia. Many of them, to my own certain knowledge, had left lucrative businesses and employments. Some of them had abandoned all they had in different parts of the country to throw in their lot with us, not for what they could gain but simply because they wished to give a helping hand to those in much need of it; and right nobly and willingly did they perform their self-allotted work. Most of them were sportsmen, good riflemen, and good horsemen, imbued with a loyalty and patriotic sense of duty which reduced discipline to pleasure and elevated my command to an honour.

When the relief of Belingwe was completed and all the different parties fused into one, it formed what might be called a truly Imperial force, composed as it was of members from every part of the British Empire—England, Ireland, Scotland, Canada, Australia, New Zealand, Natal, Cape Colony, and India. All had their representatives, even the Free State and Transvaal furnishing a quota; and I must not forget to mention that Germany, Sweden, Russia, and Italy had representatives in the force.

Of course, amongst such a mixed assemblage there were a few who did not quite conform to the necessary rules until these had to be forcibly explained. Three very good men, I am sorry to say, had to be discharged on the march. They mistook insubordination for independence. Yet, when there was so much good in the column, the little leaven of dissatisfied spirits had not the slightest effect, and altogether we got along admirably.

Their loyalty to the queen and to the Chartered Company was proved throughout, and although the column has been disbanded and its deeds are now relegated to the past, I believe that there is one who remembers that there was Such a body of men, and to him. the Right Hon. C. J. Rhodes, the officers, non commissioned officers, and men of the Belingwe Field Force, I dedicate this work. In doing so I wish to thank them all for conforming to my wishes and orders, and enabling me to be of slight service to the cause of civilisation and the expansion of the British Empire.

As my personality was to a considerable extent affiliated with all the moves of the Belingwe Field Force and garrison, I trust that, under the circumstances, the perhaps too frequent use of the personal pronoun will be excused.

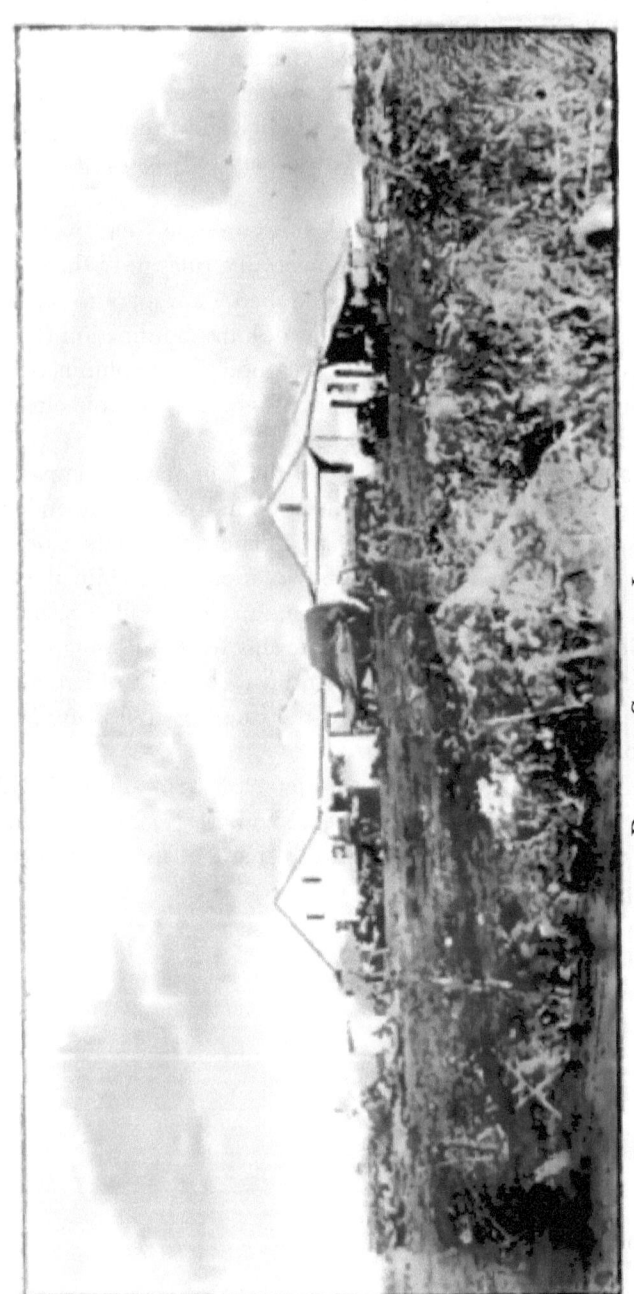

Belingwe Store and Laager

CHAPTER 1

Apprisal of Rebellion

The first intimation we, at Belingwe had of any real danger from a rebellious rising of the natives in Rhodesia was on the morning of the 26th of March, 1896.

About 7.30 a.m., whilst at breakfast, Mr. A. J. Wilson and myself were surprised by a visit from Mr. S. N. G. Jackson, the acting native commissioner at Belingwe, who appeared rather excited. After having been asked to take a seat, he explained to us that he had just received, by a native police runner, a letter from Mr. Fynn, acting native commissioner at Inseza, which he handed to me. It was as follows:—

> Sir,—I regret to have to report to you that the whole of the Cunningham family have been brutally murdered, and also Maddocks, manager of the Nelly Reef. Two of his miners got off, severely cut about. These two miners tell us that about thirty natives came up to their camp in a friendly way and sprang upon them with *kerries* and battleaxes. This happened the night before last, between six and seven.
>
> All the Europeans in this part of the district have concentrated here, as things look very serious as regards the natives. All the natives have cleared out of their *kraals*, probably fearing that the murders having been committed in their district they will be blamed.
>
> It is hard to say whether this organisation has been general throughout the country, which I fear is the case. We have received no communication from either Buluwayo or Filabusi yet.
>
> I would advise you to see Captain Laing and get all the prospectors to concentrate at the Belingwe Store, until we can get fur-

ther news. We expect someone over this morning from town. One of the murderers was shot by the police I sent after them. They came across five of them, all with guns, and that these men were Maholes I cannot believe. That the gang were composed of Matabeles—I should rather think they were Matabeles. Coach has not arrived yet.

    I have the honour to be,
        Yours obediently,
            (Signed)   H. P. Fynn, A.N.C.

After discussing the situation for a few minutes it was decided to send out information to all the outlying camps, as soon and as quietly as possible—Jackson sending out his two mounted white police and several native police, and I despatching my engineer, Edwin Vallentine, who happened to be at hand at the moment, on one of the company's best horses, to call in all the miners working for the company, and all others on his route to and from the different camps. His instructions were to ride as hard as possible, see the men at the various camps, tell them to take their bandoliers and rifles, go to the different works and order the natives employed to put all provisions and light stuff into the company's wagons, all the heavy and less dameageable material down the shafts, bring the ropes away, inspan the wagons, and get back to headquarters camp as quickly as possible, fetching as many natives as they could with them, but under strict surveillance.

I strongly advised Mr. Jackson to disarm his native police at once, but he had great faith in their loyalty and demurred; and as I was not then quite sure of the position, I did not think it advisable to interfere with one of the Chartered Company's officials—especially when he was doing his very best to assist—although at the time I felt certain that the native police would be on the side of any rebellion in Matabeleland. I, however, came to the conclusion to leave Mr. Jackson to carry out his own ideas for the time being, but made up my mind to watch the police under him very closely.

As soon as the messengers were sent off I went up to the camp of Sir Frederick Frankland, Assistant Mining Commissioner of Buluwayo, which was only about a hundred yards from my house. Wilson went over to the general store to warn the men there and get the ammunition and rifles in readiness. Sir Frederick had only arrived in Belingwe from Inseza, two days before the outbreak, accompanied by his assistant, W. C. Beaty-Pownall, and were engaged in inspecting the different mining properties in the Belingwe district for the Chartered Company. They were just about to saddle up and go out for the day when I got to their camp. I could see at once that they had not heard of the native rising. I told them what I had heard and had already done. Sir Frederick was very much upset when he learnt of the fate of the Cunningham family. He had been a guest at their house only a few days previously, and had been all over the Inseza district, where most of the murders had been committed, and knew nearly all the people there. He and Pownall at once decided to throw in their lot with the Belingwe men, and volunteered their assistance on the spot.

The disarming of the native police was then discussed, and Sir Frederick coincided with my opinion. We then rode over to the police camp, unarmed, so as not to cause any suspicion. Mr. Jackson had gone off, leaving Mr. W. R. Wilson, his assistant, in charge. We told Mr. Wilson we were in favour of having the native police disarmed, and he thought it was advisable, but would not do anything in the absence of his chief. We then decided to leave matters as they were for the time being, and proceeded to the general store, which was about a thousand yards from the police camp. Here we found all my company's employees busy getting their rifles and ammunition ready for the men coming in from the outlying camps. Sites were then selected on which to erect two small redoubts, to protect the store and cover the defenders.

About 11 a.m. Mr. Malcolm McCallum, manager for the "Buluwayo Syndicate," rode up to the store to see me. He said, "I have had notice from the police, and have put my men on their guard, and have come to see you and find out what is to be done." The situation was explained to him, and he departed at once, to bring in his men and supplies.

Shortly after midday my company's wagon, with the miners from "The Bob's Luck" and "Wanderers' Rest" and a Mrs. Mitchell, came into camp. Mr. Mitchell, who was in charge of "Bob's Luck," reported that he had tried to carry out the instructions sent, and had succeeded in getting most of the mining plant under cover before the natives deserted. This they did at the very first opportunity, disappearing in the bush in every direction. James Low, who was in charge of the "Wanderers' Rest," reported that the natives worked well and got all the mining material down a deep shaft, but when carrying the food stuff to a spot where the wagon had to pick it up, they waited a favourable opportunity, destroyed most of it, and disappeared in the bush. The above reports left no doubt in my mind as to the seriousness of our position. It appeared very plain that all the natives had an idea of what was going to happen.

Towards evening Harry Posselt, W. Lynch, and C. F. W. Nauhaus, farmers, who lived close to the Doro Mountains, about twelve miles away, came into camp and reported that fifty-six of their trek oxen had been looted during the previous night.

At 8 p.m. a meeting was held in the Belingwe Hotel, at which there were thirty-three present. This number was about ten men short of what we had estimated to be in the district at the time. Five of these we knew were at the "Sabie," twenty-five miles distant, and could not possibly be in for another day. Two others were at a camp about three miles away, who pooh-poohed the idea of a native rising; the remainder we expected were on their way in. Some of the men present had walked in eighteen miles, and it was very gratifying to notice the readiness with which most of the men in the district had grasped the situation and come in at once, to give all the assistance they could. The meeting appointed me their chairman. I read Mr. Fynn's letter and explained all that had been done and what had actually happened during the day as far as my knowledge went.

As the commanding officer of the volunteers in the district addressing them, I said that I would at once place them on an active service footing. With regard to the burghers, it was explained to the meeting that they had been asked to concentrate solely for the purpose of protecting life and property, and that the camp, as far as they were concerned, was purely a voluntary one. I asked them to do what they thought best, under the circumstances, and to co-operate with the volunteers, for the mutual defence of all. They unanimously agreed to place themselves under my command, and elected Sir Frederick Frankland to be their lieutenant and second in command.

A portion of the white men were then detailed to superintend the erection of the redoubts by about seventy natives, who had been brought into camp. The natives worked with a will when they were told the white men knew all about the rebellion, and that if any of them attempted to escape until the works were completed, they would be fired on. They were also informed they would be at liberty to go or stay with us as soon as the works were finished. The moon was just about two days from being full, and served us beautifully, and it was a stirring sight to see the natives hard at work, under the white guards, who, on this occasion, had a trying duty to perform, namely, to keep a look-out for a possible enemy in front and treachery from the enemy employed within.

By the time the moon went down, about 3 a.m. the following morning, the redoubts were so far advanced as to offer good cover for the defenders. The work was then stopped, the natives marched into the store paddock, and sentries were placed over them. A guard was mounted and sentries put on wherever it was considered the best positions were. The remainder of the white men laid down close to the earthworks, with their arms handy, and patrols were sent round the cattle *kraals* at intervals; but nothing of any importance happened. Thus, through the timely warning sent from Inseza by Mr. Fynn. most of the men in Belingwe were banded together and in a position to protect themselves and public property in less than twenty-four hours from the time the warning was received.

The acting native commissioner and his assistant slept at their own camp, about a thousand yards from the position we had fortified. When morning came they found the native police had built a bush *scherm* between their own quarters and those of their officers. This rather damped Mr. Jackson's belief in their loyalty. He came in and reported the matter, and then he and his assistant joined the other white men in garrison. The police were brought down and placed under cover of one of the forts, about a hundred yards away, but as several of them had faithfully carried the despatches entrusted to them, and had been the means of advising many of the white men, it was very difficult to decide what to do with them. They protested that they were not a party to the rebellion, and that they wanted to be faithful to the white men. They were strictly watched, but allowed to keep their arms.

All hands were kept busy during the 27th, putting the finishing touches to the forts and covering their approaches with a strong abattis made of the large hook thorn and other trees.

Towards the evening W. Sheldrake came into camp just as the men were being told off to their posts for the night. He reported that Stoddart's camp at the "Great Belingwe" mine had been looted by the rebels, and nineteen trek oxen were missing. He had had to run the gauntlet of the rebels' fire as he was on his way to the fort. Bergqvist, his comrade, had gone to look after the missing cattle. I felt very much annoyed with these men for not taking the timely advice sent to them, and acting in concert with the others. Had they done so their camp and cattle would have been saved, for they were the first men Vallentine saw on his way out. It was pure selfishness that kept them away from the other men, and when it was suggested that a party should be sent out to try and find Bergqvist.

I did not think it was proper that any lives should be risked for him, seeing that he had had the best chances of any at first; and it was only when a party of volunteers came to me on the morning of the 28th and said that they wished to go out and endeavour to find out what had happened to Bergqvist, that I agreed to let them go. I admired the sentiment that prompted the volunteers to go in quest of their comrade. The following men were allowed to depart, namely, W. R. Wilson, H. Posselt, Corporal Daniell, Corporal Le Vierge, H. Paulsen, and C. Paulsen. They were mounted on the best horses we had in the camp, and left about 6.30 a.m.

They had not gone half an hour before Bergqvist came into camp and reported that on the evening of the previous day he had followed up the spoor of the missing cattle and come up with them before sundown. They were then being driven to the southwest by a large party of armed natives, who laughed at his vain endeavours to drive his cattle back, evidently enjoying his discomfiture. Although they were all armed, they did not attempt to hurt him, only driving the cattle along a little faster and jeering at him when he gave up his efforts to recover his oxen. The patrol returned about 1 p.m.. and reported that all the provisions at Stoddart's camp were destroyed and scattered over the *veldt*.

CHAPTER 2

Treachery and Desertion of Native Police

The defence works at the store were still being carried on and improved, and the men told off into two divisions—No. 1 division for No. 1 fort and No. 2 division for No. 2 fort. A guard was mounted at sunset, and six sentries posted round the *laager*. The native police were posted and had charge of the cattle, four hundred of which were *kraaled* about a hundred yards northwards from the *laager*. They also had a few sentries posted outside the white sentries.

This brings us to the evening of the 28th. Shortly after sundown two shots were fired by the police sentries. The white sentries at once retired on their forts, according to orders, and the forts were manned. Mr. Jackson and Mr. Wilson went immediately to find out what the native sentries had fired at. The sentries said they saw several *kaffirs* moving about in front of their posts, and that they fired on them. Shortly afterwards the native commissioner and his assistant again went out to the cattle posts, and returned to report that all the native police, with the exception of three, had deserted, taking with them twenty rifles and ten rounds of ammunition per man. Not long after this several signals were heard by the white sentries near the cattle *kraal*. I then took out a patrol of eight white men, in skirmishing order, and got past the cattle *kraal* without finding anything in the shape of a nigger.

The inside of the *kraal* was examined and two natives were found hiding. They said they were hiding from the police, and, on being identified as herds, were allowed to join the other natives in the compound. I was under the impression that they were placed inside the *kraal* for the purpose of driving out the oxen when the proper moment came, but as our sentries were too much on the alert, the police had decided to go without the cattle for the time being.

The three native police who remained were disarmed, but they could, or would, give no information. Two days afterwards they were allowed to go out to bring in some mules from Posselt's farm, but, needless to say, they never returned.

I am quite sure that many people who may read this will think I was wrong from the beginning in not having the police arrested and disarmed. At the time I felt convinced I was wrong; but what otherwise could anyone have done when everything is considered? First, a native policeman brought us the warning; then, after they knew we were on our guard, they took our messages to isolated white men—some of whom were twenty-five miles away from our *laager*—and as we had no information from outside, I think it would have been very unfair to have treated them as rebels until they proved themselves such.

On the 29th we still went on strengthening our defences, the cattle *kraal* was moved close up to the *laager*, an abattis put right round the whole place, and several dynamite mines were set, to be fired by electricity Luckily my company had three strong electric batteries and any amount of wire and connections, which were of great utility under the circumstances.

This evening H. Posselt and W. Lynch, two of the troopers, who knew the country well, volunteered to try and get through, if possible, to Buluwayo with despatches, in order to let the authorities know we were all right in Belingwe, and to bring back all the information they could in regard to the rebellion. They left after dark, mounted on two of our best horses, and returned on the morning of the 31st, just as the sun was rising.

They reported that they got as far as the Inseza, which is about fifty miles west of Belingwe, on the road to Buluwayo, and found that place deserted by all white men.

A small *laager* had been formed at Cummings' store, which had evidently been attacked. There were several dead bodies of natives lying about, but none of white men. The brick walls of one of the houses bore bullet-marks in many places. About three miles beyond Cummings' store they saw the bodies of a *kaffir* woman and child, both disembowelled. As they approached the river, at the foot of the western slope of the Inseza hills, they were fired upon from the thick bush by a body of native police, who were evidently stationed to guard the *drift*.

A GROUP OF SCOUTS

Posselt and Lynch were forced to return. It would have been useless to have gone further, as they would have been overpowered. Luckily they got off clear—Posselt only losing his hat. We were all very pleased to see them back, and although they had failed to accomplish their object, we knew it was not their fault. The fact, however, of their not being able to get through made us think more seriously of the position we were in, and very anxious to know what was happening in other parts of the province.

Every morning and evening mounted patrols were sent out in different directions to watch the approaches, and patrols of Cape boys were sent up and down the river-beds every morning before the cattle were let out to graze.

On the same morning, the 31st, the mounted patrol caught a native hiding in the bush, about three miles from the fort, and brought him into camp. On being questioned, he said—

> I am one of the cattle herds, who ran away with the police from Belingwe. The police ran away because the Maholes had raided Bergqvist's cattle. They went to Um'Nyati's. The police wanted me to go further with them, but I refused, and said I wished to return to my master, the Native Commissioner. At Um'Nyati's I heard that all the white men in Buluwayo were to be killed and also those at Inseza. I heard that the *impi* was to kill all in Buluwayo first, and then come down this way and kill all here, and then on to Victoria. I also heard that ten white men had been killed at Inseza and that the others were in *laager*. I left here with four of us herd-boys and five police. I do not know who is supposed to be heading the rebellion. Um'Nyati's people are at their *kraal*. They are not armed. I ran away from the police in the daytime.

The information got from this boy proved how very serious matters were, and did not tend to make the men in the little garrison of Belingwe feel any more comfortable than they were before the lad arrived. In fact this information had quite the opposite effect, and it was not long before I heard rumours that several of the more nervous men in *laager* had been discussing the advisability of moving the camp to Victoria.

I called a general meeting in the store, and explained to those present that I considered the position we held a very strong and safe one and that it was the intention to continue strengthening it every day, and in doing so I would be glad to receive any suggestions from any one that might tend to that end.

With regard to the suggestion to move camp to Victoria, I said I was very sorry to think that there was anyone present who had so little faith in himself or his comrades as to insult them by insinuating that they were not able to hold the position against anything in the shape of an *impi* of savages, and that I was really surprised to learn that any of the men were becoming alarmed; that it appeared to me quite evident that the man who would advise the deserting of Belingwe did not know the difficulties that lay before him on the way to Victoria. I further pointed out that we were strongly fortified, in a good position, with plenty of water and provisions to last at least three or four months. I also stated plainly that if any man, or section of men, thought it best to move, he, or they, were at perfect liberty to do so, but once away from the range of our forts they would have to look after themselves, and that so far as the volunteers and myself were concerned, we would stay where we were, or if we were forced to vacate we would take the road for Buluwayo, because it was much more easy to travel on than the one to Victoria.

I also had the pleasure of informing the meeting that two of their number, who knew the different ways to Victoria, had volunteered to try and get through, and bring about three thousand rounds of ammunition—the only thing we wanted to make our position absolutely secure.

The men were invited to speak their minds freely and openly, and after considerable deliberation all agreed to remain where they were.

F. Luckhurst and W. Lyle, the two men who had volunteered to ride to Victoria for ammunition, left after dark on two good horses.

Just as the meeting ended, the signalman reported several white men coming in from the north. They were in the thick bush and evidently scouting the store. As soon as they saw white men moving about they came straight up, and we were very glad to welcome John, James, and Archie Cook, Walter Laidlaw, and C. C. Pike, from the "Sabie" district. The native policeman had delivered the message to them safely. They had started for the camp the following morning, coming slowly, and taking bypaths, in case of being surprised. They were all very tired and glad to get into camp.

On the 1st of April I had all the dynamite removed from the magazine, close to the store, and put down a shaft, about one mile away.

On the 3rd of April, shortly after daybreak, the sentry reported the approach of a white man. This proved to be James Stoddart, who had, on learning the seriousness of the rebellion in Matabeleland, decided to come in from Victoria, in Mashonaland, to warn his men in the "Sabie" district. His horse broke down before he had got over the first thirty miles, and he had to walk the remaining fifty, doing the greater part of the distance at night. He was surprised when he reached the "Sabie" camps to find them deserted, but, nothing daunted, came on with the intention of warning Belingwe, not knowing that we had already been advised. When he came in he was very footsore, hungry, and soaking wet, having lain the greater part of the previous night in the bush, on a small rise, about a mile east of our position, watching for any signs as to whether the store was deserted, or inhabited by natives or whites. He was very happy indeed when daylight came and he saw the white sentries on their posts and the place in a state of defence.

After he had partaken of some refreshment he made the following report:—

When I left Fort Victoria there were about one hundred and twenty men, and sixty women and children in *laager*. They had between twenty and thirty horses, and provisions for all, to last about six weeks, and plenty of arms and ammunition. They were still in telegraphic communication with Buluwayo and Salisbury, and had received the following information *re* the rebellion. It was generally supposed that the rising was general throughout Matabeleland, and that one of Lobengula's sons was at the head of it. The headquarters of the rebels was in the Matopo Mountains. Several small patrols of white men had been sent out from Buluwayo to help in prospectors and others from the outlying districts. The leaders of these patrols were Spreckly, George Grey, Gifford, Napier, and Selous. A large patrol of about four hundred men was being raised to go out and strike a decisive blow at the rebels, if possible, and the Chartered Company had ordered reinforcements from the Cape Colony of five hundred men, and Khama had offered his assistance. So far the telegraph wires had not been tampered with. About forty white men had been murdered so far as could be ascertained at present.

To us, in Belingwe, the information brought by Stoddart was most acceptable, because it showed us that, at all events, our comrades in other parts of the country were organising and defending themselves, and preparing to strike a decisive blow. Stoddart's report was read to a full-muster parade at 8.30 a.m., and he received the thanks of the garrison and three hearty cheers for his gallant endeavour to bring the tidings of danger to Belingwe. He was unanimously elected a lieutenant, and taken on the strength of the garrison.

On the same parade the minutes of the first meeting were read to those who were not then present, and they were asked to decide whether or not they would join the garrison as effective members and stay under its protection. All agreed to serve, and forthwith joined the ranks.

The following is the muster-roll of the Belingwe garrison as it was on the 3rd of April, 1896:—

		Nationality
1.	Capt. D. Tyrie Laing	Scotland
2.	Sir Frederick Frankland, Bart.	England
3.	Lieut. James Stoddart	New Zealand
4.	Sergt. W. Lynch	Cape Colony
5.	„ L McCallum	America
6.	„ A. J. Wilson	Scotland
7.	„ W. R. Wilson	Natal
8.	„ S. N. G. Jackson	Cape Colony
9	Corpl. Le Vierge	England
10.	„ Daniell	Australia
11.	Trooper E. Vallentine	Scotland
12.	„ J. Low	Scotland
13.	„ W. C. Beaty Pownall	England
14.	„ A. D. Cameron	Scotland
15.	„ N. Posselt	Natal
16.	„ C. Cremer	Germany
17.	„ R. Douglas	America
18.	„ G. G. Descalzie	Italy
19.	„ A. B. Inverdale	Scotland
20.	„ M. Huband	England
21.	„ P. Levine	Russia
22.	„ J. C. Mitchell	Cape Colony
23.	„ W. Miller	Scotland
24.	„ J. A. McGilvray	Scotland
25	„ C. F. W. Nauhaus	Natal

26.	,, H. Posselt	Natal
27.	,, C. H. Paulsen	America
28.	,, H. Paulsen	America
29.	,, F. Luckhurst	England
30.	,, F. H. Snowdon	England
31.	,, S. Roodts	England
32.	,, W. K. Warham	England
33.	,, W. Sheldrake	England
34.	,, J. C. Bushnell	Cape Colony
35.	,, R. Bergqvist	Sweden
36.	,, B. Yorke	England
37.	,, John Cook	Scotland
38.	,, James Cook	Scotland
39.	,, Archie Cook	Scotland
40.	,, Walter Laidlaw	Scotland
41.	,, C. C. Pike	England
42.	,, W. Lyle	Cape Colony
43.	Sergt.-Farrier W. J. Clifford	Australia
44.	Quartermaster F. J. Pope	England

And Mrs. J. C. Mitchell, wife of J. C. Mitchell, who was in charge of "Bob's Luck" mine.

To be added to the above, we had ten Cape boys, who were armed and did duty with the white men, and very useful we found them. We had also fifteen Zambesi boys, who were used as cattle and horse guards by day.

CHAPTER 3

Capture of a Native Spy

About 8 p.m. on the evening of the 3rd Sergeant Lynch brought in a native prisoner, who had been caught inside our outer line of defence. I questioned him, and he willingly gave a glowing account of a journey he had just made from Buluwayo. He had left there only three days before with a message from W. Slade to his partner West, whom he expected to be in Belingwe, but, if not, he (the prisoner) was to proceed to Gondogue and deliver his message. He professed to be surprised at finding us in *laager*, and asked the reason why. He said the people in Buluwayo were going about as usual, that so were the people at Bembesi, as he came past, and at the Inseza. He had heard there had been some slight disturbances among the Maholes at Inseza, but that the native police had put a stop to it.

The self-confident effrontery with which the prisoner answered all the questions put to him might have put us off our guard had Lieutenant Stoddart's statement not been made before, but being in possession of that it was quite easy to discern we had a very bold spy to deal with. After putting a few questions as to Gifford's fight at Inseza and telling him that we knew what had taken place at Bembesi, and that the people in Buluwayo were in *laager*, he was slightly nonplussed, and went away quite dejected when he found that we did not believe his story and that his visit had proved futile.

From the time we had formed *laager* up to the present the general defence works had been continued daily, and the men were drilled twice a day as well.

The fact of natives being able to get through the outer fence and come close up to the forts without being noticed suggested the idea of an automatic sentry, in the shape of a signal-gun, which was erected forthwith on the top of the guard-room. It was connected with wires

to the outer fence, which was divided into seven sections, each with an indicator, which dropped and fired a gun if anything attempted to force an entrance or pull away any of the bushes of which the fence was constructed. In about three days' time this automatic sentry worked so well that it was next to impossible to tamper in the slightest degree with any part of the fence or to get through it without first firing the signal-gun. In fact it worked so well, and we placed so much confidence in it, as to withdraw the seven sentries who were posted, previous to its erection, round the *laager* inside the outer fence. This proved a great boon to the men, and relieved them from a large amount of night duty, which had been very hard on them before, in consequence of many of their number being down with fever, caused by hard work during the day and having to sleep in the earthworks at night.

After this the men in each fort divided the night-watch amongst them, which generally ran to about two hours for each man per night. Three men at a time were on duty, sitting up on the ramparts of the redoubts, facing in different directions, the only outside sentry being one on the river bank, about twenty yards from No. 2 redoubt. The automatic sentry was always on the alert, and considered it his duty to turn out the guard, if only to a jackal or wolf, should any of the latter, as they often did, attempt to come through.

The defence works had advanced so far now that most of the garrison had thorough confidence in being able to repel any attack the rebels in the district might make on the position. Besides the earthworks and bush fences, twelve dynamite mines had been laid to command positions where an attacking force could get cover to concentrate before charging. These mines were attached by overhead wires to each fort, and operated by an electric battery, used for blasting purposes at the mines. We were the happy possessors of three such batteries, strong enough to explode a mine several miles away, and they were so arranged that one mine or all could be fired with one shock, if considered necessary.

It gives me great pleasure to mention that the advent of the Cooks' coming into *laager* was a great piece of good fortune, for not only were they good shots and all-round men generally, but two of them, John and James, were qualified electrical engineers. To them the arrangement and setting of the mines was left, and they worked at them every day until in all they had twenty-seven placed round the *laager* in every available position. The system they adopted was so simple and complete that any of the men could have fired the mines as ordered without explanation. It was considered advisable to mount guard every evening about sundown, as was done before the automatic sentry was erected, for the sake of appearances, in case any of the rebel scouts might have been about and noticed our change of programme. There was a full parade of the garrison held at the same time, and the men were then marched to their posts and the redoubts manned. As soon as it was dark the night-watch was set and the sentries recalled.

On the evening of the 4th, when the men were on parade, the sentry on the look-out reported two horsemen approaching on the Buluwayo road. They were coming along very slowly, but gradually increased their speed as they got near to the fort. They proved to be two Cape boys sent on with despatches from Mr. Duncan, the acting administrator in Buluwayo. Mr. Duncan's despatch was very short. He trusted we were all right, and requested me to bury all the ammunition the men could not carry and march to Buluwayo as soon as possible. The verbal message given to the despatch riders was most consoling. They had been instructed to try and get to Belingwe, and if possible to try and recognise any of the dead white men, and cover them up if they had time and an opportunity.

The boys were very well treated and petted by the men of the garrison. They got ready and started on their homeward journey at 6 p.m. on the evening of the 5th. They had travelled mostly during the night on their way down, and intended doing the same going back. By avoiding the main paths and taking across country, they hoped to be able to get in all right. Everyone wished them God-speed as they started on their adventurous journey, carrying a despatch from me to the acting administrator at Buluwayo, describing our position and showing the advisability of our remaining in possession of Belingwe.

The following extracts from the despatch above referred to may not be uninteresting to some readers:—

> We have eighteen men armed with Lee-Metfords and a good supply of ammunition for same. The rest of the men, with a few exceptions, are armed with Martini-Henrys, the supply of ammunition for which is. at present, limited to thirty rounds per man. We are expecting the return of the two messengers we sent to Victoria at any moment, but until they return it is, of course, impossible to leave.
>
> I have written to you at this length in order that you may thor-

oughly see our position and then decide whether you still wish us to march to Buluwayo. I should point out to you that in the event of us marching, in all probability the surrounding tribes will rise, thinking that this is a retreat. It will also be impossible for me to bring the cattle, and their gaining possession of these would strengthen the position of the rebels, as I hear that Um'Nyati, a neighbouring chief, is at present supplying arms and cattle to the Matebele.

In my report which was sent to Victoria, and which I requested to be forwarded to the acting commissioner at Salisbury, I pointed out how highly undesirable I considered it to leave this position. The mere fact of our staying here (although the smallness of our numbers prevents us from taking the offensive) keeps a large number of natives from joining the main body of the rebels, and the geographical position is such that it would form a good base for the concentration of any troops, from either Victoria or the South, in which case we could give active support to Buluwayo operations, being near to Shamba and Filabusi. The country here is easy to travel, and the majority of the men are intimately acquainted with it. Had I thirty more men here, horsed and fully armed, I could send out patrols and keep this district secure. On the other hand, if the addition of our small force to those already in Buluwayo would be of service, I feel sure that the men under my command will cheerfully march in. In the latter case I do not consider it necessary that you should weaken your own strength by sending any patrol to escort us, as we would travel light.

I am in hopes you have already received the news of our safety through Victoria, and think it might be advisable for you to cable to England the names of the men here and of their safety.

I may also mention that sickness has prevailed in the camp, but am glad to say it is easing off.

I must draw your attention to the fact that the value of private property at present in our charge in this *laager* is close on £10,000.

I cannot close this letter without bringing under your notice the very able assistance I have received from Lieutenant Sir Frederick Frankland, who has from the beginning of my operations co operated with me most willingly and cheerfully, sparing neither time nor trouble in the daily work of the camp;

also from Lieutenant Stoddart, who since he came into camp has rendered me much valuable assistance from his previous experience of former campaigns. I must also add that all the sergeants and corporals work faithfully and diligently, as well as the whole of the men, who are very loyal, turning out to their parades and drills without a murmur, and thereafter proceeding to the work detailed to them cheerfully.

The mere fact of our remaining in *laager* kept a large body of the rebels watching us, ready to rush for the spoil when we vacated, and equally ready to follow us up and harass us at every available opportunity which might offer itself We were much better off in Belingwe than we should have been anywhere on our way to Buluwayo; in fact it would have been madness to have attempted to reach Buluwayo. I don't believe it would have been possible, even if all the men had been fit to march. As it was, ten of them were down with fever, which would have compelled us to carry them in very slowly. This would have rendered our march all the more difficult, and I feel certain, had we been foolish enough to move, not a man would have reached Buluwayo. In any event we could not have gone until we had news from Lyle and Luckhurst: but luckily we had not long to wait for them. They turned up about 4.30 p.m. on the afternoon of the 6th. with 3,000 rounds of Martini-Henry ammunition and a despatch from Captain Vizard, who was in command of Victoria.

The despatch-riders made the following report, namely: That they left the Belingwe *laager* on the evening of the 31st of March, and got about twenty-five miles on their way to Victoria, when one of their horses broke down. They off-saddled for some time and went on again about 2 a.m. the following morning, and walked on to the east bank of the Lundi River, where they halted for a short time, then walked on again to Goddard's store, and from thence to Meeks, the missionary's, expecting there to get a fresh horse, but as all his horses had been sent away they had to walk the greater part of the way, reaching Victoria on the 2nd of April, where they at once handed their despatches to Captain Vizard. They left Victoria on the 3rd with four horses and 3,000 rounds of Martini-Henry ammunition.

At sunset on the evening of the 5th they reached the Sand River, and off-saddled their horses to give them a rest till the moon rose. The horses were knee-haltered, and Lyle had just started to gather some firewood, when two lions made for, and scattered them. Lyle, as soon as he saw what had happened, made for the horses, and succeeded in catching two of them. These Luckhurst held, whilst Lyle again went after the other two for some distance, but did not get up to them. They had stampeded on the road back to Victoria. The lions did not give chase but hung around the spot where the other horses were; that they cooked some food and coffee, and waited until the moon rose, and then put all the ammunition on to the two remaining horses and resumed their march on foot, between 2 and 3 a.m., getting to Belingwe about 4.30 the same afternoon. The natives they met on their way were Mashonas, and at that time friendly.

At 5.30 p.m. a full parade was held, and the despatches which had been forwarded by Captain Vizard, were read to the men. Those from the administrator contained a brief account of all he knew about the rebellion, its supposed cause, the efforts then being made to put it down, and concluded with congratulations to myself and the garrison of Belingwe for holding our own, giving me an entirely free hand to do what was considered best, either to hold the position or retire on any other one, until the government were in a position to send us aid.

When the men were dismissed they cheered the two despatch-riders heartily, and praised them for the plucky manner in which they managed to get the ammunition through. The men, having now plenty of ammunition, felt more confident than ever of holding their own, and were very anxious to get out and try to have a brush with any straggling parties of the enemy who might be about, but, further than the ordinary patrols, I would not consent to any party going out to look for adventure. We all knew very well that our position was closely watched during the day from a hill called Fondoque, about one and a half miles from our *laager*. The camp fires of large parties could be seen at night about eight miles to the north of our position, and often the ashes of a small fire were discovered at the back of one of the hills close up to the forts by the morning patrols. This proved that the scouts of the rebels were always on the prowl.

My plan was to leave them alone, until they got tired of waiting for us to vacate our position, and I concluded that then they would be sure to come and try to rush us out of it. I was very much averse to small parties going more than a mile or two from the laager, in case they might get cut off by a large body of the enemy, whose favourite mode of fighting is, if possible, to surround isolated bodies with overpowering numbers and annihilate them. I often had to tell the men, when they came to me for permission to go out, that they had only to wait until the enemy got tired of watching us doing nothing, then they would have plenty to do. We could not afford to lose a man until they made their attack. When that came off we should want all our strength, and that behind the walls of the redoubts and mines, for I fully expected them to attack our position in great strength.

By this time the defences were as far advanced as was really necessary and the men had little to do during the day except their inlying picquet, the sentry of which was posted on a platform erected on the top of the large iron store, and a commanding position, from which a very good view of the surrounding country was obtainable, especially with the aid of a very good pair of field-glasses, which were commandeered for the purpose from Trooper Snowdon. The only other duties were the ordinary camp fatigues, bringing in wood, &c. The water was pumped up from the river every evening, and three iron tanks, four feet square each, were always kept full. So far as rations were concerned my garrison was very well off. There was an abundant supply of bread stuffs, and we had a large troop of cattle, over four hundred head, to start with, many of them being young Matabele oxen, most of them in good condition, and, as good luck would have it, the dreaded *rinderpest* had not reached them.

We had also sixteen horses, twelve of which were in very good condition and up to despatch-riding on an emergency. We had a plentiful supply of mealies for them, with good grazing along the banks of the river, just under cover of the guns. The only thing the men wanted was work, or some excitement to break the monotony of a garrison life. The despatch from the administrator had set our minds at rest as to the ultimate end of the rebellion, and knowing the worst had happened with the murders at Inseza and other parts, any anxiety we had felt for the security of Buluwayo and other towns was dispelled when we knew that our comrades were organised and holding their own, at least, against the rebels.

As soon as the heaviest works were completed, principally for the purpose of saving our provisions as much as possible, and to get rid of what would have proved a very dangerous element in our midst in case of an attack, and likewise for the purpose of carrying and explaining a proclamation to the neighbouring tribes, it was decided to parade all the natives who had been kept to assist in erecting the fortifications, and explain to them that their services were no longer required, that they were at liberty to go home if they wished, or to stay

A GROUP OF "A" TROOP

with us if they were afraid to do so. Native Commissioner Jackson and his assistant accordingly paraded the natives, explained the position, and gave them to distinctly understand that they were at full liberty to go or stay, but that those who elected to go, if found about the camp after that night, would be treated as rebels, and that those who elected to stay would have the protection of our *laager* as long as they deserved it, but if any of them were found attempting to escape, or holding communication with any natives outside, they would be treated as spies. About seventy boys decided to leave at once, and about twenty-five decided to remain.

Knowing the localities from which most of the boys came, we were in a position to judge of the loyalty, or otherwise, of their *kraals*, and we came to the conclusion that there were very few loyal natives to the west, south, or north of us. The natives who had decided to go were instructed to inform all the people in the districts they passed through that if any of them wished to communicate with us, they were to advance along the main roads unarmed, but that if any of them were found in the bush near our position they would be treated as spies and shot, unless they could prove they were there for a purpose friendly to us.

CHAPTER 4
Attack by Matabele

On the evening of the 9th, shortly after dark, the night-watch had not been set, and most of the men, except the flying sentries and guard, were at their evening meal, when the sentry on the river post challenged rapidly, and then alarmed the forts. Captain Frankland and myself happened to be in our mess-room, quite close to the post. We both rushed out to ascertain what was likely to happen. The sentry reported that he had seen several *kaffirs* crawling along, under cover of the fence of the cattle *kraal*, and pointed out the position. By this time every man was at his post and all ready. Mr. Jackson, Captain Frankland, and myself went up to the place indicated, with our revolvers ready, but at first could not see anything. The bottom of the fence was under shadow and very dark. By mere chance I happened to observe something move close to my foot, and ordered it to stand up. It proved to be a *kaffir*, whom we at once laid hold of.

At the same time several others jumped up and ran off, taking good care to run between the men in the forts and ourselves, thereby preventing us from using our firearms, for fear of shooting each other. They got under cover of the shadow, and the next thing we heard of them was from the Cape boy sentry. Hans, challenging and firing. Immediately afterwards the signal-gun on top of the guard-room went off. This was caused by the runaways breaking through the outer fence and disturbing the signal wires. The alarm was complete by this time; even the sick men were in the forts, with their rifles ready for action. The last we heard of the runaways that night was when they got about five hundred yards away. They then commenced to signal by whistling, which was answered from several directions, showing clearly that there were others of the same tribe about. Then all was quiet.

The runaways left their arms where they were first discovered. The following morning the prisoner was tried by court-martial. At first he would not give any evidence either in favour of himself or against his confederates. On being asked if he knew he had forfeited his life, he said:

> I know that, and am sorry you caught me. I came from Wedza's, and so did those with me. He was going out to meet some more of his men. Wedza wishes to take away all cattle. Other *kaffirs* leave your *laager* at night with information, and some do it through the day, I have been very unlucky. There are a lot of our people watching Belingwe, to get it when you white men are all dead. There will be quite enough of them to eat up all of you white men.

The prisoner was condemned and shot.

Whilst the men were at their midday meal three other natives broke away and got off. They were not fired on. The Cape boys tried to run them down, but failed. It was not worth while sending horsemen after them. I would have been very glad if they had all gone, for it was impossible to tell whether they were spies or loyal. The mere fact of the natives trying to go off in this manner led us to believe that they knew something of importance was likely to happen soon and they did not want to be with us when it did take place. This made every one more alert than ever, and several shots were fired the following evening by the flying sentries, but most probably at wolves or jackals. The signal-gun also went off on the night of the 11th, but I was unable to ascertain the cause.

Sunday, the 12th of April, like all our Sundays, was a lazy day—no drills or fatigues to do by either whites or blacks—and was spent by most of us with a book or some other amusement to pass time. Very probably the Sunday's midday meal was a heavier one than those of other days, and I daresay that by 2 p.m. most of the men not on duty were taking a *siesta*. Sir Frederick Frankland and myself were preparing to do the same at about 2.30 p.m. when the sentry on the lookout alarmed the garrison and reported that the cattle posts were being driven in by a large body of *kaffirs*. We at once jumped to the ramparts of the nearest redoubt and saw that the sentry's report was too true. The cattle had been grazing about a thousand yards to the south of our position, close to some small hills, thickly covered by bush, and at first sight these hills seemed to be one mass of *kaffirs*, all rushing towards the cattle.

Sergeant McCallum and Corporal Paulsen at once got out the two emergency horses, which were always kept ready saddled and bridled, and rode off to assist the cattle guard. They did very good work on their horses until we were able to get the other horses in and saddled up. Luckily they happened to be close by, as we had had them driven into the *laager* every day at noon and let out again at 2 p.m. They were in, saddled up, and mounted in less than five minutes. By this time there was quite a fusillade going on all round our south and west front, and the bullets were whizzing high over the forts. All the dismounted men, sick included, were in the forts. Leaving Captain Frankland in charge, with instructions to keep a sharp look-out to the north and east, and to commence fire at once if any of the enemy showed up in those directions, to draw our attention to the *laager* in case of a general attack, I rode off with nine mounted men to assist the cattle guards.

By this time the rebels had succeeded in breaking up the cattle into small herds and stampeded them away to the east and south. When we came up to where Sergeant McCallum and Corporal Paulsen were, they pointed out the direction in which the largest body were driven. This was done when we were going at a good hand-gallop and under a heavy fire from the surrounding hills at the back of the police camp. The line, in skirmishing order, wheeled to the left, and went straight for the rebel fighting line, those in front breaking away before a shot was fired at them; but the horsemen soon got close up and shot a few from their saddles. As the hill at the police camp was passed three men halted, took cover, and returned the fire of the rebels, who at once left their position and retreated rapidly to the north. Lieutenant Stoddart, with two men, did the same, whilst the men in the centre came on with me to an open flat which was immediately in our front.

As soon as we cleared the bush we saw several herds of cattle only a hundred yards or so in front of us being driven as hard as they could go, but as they were being driven away from their usual grazing ground they were trying to break back again. When the men with me saw the position they all seemed to yell at once, and this drew the attention of the rebels in front on to us. They evidently had never thought that the white men would attempt to get through their fighting line, and as soon as they saw us coming down on them they became a confused mass, fired off their rifles in every direction, at anything or nothing, and made for the dense bush, about five hundred yards in front of them, as hard as they could go.

Before they got to it we were well in amongst them, and had a certain amount of satisfaction before we retired from a heavy fire which was opened on us from the bush already mentioned. By this time Lieutenant Stoddart, with the men who remained behind to watch the flanks, came up, and a few more shots were fired by ourselves into the bushes. Whilst this was going on I had time to look up and down the valley, and for a mile on each side the rebels could be seen retreating as hard as they could for the bush in front of us. Presently the order was given from a hill about two hundred yards in advance of us for the rebels to concentrate. I then thought it advisable to retire, with the cattle we had recaptured, as quickly as possible, to the forts, from which we had not heard any firing worthy of mention.

As soon as we commenced to retire the bush and hillsides, which we had just left in our rear, got quite animated, and a brisk but very harmless rifle fire was sent after us, some of the rebels being so anxious to get in their shots that they were firing from the top of the Fondoque hill, a good mile away. We succeeded in getting back to the forts with 190 cattle, out of about 380 head, and during the night a lot of milch cows came back to their calves. We lost about one-half of what we had that morning and most of the young cattle were taken by the rebels.

When we got back, which we did without further trouble and no loss on our side, our comrades had been having a very anxious and excitable time. They had heard and seen most of the firing, and had a lot of shots over them, but only got in a few in return. They could not open fire while we were in sight, and when we got out of sight they had chances but did not take them, because we might have been in their line of fire. However, they did their duty, and were delighted to see us all come back again. Captain Frankland was on the platform on top of the roof of the store all the time, and had a splendid view of the whole affair until we got behind the hill at the police camp.

The natives in our *laager* were most effusive with their congratulations, which were cut short by one of the white men reporting that he saw several of them signalling in the direction of the cattle shortly before the attack commenced. He watched to see who they were signalling to, but saw nothing but cattle herds, and concluded at the moment that they were signalling to some of them to come home for food. They were all ordered into the compound, and those that had been guilty of signalling pointed out.

On being questioned, one said he came from M'Posi's; another, who had evidently lost his presence of mind, said he came from Godhlwayo, as also did the other two. They admitted that this boy had told the truth—the three of them came from Godhlwayo and knew and were connected with the rebels—Godhlwayo being the place where the rebellion originated. They were all tried, condemned, and shot. After this every native in the *laager*, except those that came from the Zambesi, Cape Colony, or Natal, was turned out of it at once. They all went willingly, except one very big Basuto, who said he would rather be killed by us than by the rebels; he was an utter stranger among them, knew nothing of the rebellion, and was an enemy to their race. He was allowed to stay, and was very faithful all through.

The men of the garrison had now something to talk about for the next few days. The monotony that had bored us all was broken up for a time, and we were all rather glad we had got our first big job over, and watched, more keenly than before, for the next.

The rebels at the first onset fought well for the cattle. McCallum and Paulsen shot three of them before we came up. One horrid-looking old witchdoctor was at the head of the attacking party. At first he had only a battleaxe and charms, and laughed at the white men, saying they could not harm him, and that they had no shot that could kill him. He had three bullets before he dropped. After that his followers seemed to lose a lot of their dash and became rather an easy prey for us for a short time. I have little doubt that had we been foolish enough to go on they would have made a new plan and attacked us again.

The Zambesi boys, who were with the cattle, behaved very well, and did their utmost to save them until we came out to their assistance, by heading them off towards camp. One of them, through force of habit I suppose, or perhaps to show his zeal, marched into the *laager*, whilst the fight was at its hottest, with a week-old calf on his back. Another one was missing after the fight and put down as dead. Some of the white men went out with his brothers to look for his body where he was last seen, and found it after a long search, in the bottom of a dry water creek, covered up with grass. They had some difficulty in getting it out. When, however, they did, and it found it was in the hands of friends, the body came to life again, and by the time the camp was reached the supposed dead one was quite lively.

One of the rebels, who had his position on the top of the hill close to the police camp, seemed to have charge of a rifle of no ordinary calibre. He directed all his fire over the *laager*, and at regular intervals of about five minutes sent a missile over the heads of its defenders. This practice, after a while, became rather amusing to some, irksome

A Group of "D" Troop—Cape Boys

to others, and frightened a few. Corporal Paulsen informed me it took three men to work this gun, and whilst they were in the act of loading it the last time he shot one of their number, the other two immediately decamping, taking the piece with them.

CHAPTER 5

Strong Patrol Goes Out

On the morning of the 13th, with the strongest mounted patrol we could muster, I went out in hopes of being able to gather some information as to the direction the rebels had taken, or whether they were still about, and also to bring back any stray oxen we might drop across. On the previous afternoon, shortly after the fight, a very severe thunderstorm passed over the district, drenching everything and obliterating all tracks of the rebels and cattle, and making it impossible for us to get any information as to their movements. The patrol made a big detour and came round by Stoddart's camp. "The Great Belingwe," down past "McPhee's camp," home along the "Bob's Luck" road, and across the field where we had the skirmish the previous afternoon. I then understood, for the first time, that the rebels had got a greater fright than we thought.

For a mile beyond the point where we left off pursuit the *veldt* bore evidence of their very hasty retreat. Blankets, great-coats, food, and arms had been dropped, to enable the owners to run with more freedom to the friendly cover of the bush-clad hills. They had been so thoroughly surprised that they did not dare to venture into the open to get back their property, even at night. They even left their dead on the field, a thing I had never known the natives of Matabeleland to do before when there was the least possible chance of getting the bodies away. Among the articles they abandoned were several police great-coats and bandoliers, full of ammunition, blankets, and provisions. Each man had evidently carried about from 5 lb. to 6 lb. of raw meat and about 5 lb. of mealies.

All the dead had a piece of oxfat tied to their throats. This I afterwards learned was fat taken from oxen killed by the "*M'limo*" and given to each man, after it had been "*Umtigatied*" (bewitched), to render the man impervious to harm from the bullets of the white man. Amongst the dead left on the field was the before-mentioned witch-doctor, dressed up in all the paraphernalia necessary for his calling, and a most hideous brute he looked, even in death, which, as a rule, modifies the expression on the face of most natives.

During the forenoon of the 14th two of Chebi's boys arrived with a despatch, dated the 8th, from Captain Vizard, Victoria. The following information was obtained from these boys:—

> We were given the letter by the white chief at Victoria, and were told to try and get here with it and to find out whether the white men were alive or dead. We have been seven days on the road. We have had to come slowly and carefully, because it is difficult to tell who are friends or foes. Most of the way we travelled at night. At Marandella's *kraal* we were told that the natives of this district were banding together to immediately attack Belingwe. The chiefs Wedza, Buschelli, Mapanzula, Mazezeteze, Impopote, and Senda have risen, and are being led by a band of Matabele from Godhlwayo, who are headed by Maduna, the son of Marqua, Lobengula's sister. These forces are located somewhere between Wedza's and the Bungwe Mountain, and their instructions are to wipe out Belingwe.
>
> The attack was to have taken place some days ago, during the afternoon. All the cattle which have been stolen from the farmers in this district have been taken to the Matopos, by way of Shamba. A great many of the Matabele women and children are hidden away in the Impatini Mountains. The *impi* that is gathering here has instructions to march on Victoria as soon as they have wiped out Belingwe, and treat that place in like manner before returning. These are the orders of the 'M'limo,' who lives in the Matopos. We do not know the strength of the attacking force, but Maduna has about three hundred Matabele with him, and his party have been killing white men all over the country by Inseza and Filabusi. Um'Nyati has not left his *kraal*, but all his men are armed. The only chiefs who are remaining faithful are Chebi's and those between him and Victoria. Indeema has destroyed all the white men's houses, &c., at Selukwe.

The boys could give little more information, and expressed a wish to be allowed to depart as soon as possible. They said they did not consider Belingwe a safe place when an *impi* was ready to attack it. They were then informed the place had been attacked two days previously and the rebels beaten off. This information surprised them a little, and they advised us strongly to march for Victoria before the rebels had time to re-form and make another attack. They were quite sure we were mad to stay any longer when we had a chance of getting away.

A despatch was written and handed to them, and they left at 4.30 p.m. About half an hour after their departure the inlying picquet gave the alarm and reported the rapid approach of several natives and a considerable shouting from others in the bush behind the police camp. The cattle and horses were at once turned into the *laager*, the forts manned, and several shots fired close to the approaching natives, two of whom at once showed friendly signs by holding their hands up. The remainder disappeared into the bush. Our horsemen advanced to meet the natives, and found that they were the despatch-bearers, who reported that they came into contact with a large body of Matabele, some of whom had on police great-coats. They were evidently examining the ground over which the skirmish took place. When they noticed the despatch-bearers they gave chase, and pressed them so hard that the boys had to throw away their blankets, in one of which the despatches were rolled up. They were rewritten, and the boys left again after dark by another route.

The presence of the Matabele increased our anxiety, and every precaution was taken to repel an attack, if necessary, during the night, all the men sleeping at their stations, but nothing occurred.

On the 15th a boy came in from Gondoque with a letter from a Mr. Carruthers to Mr. Lyle, asking him to forward a rifle and ammunition, and asking for information. Gondoque is about seventy miles south of Belingwe. To have given the boy a rifle and ammunition meant giving it to the rebels, so he left with a letter only, to Carruthers, telling him to try, if possible, to reach Victoria direct, from where he was, as M'Tipi's natives were friendly. He succeeded in getting to Victoria.

Nothing of any consequence happened until Sunday, the 19th, at 12.30 p.m., when it was reported to me that Trooper W. C. Beaty-Pownall had been shot by accident. Trooper Roodts had taken up Sergeant McCallum's Winchester repeater, and was showing the action to some comrades, when the rifle went off. The bullet, grazing the back of Trooper Yorke's left hand, entered the left leg of Beaty-Pownall on the inside, and, travelling obliquely down, passed out on the other side. I at once set to and stopped the bleeding, bandaged the leg up in splints, and had Pownall placed inside the airiest room in the large store. I then asked if there was anyone among the men who knew anything about surgery, but found I was the only one present who had even been taught in that line, and I am very sorry to say that the short course of field surgery that I went through whilst at Gibraltar was not sufficient to enable me to save the life of this brave young man. Had he been shot in action on the previous Sunday, when he did brilliant service, his case would not have been so hard, but to be laid out by an accident was too bad. He was a splendid fellow, and a great favourite in the garrison. The first thing he did, after being put to bed, was to pray that his unfortunate comrade who caused the accident should not be punished in any way; and his wish was adhered to.

Next Sunday, the 26th, Trooper Bergqvist died. He had been suffering from fever for some time previous, but on that morning he reported to me that he felt all right again. He had a cup of Bovril and a little meat at lunch, and shortly afterwards he was observed by Sergeant W. R. Wilson outside his wagon retching and gasping. Sergeant Wilson sent at once for myself and Lieutenant Stoddart, but Bergqvist expired before we could assist him. Death apparently resulted from suffocation.

That same day Mrs. Mitchell, wife of J. C. Mitchell, contractor, died. She had been ailing for some time, and fever had weakened her considerably. The shock she got on hearing of Bergqvist's sudden death upset her nervous system entirely, and she never recovered. Sunday seemed to be the special day for great misfortunes, since for three running we had had fighting, accident, and now two deaths. These facts did not tend to make the life in our little camp very cheerful, and I believe I felt the position as keenly as any one, and looked anxiously every day for the relief. Fever again had set in among the men, and sometimes as many as seventeen were unfit for duty. With no doctor present this was very unpleasant, and it was rendered doubly so by the constant growling of some of the more selfish of the men.

On the morning of Monday, the 27th, Robert Bergqvist and Mrs. Mitchell were buried in a small clearing about a hundred yards from the fort.

On the 28th, I am sorry to say owing to the growing discontent amongst a certain class of the men, I had to parade the whole and warn them that if any one was found deliberately shirking his duty, or in any way trying to upset the discipline of the garrison, they would be put back for a court-martial and tried as soon as any strange officers came into camp, and I warned them of the penalties.

On the morning of the 28th Beaty-Pownall asked me to amputate his leg. I had looked after him as well as I could, and cleansed and bandaged the wound twice daily. Everything else that could be done by his comrades was cheerfully fulfilled. From the beginning I was certain a doctor would have amputated the leg at once, and was in hopes that, as I had in several despatches asked for a doctor, one might turn up at any minute. But as day after day went past without bringing the required aid, I knew from the outward appearance of the leg that poor young Pownall had not long to live. When he asked me to cut off his leg I felt certain he also knew what was likely to happen. I formed a board, composed of Captain Frankland, Lieutenant Stoddart, and Orderly-room Sergeant A. J. Wilson, to examine Pownall, and decide what was to be done. In their presence he proposed the amputation of his leg.

The board asked him if he fully understood what he proposed, and whether he thought he could stand the operation. He answered that he thought he would, and begged that it might be done, to give him the last chance. He said he knew the lower part of his leg was dead, and that his life could only be saved by cutting it off. The board decided the amputation should take place. It was performed at once, and apparently successfully, the patient bearing up very well all the time. For the next two days he appeared to be recovering, the leg healing nicely, but on the morning of May 2nd he succumbed, without pain; having slept well the previous night, he never awoke. This was one of the heaviest blows our little garrison had to sustain. Beaty-Pownall was buried with military honours, beside the other victims of the rebellion.

On the 1st of May Lieutenant Stoddart and Trooper H. Posselt volunteered to try and ride through to Buluwayo, with despatches and bring back information as to the general disposition of the rebels and whites, we at Belingwe being entirely ignorant of the true position and very anxious to ascertain what had been done, or was likely to be done, to reduce the rebels.

Stoddart and Posselt left with three of our best horses, to try a hazardous ride, at 12.15 midnight. It is always safest to travel at night and avoid the main footpaths and hide during the day when dealing with natives on the warpath.

May 4th brought two boys with despatches from Victoria—one from Mr. Rhodes in answer to mine of the 14th *ultimo*, thanking me, and congratulating the men of the Belingwe garrison for the determined stand they had made against the rebels, and finished by saying that he (Mr. Rhodes) would be glad to assist in every way, and adopt any suggestions we could send him. and that he would very probably be close to Gwelo by the 10th. This was the most pleasant and interesting information we had yet received, for we all knew Mr. Rhodes would keep his word, and that relief would soon be sent if possible. The despatch-bearers also brought the following information in regard to the rebellion:—

That they had heard of several big fights between the white men and the rebels, near Buluwayo, in which the white men had always got a little the best of the battle. They also heard that we had defeated the Godhlwayo Impi when they attacked us. That the rebels reported that they took away all our cattle, killed nearly all our horses and four white men during the engagement. (This was the sort of reports the rebels always kept circulating in order to incite the lukewarm ones to rise.) That the Impi was now in Belingwe, camped close to the main road near Senda's *kraal*. That they did not intend to attack again, but only to keep a close watch on the road and cut off any small parties of whites, and keep up communication between M'Patini and the Matopos. That M'Patini was full of unreaped grain, which the rebels wanted for food. That the *impi* was composed of ten *scherms* of about fifty men each. That Echlolodhlo was now the Induna in command and Endende was second in command, and that Maduna had gone to the Matopos.

CHAPTER 6

Arrival of Captain Hopper's Relief Party from Victoria

The despatch-bearers left again the following morning at daybreak with the following despatches for the Officer Commanding Fort Victoria, and for Mr. Rhodes:—

Fort Belingwe,
May 4, 1896.

Sir.—I have the honour to inform you that your despatch dated 28th April arrived here this morning.

All the men here are very pleased to know that their services are appreciated by Mr. Rhodes, yourself, and others, and send their sincere thanks for congratulations.

Re reinforcements.—Unless it is intended by the authorities to take active steps against the enemy in this district, it is not necessary to send reinforcements. I believe that the present garrison is capable of holding this position against 2,000 rebels if they give us the chance. I don't suppose they will ever be in a position to send the above number against us.

I enclose a copy of my last despatch to Buluwayo, also a copy of a statement made by a Matabele spy caught by our cattle guard. We had great difficulty in getting any information out of him. At first he pretended to be a fool, and it was only when he found out that he was a prisoner, and to be treated as a spy, that he came to his senses.

I also enclose a letter for Mr. Rhodes, contents of which please wire to him, as well as the Belingwe despatch and your own letter.

Re ammunition.—We are still well supplied, but if not inconvenient to you, could do very well with a few thousand rounds of M.-H. and Lee Speed. We are not strong enough to send for them.

Very sorry to have to report the death of W. C. Beaty-Pownall. from the effect of bullet wound, on Sunday the 2nd inst. I have the honour to be, &c.

 (Signed)   D. Tyrie-Laing,
            Capt. Commanding Belingwe.

To H. Hopper,
 Capt. Commanding Victoria.

              Fort Belingwe,
              May 4, 1896.

C. J. Rhodes, Esq., Gwelo.

Dear Sir,—I have the honour to inform you that your wire dated 21/4/96 got here this morning, with despatch-bearers from Victoria.

The men of the garrison wish me to convey their thanks for your kind recognition of their services, and all trust that you will give them the chance of reducing the rebels of this district to proper order, when you have had time to make your arrangements.

I have enclosed a copy of the despatch forwarded to the administrator at Buluwayo on the evening of the 30th *ult.* Very probably you have already had .it wired to you from Buluwayo. You will see by it that I think a good patrol working in this district would help, to a considerable extent, to put down the rebellion. Knowing that men and horses are very scarce I asked for thirty mounted men only. If reinforcements are being brought from the south I think it would be better to send them to Belingwe, which appears to me to be a more convenient base, under the present circumstances, than Victoria, as it is one hundred miles closer to the strongholds of the enemy, it would save the marching of men to Victoria, and the counter marching of them to Belingwe, and prove a great saving of time and energy.

The wagon road from Gondoque to Belingwe leaves the Victoria road about two miles on the Victoria side of the middle drift road, and was made last year by a road party formed by my company. Mr. Lyle came along it from Gondoque, about a month ago, and reports it in good order. The only difficult part is about twenty miles south of Belingwe Peak, where a very nasty pass, through the granite formations, has to be got through. This pass is about four miles long, but only difficult at one point, which is an elbow about thirty yards long. The pass is not half so difficult as the Mangwe pass, which you will remember.

The distance from Gondoque to Belingwe fort is about sixty-five or seventy miles by the wagon road. The distance from Gondoque to Victoria is about ninety-three miles, from Victoria to Belingwe about ninety miles, making a total of 183 miles. Any party coming from the south to operate in the field would save 120 miles by coming direct to Belingwe. Should it be considered advisable to order a party by the route suggested I would advise them not to come to Belingwe fort, but to take up a position on the open flats to the south of Belingwe Peak, where they would be clear of all bush, and have lots of water and grass for their horses and cattle. They would also be in command of the main line of communication between Godhlwayo and M'Patini. If you send in a party, my men, who are thoroughly acquainted with this section of Matabeleland, from here to Gwanda, and all the intervening country to Buluwayo, will be found very valuable as scouts.

If you don't consider it advisable to send a small force through this way from the south, and can spare a small, well-mounted patrol from either Gwelo or Victoria, I feel certain they will do very good service.

"From Gwelo to Belingwe is about ninety miles, and the best road is *via* Selukwe, and then on to the Belingwe road, from there to Wedza mountain, which is about eighteen miles from here. Most of the Selukwe men would be able to point out the road, which is comparatively easy. There are no difficulties on the road between Victoria and Belingwe.

(By this time the loyalty of Chebis and his men was assured and the road was safe.)

If you do send a patrol and can spare a small field-gun it would be of great service.

Any small patrol, of say fifty, coming from Victoria, or Selukwe. could travel light, and get provisions here, to serve until other arrangements can be made. It might be advisable to send an officer, junior to myself, in charge, but it is all the same to me. I wish to do what I can for the best, under any circumstances.

If active measures are not intended in this district and I can be of service elsewhere I shall be very glad. Trusting that success is being met with by your patrols everywhere,

I am, &c.,

D. Tyrie-Laing,
O. C. Belingwe.

To make doubly sure I decided to send off two despatch-riders, on horseback, to meet Mr. Rhodes at Gwelo. Two Cape-boy drivers volunteered to go. Harry Pick, a very reliable and intelligent boy, knew the road well, and also several bypaths. He and September, his comrade, were mounted on two good horses, and left after dusk. They got through in three days, but had a hard struggle, and were all but captured by the rebels close to Selukwe. Being mounted, however, they managed to get away, after shooting seven of the fleetest and most persistent of the rebels.

On the same night at 11 p.m. Lieutenant Stoddart and H. Posselt returned to *laager*. They reported that they got to the coach stables at Thabas Induna at 8 a.m. on the 2nd inst., where their advance was stopped by a large body of *kaffirs*, mostly armed with rifles, who at first attempted to encircle them. That they (Stoddart and Posselt) retreated and attempted to pass through to Buluwayo by Selous road, but were hotly pursued, and as the bush all along their route was full of *kaffirs* they were compelled to turn back on the road to Belingwe. That at Graham's store they saw the remains of a small *laager*, which had apparently held about sixty men, and there were signs of an engagement, empty cartridge-cases lying about. They further reported that they saw no fresh tracks on the road from Buluwayo to Gwelo. That they got as far as the west bank of the Inseza on the 3rd inst., and had to hang about there all day and shift their position three times, owing to some *kaffirs* getting round them. That late in the afternoon they noticed smoke signals sent up from the *kraal* on the northern side of the drift, and after dark a large beacon fire on the Bembesi hill was answered all along the Inseza range.

They had to wait until about 11 p.m. before they got across the Inseza River, and it took them three hours before they got through the line of *kraals* on the east bank. They also reported, that the *kraals* were inhabited by women and children, and that work was being carried on in the lands adjoining these *kraals*. Cumming's iron store at Inseza had been burnt down, and his sixteen donkeys killed. The coach stables at Malomachopie were intact as they passed by, but were burned down when they returned. They saw a few signs of cattle having been moved along the country, but at several places along the route they noticed tracks where large bodies of *kaffirs* had crossed their path. They were of opinion Buluwayo was environed by the rebels, but as to whether they were close up to the town or only holding the approaches at a distance of about twelve miles, they were not in a position to say. That Thabas Induna was full of *kaffirs*, and they heard the report of a seven-pounder before they came in contact with them there.

On the morning of the 6th at 7.15 a.m. two boys came in with despatches from Captain H. Hopper, who had come on from Victoria with twenty mounted men, one Maxim gun, and two Scotch carts, carrying provisions and 15,000 rounds of Martini Henry ammunition. I could scarcely credit the news; it seemed almost too good to be true that assistance should come so soon. Nevertheless, it put new life into the garrison, and even the sick men got out and tried to catch sight of the column of dust indicating the approach of our friends. I at once sent Captain Frankland with several mounted men to assist Captain Hopper and his party to cross the Umchingwe River, which had a very bad *drift* unless one knew it well.

I also sent on fresh oxen to pull in the carts. We had been told that the Victoria oxen were suffering from *rinderpest*, and as we were then still free from it in Belingwe it was thought advisable to take precautions to remain so if possible. Accordingly fresh spans with fresh trek gear were sent forward, and the sick oxen sent away to leeward of the *laager* a few miles. They were visited every day until it was discovered that they were all more or less affected, then the order was given to destroy them; they were first shot, and then burned by heavy bush fires.

Captain Hopper's advance guard appeared on the crest of the rise about a mile north of the fort, towards 12.30 p.m. It was a great pleasure to mount and ride out to meet them, and that all the more so when I found that he and most of his men were old campaigners who had taken part in the first campaign, and most pleased of all was I to learn that Dr. Anderson, of Victoria, accompanied him. Captain Hopper laughingly said that he had come to fetch me out, but as Captain Frankland had informed him that I did not intend to leave for a few weeks yet he thought it would be best to rest his men and horses for a few days if I would kindly have him and his men as guests. We shook hands very warmly on the suggestion, and I assured him that as long as there was a bite and a sup to be divided in Belingwe he and his followers were most welcome to it. He then gave the order to march on to the fort, which was manned by the Belingwe men, who showed their appreciation of the new comers by welcoming them with three lusty cheers.

The following are extracts from the Belingwe garrison orders relating to the arrival of Captain Hopper and his men, which may not be uninteresting to my readers:—

Fort Belingwe,
7—5—96.

The following officers, non commissioned officers and men, having arrived from Victoria to assist in the relief of the garrison, are taken on its strength from this date until further orders:—

Captain Harman Hopper	Sergeant Perry
Lieut. F. R. Caldecott	„ Weale
Surg.-Lieut. W. Anderson	„ Tate
Sergeant-Major Nolan	Corporal Mcpartland
Corporal Clark	Trooper Potgieter
„ Halkett	„ Carruthers
Trooper Noakes	„ Southey
„ Wray	„ Forbes
„ O'Reilly	„ Goddard
„ Hillier	„ Whitaker
„ Van der Walt	„ Berry

The Officer Commanding Fort Belingwe wishes to take this opportunity of thanking Captain Hopper, Lieutenant Caldecott, Dr. Anderson, and the gallant fellows who have accompanied them to the relief of the garrison, for their noble conduct. He wishes them to understand that he thoroughly understands and appreciates the kind, generous, and brave sentiments which induced them to undertake their perilous journey, and he sincerely trusts and feels certain that their stay here, whether it be a short or a long one, will be made as pleasant for them as circumstances will permit.

We were now able to do some patrolling and drilling. The Victoria men had brought first-class horses, most of them salted. Our morning patrols went further out, and small scouting parties were always On the prowl, but the natives had evidently left our immediate vicinity for the time being, as none of them, or any trace of their recent presence, could be found, within an area of twelve miles.

The morning of the 18th brought two despatch-runners, with a most important despatch from Mr. Rhodes. It was as follows:—

> Please send several separate runners, each with the following message, to Laing, Belingwe, begins. Please ride down to Tuli to meet column coming in. a portion having instructions to detach themselves from Victoria column and place themselves under you, and to be led in by you to Belingwe, *via*. Gondoque, to act under you as you deem best. Ends.

This was an answer to mine of the 4th of May, and proved that Harry and September had got through to Mr. Rhodes, and that we had not relied on him in vain. About two hours after the arrival of the first despatch, the first copy came, and the second one reached us towards evening, so that the despatch-runners had all done well.

CHAPTER 7

A Prisoner is Captured

I at once set about arranging to go out to meet the Tuli column, picked out fifteen of the best horses, and asked for fifteen volunteers to ride them. They were soon found, of course. Everyone wanted to go, except the sick. The Maxim was mounted on a strong set of springs and fresh harness attached, as we had a rough country in front of us, and might have to travel fast. The stronger springs enabled us to put on a larger supply of ammunition and provisions than we could have taken on horseback. The Maxim was drawn by two smart mules, with two horses as leaders, and everything was ready to start off at sundown. Captain Frankland was left in command of the garrison. We left Belingwe at 6 p.m. just as the sun was sinking, and by ten o'clock we were camped for the night close to the foot of the Belingwe Peak, some eighteen miles south of the fort. The latter part of the journey was gone over very cautiously, because it was on a small bush-covered hill in this vicinity that we believed the rebel *impi* lay.

To have gone any further that night would have been rashness. We therefore camped close to the edge of an old working on the "Zelandia" mine, which I estimated would cover both our horses and ourselves if need be, and the old dump heap would serve as breastworks. The night wore on and nothing came of it. We were all on the watch at daybreak, but saw no signs of the *impi*. The order to saddle up was given, and before the sun was two hours high we had got another twelve miles on our way, and passed what I thought at the time the most dangerous part of our journey, until the Mapelabana portion of the Matopos was reached. There were a few signs of an *impi*, but as they were several weeks' old. I was half inclined to believe that it had gone to another part of the country.

Several fresh footpaths leading from the mealie-fields to the wood slopes of the Belingwe mountain, led me to conclude that the natives had hidden away in the bush and *krantzs* and were still in the neighbourhood. The party halted in a good position and breakfasted about 8 a.m. The march was resumed again at 10 a.m.. and by twelve o'clock noon we got to the top edge of the incline leading into the Mapelabana hills. There we found a lot of M'Posi's men and women thrashing corn. Our advance scouts were right on to them ere they noticed us. as they were working among the rocks. At the first glance it seemed as if they were barring our passage. It was impossible to tell, at first sight, whether the sticks they were using to beat out the corn were not rifles.

The men were therefore at once formed into skirmishing order, with the Maxim in the centre, and stood ready, whilst three of our best *kaffir* linguists rode forward, and called out to the people. For a few minutes their replies were insolent, and two of the men advanced a short way, until they saw the line of skirmishers. They then beat a rapid retreat and gave a general alarm, which sent the whole lot off helter-skelter into the bush. One man who was not so smart as the others was made a prisoner. On being questioned he informed us that the *impi* was still at Belingwe, hid in the mountain, and that they were collecting grain all round the district. He said the natives in front were all peaceful. They never saw us until they heard the men calling to them. Then they thought there were only three, but when they saw so many whites with rifles and horses, they knew we were on the warpath, and, being frightened, ran away.

I learned that the chief M'Posi was at home, but very sick. His son, however, was about. I was inclined to believe that this native thought the information he gave was true. He further stated that M'Posi's tribe were faithful to the white man. I also believed this statement, because Carruthers, who was with the patrol, informed me that the people at a *kraal* close by had warned him not to come to Belingwe, because it was surrounded by rebels, and gave him food to take him back to Gondoque. He got back there, but with a very hard struggle, having had his rifle stolen from him while he was drinking out of a gourd handed to him by a native at a *kraal* some fifteen miles further on than where we were, and then chased for ten miles by a band of rebels with *assegais*, all of whom he managed to elude in the bush, as it became dark—the bush in this part of the country being rather dense and affording good cover.

After getting all the information the old native seemed to be able to give, the patrol advanced again, and got on to the downward slope towards the Mapelabana range and M'Posi's gorge. The track now became very steep, and was flanked on each side by thick bush, and although the natives appeared friendly their sudden disappearance made me rather suspicious, every precaution having to be taken to avoid an ambush. Up to this point we had advanced rapidly, doing a good six miles an hour; but now our progress was rendered slow, owing to the more difficult surroundings. I don't know how the others felt, but I had that eerie feeling about me that makes one expect to see an enemy at any moment. It was not at all pleasant, and I was very glad when I noticed an open space in front, just something like one of our parks at home, with two large ant-heaps covered with bush in its centre.

There I decided to halt for a short time to give the horses a rest and drink. We took up a position between the two ant-heaps, with the Maxim in the centre, and the advance and rear-guards extended on both sides, the Maxim being our main body. The horses were off-saddled and led down to the rivulet about two hundred yards away, by one-half of the men, fully armed. The other half remained to guard the Maxim and light fires, to cook a little water for coffee, to refresh all hands. While these arrangements were going on I sent for H. Posselt, W. Lynch, W. Lyle, and Carruthers. all of whom were thorough Kaffir linguists, farmers and cattle traders, in the very district we were then in. They were thoroughly well known and personally acquainted with all the natives in the vicinity, and I asked them what opinion they had formed as to the loyalty of M'Posi's tribe.

They were all inclined to give M'Posi the benefit of any doubt and say he was loyal, although at the same time they were puzzled at the behaviour of the surrounding natives. The fact of the latter having disappeared so rapidly looked rather suspicious and showed signs of guilt, because it is pretty well known that when a *kaffir* is in the right he is always ready to show it by coming up to any white man's encampment unarmed and in a very free-and-easy manner. Here we had no such thing, for although our halt was only of about an hour's duration, no *kaffirs* approached nearer than five hundred yards, as far as we knew, and those that did appear on the surrounding hills were all armed in some manner. Shortly after the order was given to prepare to march the chief M'Posi's son made his appearance, coming up the side of the stream in a very uncertain manner.

H. Posselt went out to meet him unarmed, and after a short *indaba*, induced him to come up to our camp. Posselt introduced him to me, and I questioned him as to the opinions and loyalty of his father's followers. He said they had heard many conflicting reports as to what was going on and that they were under the surveillance of the *impi*, lying close to Belingwe Peak. That his father was loyal but at present very sick, but would be glad to come and talk to me the following morning, and that we would be quite safe where we were, Posselt said to me in English that this man was his servant for a long while, and that he knew him well, but believed he was telling lies then, whether to make us feel comfortable and allay our suspicion or not it was impossible to say. I then told Posselt to tell the young chief that I believed his story and was glad to learn his father was loyal, and that when the proper time came I would not forget to speak of his loyalty to the head chief of the white men. That I would be glad now if he would go and tell his father and all the men of his tribe that they need not be afraid of us, as we had no intention of harming them in any way.

I also asked him to thank Lusena (a petty chief whose *kraal* was situated in a very strong position about six hundred yards away) for giving Carruthers good advice and thereby saving a white man's life. He replied, "I understand and will obey; stay safely, white man." Posselt answered for me, "Go in peace." He immediately went, and after getting away about three hundred yards he called out to the natives on the slopes of the surrounding hills, "All right, go home; the white men have no designs against us." He went on a little further and was joined by several others, and after a short confab they disappeared, and all others in sight withdrew.

I felt we were in an awkward position, but knowing that the natives had been taken by surprise I understood they would not decide on action until they had had an *indaba* amongst themselves and made a plan of attack. This would take them a night at least, and until they had made a plan we were comparatively safe. Orders were given to march at once and take every precaution to guard against a surprise. Every man's rifle was loaded and the Maxim belt fitted ready for action. The track from this point turned sharp to the left and through an avenue of dense bush, down a rough incline of about 30°. for the distance of about half a mile, then sharp to the right into M'Posi's gorge.

This gorge was about two miles long, thickly wooded, with high, solid granite cliffs, two hundred yards apart, and about three hundred feet high, on either side. A small stream trundled its way through the centre. Here and there the perpendicular cliffs on either flank were broken and small canyons led off at right angles on both sides. It was an ideal place for an ambuscade, but with the exception of a strong Kaffir guard at several intervals on the ridges watching our movements, we got through without any incident worthy of mention. We got out of the gorge and camped (making everything as safe as possible for the night) alongside a large ant-heap, which was levelled in the centre and a space cleared for the Maxim on top, with a slight breastwork, or rather shelter trench, all round it. The men were formed in two lines at two paces' interval—the advance-guard facing the front and the rear-guard the rear.

The horses were picketed to a rope stretched between two trees in the centre. A space for the fire was left between the horses and the men—the ant-hill and Maxim were on the flank and a stiff thorn fence was thrown up all round. I may mention here, that every officer and man carried a small serviceable hatchet, attached to his saddle, and they proved most useful implements. With their assistance it did not take the men who were in camp half an hour to fix up a very secure position.

When we encamped I was very pleased to see the women from M'Posi s *kraal* come down for water to the stream, within a hundred yards of where we were, yet was surprised that none of the men came near or were to be seen about anywhere. This made me feel uneasy, and if it had not been that our horses were in want of rest I believe I would have marched again after a short halt. As it was we had done a good forty-five miles and had got through what was considered the most difficult part of our route without firing a shot. I was very glad to notice that the men got quite cheerful round the bivouac fires—each section of four by themselves—their heads all in line with the saddle, sitting on its pommel, at the outer end, to serve as a slight shelter, if necessary, with the rifle and bandolier on top of all, ready at a second's notice. The old instincts of the soldier commenced to warm my heart again and I almost wished, as I believe all that were with me did, the rebels would show and have a try.

We were very lucky in having first-class weather and a moon nearly full. Under such circumstances as these night in our part of South Africa is nearly as bright as day, and an object, such as a man or horse, is quite discernible two hundred yards away.

We had everything snug before sundown, and shortly after the horses had been fed and the men had eaten their slice of bread and bully beef and washed it down with a draught of coffee and stretched themselves out for the night. Captain Hopper and myself were having a quiet chat on the top of the ant-hill, alongside the Maxim, when our attention was drawn to M'Posi's *kraal* by the sound of many voices, evidently in altercation. This put us very much on the watch, and presently we were advised of the approach of several natives, talking loudly, with the intention of letting us know of their approach. I sent Posselt and Lynch out, armed with their rifles, in the direction in which the natives were advancing, with orders to lie down about fifty yards out, challenge, and find out what was wanted by the natives. This was done, and the advancing party answered at once that they wanted to speak to the white chief.

The party were ordered to halt where they were, about two hundred yards off, and for two of their number to advance unarmed. After a short consultation they agreed to do this, and two advanced, one of whom was the young chief we had met at our midday halt, and the other his brother, a younger man, who had travelled as far as Kimberley and worked there as a domestic for several years. He had only returned about a fortnight, and was decked out in a tricky yachting suit, a nice straw hat, and spoke the English language fairly well. He seemed quite proud of his clothes and his English, and I was very glad that his vanity let out the knowledge of our language before we entered on the business they had come about.

CHAPTER 8

Arrival at Dooboolelo's Kraal

The young chief commenced by saying that his father, M'Posi, sent greetings to the white man, and that he was very sorry he was not able to come down and speak for himself, but that he trusted his son would be taken as his mouthpiece, and that whatever he said or promised would be as if he, M'Posi, had done so in person. I thanked the young man, and asked what further he had to communicate. He answered:

> My father wishes me to inform you that he is very glad the white men have got away from Belingwe, because the Matabele are now seeing nothing but blood, and it is death to live in open spaces. My father trusts that you will not waste any time in getting from this, for he is certain that the *impi*, lying on the bush-covered slopes of Belingwe, has seen you pass today, and you may depend upon it they will soon be on your trail, but your horses will soon take you far beyond their reach. My father trusts you will take his advice, he being a very old man, and of much experience with the Matabele, because when their eyes see only blood there is no reasoning with them, and if the *impi* comes here and finds you amongst us we also will have to suffer.

I replied:

> Yes, I see what you mean, and understand the position; but your father does not. You must not think we are leaving Belingwe for good. We are only out to see what your father and his people are doing, and others like them. I shall be back here again before a new moon comes round, and I shall judge of your father's loyalty by his actions. Before I come to the Nuanetsi River, on my return journey, I shall expect to find two wagon-loads of grain

lying there. If I find them, then I will know that your people are our friends, but if the grain is not there you will be treated as enemies, if you come in our way. Now you must go back and tell your father what I have said, and also disperse the crowd of people we can see from the ridge alongside your father's *kraal*. Tomorrow morning, before the sun is so high (pointing to a place in the sky indicating about 8 a.m.) I expect you to send down at least two bags of mealies to feed our horses. Of course I will pay you for every bag of grain.

He said, "I will carry your instructions to my father, and you will have the grain."

We parted company with the usual salutations. As soon as they had gone one of the interpreters, who had been sitting down beside me watching, said, "Captain, these niggers are false; they are lying."

I asked Posselt what he thought. He replied, "I also think they mean treachery, sir."

When the envoys got away about four hundred yards they called out to the natives clustered round the *kraal* to go away. This they did, but during the night the sentries reported several times that the buzz of many voices could be heard occasionally. An hour before daybreak the following morning the horses were fed and every man set to watch his immediate front, till there was enough light to see the surrounding country. Then the horses were saddled, and we marched off at a brisk canter, which was kept up on every bit of favourable ground for three hours. This brought us in the vicinity of Dooboolelo's *kraal*—the people who had tried to murder Carruthers.

When we were about three miles from the head *kraal*, we left the main track, cut a *drift* over one of the many small streams in the vicinity, and keeping well under cover of the thick mimosa bush, with which the country was covered, approached the *kraals* cautiously. We found the natives were all on the alert, but evidently taken by surprise. They very probably expected us to keep the main track. We camped about three hundred yards away from their *kraals*, which were situated at the foot of a high granite hill, in a strong position, amongst huge boulders and thick bush.

Chapter 9

A Slight Brush with the Enemy

Before sighting their position our right flanking files had a brush with a small number of the enemy, and killed one of them. His arms were a rifle and three very sharp *assegais*. As soon as the camp was in order, Posselt, Lynch, and Carruthers went forward to communicate with the people at the *kraals*, and asked the chief to come down and speak with me. This the chief declined to do, and defied us. We gave him an hour to consider, while we were having breakfast. At the end of that time he was still defiant, so his position was attacked and his *kraals* destroyed. All the *kraals* under him were treated in the same manner as we went along.

The name of this chief was Dooboolelo. He was a Maholi, and honorary chief of one of the old Matabele regiments during Lobengula's time. It was the duty of this chief and his followers, who were all located along a narrow fertile strip well adapted for the cultivation of mealies, *kaffir* corn, &c., to keep a store of grain always on hand, to supply the wants of his regiment when necessary. It was Dooboolelo who ordered Carruthers to be chased and killed, and as he was the first chief I had come across on the march who could be proved a rebel I decided to chastise him and his following. He was, however, too clever for us, and all his people except two were out of harm's way, in the covers, alongside his own *kraal*. As we had no time to waste we left them there and continued our march, destroying several *kraals* under his sway as we proceeded.

We camped for the night about seven miles north of the Nuanetsi River, and as on the previous night, made our position as strong as possible; but except for the occasional howl of a wolf or jackal our slumbers were undisturbed. Daybreak the following morning found us all ready for the march again, and eager to get on. We reached the

Nuanetsi River, made a good drift, and halted for breakfast on its south bank by 9 a.m. During the march the advance party surprised and ran down an armed *kaffir*, who declined to give us any information as to the movements of the natives of the district. He was a fine, strapping fellow, and had the appearance of being a Matabele of good blood, and spoke their language fluently. He was accused of being a Matabele spy, but denied the accusation very emphatically, at the same time admitting he had served for many years in one of the Matabele regiments; having been captured in his youth and made a slave, serving from the day of his capture till the white men took Matabeleland three years previously, and when his regiment was broken up he made his escape, and came back to live with his own people again. M'Tipi's people he was sure would corroborate his statement if asked to do so. The men offered him some preserved meat, but he would not eat. He said he knew the white men suspected him, and probably they wanted to poison him, and he would not eat until the white men had found out he was not a spy.

We marched again at 12.45 p. m., and reached Gondoque at 3 p.m. Gondoque is on the main road from Tuli to Victoria, and seventy-two miles south of Belingwe. The natives in this district are of the Basuto race—a very strong tribe under M'Tipi, and generally known as M'Tipi's *kaffirs*. They have always been very loyal to the Chartered Company and friendly to the white men; but nevertheless I looked forward with a considerable amount of anxiety to an interview with M'Tipi or his representatives. All the people on our line of march in this district fled on our approach, but, with the exception of two old men, they were all unarmed, and the latter handed over their rifles at once on being asked to do so by the advance-guard. They also consented to guide us by a shorter path than the cart-road to Gondoque. We followed them and found they were quite right.

We halted, formed a camp, and sent for the neighbouring chiefs, only one of whom turned up that evening, the remainder not being at home. At Gondoque we found Mr. West's storekeeper still there, but his supply of provisions had almost disappeared. This was a disappointment, for the men of the patrol had travelled with as little impedimenta as possible, and had taken only enough rations to last until they could reach Gondoque believing that once there we would be able to get supplies. As all traffic, however, had been stopped for some time, Mr. West had not been able to obtain any food-stuffs from Victoria. All he could furnish us with was an ox or two and a few bags of mealies. The latter were very acceptable for the horses and the men also, for they had to boil them and use them in lieu of bread for the next few days.

Early on the morning of the 22nd, M'Kati, one of M'Tipi's sons, came down to speak with me. We had a short *indaba*, and he left to send off messengers to bring the other chiefs together. As soon as M'Kati left I moved the men up to West's store and formed a camp. The verandah round the store provided excellent shade, and the men made the best of their stay to rest after the rapid march we had made. The grass close by was very good, and the horses made the most of it. Altogether we were comfortably off, and only wanted information as to the movements of the column we were looking for to set us completely at rest.

M'Kati knew our prisoner, said he was one of the tribe and a good man. He was released at once.

About 8 a.m. Umcheti, the eldest son of M'Tipi, turned up with a small following. He said he had not heard of any column coming up from Tuli, and he volunteered to send off six of his young men to look for it and bring back information. This was at once done, the runners taking a despatch from me to the officer commanding the Tuli column.

On the 23rd we remained at Gondoque. A great many of the natives came from the surrounding country and brought presents of mealies, potatoes, &c., to us. This assured us to a certain extent that they were friendly, but we could gain no information from them, either about the column we expected to meet or the rebellion. This made me rather uneasy, and inclined to mistrust them altogether.

On Sunday, the 24th, three of M'Tipi's sons, with a following of about seventy men, turned up, unarmed. Umcheti, the eldest, represented his father, and said that he had been instructed by the latter to come and greet the white chief and offer the services of M'Tipi and his followers. He said:

> The white man knows that my father's people have been friendly to the white people. We have kept the roads open, and have always given food and cattle to the white man when passing through our country, and when the white man went into Matabeleland to fight the Matabele *impis* two years ago we also wished to give assistance, and you know that a party of us went with five policemen as far as Godhlwayo's, and brought back

the coach mules which the Matabele took from this district. We were very much annoyed then because the white men would not let us fight, so that we could prove our loyalty. We have all looked at the *induna* in charge of the white men here now, but we do not know him, or remember ever having seen him before, although we know several of his followers (here Umcheti pointed to Posselt, Carruthers, Lyle, and several others) and we are glad that they remember us and know that we are speaking the truth, and they will tell their chief that they know us, so that he may understand we are loyal. Harry (pointing to Posselt) has told me you are very angry with my father's people because they have not given you any information. It is not their fault. They were ordered not to say anything until the chiefs came to have a proper *indaba* with you, and now we have come, and our instructions are to tell the white chief all we know and give him all the assistance in our power.

I thanked Umcheti. and asked him to tell me everything he knew about the rebellion and what had taken place in Matabeleland. The first part of his story was pretty much what we had heard from Buluwayo and Victoria, and was not of special interest. He introduced his brother M'Kati, saying, "As my brother is more active than I, being younger, he may have a more interesting narrative for you."

M'Kati took his seat in the centre of the circle and said:

This boy, Tshaleja, and several others of my tribe have been away for some days scouting and watching the movements of the Matabele in the district to the north of our own country, that is the Weza district, and they tell us there are two small *impis* south of Belingwe—one in the Weza and Mapelabana about two hundred strong. They are collecting cattle and grain and trying to force the natives there to take up arms against the white man. They have also ordered all the grain to be reaped and stored for them at different places in the Weza range of hills towards Inyamandi's *kraal*. Inyamandi, as you must know, is a Maholi and an agent of the Matabele, and his people are dangerous to the white people at present.

The other *impi* is close to Belingwe. It is much stronger, and had a great many women and children with it, most of whom have come from Godhlwayo and the Lower Inseza. There are also a great many Matabele women located in the hills close to

M'Posi's. The hills they are located in are called 'Sibua.' These women are there for the purpose of gathering grain and storing it at convenient places in case it should be wanted by the large *impis* who are now in the Matopos. There are two of them— one on the hills close to the Tuli Buluwayo road and the other further west and close to the Palapye Buluwayo road.

The Matabele say these *impis* will fight the columns of the white men and beat them if possible, but if they are beaten instead one *impi* will retreat down the Guai River, and get into the thick thorn bush country where the whites will not be able to follow, and the other *impi* will retreat by Shamba, through the Mapelabana. Weza, and Inyamandis, and on to Gazaland. This *impi* will take all the cattle, because they will live in Gazaland, and this is the reason they have their women and children already along this probable line of retreat. You have now been told all we know about the Matabele and their intentions. We have not heard of any *impi* of white men coming this way, but believe that there is one coming when the white man says so.

I again thanked the chiefs and their followers, and told them I would make a good report of them to the head chief of the white men, and finished by saying that when the column came up I would want three hundred of their young men to go with me and fight the Matabele. Umcheti said, "The three hundred men will be ready, armed with the rifles they had received from the great white chief several years ago when the white man first passed through this country, but as their ammunition was finished I would have to supply that." I promised them all the ammunition they would want and the *indaba* ended.

The chiefs and several of the older men stayed with us for some time conversing with the men. The young men went off at once towards their different *kraals*, shouting their war-cries and having mimic battles with each other on the way, evidently delighted at the prospect of having a chance of trying their strength with their natural foes, the Matabele.

The runners who had been sent on to meet the Tuli column had not returned or sent back any message. It was quite evident the column was at least thirty miles off, and I therefore decided not to wait any longer at Gondoque, and gave orders to march at 5,45 p.m. The moon was nearly full and the night cool, so that marching was much

A GROUP OF "B" TROOP

more comfortable during the night than through the day. Taking the old coach road from Gondoque to Tuli we got along at a smart pace for about three miles when the pole of the Maxim carriage broke short off. This brought us to a halt until another was cut from the bush and fitted. This operation delayed us about an hour, and whilst the repairs were going on, two of the runners turned up. They reported they had been as far as Goma, about thirty miles ahead, but had not seen or heard of the column we were expecting. Moreover, they had overtaken two Basuto police, belonging to the Chartered Company's service, who had been sent out from Tuli, to scout the country as far as M'Tipi's, and they denied any knowledge of a column of men coming towards us. They said all wagons and men were sent on from Tuli by the Semokwe road to Buluwayo.

The day before they left Tuli, thirty wagons and a lot of men had left for Buluwayo by the route mentioned. This was rather disheartening information. I was very much afraid that circumstances had occurred in other parts of the country sufficient to cause the Tuli-Victoria column to be sent in another direction. I was rather sad over this, but determined to march on to Tuli, if need be, and perhaps arrange there to get another column to go into Belingwe.

We reached M'Tipi's at 10.15 p.m., and bivouacked for the night. Starting off again the following morning before daybreak we arrived at the Bubye River shortly after 8 a.m. and stayed there to rest the men and give the horses the benefit of the good grazing along the river banks. On the march I was surprised to find most of the native *kraals* deserted and no signs of natives about. This made us suspicious, and naturally a sharp look-out was kept. We marched on again at 4.45 p.m., the horses being in very good form, but the men rather out of sorts. The boiled mealies were not agreeing with them, and I was afraid the bad water we had to use along the route would cause dysentery. I remembered that the same feeding occasioned a great deal of illness amongst the men on the Bubye patrol towards the close of the 1893 war.

I was therefore most anxious to get to Tuli or meet the column, so that the men might have a change of food, and had proposed to make three long marches during the night, expecting to be within thirty miles of Tuli by daybreak. The country we were marching through was covered with thick bush, and the only signs of human beings about, except ourselves, was the spoor of what we presumed were the Basuto police, who had been carefully followed up by a pack of lions from the Bubye River. This was a source of speculation and amusement for the men. The off chance of coming up with the pack helped to break the monotony of the march. However no lions made their appearance, but towards sunset the advance files signalled the halt, and one came back to report the discovery of fresh tracks of horses on the road in front. This was much more interesting.

Chapter 10

Captain Brabant Arrives with Despatches from Earl Grey

I rode forward with the advance files and found that two horses had come along from the Tuli direction as far as the point where we were and then they had turned back again. It at once occurred to me that the scouts from the advance party of the column had been as far forward as this, but what distance they were in advance of the column it was not possible to judge.

Our march was resumed at once, and was continued until 6.45 p.m., when I decided to halt for a time. I had ridden ahead with the advance files the greater part of the way from the point where it was observed that the horses had turned round, and when we halted to close up we thought we could hear noises in front, but they were so indistinct that we were inclined at first to put them down to our imagination. Nevertheless, we were induced to advance a little further, and soon became quite certain that there were people a short way in front of us. We proceeded cautiously for another half-mile, and could then see camp fires, and felt certain we had struck the advance of our relief column. I had just instructed Trooper Mitchell to ride forward a little way and challenge to draw the attention of their sentries in case of accident, when we were surprised by a challenge, in good English, from behind a large ant-heap on our left front, and by a second challenge from the bush on our right front.

We, of course, answered in the usual manner, and then our friends, eight in number, showed themselves. They were all round us in skirmishing order, and it was just as well we were friends. They had been out digging in the dry river-bed, close by, for water, and had heard us before we had heard them. Not expecting to meet anyone, they at once sent word back to camp, had their horses in, and took to the bush in order to find out who we were. The sergeant in charge reported that the scouts, twenty strong, under Mr. Natrass, were encamped there for the night, and were making water-holes for the horses and mules of the column to drink at when they arrived the following morning. The column was *laagered* up about eight miles behind. This was, indeed, very pleasant information, and by the time it had been delivered my patrol had closed up, and we marched on to the camp with our comrades. I was very pleased to see a great many well-known faces among the scouts of the column—faces I had seen in several tight corners before—and I believe the hearty greetings which passed between old comrades in both parties sent a glow of enthusiasm through the hearts of all who were present.

For myself, I scanned the sunburnt countenances of the advance party, shown up, as they were, by the glimmering light from their camp fires, with a more intense interest, I believe, than anyone, else. To me they were more than old and trusty comrades. They were the men I had been ordered to meet, command, and lead to the end of the campaign. The thought passed through my brain as I watched them cooking and handing round a liberal share of their rations to the men of my patrol, that if these were a fair sample of the men composing the relief column, no matter what hardships were in front of them they would prove equal to overcoming them, if it were possible, and I wished from my heart then that I might be enabled to lead them carefully and successfully, without sacrificing any of them unnecessarily.

Many were the questions asked and answered round the camp fires that evening, and many a strong expression escaped the lips when the brutal slaughter of some old pal was related. The murders of women and children were commented upon, and condemned in anything but modest terms by all, and it was very evident that the dearest wish of every one was to meet with and punish the murderers.

About an hour after our arrival Lieutenant Yonge, accompanied by Captain Brabant, rode in and reported themselves. Lieutenant Yonge was in charge of the column. He had little to state further than that the column had been delayed at Tuli three days over the original time fixed for starting, and that the horses and mules were suffering very much and dying from horse-sickness. Captain Brabant had just ridden from Buluwayo *via* Mangwe, Semokwe, and Tuli, with despatches from Earl Grey, the administrator. The despatches simply gave me the entire command of the column with instructions to use it to the best advantage in quelling the rebellion. Captain Brabant was to remain with me and help to organise any native levies I might wish to have employed. I was delighted to have Brabant with me, because, I believe, without exception, he is one of the best leaders of native troops in South Africa. He had proved himself such on many occasions, and during the 1893 war was invaluable.

Away from despatches, his narrative of what had been done and was being done was most interesting information, eagerly sought after, and very acceptable to us who had been caged up so long in Belingwe. The list of those murdered and missing was much greater than we anticipated, and left an impression on every mind anything but amicable to the rebels. To say that we were shocked would be putting it very mildly. Disgust took the place of surprise, and revenge was the most natural sentiment under such revolting circumstances. Captain Brabant was very tired, having ridden 270 miles in less than nine days, picking up fresh horses and rations wherever available along his route, which was anything but a convenient one. After Lieutenant Yonge had rested his horse for a time he rode back again to bring on the column the following morning.

On the morning of May 26th the relief column arrived at Setoutsi's, where I took over command from Lieutenant Yonge. The strength was about 130 white men, 70 Cape boys, 150 horses, 25 wagons, and 350 mules. The latter, thanks to "Doel" Zeederberg, were in first-class order. The horses were a very mixed lot, and not in very good condition. The wagons were loaded with provisions and munitions of war, and eight of their number were under orders for Victoria for the garrison there. The horses and mules had suffered from want of water during the march on the day previous to reaching Setoutsi. At this point the dams made by the advance party had collected enough to water them all well.

After taking over command I decided to rest that day and organise the force. Three mounted troops were formed, namely, Maxim Troop, under Colonel Hopper, with Lieutenant Stoddart; A Troop under Lieutenant Yonge, with Lieutenant Bates; B Troop under Lieutenant Beisly, with Lieutenant Bell. Each of the above troops were about thirty strong. The remainder of the white men formed an infantry or *laager* troop. The Cape boys, some seventy strong, were also formed into a laager troop under Lieutenant Donald Campbell, with Lieutenants Howe and Moore. Lieutenant W. Lynch was appointed chief of the scouts. The remainder of the force was told off to conduct the eight wagons to Victoria under Captain Sporssell.

Lieutenant Chivers was appointed remount officer, and Lieutenant Lichtenstein ("Jumbo") Quartermaster. Mr. H. Posselt was appointed Lieutenant to assist Captain Brabant with the native levies, and Troopers Carruthers and Southey were attached to their staff.

On inspection of the men I found I knew a great many of them. They had come from all parts of South Africa to render assistance to their countrymen in distress. Many had given up lucrative employment in the Transvaal and elsewhere to answer the call for aid, and, taking them all in all, they were a first-class lot to look at, and I had every confidence they would do the work in front of them well.

Captain Brabant. Lieutenant Posselt, and Trooper West rode ahead on the afternoon of the 26th to M'Tipi's to find out what was going on there and gather the feeling of the natives now that they had had time to think over the prospect of a fight with the Matabele.

On the morning of the 27th the reorganised column, with the Victoria convoy in front, marched from Setoutsi, and reached the Bubye River in the first trek. The column marched again during the afternoon, and laagered for the night on the west bank of the Umquqe River.

On the following morning, the 28th, M'Tipi's was reached and *laager* formed by 8 a.m. I resolved to remain here long enough to give the men some drill and musketry practice, whilst the M'Tipi contingent was being got ready.

The Victoria convoy marched on again during the afternoon, but before this took place Captain Brabant had returned and reported that he believed the M'Tipi natives loyal and very friendly but disinclined to take the field; that he had not pressed this point on them, and that as the *indunas* were coming to have an *indaba* with me shortly perhaps an understanding would be arrived at then. That the natives were very friendly was evidenced from the fact that the women and children brought down presents of food, &c., to us, and chatted quite freely, apparently not in the least alarmed. This led me to believe that the men meant well, because if they had intended mischief the women would have been kept well out of the way.

Shortly after Umcheti came up with several minor chiefs, the principal one of whom was a man named "May," who had served with the British in Zululand, Basutoland, and also at Sekonis. He spoke English, and remembered Sir Garnet Wolseley and Sir E. Wood, and most of the principal officers. Umcheti said, "This man will represent me, as I am too old to go to the front myself. He will lead one hundred of my young men, but M'Kati, my brother, will have the supreme command of all M'Tipi's men under you."

I thanked Umcheti, and said, "Where are your brother and the other chiefs, and where are the three hundred men? I expected to find them here, according to your promise of last Sunday."

He answered, "As soon as you give the order for them to come here I will send for them. M'Kati is now at his *kraal* ten miles away waiting your orders. He will come at once, and by the time he is here all the others will have come. They will all be here before midday tomorrow."

I again thanked Umcheti and gave the necessary orders, and at dusk that evening on the top of every hill a beacon fire was lit and answered by others from every hill in the district for a good ten miles around.

The following morning the men were paraded shortly after sunrise for skirmishing drill, and again at 11 a.m., when ball cartridge was served out to them for rifle practice. A large rock background was fixed on to fire up against, and smaller ones pointed out to fire at. The different troops were put through a practical skirmish, and the shooting was very good. On the whole I was quite satisfied with the performance. Whilst this work had been going on M'Tipi's men had been rolling up in small detachments from every direction, all of them armed, the greater portion with Martini-Henry rifles, and the remainder with the old Enfield of different patterns, *assegais*, and battleaxes. The fighting men kept away by themselves, and were a fine lot of young warriors. They were very quiet and orderly, and seemed to take no notice of anything outside their own lines. With them came many others of all sorts, from the grey-bearded, limping old man down to the child in arms. The women and children brought presents of potatoes, milk, &c., to the men, and showed any amount of friendliness.

About 2 p.m. M'Kati turned up in full war-paint, which consisted of an old frockcoat, a very old silk hat, and a strong walking-stick. He wore the happiest of smiles, and altogether seemed to be in the best of humours. He reported that all of his men had not turned up, but that they would be present before the sun set. I asked him how he and his followers liked the idea of fighting the rebels. He answered, "If you will only let us fight when we get to them, you will be able to form your own opinion as to our likes and dislikes. All I can say at present is that my people and myself have every reason to hate the Matabele. They have been our mortal enemies for years, and we only wish to

MAXIM TROOP

have the chance of paying them back in part for the harm they have done us on several occasions."

I replied, "Very well, M'Kati. I shall do my best to let you and your followers have full satisfaction, but you must keep those young men of yours under firm control, otherwise they may spoil our plans. Captain Brabant will draw ammunition for your men and they must be ready to march at daybreak tomorrow."

Towards dusk a council of war was held, to decide upon the best route to take for Belingwe. There was every reason to suppose that the rebels would have blocked the route which we came by, as it was the only route used by the white men to get in with their wagons through the Mapelabana Mountains (which to my mind are an extension of the Matopos). The Basuto chiefs said they knew of another easier and more direct route, along which wagons had already gone to Belingwe, and that it would be shorter and quicker to strike straight from where we were for Belingwe. The native contingent would cut the trees down and clear the way where necessary. This suggestion appealed to me as being a good idea to work on, and that for two reasons. It would shorten our march by about twenty miles, and as the new route would be about twelve to fifteen miles east of the old one, the chances were that we would be close to the worst part of the country we had to pass through, before the rebels knew of our intention.

They were almost certain to watch the route we had come by, expecting us to return that way. It was then arranged that M'Kati should send off about twenty of his most intelligent young warriors to act as scouts and spies. They were instructed to get in contact with the rebel spies if possible, obtain all the information out of them they could and misinform them as to the movements of the column—in fact, if they found it possible they were to deny any knowledge of a column coming in that way and were to find out if the Matabele or their allies knew of a convoy of wagons being sent on to Victoria. If so, they were to exaggerate the strength of it and not lose a minute in sending back word to me if they found the Matabele meant attacking it.

M'Kati said he felt certain there were no Matabele spies among his people, and as his country extended to the banks of the Nuanetsi River, which was about thirty miles north of our present position, he was sure no Matabele would be found south of it, and that they would be ignorant of our movements until we were in sight of the river. He concluded by saying, "My father's men have all been warned to keep their eyes open and their mouths shut, and where the Matabele are concerned you can depend upon them following the advice of their chief."

Everything was ready for the march now. Lieutenant Lynch and his scouts had gone on in front with a light wagon to mark out the way and select convenient places for laagering. He was accompanied by Captain Brabant and about fifty of M'Tipi's men. The remainder of them, close on three hundred, stayed with the column.

The strength of the column as it now stood was roughly as follows:—

	Officers.	N.C.O.'s	Horses.	Mules.
Staff	3	3	8	—
Maxim Troop	2	28	30	4
A Troop	2	28	30	—
B Troop	2	27	29	—
Laager Troop (including hospital)		20	2	—
Cape boys	3	65	4	224
Scouts	1	6	10	—
Remount	1	3 (sick)	35 (sick)	20
	14	180	148	248

Sixteen wagons for transport.

	White Officers.	N.C.O.'s	Men.
Native contingent	2	2	330

324

CHAPTER 11

M'Tipi's Men Score a Victory

The march from M'Tipi's commenced at 6.30 a.m. on the morning of Saturday, the 30th of May. Lieutenant Lynch and the scouts kept a good trek ahead for the first two days, making a road and selecting, favourable watering-places. So far nothing had happened to indicate the presence of the enemy. Several of the native scouts had come back from different directions, and reported that up to the points they had been to there were no signs of the Matabele.

The first march, on the morning of June 1st, brought us to the banks of the Umchime, about three miles to the east of Sekombi's *kraal*. Sekombi came into *laager* with M'Kati and gave the following information—namely:

> I am related to M'Tipi by marriage, and live inside his territory. I and my people are loyal to the white man. We will do what we can to prove our loyalty, but don't wish to leave our *kraals* now, because the Matabele are close by and watching us. Yesterday five of their scouts came close up to my *kraal*, but they would not enter. They were armed with Martini-Henry rifles and *assegais*. They inquired for information in regard to the movements of the white men to the south. My people told them that the white men had all passed on to Tuli. They did not stay any longer, but went off to the northward in the direction of M'Posi.
> Some of my young men have been over to M'Posi's *kraal*. M'Posi is working with the Matabele, about two hundred of whom are staying with him. They have blocked the pass that you came through, and intend to surround you in it when you go back. If you had waited another hour the morning you left M'Posi's

kraal your party would have been surrounded. You were followed until the rebels heard the Maxim firing at Doobooleolo's *kraal*. This astonished them, because they did not know you had a Maxim with you, and they decided to wait for your return, in the hopes of being able to get an advantage over your party. They have set traps at several points along the road, but as you have come this way you have avoided them.

So far, I don't think—in fact I am certain—they know your column is here; we did not know until this morning. We saw M'Tipi's scouts yesterday, but thought they were only looking for information for the tribe. In these wartimes scouts are always going and coming. I told you before, I cannot let my men leave their *kraals*, as our position is not strong, and as the Matabele are on the watch. If they found out we were assisting you they would be sure to attack us. When you have passed on, all I and my people can do will be to keep a strict watch to the westward and let you know if the Matabele intend attacking from that side. This my people can do without drawing the attention of the rebels on themselves.

I then gave the chief permission to go. He did not waste a minute, and was very soon out of sight. M'Kati laughed when he went, and said:

That man is much more afraid of the white man than of the Matabele. Although he is married to my father's sister, I do not trust him, although I believe he has told the truth, especially about the position of the rebels. I believe myself they will be close by M'Posi's, expecting the column to come that way. They will be sure to know tonight that the column is coming this route, and I am afraid we will have to fight through the other pass.

The column moved on again towards evening, and *laagered* on the north bank of a small stream called "Matope," about fourteen miles south of the entrance to the pass. This night the sentries were doubled, but nothing of any importance occurred.

Before marching the following morning the country was well scouted by mounted men and natives. I was anxious to locate the rebels if possible, and I would have been glad if they would have attacked us on the flats, although the latter were rather thickly covered with bush. Just before starting three of the natives came in and reported that they had been close up to M'Posi's, and that all his people, with about two hundred Matabele at their head, were awaiting the column. They had heard of it, and expected it to come through M'Posi's pass. That several of their comrades were still watching M'Posi's, and would come in as soon as the rebels made a move. I decided to march on towards the new pass, and sent a strong patrol in the direction of M'Posi's to draw the attention of the enemy, if possible, on to it.

The column moved forward at 8.30 a.m., crossed the Weza range, and *laagered* up again at 9 a.m. until such time as the scouts came back. When they returned they reported they had seen no signs of the *impi*. We marched on again about three miles further, and got on to what I considered a very good position, *laagered* up. and decided to show the rebels where we were by sending out small patrols to destroy, by fire, all the *kraals* in the vicinity. By doing this I hoped to provoke an attack. I was anxious to have an engagement before going into the pass. To a certain extent the ruse was successful, and brought the *impi* down from the hills about three miles to our right. Our native scouts, when they saw the fires lit by the column, set fire to several *kraals* close up to the position held by the enemy, and afterwards had to run hard to return to the *laager*. The *impi* came on with the intention of fighting, but gave up the idea when they found out that instead of twenty white men, they had a large column to attack.

On the morning of the 3rd, after scouting the country in every direction, the column marched straight forward again at 8 a.m., across the Nuanetsi River, and *laagered* on its north bank, about two miles south of the entrance to the pass.

The country we passed through during the morning's march was one vast mealie garden, the greater part of which was still unreaped. The crops were very luxuriant, and would prove of immense value to whosoever could reap them. It was, therefore, evidently part of my duty to stop any of this grain from being carried to the rebels in the Matopos. The *laager* was formed in a very strong position, and I did not intend to move from it until I had had a brush of some sort with the rebels. The scouts came in shortly after *laager* was formed and reported the road in front very difficult and that the ridges of the hills were lined by *kaffirs*. I was still in hopes the enemy might attack, and sent out word to the Cossack post and horse-guards to retire at once if the enemy showed any inclination to fight.

Towards midday the outposts reported a strong body of natives assembling on the top of a large flat hill about two miles east of our position. Field-glasses were brought to bear upon this spot, which at first had about three hundred natives on it in sight. Before sundown their numbers had increased, until the hill was quite black from one end to the other, but it was impossible to estimate the number of people on it. It then appeared to me that the rebels did not intend attacking us in *laager*. They evidently wanted to pounce on us in some difficult part. Of course the large numbers we had seen during the day made the sentries more vigilant than ever, and as most of the men had had a good day's rest, very few slept during that night. I noticed this from the fact that I went round the camp frequently during the night. I had previously, however, formed an idea that if the natives had meant to fight they would not have shown up at all until they commenced to attack, and in this idea M'Kati coincided with me. He said he thought they wanted to frighten the white men by their numbers, but did not want to come near the guns.

The position we held was one that could be seen from some distance, and towards morning I decided to send on a mounted troop and the native contingent, under Captain Brabant, to make a feint on the position held by the rebels. A Troop, under Lieutenant Yonge, and the native contingent were accordingly detailed for this purpose, and left at about 4 a.m. They got close up to the rebel position, but more than half an hour too late to catch them at rest. M'Tipi's boys tried to rush the enemy, but the rebels, seeing the horsemen behind, elected to retreat after firing a few shots. M'Tipi's boys followed them up for some distance, took one prisoner and a few cattle and sheep, which they brought back with them. The prisoner, on being questioned, said, "The Matabele had left about sundown the night before, and gone on to Belingwe Peak to bring on the *impi* lying there to block the pass, and that the natives of Mapelabana were all loyal."

This latter statement we knew to be untrue, as the men had reported that the huts where they had been to were full of stores belonging to white people, such, for example, as boxes of tea, bags of sugar, candles, &c., and in one was a chest full of white woman's wearing apparel.

Whilst the sham attack was going on the scouts were in front trying to find the pass, but were unsuccessful. As soon as the mounted troops returned I went with a party of B Troop, mounted, to reconnoitre the pass, taking two of M'Tipi's boys along with us. They succeeded in finding the proper path, and I was very glad to notice the old spoor of a wagon which had passed probably the year before. The road was easy enough, but lined on either side by rugged granite hills covered with thick bush. When we had gone about five miles, and could almost see the other side of the hills, we were startled by shots on our left. This was the scouts on the left flank engaged with some *kaffirs*, who took to the bush after a few shots were fired. A little way ahead of where we were I could see the valley open out until it was nearly a mile broad.

This was encouraging, and I determined to march the column in at daybreak the following morning. Accordingly on the 5th it started at daybreak, and took three and a half hours to reach the open valley sighted the night before. There we *laagered* in a good position, with one flank up to the rocks, and open ground in front, rear, and right flank. The scouts had come in contact with a few natives, but they took to their caves, saying that the Matabele had gone on to Belingwe. The scouts had been two miles further ahead than the point where the column halted, and reported difficult roads, but more open flats.

As soon as the horses and mules had had a drink and the men had had time to make a cup of coffee we marched on again. Half of M'Tipi's boys were sent on in front, and the remainder, on the right and left flank, manned the rocky hills on either side of our route, and we succeeded in getting through the pass without firing a shot. This was much better fortune than any of us anticipated. The column marched on about two miles north of the pass, and *laagered* for the night in open country, with good grazing for the cattle and good water for all. It was a great relief to my anxious mind to see the column safely *laagered* in the open flats at the southern end of the Belingwe Mountains, and, as we afterwards learned from the prisoners captured, good fortune favoured the column to a most valuable extent in this way.

I learned that M'Posi had not taken any active hand himself in the ransacking of the miners' camps in the Belingwe district, although several of his followers were with the rebels, but as they were in the minority and without a leader the other sections led by their chiefs, namely, Wedza, Mapelabana, and Um'Nyati, Senda, and Selemba, took advantage of the circumstances and sent M'Posi's men back with scant courtesy and less loot. This, happily for us, led to dissension among the rebels in the M'Patini, when it came to a matter of fighting the white column. M'Posi, being the principal local chief and responsible, as I have already mentioned, to the Matabele for the actions of his tribe, was very much incensed against his neighbours who, under the old *ré-*

gime of Lobengula, were subordinate to him under all circumstances.

When we passed through his territory, followed up by a body of about two hundred Matabele, he decided to work in conjunction with them and destroy us if possible, on our return, without the assistance of the neighbouring chiefs, who were threatened with a severe chastisement as soon as the white men had been driven out of the country. The Matabele leaders had taken a prominent part in all this, and it was only when they found we had changed our route that they discovered their blunder, because when it came to the point of war, M'Posi's people were more pleased than disappointed to find that their neighbours who had treated them so badly were likely to suffer more from the white column than themselves; and when the Matabele urged them on to attack the column, during the afternoon we fired the *kraals* along the Usza valley, M'Posi's men would only come as far as their own boundary.

When the Matabele found that M'Posi was obdurate, they decided to let him stay and look after his own land, and started off to the westward to raise the men belonging to Mapelabana, Senda. and others, but as they were limited to time, and as the threats they had sent on a few days before still rankled in the breasts of the people they now wanted to assist them, they practically failed to get up an organisation sufficiently enthusiastic to tackle the column. They did, however, succeed in gathering about five hundred men together on the top of the hill close to Senda's, but as none of the head chiefs turned up the greater part of the Matabele decided to rush back to Belingwe as soon as possible in order to obtain the assistance of the remainder of the *impi* lying there. They left about ten of their number with the force that Captain Brabant and Lieutenant Yonge attacked, on the morning of the 4th, and we were subsequently told that nine of them were killed by M'Tipi's men in a narrow pass which they were trying to defend.

While Senda's men were driving some cattle and sheep away, M'Tipi's men managed to cut off their retreat and put an end to them and a few of Senda's men who were with them defending the pass. Only one of M'Tipi's men was killed. He was shot through the head; but this was considered a very trivial affair by his comrades, who succeeded in capturing a good many cattle and sheep, as well as all the rifles and ammunition of the Matabele and those with them. When they returned to camp they were very elated with their success and did a war-dance in front of the *laager*, rushing up to where a few of the white officers were sitting, and shouting, "Now the white *induna* knows we can fight and beat our enemies,"

Trooper Anderson who, during the excitement of the attack, had gone on with M'Tipi's boys and kept with them all through the pursuit, reported that M'Kati showed great skill in handling his men and sent the party that cut off the disorganised rebels by a circuitous route under his son who knew every inch of the country. When the movement was complete the rebels were fairly hemmed into a narrow gorge between two perpendicular walls, from which it was impossible to escape. They were rushed by M'Tipi's men from both ends, and the fight did not last more than a few minutes. I was, of course, delighted with the result, and would have been more so had I known that the report carried to the *impi* at Belingwe was very much exaggerated. The mere fact of nine out of ten Matabele being killed would give credence to any amount of exaggeration, and this, with the disinclination of Mapelabana to come out of his caves, led the leaders of the *impi* to decide to remain where they were until a more favourable opportunity for their operations occurred.

Mapelabana's people all stayed in their caves until we passed, and in detached parties on the hills flanking the pass when the column was clearing it. A few shots fired by the flanking parties sent the rebels off under cover. After the column had *laagered*, the rebels showed up in mass on top of a hill well out of range.

I should have been glad indeed to have known all this beforehand, as it would have relieved me of two days' great anxiety.

The whole success of the undertaking in front of the column depended on its being got through the western Matopos without accident. The provisions and ammunition were absolutely necessary for success, and had they been lost the column would have been like a white elephant; but, thank Providence, the worst was all over, and now I felt confident of success. As this was really the first opportunity I had had, I watched the behaviour of the officers and men I had under me very closely, and I am glad to say it was such as to give me absolute confidence in everyone.

They all did their duty in the most careful and deliberate manner, and when a few shots were fired from the flanking parties on the heights, just as the column cleared the gorge, it was a pleasure to see the rear-guard, who were in a very nasty position at the time, at once discard their horses and take cover in the bush facing the rear. The officer in charge knew that the horses would only prove an encumbrance, and that they could not get away except towards the column where they would be captured. M'Tipi's boys, who were in the rear-guard, also doubled back and took up their position in line with the white skirmishers, but there was nothing for them to do on this occasion.

Chapter 12

Relief of Belingwe Garrison

I now considered the hardest part of our trek was over and that we should be pretty well able to arrange matters to suit ourselves in future. It was my intention, first of all, to relieve the garrison at Belingwe with men from the relief force. The men who were there were nearly all prospectors, and had a thorough knowledge of our own district and the country generally and would be of infinite service in the field. I therefore gave directions to move the relief party forward with enough rations to keep the garrison going until the field force had reduced to order the rebels in the district.

On the morning of the 6th the column moved forward about six miles and formed what was to be a permanent *laager* until the relief of the garrison was effected. The position chosen was a small granite hill, which used to be Selemba's (a Maholi chief) headquarters, his own *kraal* having been built on the top of it. The *laager* was formed hard up to this, with the hill for a base, the wagons making three sides of a square and the hill the fourth side, with the native contingent occupying a good position on its southern extension. The position generally was a strong one, with plenty of water close by and any amount of food for the horses and mules in the surrounding mealie gardens, which had only been partially-reaped.

That afternoon four wagons were loaded up with provisions for the new garrison, the relief party told off and placed under the command of Lieutenant Stoddart, who was promoted to the rank of captain, to take command of the garrison and forts of Belingwe for the time being.

The relief party to form the new garrison at Belingwe consisted of the following officers, non-commissioned officers, and men, *viz.*:—

Captain Stoddart	Trooper McLellan
Lieut. McCullam	,, Tannahill
Lieut. & Q.-M. Wilson	,, Stone, G. W.
Sergt. Douglas	,, Reece
Sergt. Coats	,, Wilks
Corp. Duffy	,, Stone
Corp. Nash	,, Walsh
Trooper Randell	,, Lyons
,, Grant	,, Jansen
,, McLeod	,, Woest
,, Nickliss	,, Coutts
,, Skews	,, Laing
,, St. Aubyn	,, Carlsen
,, Beavor	,, Palmer
,, Horwitz	,, Levin
,, Logan	,, Luckhurst

This party moved off at dusk, accompanied by a few men of the Victoria patrol, who had decided to go back to their homes, the idea beings to move during the night so as, if possible, to avoid observation. The convoy got to Belingwe the following afternoon without accident, a distance of some twenty-five miles by road to the north of our position. The first night we were in *laager* at Selemba's I sent for the three chiefs of the native contingent and gave instructions to M'Kati to keep his men scouting the neighbourhood constantly and carefully, until they located the exact position of the *impi*, and, if possible, they were to find out what it intended doing, but on no account were they to expose themselves. M'Kati said, "I understand what is wanted. My men will be instructed and will do their best."

Leaving Captain Hopper in charge of the *laager*, I started the following morning before daybreak, and rode on with a small party of horsemen to Belingwe, for the purpose of arranging the relief of the garrison there. We got there before the convoy which had preceded us the previous evening. It did not take long to make the necessary arrangements. All the men of the old garrison except five volunteered to join the field force, and were happy at the idea of leaving what had been more a prison than a home for them for the past ten weeks.

On my arrival Captain Frankland reported the death of Mr. T. J. Pope, the quartermaster of the garrison. This was very sad news to me, as it made the fourth victim out of our little lot who had succumbed to privations caused by the rebellion. Captain Frankland further reported that the health of the men generally had improved greatly under the supervision of Dr. Anderson, who had proved himself a first-class man, and had succeeded during the short time he had been at Belingwe in getting all the fever-stricken patients on their feet, many of them fit for duty. This was most welcome news. Captain Frankland also reported that Captain George Grey had ridden through from Inseza with despatches from Mr. Rhodes, one of which was practically my commission. This document is so characteristic of the founder of Rhodesia that I insert it.

Near Rixon's Store,
May 25, 1896.

My Dear Laing,—We got your despatches all right at Gwelo, and we accepted all your suggestions. We instructed Victoria to send you runners telling you to go down and meet the Tuli column and bring it to your place, *via* the Gondoque road, you taking command. In case the runners did not reach you, we instructed the Tuli column to go, *via* the Gondoque road, to you, and when it reached you, you to take command. It had instructions to detach some meal and some necessaries to Victoria with an escort. Its strength is about 150 mounted men with sixteen mule wagons. These would reach you, less the escort and wagons with meal for Victoria. Your instructions are to do what you think best, to assume the defensive, and do the most harm you can to the natives around you. If, after doing that, you think the best plan is to work up in the direction of the Filabusi and Bembesi, do so; but these matters are left to your judgment. We have every confidence in you, and do not want to tie you in any direction.

Grey, who brings this, will tell you all the news. The only thing that you must bear in mind is, that you take command and do the best you can.

Harry reached us all right. I did not send him back, as I thought wires from Victoria were quicker.

You may think that the best plan is to work through the Filabusi and Molungwana to the Matopo, where we are eventually going; if so, do so, but if you do, I suggest you take a few mule wagons with you for sick, wounded, and food. This plan of going on long journeys with only horse patrols is a mistake. You can't fight on empty stomachs, though I agree that too many wagons hamper action.

I can say no more, but thank you for all your good work.

If you can, let me know what you are doing, but for goodness' sake don't risk despatch-riders and horses. You will want every horse you have got. The nimble native you can use as a foot-runner.

    Yours   (Signed),

                C. J. Rhodes.

The new garrison marched in about 11 a.m., and the old one marched out about I p.m., the wagons being loaded with the men's kits and mealies for the horses and mules, a good supply of which was still left at Belingwe.

I had to arrange for the return of all the Victoria men who wanted to go back to their own district, and four of the old Belingwe garrison who wished to accompany them, fifteen in all. They marched on the afternoon of the 9th, with one wagon and sixteen oxen to carry their kits, rations, and ammunition, under the command of Sergeant-Major Nolan, who was promoted to the rank of lieutenant to undertake the command.

Sergeant Weale, late assistant native commissioner, Victoria, was also appointed a lieutenant, and sent off during the night to get through to Chebi, who was still loyal and anxious to support the white men, with instructions to raise as many of his followers as possible, and bring them down to reap the corn in the fields of the Impatini; but owing to the rebellion breaking out in Mashonaland. Chebi and several loyal native tribes were needed to act against the rebels in their own more immediate neighbourhood. As soon as all the necessary arrangements were made, I rode off with a mounted party to catch up the convoy, which had left to join the field force under the command of Lieutenant Caldecott. We got up to it shortly after dusk, and I was pleased to notice that the men were in high spirits, although many of them were weak from the effects of fever.

They were all very happy, and behaved more like a lot of schoolboys out for a holiday than men who would probably be in action within twenty-four hours. Most of them had suffered physically while shut up in Belingwe, but the first short march, and the pleasure of anticipating a meeting with, and punishing, the rebels for the hardships and deaths they had caused amongst the whites, had instilled new vigour into them. On the morning of the 9th myself and party rode on in front of the convoy and reached the *laager* about 1 a.m., where everything was found to be in perfect order.

Captain Hopper reported that M'Tipi's scouts had not yet quite located the exact position of the rebel *impi*, but had seen scouting parties from it, which they believed they had managed to evade, although the enemy were very vigilant and always on the prowl, coming from and returning to the bush-covered slopes of the mountain, which was about five miles from our position.

The short rest and good feeding in the *kaffir* gardens had already made a marked improvement on the horses and mules. The latter especially were in much need of a rest, as they had had very hard work all the way up. What were left of them now were in prime condition but tired. We had lost a great many from horse-sickness. The mules seemed to suffer more from this dread disease than the horses did, although the latter had not all come through it.

The Cossack post reported the approach of the Belingwe convoy about midday. They were about five miles off, and moving slowly, as the wagons were heavily loaded with mealies. The convoy reached the *laager* about 2 p.m.

Shortly after this Captain Brabant came and reported that M'Kati's boys had located the *impi*, but as the principal men had not returned M'Kati was not in a position to give a good report of the situation or strength of the enemy. "May," the *induna* of Umcheti's boys, came in and reported that he. with a small party, had gone back to the Mapelabana pass, and had succeeded in getting the natives there to talk to them from the hills. Mapelabana himself came down to within speaking distance, and said he wanted to *"konja"*—that is, "surrender"—to the white man.

"May" said, "All right; you had better come into the *laager* and do so."

Mapelabana answered, "No, I cannot do that, because my heart tells me that the white chief will kill me for the part my people and myself have taken in the rebellion; but I will do what I can to put matters right and keep my people quiet, and this pass will be open to the white man. I will also send grain and sheep as a token of submission. If you come back tomorrow morning you will find the first lot left on the rocks at the entrance to the pass."

"May" replied, "You had better send back all the cattle you took from the white men."

The answer was, "I don't have any of the cattle. They were divided between Wedza, Um'Nayati, Senda, and the *impi* which is lying at Belingwe. The most of the cattle are at Senda's. All Senda's men and a great many of Um'Nyati's are there guarding them. They are kept in the valley close to the Nuanetsi River, and I don't think the white man will get them out, the country being too difficult. The cattle have to be driven up the river-bed into this valley. I don't want to help the white man, and I don't want to fight with him. I wish to stay in peace here with my people. We will live like rock-rabbits in our caves until this trouble is over. I don't know anything about the strength of the *impi* at Belingwe, but I think the white man will find out all about it before full moon."

"May" informed me that towards the finish of the *indaba* Mapelabana was rather inclined to be insolent, and taunted M'Tipi's men for helping the whites against their own colour. To finish up, he said, "I have told you to tell the white man that this pass is open to him. but you Basuto dogs will never go through it again. Your wives will very soon be widows." "May" was very wroth with Mapelabana. and his indignation was a source of much amusement to the other members of the native continent, most of whom were young men.

Towards sunset M'Kati's son came back with a few others from a scouting expedition, in which they had been most successful. They had located the exact position of the *impi*, but could not give any idea of its strength. They were quite sure, however, it was equal in numbers to M'Tipi's contingent, and had a great many women, children, and cattle with them. The scouts said the position held by the rebels could be pointed out from the top of one of the small hills close by the laager. I at once went off with them to the point indicated, and, with their description and the aid of a pair of good field-glasses, was able to sketch what afterwards proved to be a very useful plan of the rebel *impis* stronghold. After this had been done, I asked M'Kati what he thought our chances were of making a successful attack on the rebels' stronghold.

He said, "I gather from the scouts that the rebels have picked out a very formidable position, which they have strengthened by building stone walls all over the cliffs, behind which they intend to take cover and fight the white man. They live in the gorge underneath the cliff, and have erected temporary huts for their wives and children, and *kraals* for their cattle and sheep. This gorge is covered with thick, heavy bush. The rebels have cut down a lot of the latter, and made strong *scherms* all round the place. My men think it will be hard to beat the rebels in this place, but the easiest way would be to get on the hills behind and attack from the top."

A short description of the Belingwe Mountains will give an idea of the position.

The southern end of the Belingwe mountain in the centre of which the rebel *impi* was located forms a high, rugged ridge, the crest of which varies in height from 800 to 1,200 feet above the level of the flats. The rock formation of the mountains is a hard slate, tilted on edge, the measures of which are almost perpendicular. In many places this formation stands out bold and rugged, forming precipices varying from 10 to 200 feet in height, standing tier upon tier above each other, with little flat spaces at their respective bases.

I may here mention that the position pointed out by the scouts was a *kloof* situated at the foot of a perpendicular cliff, on the southern slope of the south end of the Belingwe mountain. The foot hills, which trended away from the bottom of the cliffs to the flats, were very steep, long, and covered with trees, and a very heavy undergrowth of all sorts and condition of creepers, many of which were very thorny, and in places forming interwoven masses, which could only be got through after the chopper had been used freely. Of course there were paths cut out from the flats to the stronghold, but I concluded they would be well guarded and perhaps rendered more inaccessible than the virgin forest to an attacking force.

By the time M'Kati's scouts had explained and pointed out all they knew the sun was getting low, and in doing so had cleared the peak of Belingwe, which up to the present had cast a shadow all along the line of cliffs. Now the slanting rays shone right on to the slope and lit up the points we were most interested in observing. This was real good fortune, and it enabled us to decide on the spot, our line of action. Captain Sir F. Frankland (now staff officer of the column), Brabant, and Lieutenant H. Posselt, were present during the *indaba*, and before we left our dispositions were made.

Captain Brabant, with the pluckiest lot of M'Kati's boys, about one hundred, were to ascend the spur to the right of the rebel position, and, if possible, get into the works made by the enemy. Lieutenant Lynch was to lead the greater part of M'Tipi's boys up the gorge, straight on to the position, whilst the white men and Cape boys were to be led by myself up the left spur of the mountain and, if possible, the works on the left flank of the enemy's position, occupied by the

Cape boys under Lieutenants Donald Campbell and Howe. All this had to be done during the night, and the positions occupied before daybreak the following morning. This was our plan of attack and, as good fortune would have it, it was almost executed to the letter.

When we got back to camp the sun was all but down, and the night-watch set. I at once sent round for volunteers to attack Selemba's stronghold. Every man wanted to go, so a party from each troop had to be selected by their troop officers. The detachment from Belingwe volunteered to a man, and they were allowed to go along with detachments from the Maxim Troop under Lieutenant Caldecott. One from A Troop, under Lieutenant Bates, and another from B Troop, under Lieutenant Beisly, the whole making about eighty white men.

Lieutenant Donald Campbell had about thirty of his best Cape boys with Lieutenant Howe to assist him, and Captain Brabant about 250 of M'Tipi's boys, with Lieutenants Posselt and Lynch and the white scouts to assist him in leading them.

CHAPTER 13

A Council of War

The attacking force was ordered to parade at midnight, the white men mounted. The remainder of the column was placed under the command of Captain Hopper, with instructions to hold the *laager* until the attacking force returned. This force paraded at twelve midnight, when the plan of attack was explained.

Orders were given that there was to be no talking or smoking on the march, as the whole success of the attack depended upon being able to get into the enemy's defences on the hill without their knowledge. If this were accomplished, the rebels would be in a bad position.

The march commenced at 12.15 a.m., and about an hour brought us to the first part of really thick bush, at the foot of the Belingwe slopes. Here the mounted men gave up their horses—Sergeant Burnett being left with ten men to guard them. They were not very well pleased at being left out of the fun. I considered, however, that their duty was a most important one, for if the attack proved a failure, the safety of our horses would be very necessary for the preservation of all, if we had to make a hurried retreat. A short halt was then ordered to give the footmen and M'Tipi's boys a rest. Then the ascent of the first foot hill was commenced. Another hour of silent marching through dense bush brought us to the point where the attacking force was to divide into three divisions, climb the steep slopes, and surround the enemy's position.

All necessary arrangements having been made, the parties separated and moved away from each other a short distance, and lay down to rest and listen for any sound that might serve to betray any movement of the enemy's outposts. The only audible sounds that reached us, however, were the cry of the night-birds, the occasional howl of a wolf, or the baying of a pack of jackals. There was not the faintest indication of the presence of an *impi*, not even the barking of a dog, and it appeared that up to the present our approach had not been detected by our foes.

While the men were resting, the officers met and held a council of war, at which it was decided that no signals were to be made until Captain Brabant had got into position. His party having furthest to go, it was reasonable to expect that the other divisions would be in their appointed places before him.

As soon as he was ready he was to cause the "Alert" to be sounded, and then wait for my bugler to sound the "Advance" and "Commence firing."

We wished each other God-speed, and took command of our respective divisions, and moved off in different directions as silently as possible. I led the white men and Cape boys, Captain Frankland being next in command. For the first half-hour we skirted along the foot of a gentle slope, where the bush was not very thick, rendering our progress comparatively easy. Then we had to negotiate the crossing of a very steeply banked *donga*, which was covered with very thick bush and heavy undergrowth. Hatchets had to be brought into use, and a passage cut through this tangled mass. The bottom of the *donga* being reached eventually, the scramble for the top on the other side commenced, and the bank was gained, after close upon an hour's hard work. The Cape boys were now placed in front and in single file, and laid down to wait for the word from the rear that all were through. The intense darkness added to our difficulties, but I believe proved our best friend on the whole.

We were now on the spur which we had to follow to get to the position we intended to occupy before attacking, but we had still a good mile and a half of stiff hillside to climb over, rendered very difficult by a heavy growth of *Mahobo* trees, whose great leaves had commenced to fall and cover the ground with a thick carpet, which slipped away from under our feet on the slightest provocation. After a short but very tedious lapse of time, the word was whispered from the rear "All through," and then we moved on up the hill under the direct guidance of two of M'Kati's sons, who did their duty in a most admirable manner, and succeeded in getting us on the top of the first ridge, where we could then see the watch-fires of the enemy. The latter, of course, we intended to avoid. Here we again halted for a short rest, and listened for any sounds that might betray the whereabouts of our friends or enemies; but not a sound or sign reached us. Meanwhile our guides had gone forward under cover of the bush, and got close up to the first watch-fires, which had been deserted. The guides were now at a loss, and were not able to form an opinion as to the intentions of the enemy. They said the outpost might have heard our approach and gone back to report, or they might have gone back to headquarters, thinking that all was safe.

I did not like the absence of the rebel outposts nor yet the silence. I was afraid that the enemy knew what we were up to, and that very probably they were already arranging a surprise for us. The order was sent back to be more on the alert than ever, and if attacked, the men were at once to lie down, the Cape boys facing the front, the Maxim Troop to the right, A Troop to the left, and B Troop to the rear.

After the first ridge was passed, our advance became more easy. The slope was not so steep, and we had got out of the *Mahobo* on to bare soil which gave a much better foothold. This continued until the top of the next ridge was gained. Our guides now reported that we were very close to the position we wanted to occupy, but as the intense darkness was so deceptive they would like to go forward with only one white officer to make sure. This I agreed to at once, and Lieutenant Howe, a very intelligent and trustworthy officer, went with the guides. After what was to me a very anxious half-hour, they returned as quietly as they left. Howe reported that we were within 400 yards of the *kloof*. He had been quite close up to the position held by the enemy and believed they were altogether off their guard. The only signs of life to be heard were the movements of the cattle and goats inside the enclosures. He was confident the *impi* was asleep, and so were the native guides, one of whom had advanced and got into the first breastwork, on the lower edge of the *krantz*. This was very exhilarating information and not a minute was to be lost before we made sure of our position. The darkness was already showing signs of giving way to the first glimmer of daybreak, and Brabant's bugle might be expected to sound within the next half-hour.

A GROUP OF "C" TROOP

CHAPTER 14

Description of the Engagement

Lieutenants Donald Campbell and Howe advanced with the Cape boys, with instructions to man the first breastworks, facing the main exit from the gorge in which the *impi* lay, and to hold it at all hazards; it being very desirable to keep the enemy out of the *krantz*, and away from the stone breastworks which they had erected at every place of vantage. We again advanced, and whilst Campbell and Howe were posting their men the Maxim Troop was extended along the ridge facing the enemy's position. B Troop then prolonged the line to the right, with their right flank thrown forward to form a half circle. A Troop's turn came next, but they could not be found, and it was then discovered that nearly half of the white detachment had diverged and gone astray. Captain Frankland had evidently noticed this while I was busy getting the others into position and had gone off to try and find the stragglers.

Sergeant Halkett was sent off to try, if possible, to guide them up to where I was in time to form into position before Brabant sounded. This I am glad to say was accomplished, and the cause of the straggling cleared up. One of the men, overcome with fatigue, had fallen asleep, and when the last advance took place had failed to pass the word on to the rear. The officer in charge acted very wisely. As soon as he found he was not in touch, he halted and listened, and was guided by the sound made by those in front to advance towards us. Luckily he got up in time, and his troop extended in rear of the fighting line to act as a support, or to engage any of the enemy that might attack from the left flank, for we were not certain there was not a division of the *impi* lying in the adjoining gorge. So far all had gone better than I had anticipated, and I felt pretty secure and certain of success.

All that was wanting now was Brabant's signal to establish absolute confidence. The men were ordered to lie down but to keep on the alert. They were all very tired, some of them almost knocked up. My sergeant-major, a fine athletic young fellow, who had had more than a fair share of the work to do, came to me just as everything was completed and said "I am dead beat. sir. I must lie down for a short time." Captain Frankland was also very much exhausted, having had a lot of extra work to do.

I believe nearly all the men were in a similar condition. However, all the climbing had been done and it was yet a good half-hour to daybreak, which would give every one a beneficial rest. Frankland and I sat down together, to talk over matters, but neither of us could keep from nodding, so we had to get up and move about.

I was now beginning to grow anxious about Brabant. It was high time he sounded, to let us know his whereabouts. Daylight was coming in rapidly, and objects at a distance of fifty yards were becoming quite distinct. Campbell sent down to say he had manned the first breastwork and had thrown a line of skirmishers across the main footpath from the gorge. Silence reigned supreme, and I hardly ever remember a more beautiful daybreak. As daylight became stronger the line of skirmishers grew more distinct, and many irregularities could be noticed. I decided to wait for Brabant before correcting them. It was quite plain that most of the men were fast asleep, stretched out face down, with their rifles clasped in their right hand and a few loose cartridges in the left, all ready.

Many of them had stripped off their jackets and only waited the word to advance. I was pleasantly, and perhaps I may be pardoned for saying proudly, contemplating the scene, when, welcome sound, from far up the mountain on the other side of the gorge came the first note of the bugle from Brabant. The bugler must have been a little nervous, because his first attempt at sounding a call ended in a most discordant wail, but, evidently recovering himself, the next blast brought the "Alert" ringing clearly across the gorge. Frankland and myself burst into a hearty laugh, and anxiety fled from me. The men all jumped to a kneeling position, and kept an anxious and expectant watch to their front.

After the last sound of the bugle had echoed itself out along the *krantz* on either hand, silence again took command, but only for a few seconds. During that short period, however, it was very distinct, all eyes and ears being fixed on the gorge in front. Presently from the thick cover of the bushy slope a buzz as of many voices commenced to reach our ears. This gradually increased until it was quite an uproar, and then it subsided, when the distinct calls of two or three chiefs could be heard giving orders and shouting, "The white men are coming! Make for the *krantzes!*"

I now gave orders to advance the skirmishing line fifty yards, to correct intervals, and to lie down under best available cover. This was done and a second similar advance made, which brought us to within two hundred yards of the bush *scherm* of the enemy. Just as the fighting line took up position for the second time, a volley of musketry was poured from the first breastwork, and the Cape boy skirmishers opened fire all along their front. Another volley from the breastwork and then comparative silence. Lieutenant Campbell now sent along word that the breastwork had been rushed from the bush by a large body of rebels, but that he had driven most of them back into the bush again, and from where he was he could see large numbers of the enemy scrambling up the rocks to get to the stone walls they had made to fight behind. I concluded that now it was time to make a general attack. Accordingly the "Advance and commence firing" was sounded, and responded to by a cheer from all sides. The sun had now made its appearance, and everything seemed to be in perfect order, and from the position I took up about the centre of the line of white skirmishers I could see all that was happening.

Brabant's men now opened fire from the *krantzes* opposite, and M'Tipi's main body emerged from a large patch of bush, and advanced rapidly over an open space of about two hundred yards and halted when they got in line with our right. M'Kati and "May" shouted out, "What are we going to do now? Are the white men afraid to advance?" This caused a laugh along the white line. One of the white men answered that we were not afraid to advance, but would not like to go in before the Basutos were ready.

As our advance was converging I now pushed forward the Cape boys on the left into the bush, and supported them with the Maxim Troop, ordered a few rounds to be fired, and moved the whole line forward about thirty yards. Halting the white skirmishers where they had a good view of the *krantz* over the tops of the trees, our advances roused up M'Kati's men, and after firing a volley into the bush in front of them, they charged it in a body in a most gallant manner. They were checked at the fence for a few seconds, but the rifle fire from the Cape boys cleared the front, and very soon Cape boys and Basutos were out of sight in the thick bush. Then the rattle of musketry with a mixture of savage yells was all that could be heard, but it was soon evident the rebels were not holding their own.

The attention of the white skirmishers was drawn to the *krantzes*, upon which large numbers of the enemy were seen swarming, firing their rifles at anything and covering their retreat by a shower of large stones, not being at all particular whether they struck friend or foe as long as the individual made good his retreat and got in behind a stone barricade, from which fire was opened, but did no harm worth speaking of, and as they were surrounded on three sides and exposed to a cross fire from good shots under cover, they soon gave up attempting to return our fire. It was, moreover, amusing every now and again to see one of their stone walls commence to move down the cliff; solid at first, but shortly to become a scattered shower of huge stones which went crashing to the bottom of the cliff, doing far more damage to themselves than to the attacking force.

At the end of an hour resistance was practically finished. The white men were kept in their position, and Brabant's men moved off to the right, and getting on top of the mountain, advanced along the zigzag on to the breastworks. As they approached some very exciting hand-to-hand encounters took place on the cliff, in which *assegais*, battle-axes, and shields played a prominent part. The attack virtually ended in a proper *kaffir* fashion, the white men and Cape boys having been drawn back and not allowed to enter the enclosure. By nine o'clock the position was taken and the *impi* which had contributed to organise the bands that committed so many cruel murders amongst the white people in the Lower Inseza and Filabusi districts was practically disbanded.

M'Kati and his people captured a good many oxen and sheep and about a hundred women and children, nearly half of whom were Matabele from the Inseza and Filabusi districts. One man, disguised as a woman, was taken prisoner, and although he was very cunning, his little trick was discovered by the Basutos at once. He was reported and pointed out to me. I advanced to interrogate him, but one of the young Basutos got excited, having noticed what he took to be the shaft of an *assegai* under the sheepskin, he shouted out, "Be careful, N'Kos, he will kill you," and advancing with his *knobkerrie* he made a stroke at the rebel's head, which the latter cleverly parried and dashed off through the crowd of women and children, only to fall a victim to a Martini-Henry bullet, which put an end to his flight and existence.

M'Kati was highly delighted at his success, and it was most amusing to see him leading the war-dance, in an old frock-coat and bowler hat, with a rifle in one hand and a bunch of *assegais* in the other.

The enemy's loss was not estimated; it would have taken too long to find out in the thick bush, but it was pretty severe.

Our loss was trifling, considering the work undertaken. Paul Zandvogle, a Cape boy, was killed. Captain Brabant and a few others slightly wounded. A few of M'Kati's boys were killed, several wounded, one severely.

As soon as the Basutos had destroyed the enemy's stronghold, we buried our dead, and retired, getting back to our horses by 10 a.m., all very tired after the trying night march and excitement. I noticed that many of the men went to sleep in their saddles on the way back.

We reached the *laager* before noon, and found everything correct. The men were at once dismissed, and went to rest.

The wounded—friend and foe alike—were handed over to the care of Dr. Anderson and his staff.

CHAPTER 15

The Rebels Send Peace Offerings

Of course everyone was delighted with the result of our attack on Selemba's, and for myself I must say I was pleased beyond all expression with the manner in which all ranks behaved in action. I had had every faith in the men of the column before, and now it was confirmed. My only wish was to be able to provide them with more work as soon as possible, and to restore law and order. Orders were given to M'Kati to interview the women and children, and find out as much as possible from them about the movements of the rebels everywhere. He did not get much information from the prisoners for some hours, but at last one elderly woman came to him and said she was willing to tell all she knew.

The narrative was interpreted to me as follows:—

I with about fifty other women and children and perhaps thirty men arrived at Selemba's the evening before last. We came from the Lower Inseza, which has been visited by a very strong body of white men, who have scattered everybody and destroyed all our *kraals*. Most of our young men have gone to the Matopos. Only a few came with us. They were all at Selemba's this morning. They were led by Meshlointombi, who was among the first killed. Selemba had his own following, about one hundred men; and the Matabele, under Gota Monzie, about four *scherms*, probably two hundred men and a few petty chiefs with a small following each. They were all taken by surprise, and never expected the white men to get up to them during the night.

The sentries had all come back when the night got very dark, thinking it was impossible for anyone to come up the stronghold except by day, when they would have been seen a long

A LAAGER AND READY FOR ACTION

way off. We should all have then got into the cliffs behind the breastworks, where you would have found it very difficult to have beaten us. Nearly all our leaders were shot at first while trying to get to the breastworks. I have told all I know.

The women and children were handed over to his charge, with orders that they were to be well treated and cared for. M'Kati said, "I promise you they will have the same treatment as our own wives and children."

The Cape boys, under Lieutenants D. Campbell and Howe, did splendid service.

The men from Belingwe were now distributed among the troops already formed, and what was afterwards known as the Belingwe Field Force was constituted.

The distribution was roughly as follows

	In Command.		N.C.O. and Men.
Maxim Troop	Capt. Hopper	Lt. Caldecott	30 mounted infantry
A Troop	Lt. Yonge	,, Bates	25 ,,
B Troop	,, Beisly	,, Bell	26 ,,
C Troop	,, Jackson		30 infantry
Lieuts. D. Campbell, Howe, and Moore			70 Cape boys—Infantry.

On the afternoon of the 10th, "May," with a party of M'Tipi's boys, was sent off to scout the neighbourhood of Senda's position, with instructions to remain in the vicinity until the arrival of the column.

Towards evening a messenger was sent back from "May" to say that Senda's people were defiant, and had strengthened a naturally strong position by every available means, and challenged the white men, to take them out of it. The scouts could not find any trace of the cattle formerly reported by Mapelabana, and thought it was most probable they had been removed to some other part of the country.

On the afternoon of the 11th the column moved up to within two miles of Senda's stronghold, and *laagered* up in a good position.

I rode on towards Senda's with a small mounted party, under Lieutenant Beisly, to make a reconnaissance, and try, if possible, to find out the designs of the enemy.

The position the rebels held here was a high granite hill, with a small oval-shaped ball top, about a mile long, and five hundred feet high, the slopes of which were covered with a jumbled mass of high boulders piled on top of each other, in all sorts of fantastic shapes, forming large spaces or cavities, which were termed caves.

It was quite possible to move about among these rocks and get from one end of the hill to the other without exposing oneself. To add to the physical strength nature had provided a luxuriant growth of thorn scrub, which grew up and intermingled with the rocks, forming an almost impenetrable barrier through which the rebels had cut numerous footpaths, which zigzagged about among the rocks from one end of the position to the other. These footpaths had all been blocked by large thorn-trees and made next to impassable. A thickish bush covered the flats up to within about five hundred yards of the hilltop, then there was an open space which had been cleared and cultivated. Our party rode on to the edge of this open space, and then along it for about half a mile, keeping a sharp look-out in case of getting cut off, but we learned afterwards that the latter event was not likely to happen, it being the intention of the rebels to keep to the rocks. With the exception perhaps of about ten natives perched on the top of the highest rock, evidently as sentinels, there was no sign of the position being occupied by a force of rebels. There was scarcely a sound to be heard except now and again the bleat of a goat. The rebels kept perfectly quiet.

After riding along and examining the situation as closely as a pair of good field-glasses would enable me to do, I turned towards our *laager*, not at all sanguine of being able to inflict much harm on the rebels at Senda's, but decided to make an attempt on the morrow. It appeared very evident that a night attack was out of the question and would only lead to disaster, therefore any ideas I had of making one were abandoned.

During the night the rebels made a considerable noise, but whether it was to impress us with their numbers, or whether they were moving out and in, I never learned, but probably they were strengthened during the night by recruits from the surrounding hills.

The following morning, shortly after daybreak, Captain Hopper, myself, and a small mounted party, rode forward again to reconnoitre the position from a different point of view. On our approach the sentinels commenced to blow their horns, and we could see a distinct commotion all about the hillside. The natives seemed to be everywhere about, and commenced to shout insulting and defiant threats to us.

It was now quite evident that they were in force, and meant fighting if their position was attacked.

I decided therefore to move the *laager* on to a small rise, about five hundred yards from the foot of the hill, and nearly opposite to its centre. This would bring the greater part of the hill under fire from the *laager*; and the centre part, which seemed at present to be more thickly populated, would be within easy range of the Maxim. The *laager* was moved up accordingly on to the desired position.

As soon as *laager* was formed, the Cape boys, under Lieutenants Campbell and Moore, were sent off to the right, so as to turn the left flank of the enemy's position, and, if possible, to climb a good way up the ridge and attack downwards on the centre. As soon as they were ready C Troop was extended and advanced on the centre, to within two hundred yards, where they had a fairly good view. It was of no use going closer up as the rocks and bush obstructed the vision. The Maxim gun was trained to work over them, and had a splendid field, varying from five hundred to a thousand yards. M'Tipi's boys, under Captain Brabant and Lieutenant Posselt, were sent off to our left flank, to attack from the enemy's right, in a manner similar to the Cape boys on the left

Before they were marched off about fifty of them were armed with three dynamite *assegais* each. These *assegais* were so constructed that when they were thrown they always fell point downwards. A detonating cap, with a French nail fixed into it, then caused an explosion. They were dangerous weapons, and only the boldest men would handle them, after they were shown the effect produced by the explosion.

Captain Brabant and his lieutenants reported that the men armed with the dynamite *assegais* were so confident of the efficiency of their arms that it was very difficult to keep them back. It was most amusing to see the bearers dash forward, throw their *assegai*, and dodge behind a rock, with a diabolical expression on their faces, to listen for the explosion, and then dash out again and discharge another. I am not aware that any actual damage was done by these *assegais*, but the moral effect on the enemy was indescribable.

M'Tipi's boys had not been in action on the left half an hour before the rebels gave way and vacated the left flank of the hill; many of them succeeding in escaping to the hills behind.

Every arrangement for making the attack was completed by 11 a.m. Then the "Commence firing" sounded. M'Tipi's men were the first to open fire. They had come rather unexpectedly on a party of the enemy, who were guarding a large number of sheep and goats on the right of the position. This, of course, led to a short encounter, which ended in a grand success for M'Tipi's boys. The firing on the right caused a commotion among the rebels in the centre. Many of them clambered up the rocks to see what was going on, and exposed themselves to the fire of C Troop and the Maxim. Then the Cape boys commenced to attack downwards from the left flank. This evidently upset the philosophy of the defenders, who began to yell and move about rapidly amongst the bush and rocks, letting loose their rifles and blunderbusses, but doing no harm. A few pot-legs were sent over the *laager*, but they only served to amuse the men by their peculiar musical accompaniment.

All we had to do now was to watch the development of the attack, which was, owing to the difficulties to be overcome, very slow. At times the rattle of rifle fire was very sharp, but often died away to a dead silence, starting off again suddenly when some fresh nest of rebels was struck.

The skirmishers of C Troop were almost always engaged along some part of their line, only firing when they saw the rebels on the move. After a time they got used to the passes, or gangways, which seemed to be the main lines of communication between different parts of the rebels' stronghold, and as soon as a party of natives appeared they were saluted with a shower of bullets.

This sort of thing went on for about three hours, the Cape boys and M'Tipi's men gradually working to the centre, clearing everything in front of them and destroying all the rebels' huts and stores.

By 3 p.m. the position was taken. All the rebels remaining had gone to earth in a cave under a high boulder, which was between 100 and 200 feet long by 50 broad. A large party located themselves there, and kept firing from that point of vantage. Lieutenant Campbell called on them to surrender and give up their arms, but this they refused to do. He then sent to the *laager* for dynamite, a few charges of which put an end to their firing, and although they would not come out of the cave themselves, they sent up a great many sheep and goats, and a very humble entreaty to be spared, promising not to interfere with the white men any more.

As soon as this was reported I went over to the cave and held an *indaba* with these people, who were evidently far down under the huge rock. They said they did not know where Senda was. They thought he was in a cave on a hill, or that he had perhaps escaped. That the cattle had all been taken off on the approach of our column, but that all the sheep and goats would be sent down if the white men would draw off a little way.

The man who did the talking wound up with an appeal for mercy, which I promised would be granted, provided their promises were kept. The attacking party was then withdrawn. Lieutenant D. Campbell reported having seen forty rebels dead; Captain Brabant that on the first brush a good many fell on both sides, but he could not give any numbers. The loss sustained by M'Tipi's men was trifling, and they treated it in the most offhand manner, being much more delighted with their success than interested in their losses. They were to be seen straggling out of the rocks, laden with all sorts of loot. Among the Cape boys a few had sustained slight injuries, but no deaths occurred. There were no casualties among the white men.

As soon as the attacking force withdrew, armed fatigue parties were sent in to bring away as much grain as possible and destroy the remainder. Nearly all the grain found was in the husk, it being harvest-time, and the reaping little more than commenced.

The rebels kept their promise to a certain extent and sent down about twenty goats and sheep from different parts before night set in.

The *laager* remained where it was during night. The following morning a search party was sent into the hill. On their return they reported that the position was deserted. This practically ended the attack and the breaking up of the rebels at Senda's. I was sorry the rebels still held the cattle, but decided to let them keep them for the time being and push on to where the services of the column would be of more benefit to the public welfare.

CHAPTER 16

March to Buluwayo

A council of war was now held to decide upon the course to be followed with M'Tipi's men. So far they had proved themselves most valuable, and had done excellent work, especially as scouts, and the information they had brought in had led to a great success at Selemba's. Their work in the Mapelabana pass was also most beneficial to the welfare of the column, and altogether they had shown themselves to be a loyal and valiant lot of natives. The amount of loot they had collected, and the wish to keep it, made them anxious to get home. This wish was hinted to me by Captain Brabant, and confirmed by Lieutenant Posselt. I came to the conclusion that it would be better to part with them on good terms.

I was all the more anxious to do so because I now contemplated a march through the Lower Inseza, Filabusi, and on to Buluwayo, and because the continued presence of three hundred natives would have been a great draw on our supply of provisions. I therefore sent for M'Kati and told him he was at liberty to march back home or to come on with the column. He decided to go back, and Captain Hopper, with twenty mounted men, went back with the native contingent for a distance of about five miles, until they were nearly through the Mapelabana Mountains. The passage at this point becoming somewhat difficult for horses, and there being no signs of any rebels about, Captain Hopper left them and returned, destroying a few *kraals* on his way back.

Three of our white scouts were sent on with M'Kati's men to go as far as Is'Iknombo's, to try and get a hundred of his boys to act as guides, herds, &c. They returned on the 16th instant without any, and reported that as M'Tipi's fellows got towards the end of the gorge (which they were about to enter when Captain Hopper left them) they were set upon by a large party of rebels, who attacked them on the flanks. After a very severe encounter the rebels were defeated with severe loss. M'Tipi's men lost a few. Sergeant Wilson said M'Kati behaved splendidly, and practically saved his men by his coolness and bravery. He was the last man to leave the pass, and all his dead and wounded were borne off the field. They saved all their cattle and sheep.

M'Kati sent messengers to Is'Iknombo, but was not satisfied with the answer he received. He advised the white scouts not to go near him, and sent an escort back at night to guard them through the pass. This was our last communication with M'Kati, who was certainly one of the finest specimens of a *kaffir* chief I have ever come in contact with.

On the 15th inst. the column moved northward towards Um'Nyati's stronghold, and *laagered* up on the west bank of the Nuanetsi River.

On the following morning two wagons were sent back with an escort to Belingwe, to bring on grain for the horses and mules.

Captain Hopper, with Captain Frankland and thirty-six mounted men, were sent off to try and find out Um'Nyati's strength. The patrol returned during the afternoon. Captain Hopper disconsolately reported that Um'Nyati, after fortifying his position, had decamped, leaving nothing but empty *scherms*, stone breastworks, and huts, all of which were destroyed by the patrol.

Um'Nyati's spoor went in the direction of Shambo, but as the column was now to march by that route, I decided for the present to leave him alone.

On the 17th despatches were sent off to the administrator, detailing the work done by the column.

As I had now no native contingent I arranged to send off Captain Brabant, along with Lieutenant H. Posselt and Trooper Southey, to endeavour to raise about five hundred of Chebi's boys and bring them into the M'Patini district, for the purpose of reaping the crops, and thereby keeping the rebels from benefiting by them.

Whilst waiting for the return of the grain wagons from Belingwe, the men were exercised in skirmishing on horseback and defence of the *laager*.

On the afternoon of the 19th the wagons returned with thirty-six bags of grain. This, with what we expected to pick up on the way, I reckoned would ration the horses and mules until Buluwayo was reached.

On the morning of the 20th the column marched from the west

bank of the Nuanetsi along Cunningham's trading route, in the direction of Shambo, The reason I had for taking the trade route was because it led to all the principal *kraals* between Belingwe and the Lower Inseza. The horses and mules were fresh after the two days' rest and good feeding on the banks of the Nuanetsi. The weather was simply delightful, it being now mid-winter. The men were in high spirits and looked forward eagerly to having a slap at the arch-rebels in the Inseza. The country we were passing over was open, undulating, and well-watered. Um'Nyati's spoor was discovered by the scouts. He had only gone a few miles in the direction of Shambo, then turned sharp off to the northwards, having evidently made for the bush-covered hillside of the Dora Mountains, where I thought it best to leave him unmolested for the time being, trusting to his natural greed and love for cattle to find him and them at some more convenient time in the near future.

I may here mention that up to the present the dread *rinderpest* had not taken hold of the Belingwe district.

We advanced by easy stages, doing about fifteen miles per day. Everything in the shape of *kaffir kraals*, &c., *en route* were destroyed, most of them being deserted on our approach.

Nothing of any consequence happened until we got to the west most part of the Shambo Mountains. There the presence of a considerable body of natives was indicated by sleeping *scherms* for about three hundred men, and fresh spoor showed that they had been in use but lately. Only one native, however, was seen, and he was far up the slopes of the mountain, keeping perhaps a close watch on our movements. The scouts were lucky in capturing a few young cattle and sheep here, which were rolling in fat. We left Shambo behind on the afternoon of the 21st, and *laagered* about five miles further on, on the Lower Inseza road.

All the spoor of cattle, &c., we came across went westwards towards Godhlwayo, from which, on the afternoon of the 22nd, we could see a large and very dense column of smoke ascending. I was in hopes this was the result of the work of one of the Buluwayo columns. If so, I conjectured that our task would be made lighter, and that we might have the good fortune to drop across an *impi* retreating over the flats.

Towards evening on the 22nd *laager* was formed on a large grassy plain, a good fifteen miles broad, lying between the Shambo and Tandodzie ranges. The weather having been particularly good for several weeks made everything as dry as possible, and on this particular afternoon the wind was strong and from the east. Shortly after the *laager* was formed and the cattle turned out to graze, the quarter-guard sentries reported several small columns of smoke about two or three miles away to the windward. At the first glance there did not seem to be anything very particular about this, but as I watched I noticed others springing up.

It was at once evident that the flats were being premeditatedly set on fire for the purpose of endeavouring, if possible, to destroy the column. It was quite plain that there were a great many hands at the devil's work, for what at first were only a few columns of smoke soon increased into a dense black cloud, nearly three miles long, advancing rapidly, and growing denser every second. The sight was very appalling, and frightened me more than anything I had ever seen before. There was not a moment to be lost. The grass all over the flats was at least three feet high, and as dry as matchwood, and the stiff breeze blowing was bringing the fire down on us at a great pace.

The bugles at once sounded the "Alarm" and "Horses in." The men were equal to the emergency, and rushed out to get branches of trees, &c. A circle of fire, about a hundred yards out from the *laager*, was started, and kept in check on the inner side. In less than a quarter of an hour a good big band had been burnt round the *laager*. This was accomplished not a moment too soon, for a roaring mass of flames, about three miles long, twenty yards broad, and thirty feet high, swept past our position, with a noise like a river in flood. Had the *laager* been enveloped in that enormous flame not a thing would have been saved. As this fire-storm passed the faces of the men expressed their feelings beyond any doubt. Every one knew we had had one of the narrowest escapes possible. The horses and mules in the *laager* were huddled up together, all quaking with terror. A sigh of relief escaped from every one when the danger passed us and rolled on, destroying everything it came in contact with. Our enemies had all but scored against us. Yet luckily all the harm they did by their diabolical attempt was to rob our poor cattle of a good feed.

The column moved forward again on the morning of the 23rd inst., and as it was now nearing the Lower Inseza district, one of the most populous and fertile in Matabeland, and being the locality in which the first actual signs of the rebellion were discovered, native *kraals* became more numerous. The scouts and the advance and flanking parties had lots of works to do, burning and destroying everything that was likely to afford shelter or be of the least service to the rebels. There were a few signs of natives having been about lately, and towards the end of our second trek a large, well-beaten track was crossed, along which it was quite evident a great traffic had recently been carried on. Several of the scouts were sent along this path to try and discover the whereabouts of any rebels that might have happened to be close by, and one of our flanks (James Cook) in following up a small footpath, which struck him as being very new, found a large quantity of grain, hidden away in the thickest part of the bush, about a hundred yards to the left of where the wagons of the column would pass.

This grain was all stored in grass bags, each, of which contained about two ordinary sacks full of grain. The bags were all sealed with clay, and covered with flat stones. This was a most welcome and valuable discovery in more ways than one, because it not only enabled us to replenish our stock of food for the horses and mules, but it reduced the rebels' store to a very considerable extent, and showed us very plainly that they had still a line of communication open to Inseza, along which we might find similar stores of grain. After loading up our wagons with the grain the column moved forward again, and *laagered* up for the night on the west bank of a rocky *spruit*, about one and a half miles east of Cunningham's farmsteading. Some of the scouts had been forward as far as the latter and reported its utter destruction, and also that the remains of the family were still unburied.

The scouts employed in following up the "grain track" (the name given to the large path discovered during the afternoon's march) reported that they had seen a few *kaffirs* on the hills, watching the movements of the column, and that, at the sand drift of the Inseza River, quite recently a large quantity of cattle, goats, men, women, and children had crossed over, going to the westward—*i.e.*, towards the Matopos.

The column moved forward early on the morning of the 24th, and *laager* was formed up within a hundred yards of the ruins of Cunningham's farmsteading. As soon as the halt was ordered I went forward with several officers to examine the ruins, and I may safely say it has not been the lot of many to behold a more melancholy, heartrending, and revolting spectacle.

The Cunningham family consisted of an aged father and mother, a son, and several grown-up daughters. The son was a married man, and his wife and children were with him. The family party, so far as I could gather from the men who knew them, consisted of nine persons, all of whom had their home at "Kildare," the name they had given the farm. They were attacked about midnight on the night of March 24th, and brutally murdered by a band of rebels, who used *knobkerries, assegais*, and battleaxes to do their devil's work. The roofs of the various huts, in which the unfortunate family had been sleeping, had then been set on fire, and to a certain extent had consumed the bodies. It was impossible to distinguish any of them. We could only judge by the size of the bones whether they were those of an infant or adult. It was evident that in one room one woman and three children had perished together—the children having evidently been killed in the arms of their mother—for the four heads and the bones of the fingers of four persons were all together in one little heap. In two adjoining rooms the remains of what were probably two men, were found in one, and those of two women in another.

I was afterwards informed by a prisoner that one of the young girls, aged about seven years, escaped unhurt, by some means unknown, on the night of the murders, and got down to the banks of the Inseza River, which was about five hundred yards away, and lived there for a few days until discovered by a party of *kaffir* women, who had come to reap the grain growing in Cunningham's fields. These women caught the child, and one of them, with a degree of cruelty that I trust has seldom been equalled, held the poor child's head on a large stone with one hand, and with the other picked up another stone, with which she, infernal fiend, smashed the child's head to pulp.

The slight glance I had at Cunningham's was too much for me. I went back to the *laager* very sad indeed, and asked the men to go as soon as they had breakfasted and gather the remains of all the bodies, and place them in an iron box, so that they could be buried. The men did not wait for breakfast, but set to at once, and, with the assistance of Dr. Anderson, every particle of human bone to be seen was picked up and enclosed in a box. Captain Hopper read the funeral service, the remains being interred about 11 a.m., about fifty yards to the east of the homestead. A large pile of stones was raised over the grave, every man of the column contributing his stone to the pile.

The Cunninghams were proverbial for their kindness and hospitality, and their home had always offered a hearty welcome to the wayfarer or straggling prospector who might have happened to be about after dark. Many of the men of the column were intimately acquainted with the family, and they were very much affected. Captain Frankland had been their guest about ten days before they were murdered, and spoke in unmeasured terms of their kindness to him.

He had lost his way, but had the extreme good fortune to reach their homestead after nightfall. A very slight glance at the faces of the men around the grave, whilst the service was being read, would have convinced the most casual observer that mercy would be the last thing the rebels might expect to get from them.

Several watches and articles of adornment were recovered from the ruins and placed in a small box for the purpose of being conveyed to Buluwayo, and there handed over to the authorities.

During the afternoon I took out a strong mounted patrol and destroyed several *kraals*, which were located in the hills to the south. At one *kraal* a dead body was found, but it was impossible to say whether it was that of a white or black man. A bullet had passed through the skull. We were inclined, however, to think it was the body of a *kaffir*, who had met his death at Cunningham's or somewhere close by.

After destroying several large *kraals*, every one of which had been deserted some time, and all grain taken away, I followed up the footpath we passed the night before, until it crossed the Inseza River. There was fresh spoor on it of both *kaffirs* and cattle, the latter probably pack oxen used for carrying grain, &c.

I had now become convinced that this path was the one most in use between this part of Inseza and the Matopos, and decided to follow it up as closely as possible with the column, in the hope of finding more stores of grain, and perhaps dropping across a foraging *impi*.

Chapter 17

A Brush with the Enemy

The morning of the 25th the column crossed the Inseza River, and making a trek across the country to the westward, about a mile to the north of the grain path, had not gone far before it struck the spoor of a large column which had preceded us. I decided to follow this spoor until it crossed the grain path, and then to make after the latter again.

Sir Frederick Frankland, who knew the district we were in very well, was anxious to take a small scouting party to the south, about two miles, to find out what had happened to Croft's store. I allowed him to take four of the best mounted men, with instructions to undertake no risks and to get back to the column as soon as possible.

We had to make a long march because water was not very plentiful, and after doing about seven miles the Buluwayo Filabusi road was struck. The column now changed direction and marched along that road to the south. Shortly after we got on the road the scouts reported rebels on the high granite hills in front and on the right flank, but only in small parties. Not long afterwards shots were heard in the direction of Croft's store. It was evident Frankland had come in contact with a party of rebels. The firing increased rapidly and I became rather anxious, being afraid that perhaps Frankland's party had been cut off, but as they were well mounted there was every chance of their getting back, even if they had to make a detour. I could not send back to their support without halting the column, and as it was then marching through thick bush and no water handy it was undesirable to halt.

The natives on the granite hills to our right were numerous, but did not make any attempt to molest us, although we could see plainly they were all armed. At last water was reached, at a place where a fairly good position was selected and *laager* formed, the Cossack post sent out, and everything got ready to repel an attack. The rebels on the hills kept moving round to our right, and shortly afterwards commenced to fire at the sentries from longish range, makings fairly good shooting, but killing no one. I now became most anxious about Frankland and his party. An occasional shot from his direction showed there was still something doing. The column had marched about ten miles during the morning, but in a circular manner, and this had again brought us to within about two miles of Croft's store.

Presently two of Frankland's party rode in and reported that they had come across a small party of rebels on a little *kopje*, which they pointed out. The rebels had taken to the rocks, where Sir Frederick intended keeping them until a strong party could be sent on to collect the grain and cattle the natives had stored there. I at once ordered out a patrol of thirty men and a team of mules to bring back a cartload of grain, there being a Scotch cart at Croft's store.

I went off to assist Frankland, leaving Hopper in charge of the *laager*. I half expected he would have had a fight before I got back, but as the *kopje* was not far off, if such had been the case we should have heard the firing as soon as it commenced.

Our progress to the *kopje* was not interrupted, and when we got there we found Sir Frederick and his two men all right. The place was at once surrounded, but we could not get at the *kaffirs*, who had taken to the cover formed by the disjointed rocks on the highest part of the hill. We, however, got at their main store of grain, which was a large one, although of not much use to us, being principally *Poco*, a small class of *kaffir* corn, rather like mustard-seed, and very bad feeding for horses and mules. We did succeed in getting a cartload of good grain, and destroyed everything else. This position was entirely a depot for storing provisions from the surrounding districts, and had been garrisoned by about three hundred rebels, whose sleeping and defence *scherms* were still there. These we destroyed, as well as the huts of three large kraals, all of which had been occupied very lately. We also succeeded in capturing about fifty sheep and goats before making for the *laager*, which we reached in safety.

Captain Hopper reported that he had sent a small party round the foot of the hills to dislodge the rebels, who were firing at the sentries when the patrol rode off. He also reported that he had had no trouble since midday, as all the rebels had disappeared. This fact, with the information we had got from the *kaffirs* in the caves at "Freddie's kop," led me to believe that we were now on the heels of a retreating *impi*, which I decided to follow up if possible.

Our laager was formed within two hundred yards of the grain path which still went straight for the Matopos. This the scouts followed up for a mile or so, reporting that they could not get any further because the rebels were in force on the hills beyond, and that it would not be possible to follow the path with the wagons, as it went in between the granite hills, through a very narrow pass, which was guarded by rebels. This was getting much more interesting, and looked like business, with every prospect of a brush with the rebels.

The column moved on to the south the following morning and halted about three miles from the hills. The scouts were sent away to the westward and to the south of the hill for the purpose of finding out if it was possible to get the column through in that direction. They returned and reported that the only impediment would be the thick bush, and that they had seen no rebels.

I decided to try along the south edge of the hills and marched again at 1 p.m. in double column of wagons, with a party of dismounted men carrying axes to clear the bush in front of each. We had not gone more than two miles in this direction before it became apparent that the movements of the column were closely watched from the hills. On the hill nearest to us, along the base of which we had to pass, many natives could be seen on the sky-line. They were much disturbed and soon disappeared over a rise. Shortly after, some stray oxen, in an excited state, were rounded up by the scouts, who reported that others were being driven on in front. This accounted for the commotion among the niggers on the hill. The progress of the column had been retarded by the thick bush which, however, now became more open and the country more accessible as we got past the shoulder of the first hill, which terminated in a deep gorge.

On the other side of the gorge a long, flat hill, composed of smooth granite and covered with patches of dwarf scrub, rose and trended away to the westward. Behind this flat hill a high peak rose, on top of which a large body of rebels were perched, watching our progress, and perhaps from their point of vantage were directing the movements of others, who were not yet discovered by us. After passing the gorge, which had a thickly bushed entrance, Lieutenant Beisly, who was in charge of the main body of the rear-guard, sent in to say that a small troop of cattle were being driven across our line of march into the gorge, and asking for permission to take a few of his men to capture them. I sent him instructions to do so, and halted the column with the intention of waiting Beisly's return.

As soon as Beisly moved off a large body of rebels showed up on the flank of the hill which we had just passed, and made for the sides of the gorge as fast as they could. The old game was being played with us. The cattle were the lure. I at once sent Captain Hopper off with one-half of the Maxim Troop to assist Beisly, to capture the cattle if possible, and guard against an ambuscade. At the same time *laager* was formed without outspanning the mules, and the "Halt" and "Alert" sounded to put the advance and flanking parties on their guard. This had hardly been done before a rattling volley of musketry was fired from the gorge. followed immediately afterwards by several others. Hopper and the rebels were engaged, at the same time, on the flat hill on our right flank.

The rebels now commenced to show up, dodging from one clump of bush to another, and in a sort of general irregular advance. All this looked like the commencement of a fight. The "Retire" was sounded, the picquet lines stretched between the wagons, and the infantry and Cape boys extended round the laager, at which the enemy were now directing their fire. Captain Hopper's party got back simultaneously with the advance and flanking parties. Lieutenant Yonge with A Troop mounted, was ordered to advance in skirmishing order against the hill on our left flank. His instructions were to engage the enemy and then gallop back to *laager*, to draw the rebels on to it if possible. This he tried three times, but the enemy would not leave cover. He was then ordered to make a stand against them at about two hundred yards from the foot of the hill. The Maxim was trained and opened on the clump of bushes, wherever the whereabouts of the niggers was discernible by the smoke from their rifles.

This had the desired effect, and very soon cleared the slope of the hill immediately on our flank, and gave the skirmishers some good practice as the rebels retired from cover to cover. Scouts were then sent out to the front, left flank and rear, for the purpose of ascertaining if the rebels had any force in the bush surrounding our position, but so far as we could learn they had not. The march was again resumed, and for two hours a dropping fire was kept up on us from the hillside. This kept the right flank engaged all the time, but little damage was done by the rebels. Whether our fire had done any damage it was impossible to say, but it had kept the enemy at bay.

The party that Hopper encountered had lined the bush at the entrance to the gorge and fired three volleys, which Hopper returned and cleared the entrance. He at once gave the order to retire, when he discovered he was just at the entrance to a deadly trap.

Out of his party he had one man—W. Potgeiter—wounded through the thigh, one horse shot dead and three wounded.

I congratulated Hopper on the excellent manner in which he got his wounded and dismounted men away from the gorge.

Towards dusk a fairly good position was selected to *laager* in for the night and a thick thorn-bush *scherm* cut and set all round it. The rebels still hung about on the hill, exchanging an occasional shot or two with our outposts. Needless to say the watch was very much on the alert all night, but nothing happened further than that one of the sentries reported having seen three natives make a detour round the laager. Morning came but did not bring the expected attack. The bush was carefully scouted in front, rear, and left flank, but no signs of the enemy being in any strength the column was moved forward again.

Shortly after marching the rebels showed up on the hill to our right, and the rearguard was engaged in a slight skirmish, but this did not delay the march. Captain Frankland went back and strengthened the rear-guard with the Cape boys. The rebels were only playing a harassing game, which lasted nearly two hours. Then they took to the hill on the right, and disappeared over its crest to the northward. Thus ended our experience in the "Glass valley."

Still cutting our way through thick bush, the column continued its march until the Umzingwani-Buluwayo road was reached, about a mile south of Wier's store on the Umzingwani River. Here a halt was made. We found the rebels had wrecked the store, and killed everything they could lay their hands on, in the shape of man and beast.

CHAPTER 18

Attack on Matopos Postponed

We marched again at 2 p.m. taking the main road for Buluwayo. After crossing the river we came upon the *laagering* ground of a large column—"Spreckley's," I believe.

The "grain track" was again crossed, still keeping straight for the Matopos. Along it, probably the same day, had passed a large party of men, women, and children, cattle and sheep, all going towards the Matopos.

I did not think it advisable to follow up the path any further. The retreating rebels, if they wished to, would reach cover of the Matopo hills before I could stop them, and if they wanted to fight the column they knew where to find it.

The harassing attack they had made on the column yesterday and this morning only meant to retard it until the women and children were got out of the way, for as soon as the rebels had accomplished this they left us alone.

I was determined to make for Buluwayo as fast as possible.

On the evening of the 27th the Makukupen Drift, on the Umzingwani River, was reached, and *laager* formed on its south bank. During the afternoon march, small parties of the rebels had been observed on our flanks, but well out of range. I was told afterwards that there was an *impi* on either flank of the column with orders to attack if circumstances were favourable. As the column which had preceded us took the Makukupen road to Buluwayo, I decided to march along an old prospector's road which runs along the south bank of the Umzingwani River. This I thought would give the column a chance of breaking fresh ground until the Tuli road was reached and bring it in closer touch with the Matopos. All the *kraals* along this route were deserted, and we destroyed all that came within our line of march. Many fresh spoors were observed, all leading to the Matopos, and a few niggers, presumably rebel scouts, were still hovering about on the *kopjes* on our flanks.

The Tuli road was struck in due course, and the column passed over the northern portion of the ground, where Captain Brand's Gwanda patrol had had a stiff engagement some weeks previous.

The skeletons of his horse and several mules, and a few bodies of what we took to be rebels were lying about. I did not then know that Brand had to leave his dead, otherwise I would have caused a closer examination of the remains to have been made; but as most of the bodies were lying close up to the *kopjes*, where it was most likely the rebels would attack from, and a good way from where the horse and mules were lying, I felt certain the remains were those of rebels.

On the evening of the 29th the column *laagered* at "Dawson's" store on the Umzingwani, twenty-three miles south of Buluwayo. All day the rebel scouts had been oftener reported than on previous days, but large bodies of them were not observed.

On the evening of the 30th the column *laagered* on a small *spruit* about four miles south of Buluwayo, and on the morning of the 31st it moved up to within two miles of the town. I rode in and reported my arrival to General Carrington, who received me very kindly, congratulated me and the column for the work done, and gave orders for the column to rest for a few days.

During the afternoon the column moved close to the "Eureka" mine, where good water and grazing were plentiful, and *laagered* up for a rest. Here we remained for the next ten days, doing a lot of small patrols, mostly in the direction of Thabas Induna, where the spectre of a huge *impi* always hung round.

Although my men tried hard, both night and day, to get a glimpse of it, the sight was denied them, but was reserved for the vision of a few more favoured mortals who never lost a chance of letting the whole country know when they had seen the *impi* on the warpath, and by their reports succeeded in keeping the inhabitants of the town in a nervous state of excitement, and gave the men who had the work to do a heap of extra marches, presumedly to keep them from getting rusty. The men of the column and myself were indeed very glad when this mythical *impi* took up its quarters on the brickfields, which were on the other side and much closer to the town than ourselves. But with all this the most of the men had time to go to town on leave

General Carrington, Sir R. Martin, and officers of the Belingwe Field Force and stand a general treat to many of their old comrades. The following account of that happy occasion is taken from the *Rhodesian Weekly Review* of July 11, 1896:—

BELINGWE F. F. HOSPITALITY.

It was a merry band of guests and hosts that gathered round the festive *al fresco* board of Captain Laing's famous little force last Saturday night, in the light of a gigantic bonfire which reminded one of the Eve of St. John in the north of France. Speech and story followed in quick succession while the ample fare was being consumed by the light of an ingeniously contrived chandelier made of whisky cases. By the side of each guest was his own individual candle, and great was the fun at each man's effort to make his candle last the longest. After the Queen's health had been proposed and received with patriotic cheers, Captain Napier spoke in feeling terms of Buluwayo's admiration of the Belingwe Field Force and its gallant commander, while Mr. Holloway spoke a few words in eulogy of Captain Hopper and the merry men who followed him to join Captain Laing.

The 4th of July, which date it happened to be, was an excuse for drinking to the health of America, coupled with the name of the genial 'Jumbo.' After dinner an adjournment was made to the silvan concert hall, around the blazing fire, and there, under the sway of M.C. Donald Campbell, a right pleasant little entertainment followed, finishing up with the chairing of Captains Hopper and Laing by their enthusiastic followers, after the toasts of Mr. Rhodes and Dr. Jameson had been cheered with three times three. The guests at that Saturday will long remember the hearty, genial hospitality and good fellowship tendered by the Belingwe Field Force.

In the morning the force was inspected by General Carrington, who praised in no measured terms the bravery of Captain Laing and his men, and his appreciation of their gallant conduct.

The column was also inspected by General Carrington and Earl Grey, the administrator, both of whom highly praised the force and thanked them for the work done. The following account of that event is also taken from the *Rhodesian Weekly Review* of July 11. 1896:—

INSPECTION BY EARL GREY.

On Tuesday, 7th July, Earl Grey, the Administrator of Rhodesia, inspected the Belingwe Field Force at their *laager*. He afterwards addressed the troops as follows:—

Captain Laing, officers, and men of the Belingwe Field Force, I am proud of the opportunity which you have today given me of thanking you on behalf of the government, whom I represent, for your brave stand at Belingwe. and the services you subsequently have rendered. When in the greatest peril, Captain Laing and his force refused to come in, and under a flag made by one of the garrison (Captain Frankland designed the flag and Trooper Huband made it) taught the enemy that Britons still know how to fight. I am told that many of you have shown quite a talent for inventions and devices that have added to the discomfort of our enemies, and that, under Captain Laing, you are prepared to give further proofs of your bravery.

This chance will be given you as soon as General Carrington can make the necessary arrangements for your departure to the Matopos. I am pleased to say a victory has been won at Tabas I'Mamba by Colonel Plumer's column, where some severe fighting has taken place. A police force is in process of formation, and patrols will be sent out from various centres to scour the disaffected districts. Again thanking you for the pleasure it has given me to inspect you, I shall await with confidence your return from the Matopos, and the re-advent of peace and prosperity to Matabeleland.

On Sunday the 12th of July, at noon, an orderly from the general rode into the *laager* and handed me a note, which ordered my column off to Fig-Tree Camp.

The column marched at 3 p.m., passing through Buluwayo and taking in provisions there, then on again in the direction of Matabele Wilson's farm. As it was imperatively necessary for us to get to Fig-Tree as soon as possible, I selected about seventy of the best mounted men, three wagons for provisions and ammunition, an ambulance wagon with Dr. Anderson and a staff of hospital orderlies, and made a forced march for Fig-Tree. which we reached the following evening at 5 p.m. There we found Mr. Fergusson, A.D.C. to General Carrington, and two half troops of the new M.M.P., the men of which had formerly been in Gifford's Horse and Grey's Scouts, and a nice hardy serviceable lot they were. They were now A and F Troops M.M.P., under Lieutenants Chesney and Carney.

Having discovered that the *impi* which was about to attack Fig-Tree and ravish the district was composed of the same material as the one which hung about Thabas Induna and the brickfields of Buluwayo, an arrangement was made to remove the officer who had discovered it to a place where his powers of observation would be more appreciated and free scope given to his faculties of imagination. A new man was put in his place, and the police and my men moved on about three miles east of Fig-Tree to a position more favourable for our principal purpose, and where good water and grazing were procurable.

On the 14th of July I received orders from the brigade office to take command of the M.M.P., join my force with them, and be ready to march at the shortest notice.

On the 15th I received instructions and plan of attack for operations in the Matopos.

On the 17th a detachment of infantry, under Lieutenant Butters, and an artillery detachment with seven-pounder and Nordenfelt, arrived, along with several volunteers unattached, one of whom, Mr. Percy Hare, had a letter of introduction to me from Captain Frankland. This young fellow, like many others, had left England on the news of the outbreak of the rebellion, and hurried out to take part in subduing it. He and mostly all of them were fully equipped at their own expense, and were dying for a fight. The strength of the white force now mustered was—

Belingwe F. F.	70	Officers and men	mounted
M.M.P.	50	,,	,,
Infantry	30	,,	dismounted
Artillery	7	,,	,,
Hospital	5	,,	,,
Cape Boys	25	,,	,,
	187		

To be added to the above there was a contingent of about twenty natives (friendlies) under Lieutenant McDonald.

On the 18th I got a wire from headquarters saying that the attack planned to take place on the morning of the 19th had been postponed.

On the 19th I received despatches by rider, ordering an advance on Inugu, with orders to attack at daybreak on the 20th, and turn rebel *impi* out of their positions, and then proceed to cut off the retreat of the rebels from the Cheleli valley, and join Colonel Plumer's column by that route, if possible.

CHAPTER 19

The Battle of Inugu

The column was marched forward at 7 a.m., and reached Chawner's Camp at 9 a.m., where it halted for an hour to refresh men and horses. Marching on again it got close up to Inugu before noon, where we *laagered* up. Scouting parties were sent out, one under Lieutenant McDonald with natives, and the other under Lieutenant Fergusson, with Mr. Hare and a few men. Both parties returned and reported that there were no signs of the enemy. The natives brought back a little girl prisoner, but she could give no information further than that the men were all away, she did not know where. After some deliberation I decided to move the *laager* forward under Inugu, The class of country we had to advance through now was most difficult and dangerous for an attacking force. It verged into a narrow valley, on both sides of which ran a line of rugged hills, more like cairns of huge boulders, rising from two hundred to five hundred feet.

The space between them through which we had to pass being covered with thick bush, which helped to render the task more difficult for man and beast. However, by dint of perseverance, a good deal of whip-cracking, some language more forcible than elegant, and a sharp look-out to every quarter, the column was got through the narrowest and most difficult part of the gorge before nightfall, and *laagered* with its right flank close up to the rocks at the foot of Inugu, in a thickish bit of bush, which screened the position from front and half the rear, leaving an opening of about two hundred yards from half rear round the left flank and half the left front. The sentries were posted, and the men laid down in skirmishing order all round the *laager*, about twenty yards in front of the wagons, their rifles ready.

The native contingent was *laagered* about 150 yards in front, close up to the rocks and surrounded by a *scherm*. Every precaution was taken to guard against a surprise, and I believe every man present expected an attack. According to the story of our native guides we were just in the position the rebels wanted us to get into, it being their intention to cut off our retreat and kill us off at their leisure. For myself I felt certain that if there was any fight left in the rebels, they would show it here, but to make an absolute certainty of having an attack I had a bet of a "saxpence" with Dr. Anderson. It was always safe to bet with the doctor. He invariably lost. Yet he was all the more ready to take the bet because he had had little or nothing to do except bandage *veldt* sores since we left Buluwayo. I am, however, very sorry to say that before twelve hours had elapsed he had more than enough to do, but he was equal to the occasion, and did his duty most thoroughly throughout the action, which afterwards was acknowledged and appreciated by all.

During the night I don't suppose I slept more than half an hour; there was a good deal of wind blowing, and the sky slightly overcast. Occasional drifting clouds shut out a view of the sky, but it was never very dark. Several times the sentries reported having seen natives fleeting about on the rocks above our position, but no alarm was given. About 4 a.m. the men stood to arms, and as it was commencing to get light the mess orderlies were allowed to fall out and make coffee, the fires being inside the line of skirmishers. The "Boot and Saddle" was sounded at 5.30 a.m. By this time objects were discernible at about a distance of fifty yards. The last note had hardly left the bugle when a rifle shot was fired from our rear, and a bullet whistled harmlessly over the *laager*. Immediately after the shot came the battle-cry and yells that are the inevitable accompaniment of a Matabele charge. I dropped the cup of coffee which had just been handed to me by our mess cook, and shouting "Stand to arms," rushed as quickly as I could to the rear face of the *laager*.

I found the men all ready at kneeling position, and Sergeant Money had his Nordenfelt ready for action. All were anxiously watching the rapid advance of a yelling mass of rebels who were evidently vieing with each other to get to the *laager* first, sending out deafening shouts to cheer themselves on and frighten us, firing off their rifles as they ran. To me the sight for a second was a bit awe-inspiring. I called to the men to keep steady, and not to fire on the picquet, the men of whom were rushing towards the *laager* on the left of the attacking force, discharging their rifles into the mass as they came along, and doing their best to alarm the *laager* and stop the rebel charge.

The order was given to commence firing, and the first volley from the rear face put a check on the rapid advance of the enemy, and allowed our picquet to get in safely. The rebels halted about forty yards from the *laager*, sat down, and waited to be strengthened from the rear, at the same time pouring a hot and rather deadly fire on the *laager*. The first two minutes of this killed two men and wounded one close to where I was. The brunt of the attack fell upon the infantry troop under Lieutenant Butters, and D Troop under Lieutenant Bell, which had been wheeled round half left to facilitate their fire, as there was no attack from the open ground on our left flank.

All this time our men had been keeping up a steady fire on the increasing mass of rebels, who now commenced to show signs of charging again. This was indicated by the peculiar "burring" sound made by the Matabele before making a rush. Sergeant Perry had run the seven-pounder round and was loading with case shot when the second charge took place. The rebels got up to within twenty yards of our fighting line before they were checked. Just at this moment a very unfortunate occurrence happened.

One of the men lost his head for the second, and rising up, shouted, "Are we to get back to the wagons?" He had hardly got the words out of his mouth before he was shot through the head. The men of the fighting line, not knowing who gave the order, rose up and looked round. The order was given to advance ten yards, lie down as flat as possible, and keep up the fire.

Lieutenant Butters set a brilliant example to his men. He dashed forward the number of paces mentioned, revolver in hand, shouting to them, "Come on, boys, we will soon dust them out of this."

At this pass I also noticed that the first man to dash to the front was the young volunteer Percy Hare. He rushed up to within ten yards of the enemy, who were wavering a little, and sat down on his knee and commenced firing into them. The men, as soon as they understood what was wanted, dashed forward, and lying down flat took up the fire. Simultaneously a charge of case shot from the seven-pounder was sent right into the teeth of the enemy. This rather upset their plan of attack and their equanimity, stopping their fire for a few seconds. But again they commenced to gather.

A second and third shower of case shot from the seven-pounder, the steady grinding of the Nordenfelt, and a shower of bullets from the rifles had the desired effect. The attack from the rear was broken. The rebels scattered and took refuge in the bush and rocks on our right flank. This at once brought them on to the fire of E Troop and

EARL GREY ADDRESSING THE BELINGWE FIELD FORCE NEAR BULUWAYO

the M.M.P., who were on the left rear of the *laager*. Lieutenant Carney had his men well in hand, and poured in a steady fire, which made the rebels seek shelter elsewhere.

A slight lull now took place, and I had time to go round the *laager* and rearrange details. I had very little to do in this respect, as the troop officers had their men in good order, and Lieutenant Fergusson, A.D.C., had been about in every direction, rendering very valuable assistance.

Time flies rapidly in a fight, but up to the present I don't suppose we had been over ten minutes engaged and the worst of the battle was yet to come.

Whilst the attack on the rear had been going on the men on the front faces had not been idle—in fact, the rebels had so arranged that their heaviest attack should be delivered from the front. The party attacking from the rear were to make a great noise to draw our attention in that particular direction, whilst the main attack would rush in on us from the front. This they did attempt, but the fact of their first having to deal with the native contingent somewhat spoiled their plans, although the latter did not make anything like a good stand. Still they acted as a buffer, and by the time the enemy had dealt with them Hopper had his Maxim trained and the men on the front faces thoroughly in hand, and opened a steady and destructive fire as soon as the friendlies cleared the front. This they did by rushing out in the open ground on our left and lying down, afterwards gaining the *laager* and packing themselves away under the wagons in huddled masses. I never hope again to see such an abject lot of human beings.

The fight now developed into a rifle duel. The rebels had taken cover in the rocks and kept up a lively fire for an hour and a half or two hours, doing a considerable amount of damage to men and animals. Our men returned the enemy's fire whenever they could locate the position of a few to any certainty on the rocks. Those in the immediate vicinity of the *laager* were eventually cleared, and Lieutenant McDonald, assisted by Sergeant Wilson, Troopers Nauhaus and M. Robertson, a volunteer attached, were ordered to occupy them with the native contingent.

They had a great deal of trouble in getting the friendlies to move from the cover of the wagons where the thickness of their numbers had made them a good target for the rebels, causing them a heavy loss. At last I gave them the option of getting into the rocks as ordered, or of being shot by the Cape boys. This had the desired effect. They decided to choose the least of two evils, and went for the rocks in fairly good style.

After they were once in they did really good work, perhaps through sheer desperation, but to my mind they were chiefly inspired by the gallant behaviour of their white leaders. Their occupation of the rebels' central position caused the latter to shift about and expose themselves to the rifle fire from the *laager*, and it now became evident that the rebels had lost their vantage. The seven-pounder was employed in shelling wherever a party of rebels were seen to congregate. Sergeant Perry handled his gun splendidly, and made some excellent shooting.

By about 8 a.m. the rebels had virtually given up firing, and I gave the order to inspan with the intention of moving forward to the entrance to the Cheleli valley, when Lieutenant McDonald reported the rapid approach of a fresh *impi* from the left front. I sent him back with instructions to keep the position held by the native contingent on the rocks, and had the Maxim and seven-pounder trained on the edge of the bush, through which the fresh *impi* was advancing.

They soon made their appearance, coming on in very good style. They crouched down on the edge of the bush with their shields in front of them and commenced singing a war song as they waited for their reserves to close up. They certainly looked well, and we could enjoy the sight all the better from knowing the game was now in our hands. Their leader, a fat old Cumulo, came up at last, and the war song stopped as he commenced to interrogate the rebels on the hill. Many of my men knew what he said. The rebels on the hill shouted to him that they had been very badly beaten and did not want to fight any more, and advised the chief to be careful. A slight commotion could now be noticed in the ranks of the new *impi*. I gave the order to open fire. The seven-pounder sent a shrapnel right into their centre, and Hopper stirred them up with a shower of lead from the Maxim. The new *impi* burst and scattered in every direction; the greater part of them going straight back.

The remainder rushed to take cover in the rocks, but finding them occupied on top did not go very far. They clustered on top of a large flat stone under a *Marula*-tree, making a beautiful target for another shrapnel, which was landed in by Sergeant Perry in a splendid manner. This was evidently all they wanted. They were now helpless, and rushed for the flats, exposing themselves to the rifle fire of our white skirmishers. The party that had fled backwards had now massed under a tree about eight hundred yards away. The top of the tree could just be seen from the *laager*, and our directions were got from the leader of the native contingent.

They had a good view from the hillside. The first shell burst rather high and did not do much, if any, damage. The next one burst about twenty yards from the tree and sent the rebels flying again. They never halted until they got on to the bush-covered slopes of the hill about a thousand yards away. Here the shells found them, and they soon disappeared over the ridge of the hill.

Thus ended the Battle of Inugu, the stiffest fight I have ever been in, and I believe the only *laager* fight which occurred during the rebellion. Our force was just sufficiently weak to encourage the rebels to attack it and sufficiently strong to beat them off thoroughly. Throughout the engagement all ranks behaved in a most excellent manner and relieved me of a great deal of anxiety, for I must confess that during the first hour and a half I was at a loss to know what the upshot was to be.

When the fight was at its worst I had time to stand by the hospital wagon for a few minutes and watch Dr. Anderson and his assistants at work. At that time he had over thirty dead and wounded lying in his enclosure. The wounded white men bore their sufferings manfully, never uttering a groan or showing the slightest signs of fear, whilst the wounded friendlies were howling in a most dismal and disheartening manner.

This was the first time I fully realised the position and my own responsibility as officer commanding, and I was glad that it was not possible for the men in the fighting line to see much of the hospital enclosure. I watched with pleasure and satisfaction the demeanour of the men bringing in the wounded, and was glad to observe that as soon as they laid down a wounded comrade they at once ran back to their respective places in the fighting line, and took up the firing without making a remark.

Dr. Anderson seemed to be oblivious of everything, except a devotion to his duty. He took the men as they came; bandaging them and passing on to the next, with a few cheering words to each. He certainly proved himself the right man in the right place, and is deserving of all praise.

The fight at Shangani and Bembesi, during the campaign of occupation in 1893, were, in my opinion, mere flea-bites compared with Inugu.

The following is a list of the killed and wounded:—

Killed	... ...	Corp. J. Hall ...	B Troop
,,	... ...	Trpr. P. Bennett	E Troop M.M.P.
,,	... ...	,, W. H. Bush	,, ,,
Severely wounded		Serg. C. H. Halkett	Maxim Troop Belingwe F.F.
,,	,,	,, M. Eadie ...	F Troop M.M.P.
,,	,,	Trpr. D. Dick ...	Belingwe F.F.
,,	,,	,, T. Judge ...	,, ,,
,,	,,	,, J. R. Toulson	,, ,,
,,	,,	,, C. O. Morgan	Died July 23rd
Slightly wounded		,, A. M. Stewart	,, ,,
,,	,,	,, C. Sell ...	M.M.P.
,,	,,	,, F. H. Miller	,,
,,	,,	Corp. C. S. Roger	Belingwe F.F.

The native contingent had fifteen wounded and twenty-seven killed and missing.

We also lost nine horses, which were killed or died of their wounds, and had two wounded, with three mules killed and three wounded. After the fresh *impi* was fairly routed the order was given to inspan, and the column moved forward to try and get to the entrance of Cheleli valley, which our native guides told us was only a short way ahead now, and the way to it through fairly easy country. The last part of their information proved tolerably correct, but as they were never able to point out an entrance to the valley I am certain they were at fault as to its whereabouts.

The column advanced along a valley running parallel with Cheleli, about half a mile broad, banded on either side by a line of rugged hills, and halted at 10 a.m. with its left flank up against a rocky *kopje*, where the valley had narrowed down to about a hundred yards wide. There was a little water here, and it was decided to breakfast. The friendlies were posted on the hills on either side, and Cossack posts put out.

Laager had not been formed more than half an hour when the friendlies and Cossacks on the left flank reported the advance of an *impi* up Cheleli valley. This *impi* came on rapidly, and joined with part of the defeated one, which had followed the line of hills on our left, picking up stragglers as they went along, keeping the hills between themselves and the column. When they were joined by the new *impi* they halted, and after a short time both *impis* moved off rapidly in the direction of Umshamo.

The column moved forward again at 11 a.m., and *laagered* up about eight miles further on, well past the centre of this part of the Matopos. Our guides had failed to point out an entrance to the valley, and as the position we now occupied was a good one, I decided to halt there for the night. From the hills on our right a good view of the country to the north could be obtained. The scouts and native contingent were sent on to watch for any movements of the enemy. About 3 p.m. they reported a large body of rebels marching over the hills from Cheleli valley towards Fynn's farm, and shortly after another lot with cattle, women, and children moving in the same direction. These I took to be rebels retreating in front of Colonel Plumer's attack.

They all crossed over and disappeared behind the granite ridges, about three miles to the north-west of our position, before sundown.

CHAPTER 20

Return of Column to Belingwe

As soon as the *laager* was formed and in a good state of defence, the bodies of our comrades killed in action that morning, which were brought along on the wagons, were interred in one grave, and a large cairn of stones erected on the top of it by the men of the column.

At 8 p.m. three star-shells were sent up to indicate our position to the other column, but they were not answered.

I spent an anxious night, and made certain the rebels would attack again, unless they had been routed all round. The men stood to arms as usual before daybreak, but no rebels showed up. Shortly after it was light enough to see well patrols and scouting parties were sent out in all directions, each returning to report that no rebels were to be seen, or any signs of them. The guides were again questioned as to the entrance of Cheleli valley. They said that the entrance was now only a short way ahead to our left. The column moved forward again about one and a half miles, when Lieutenant McDonald rode in and reported that he had lost all faith in the native guides, who, he said, were leading us astray, either from fear or design.

I saw it was futile to go further under the circumstances, and the condition of our could not be got back too soon to a place where they could rest and be well looked officers together, explained the situation, and decided to return by the road we had come in. The column counter-marched at once, and shortly after sundown reached Chawner's camp and *laagered* up for the night.

From the time the rebels were observed disappearing over the hill to the eastward, on the afternoon of the 20th, we had only seen two niggers, and they, just as we left the Inugu gorge behind us, fired on a foraging party and fled. As we passed over the battlefield on our way back, many more dead bodies of the enemy were seen lying about. In all probability they were the bodies of wounded men who had got out of the rocks and endeavoured to reach a small rivulet to drink. One wounded man had hanged himself.

The friendly *indunas* were ordered to count the enemy's dead as we returned, and between them they reported having seen ninety. I presume this was a fairly accurate report.

We had scarcely been more than an hour in *laager* at Chawner's camp, before the sentries announced the approach of a large body of men and horses from the direction of Inugu, and presently a bugle sounded the general salute. Shortly afterwards Colonel Baden-Powell[1] rode into *laager* and asked who we were. He had been sent out with two squadrons to look for my column, the absence of which had somewhat disturbed the peace at headquarters. He told us of all that had taken place with Plumer's column, and that after their fight they had gone back to Usher's No. 2. This explained why our signals had not been answered on the evening of the 20th, and made me feel very thankful that my column was clear of the mountains. I had an idea that once in the hills we were to stay there until the rebels went out.

Colonel Baden-Powell took a few notes of our engagement, and returned to headquarters at once, taking the two squadrons with him. Before leaving he arranged to send an ambulance wagon and doctors to assist our wounded.

The following morning about 11 a.m. the ambulance wagon arrived under mounted escort, along with Dr. Sutcliffe, who came to assist Dr. Anderson with the wounded. After they had all been properly attended to, the column marched on to Usher's No. 2, arriving about 3 p.m.

I rode on a little in front as we neared headquarters, and met Captain Beresford with a squadron of horse coming to look for us, and render any assistance that might be required; luckily none was required.

On arriving in camp I met General Carrington, who congratulated the column and me on our successful engagement.

The following day the column moved towards Buluwayo, leaving the M.M.P., and F Troop R.H.V. at headquarters.

Our instructions now were to take provisions on to the garrison at Belingwe as fast as possible.

---

1. *Baden-Powell: the Early Campaigns* by R. S. S. Baden-Powell (*The Downfall of Prempeh, a Diary of Life With the Native Levy in Ashanti, 1895-6* & *The Matabele Campaign 1896*) is also published by Leonaur.

On arrival at Buluwayo I met Captain Frankland, who had, after fixing up our depot at Matabele Wilson's farm, marched a party of forty to join Plumer's column, and was engaged in the attack on Babyaan's stronghold. Frankland had been very busy in Buluwayo, and with his usual push had got all the wagons in good order and loaded with provisions for Belingwe. A day's rest was necessary to give us a chance of overhauling everything, and the shoeing of the horses seen to. Then we were ready to start.

I was glad in a way and very sorry in another, to have to part with two of my best officers, in Surgeon-Captain Anderson and Lieutenant Donald Campbell. As a doctor Anderson was perfect, and I don't believe a better leader of Cape boys could have been found than Donald Campbell proved himself to be. They were both promoted—Dr. Anderson to the position of District-Surgeon of Buluwayo, and Campbell to that of chief of the detective staff of Rhodesia.

On the morning of the 26th of July the provision convoy was ready, and the column marched for Belingwe. We had instructions from the brigade officer to laager up near Thabas Induna and scout the vicinity, as another *impi* had been reported hovering about in that direction.

On the 27th I signalled back to the brigade office, "No signs of *impi*," and marched on, reaching "Denendeen" on the evening of the 28th, where I again communicated with the brigade office, twenty-seven miles, by heliograph. On the evening of the 29th the *laager* was formed on the east bank of the Inseza River, fifty miles from Buluwayo.

On the 30th the column crossed the Inseza hills and *laagered* on their eastern flank. On our way through, Lieutenant Campbell, who was in charge of our signalling staff, tried to get into communication with Bembesi by heliograph, but failed, owing, I believe, to a heavy haze.

Towards sundown on the evening of the 30th two despatch-riders caught up the column bearing despatches from the brigade office with instructions to keep a sharp lookout for any retreating rebels from the Matopos.

On the 31st I sent seven wagons, with an escort of infantry under Lieutenant Caldecott, to relieve Belingwe, and moved the mounted men in the dusk, under a large hill, where we would be fairly well hid, and gain a good view of the surrounding country. We laid there for two days scouting the country in every direction, but the rebels showed no signs of being anywhere about. The whole country for miles round had been burned by grass fires and there was no food for the horses. I had therefore to move forward again on the 2nd towards dusk, and on the evening of the 3rd *laagered* up at Posselt's farm, twelve miles from Belingwe, and ninety-five from Buluwayo. Here the grazing was excellent, with plenty of good water.

I now made up my mind to leave the column and ride on to Belingwe, with a small escort, to see how matters were with the garrison there. I started on the morning of the 4th and found on arrival that Lieutenant Caldecott had got his convoy safely through and that the men of the garrison were all right, and not in want of provisions as we had been led to believe. All this was very satisfactory.

On the 5th the garrison was relieved by men from the field force. The relieved garrison joined the field force the same evening.

The following day all the farriers set to work to overhaul the horses, and see to the shoeing of them, and of the mules.

The column had a holiday which they spent in a shooting competition, troop against troop. The staff put in the best shooting team, and Sergeant Lawrence, of B Troop made the highest score.

Captain James Stoddart, who had been in command of the garrison at Belingwe, reported that all was quiet in the district, except at Wedza's, Mazezeteze's, and Mondi's, where he believed the rebels held strong positions.

I decided to march a force against Mazezeteze and Mondi, and on the morning of the 7th, leaving Lieutenant Yonge with A Troop in charge of our depot at Posselt's farm, marched a patrol of fifty mounted white men, E Troop. Captain Stoddart's infantry, and thirty Cape boys, towards Mazezeteze's. After crossing the Umchingwe River, the scouts were sent on to Mondi's, and towards sundown the patrol *laagered* within about two miles of the latter and about the same distance from Mazezetezes. The scouts reported that the rebels at Mondi were in large numbers, but did not show signs of any antagonism. They contented themselves with watching the movements of the scouts in an indifferent sort of manner.

On the morning of the 8th the column moved forward again and *laagered* close up to the south end of Mazezeteze's hill. About 7 a.m. the order was given to have breakfast and prepare to storm the position, a granite hill about two miles long, a mile broad, and in some parts five hundred feet high. The top rocks were crooked, the open fissures forming what are generally known as caves, in which the rebels are very expert in finding protection from any attacking force, using all the natural advantages such positions afford for dealing a blow in return.

Whilst the men were having breakfast, the rebels showed up very boldly on the most prominent parts of the hill and shouted down to us all sorts of defiant abuse.

As E Troop, under Captain Stoddart, had been pent up in Belingwe for over six weeks, it was only natural that they were anxious to have a brush with the enemy. I sent Captain Stoddart and his men round the south end of the mountain, with instructions to storm the *kraals* and drive the rebels out of the position on that side. Captain Frankland was sent off with a few mounted men to watch the operations and send in reports as they proceeded. Lieutenant Beisly was sent with B Troop mounted half-way up and about five hundred yards away from the east flank of the hill, to cut off any rebels who might retreat to the bush-covered slopes of the Bungwe hills, which ran parallel to, and about three miles east of, Mazezeteze's. Lieutenant Howe with twenty Cape boys was sent to cut off the retreat on the north end of the position.

As soon as E Troop disappeared round the southern end of the field, the seven-pounder was sent out, and Sergeant Perry commenced to shell the positions where the most of the rebels were to be seen. The shells soon made them take cover, and very shortly after a sharp rattle of musketry announced that E Troop was engaged. This lasted for about a quarter of an hour and then a large column of smoke rising from the side of the hill, on which E Troop were at work, showed that the first *kraal* had been taken and destroyed. This again was followed by a few more clouds of smoke and then the rebels could be seen retreating toward the north end of their position assisted on their way by an occasional shell from the seven-pounder.

Information was sent round that the southern portion of the hill had been cleared, and that Captain Stoddart was advancing to attack the northern portion, where the rebels had all located themselves and were compelled to stay and fight it out, seeing that the base of the hill was surrounded by a line of Cape boy skirmishers. The rattle of rifle fire announced the attack of this portion of the enemy's position. Shortly after midday Captain Frankland rode in and reported that the rebels had all been driven into the northern end of the hill, and that without the aid of the seven-pounder it would be impossible to take them out of the position. One man, Trooper Woest, had been shot dead, and was still lying close up to the caves.

The gun detachment were sent forward at once, and Sergeant Perry shelled the caves in rotation, until the rebels were shifted from one to another of them, and finally went to earth. Trooper Woest's body was then recovered.

A linguist tried to get into conversation with the rebels, offering them their lives and liberty if they surrendered. After many vain endeavours the attempt was given up as the rebels never replied.

It was now almost sundown and the troops were ordered back to the *laager*—E Troop very much fagged with their hard day's work.

The following morning Trooper Woest's remains were interred about eight hundred yards west of the south end of Mazezeteze's mountains and a large cairn of stones erected over his grave to mark the spot.

A light mounted patrol was sent round the mountain to try and get in touch with the rebels, but during the night the latter had retreated towards the M'Popoti Hills, taking the women and children with them.

The column then moved to the south-east, in the direction of Mondi's position, which was found deserted. The action against Mazezeteze had shattered Mondi's faith. He and his following had gone to Wedza's, where I decided to let them stay. All the *kraals* here were destroyed and the column moved to the Umchingwe River and *laagered* for the night on its north bank.

The following morning a *drift* was made through the river-bed, by which the column crossed, reaching Posselt's farm by midday. Here Lieutenant Yonge had nothing of importance to report, as no rebels or any signs of them had been seen by his patrols.

On the 11th the column marched southeast in the direction of Belingwe Peak. Scouting parties were sent out to see if Um'Nyati had returned. He had not, and there were no fresh signs of the rebels about.

On the afternoon of the 12th the column *laagered* up at A. Little's camp, about five miles south-west of Belingwe, where the wagons were dismantled and the men put on to repair them.

By the morning of the 19th the wagons had been overhauled and the horses re-shod and everything got ready for another march.

While the men had been busy repairing I took advantage of the halt, and with a small patrol, which consisted of Captains Hopper and Frankland, Mr. Percy Hare, and a few mounted men, visited some of the principal mining camps in the district. Stoddart's camp at the "Great Belingwe" had been looted and destroyed by fire, as well as the camps at "Bob's Luck" and "Wanderers' Rest" mines. The damage done to machinery alone at the "Bob's Luck" mine amounted to about £1,000. Many of the smaller mining camps had not been destroyed, and the claim pegs and beacons were all intact. No fresh spoor of rebels was to be seen anywhere.

CHAPTER 21

Arrival of Column at Buluwayo

On the morning of the 19th the column again moved in the direction of Buluwayo, but by a new route; the intention being to make a new road from Belingwe to Inseza, through the bush-covered flats close to the Umchingwe River, and to make that river, which is a most difficult one to cross with wagons, fordable, by opening out several drifts at different points. By doing this the rugged country to the north, I took it, would be made more easy of access from the main road, which ran about five miles to the south.

Lieutenant Yonge was left with a detachment of mounted men and a Nordenfelt at Posselt's farm, with the horses and mules that were unfit for work.

On the 25th Tandodzie's stronghold was to be attacked, but the first two shells stopped all resistance. The rebels in sight (there were only about thirty of them) took to their heels and disappeared in the bush.

On the evening of the 26th the column *laagered* on the open flats on the east bank of the Shangantopi Spruit, where we had again to deal with a grass fire, which the rebels had arranged for our annoyance. It was not such a violent one as the first, but it destroyed all the grass in the district.

On the 27th we *laagered* at "Finger Kop," about five miles east of Inseza, to wait for Lieutenant Wilson, quartermaster of the Belingwe garrison, who, with a small convoy of wagons and eleven men, was, at this point, expected with grain and provisions for the column.

On the morning of the 28th Wilson turned up and reported all quiet on the road between Belingwe and Inseza. He brought information from Lieutenant Caldecott, who had been left in charge at Belingwe, and Lieutenant Jackson, acting native commissioner there, to the effect that six native chiefs had come in to surrender. Jackson was instructed to accept their surrender, and send them back to their *kraals*, with orders to keep their arms for the purpose of enabling them to help the white man against the other rebels, if necessary, and to keep the garrison at Belingwe posted as to the movements of any of the latter in the district.

The chiefs said the action against Mazezeteze's had made them decide to surrender, and that as many of our shells had done great havoc in many of the caves, the natives in the district were convinced that the white man was more than able to beat them, and now wished to make peace rather than be killed. Wedza, they said, was still in his cave, and Mondi's people were in one of the adjoining hills, but as these two tribes were at loggerheads over some cattle they would in all probability fight with each other very soon.

Um'Nyati had taken all his people into the Mapelabana Mountains, did not wish to fight any more, and was afraid the white men would catch him.

Mr. Jackson had instructions to send peaceful messages to all, and to try and establish a feeling of confidence between white and black in that district.

I thought it best to allow Wedza and Mondi's people to settle their own affair, knowing full well that, with the other natives in the district friendly, they would be quite harmless.

I was aware that their position was strong—the strongest in the country. Before the rebellion broke out I had often been at Wedza's, and knew it well; but as their following was a small one—Wedza's about forty and Mondi's about fifty fighting men—I always believed they were just about so evenly balanced as to keep each other in order. They never did any harm in the district after the column left, but owing, I believe, to conflicting rumours and reports being sent to headquarters. Colonel Baden-Powell was sent against Wedza, with a force of hussars, &c., and the remainder of the Belingwe Field Force. After two days' hard work Wedza's stronghold was destroyed. An account of the taking of Wedza's was forwarded to me by an officer of the Belingwe Field Force who was present, but as he had not seen so much of the fighting as Colonel Baden-Powell, who has so thoroughly and brilliantly described the whole affair in his admirable work, I do not think it necessary to publish my officer's report.

The column moved forward again on the 29th, but before doing so we had a melancholy duty to perform. Sergeant Perry, who was in charge of the gun detachment, had contracted enteric fever, some two days before, and unfortunately had succumbed to it early in the morning. Perry was an excellent soldier, and his goodness of character in every respect had endeared him to every one of the column. His sudden death cast a gloom over all. His remains lie under a *Marula*-tree, about 170 yards south of "Finger Kop," and his grave, like all others who had gone before him, was covered with a large cairn of stones.

The column marched on after he was buried, and *laagered* up at the ruins of Cumming's store, in the Inseza hills. Here we halted for the greater part of the day.

It was here that Colonel the Hon. Maurice Gifford had his first fight after the rebellion broke out, the marks of which were still quite visible. As Gifford had to bury some of his dead under fire, their graves were not very well finished, but our men put them all to rights ere we marched on again.

On the 13th we crossed the Inseza range of hills and *laagered* at the foot of the western slope. Whilst here Captain J. Warrick came up with a detachment of police from Buluwayo, with orders to establish a post at Rixon's farm, on the Inseza. Warrick told me all about the peace negotiations going on between Mr. Rhodes and the rebels in the Matopos. This was pleasant information, and on hearing it I determined to march the column straight for Buluwayo.

On the 1st of September I left the column in charge of Captain Hopper, about sixteen miles from Buluwayo, and rode on to report myself, taking a small mounted escort with me.

Captain Hopper brought the column in slowly and *laagered* on our old camp ground two days later.

On arriving at Buluwayo I reported myself to the general and administrator.

They were both glad to hear of the column's safe arrival and that the natives in the Belingwe district were suing for peace.

Before the column got in arrangements were made for disbanding a portion of the officers and men. Captain Hopper was ordered back to the Inseza district to try and bring some of the rebels who were lurking about there to reason, but he had all his march for nothing, as no rebels were to be found.

After Captain Hopper marched for Inseza I applied to the G.O.C. for permission to resign and take up the duties of my company, the work of which was very much in arrear in every department.

General Carrington was most kind and considerate under the

circumstances, and on my promising to look after the affairs of the column when it came to be disbanded, he told me that he would accede to my request, and forthwith the following General Orders were published:—

Extracts from General Orders by Major General Sir Frederick Carrington, K.C.M.G., commanding forces. Headquarters' Office Buluwayo. September 7th:

3. A portion of Captain Laing's Belingwe Field Force will be disbanded from the 7th inst.

4. Captain Laing retires from his command and is given the rank of honorary Major. The General Officer commanding wishes to place on record his high appreciation of the excellent services rendered by this officer during the late operations.

Extract from General Orders, 18th September:

1. The following officers of the Belingwe Field Force resign their appointments from the 7th inst. inclusive: Captain James Stoddart, Lieutenant A. J. Wilson, Lieutenant Malcolm McCallum.

Captain Hopper's patrol got back from Belingwe and Inseza districts on the evening of September 29th, and orders were issued for the disbanding of the column next day.

About 11 a.m. on the 30th of September all that remained of the Belingwe Field Force, except the detachment at Belingwe, marched into Buluwayo and paraded in front of the administrator, Earl Grey, who received them most cordially, and addressed them on behalf of the Chartered Company in the following words:—

Major Laing. Captain Hopper, Captain Frankland, Officers, Non commissioned Officers, and men of the Belingwe Field Force, this is the second time I have had the pleasure of addressing you, and thanking you on behalf of the Company which I represent, for the gallant conduct you have displayed in the field on all occasions during the rebellion. I stand by what I have already said to you, men, when I first had the pleasure of meeting you, when you passed through here on your way to the Matopo Mountains; that if every district had stuck together and defied the rebels as you did, the rebellion would never have reached the dimensions it did. You are being disbanded, and to me this is a sure sign that the rebellion is at an end; the force of this fact is brought home forcibly to me, when I see your old commanding officer, standing here without his uniform, and you can retire proudly on laurels that have been bravely won. You have made your district of Belingwe famous, and the white men respected by natives in every part of it. You will now adjourn with me to the Chartered Hotel where we will drink to the future prosperity of Rhodesia and success to its inhabitants in years to come. But before doing so I will read to you the General Order for disbanding you.

Buluwayo,
September 30, 1896.

The General Officer commanding, in disbanding the Belingwe Field Force today, wishes to convey to Major Laing, Captain Hopper, and the remaining officers, non-commissioned officers, and troopers of the force, his high appreciation of the service they have rendered during the rebellion, of the gallant conduct they have on so many occasions shown on the field, especially in the action at Inugu Mountain, on the 20th July, and of the high sense of duty which has been conspicuous among all ranks throughout the campaign.

By Order.

(Signed)

C. B. Vyvvan,
Captain.

Brigade Major, Staff Officer in chief.

Earl Grey then called for three cheers for the Belingwe Field Force—a call which was responded to heartily by the bystanders, a large number of whom had gathered to see the Corps disband.

For the earl's speech I am indebted to one of the spectators who took shorthand notes and then transcribed them for me afterwards.

As soon as the men had had some light refreshment they handed in all their equipment, and were dismissed; and thus, after a short but brilliant career, the Belingwe Field Force became a thing of the past.

ALSO FROM LEONAUR
AVAILABLE IN SOFTCOVER OR HARDCOVER WITH DUST JACKET

THE ART OF WAR by Antoine Henri Jomini—Strategy & Tactics From the Age of Horse & Musket.

THE ART OF WAR by Sun Tzu and Pierre G. T. Beauregard—*The Art of War* by Sun Tzu and *Principles and Maxims of the Art of War* by Pierre G.T. Beauregard.

THE MILITARY RELIGIOUS ORDERS OF THE MIDDLE AGES by F. C. Woodhouse—The Knights Templar, Hospitaller and Others.

THE BENGAL NATIVE ARMY by F. G. Cardew—An Invaluable Reference Resource.

ARTILLERY THROUGH THE AGES—by Albert Manucy—A History of the DEvelopment and Use of Cannons, Mortars, Rockets & Projectiles from Earliest Times to the Nineteenth Century.

THE SWORD OF THE CROWN by Eric W. Sheppard—A History of the British Army to 1914.

THE 7TH (QUEEN'S OWN) HUSSARS: Volume 3—1818-1914 by C. R. B. Barrett—On Campaign During the Canadian Rebellion, the Indian Mutiny, the Sudan, Matabeleland, Mashonaland and the Boer War Volume 3: 1818-1914.

THE CAMPAIGN OF WATERLOO by Antoine Henri Jomini—A Political & Military History from the French perspective.

RIFLE & DRILL by S. Bertram Browne—The Enfield Rifle Musket, 1853 and the Drill of the British Soldier of the Mid-Victorian Period *A Companion to the New Rifle Musket* and *A Practical Guide to Squad and Setting-up Dtill.*

NAPOLEON'S MEN AND METHODS by Alexander L. Kielland—The Rise and Fall of the Emperor and His Men Who Fought by His Side.

THE WOMAN IN BATTLE by Loreta Janeta Velazquez—Soldier, Spy and Secret Service Agent for the Confederancy During the American Civil War.

THE BATTLE OF ORISKANY 1777 by Ellis H. Roberts—The Conflict for the Mowhawk Valley During the American War of Independenc.

PERSONAL RECOLLECTIONS OF JOAN OF ARC by Mark Twain.

CAESAR'S ARMY by Harry Pratt Judson—The Evolution, Composition, Tactics, Equipment & Battles of the Roman Army.

FREDERICK THE GREAT & THE SEVEN YEARS' WAR by F. W. Longman.

AVAILABLE ONLINE AT **www.leonaur.com**
AND FROM ALL GOOD BOOK STORES

ALSO FROM LEONAUR
AVAILABLE IN SOFTCOVER OR HARDCOVER WITH DUST JACKET

THE 9TH—THE KING'S (LIVERPOOL REGIMENT) IN THE GREAT WAR 1914 - 1918 by Enos H. G. Roberts—Mersey to mud—war and Liverpool men.

THE GAMBARDIER by Mark Severn—The experiences of a battery of Heavy artillery on the Western Front during the First World War.

FROM MESSINES TO THIRD YPRES by Thomas Floyd—A personal account of the First World War on the Western front by a 2/5th Lancashire Fusilier.

THE IRISH GUARDS IN THE GREAT WAR - VOLUME 1 by Rudyard Kipling—Edited and Compiled from Their Diaries and Papers—The First Battalion.

THE IRISH GUARDS IN THE GREAT WAR - VOLUME 1 by Rudyard Kipling—Edited and Compiled from Their Diaries and Papers—The Second Battalion.

ARMOURED CARS IN EDEN by K. Roosevelt—An American President's son serving in Rolls Royce armoured cars with the British in Mesopotamia & with the American Artillery in France during the First World War.

CHASSEUR OF 1914 by Marcel Dupont—Experiences of the twilight of the French Light Cavalry by a young officer during the early battles of the great war in Europe.

TROOP HORSE & TRENCH by R.A. Lloyd—The experiences of a British Lifeguardsman of the household cavalry fighting on the western front during the First World War 1914-18.

THE EAST AFRICAN MOUNTED RIFLES by C.J. Wilson—Experiences of the campaign in the East African bush during the First World War.

THE LONG PATROL by George Berrie—A Novel of Light Horsemen from Gallipoli to the Palestine campaign of the First World War.

THE FIGHTING CAMELIERS by Frank Reid—The exploits of the Imperial Camel Corps in the desert and Palestine campaigns of the First World War.

STEEL CHARIOTS IN THE DESERT by S. C. Rolls—The first world war experiences of a Rolls Royce armoured car driver with the Duke of Westminster in Libya and in Arabia with T.E. Lawrence.

WITH THE IMPERIAL CAMEL CORPS IN THE GREAT WAR by Geoffrey Inchbald—The story of a serving officer with the British 2nd battalion against the Senussi and during the Palestine campaign.

AVAILABLE ONLINE AT **www.leonaur.com**
AND FROM ALL GOOD BOOK STORES

www.ingramcontent.com/pod-product-compliance
Lightning Source LLC
Chambersburg PA
CBHW021957160426
43197CB00007B/165